BUSINESS LAW GUIDE
TO GERMANY

BUSINESS LAW GUIDE to GERMANY

Strobl, Killius & Vorbrugg

Munich Law Firm

CCH Editions Limited

TAX, BUSINESS AND LAW PUBLISHERS

Published by CCH Editions Limited
Telford Road, Bicester, Oxfordshire OX6 0XD
Tel. (0869)253300, Facsimile (0869)245814.

USA	Commerce Clearing House Inc., Chicago, Illinois.
CANADA	CCH Canadian Limited, Toronto, Ontario.
AUSTRALIA	CCH Australia Limited, North Ryde, NSW.
NEW ZEALAND	Commerce Clearing House (NZ), Auckland.

This publication is designed to provide accurate and authoritative information in regard to the subject-matter covered. It is sold with the understanding that the publisher is not engaged in rendering legal or other professional services. If legal advice or other expert assistance is required, the services of a competent professional person should be sought.

Ownership of Trade Marks

The Trade Marks

COMPUTAX and **COMMERCE CLEARING HOUSE, INC.,** are the

property of Commerce Clearing House Incorporated, Chicago, Illinois, U.S.A.

ISBN 0 86325 063 7

Typeset and printed in the United Kingdom by CCH Editions Limited.

Preface

Since the early 1970s, when CCH first published a Business Guide to Germany, most fields of business law have become more complex, while international business transactions have increased in frequency. In addition, foreign investment into Germany has continued to be impressive, benefiting from the political stability, low inflation rate and, last but not least, the comparatively reliable and predictable legal system of the Federal Republic of Germany. Although there is now much English-language material available on German business and tax law, such material confines itself mainly to selected areas. The need of foreign executives, businessmen, legal counsels and tax advisers for practical, concise and current information about the fundamentals of conducting business in Germany therefore remains largely unfulfilled.

As suggested by its title, *Business Law Guide to Germany* is primarily meant to be a handbook for general use rather than a specialised manual for the legal or tax professions (which, nevertheless, should find the book of considerable interest). The Guide is not restricted to purely national law, but also includes developments at European and international level to the extent that they are of practical importance to foreign business or 'local' subsidiaries of foreign legal entities.

Strobl, Killius & Vorbrugg
August 1986

About the Publisher

CCH Editions is part of a world-wide group of companies that specialise in tax and law publishing. The group produces a wide range of books and reporting services for the accounting, business and legal professions. The Oxfordshire premises are the centre for all UK and European operations.

All CCH publications are designed to provide practical, authoritative references and useful guides, and are written by CCH's highly qualified and experienced editorial team and specialist outside authors.

CCH Editions Limited publish bound books and loose-leaf reporting services specific to the United Kingdom, as well as distributing the publications of the overseas affiliate companies.

Contents

CONTENTS

CONTENTS

Glossary of Terms

The following list explains those terms most commonly used throughout this work, and gives the accepted abbreviations for some of the most important bodies and institutions in West Germany.

Abmahnung	advance warning (in cases of dismissal and unfair competition)
Aussperrung	lock-out
Aktie	stock certificate
Aktiengesellschaft (AG)	public stock corporation
Amtsgerichte	local courts
Angestellte	salaried employees (white collar workers)
Arbeiter	wage earners (blue collar workers)
Arbeitsamt	Labour Office
Arbeitsbescheinigung	certificate of employment
Arbeitsgericht	Labour Court
Arbeitslosengeld	unemployment benefit
Arbeitslosenhilfe	unemployment assistance
Arrest	seizure
Aufsichtsrat	supervisory board
Ausfuhrbescheinigung	export certificate
Bundesamt für gewerbliche Wirtschaft	Federal Office for Commercial Business
Bundesamt für landwirtschaftliche Marktordnung	Federal Office for Agricultural Market Organisation
Bundesanzeiger	Federal Gazette
Bundesarbeitsgericht (BAG)	Federal Labour Court (highest labour court)
Bundesaufschitsamt für das Kreditwesen	Banking Supervisory Authority
Bundesfinanzhof (BFH)	Federal Court of Justice
Bundeskartellamt (BKartA)	Federal Cartel Office (FCO)
Bundespatentamt	Federal Patent Office
Bundesverfassungsgericht	Federal Constitutional Court
Bundesverwaltungsgericht	Federal Administration Office
Bürgerliches Gesetzbuch (BGB)	German Civil Code
Beschluß	(court) order or resolution
Betrieb	firm, plant or shop
Betriebsstätte	permanent establishment
Bilanzsumme	balance sheet total
Brutto-Gehalt	gross salary
Brutto-Lohn	gross wage

Brutto-Vergutüng	gross remuneration
Bundesamt für Ernahrung und Forstwirtschaft	Federal Office for Food and Forestry
Datenschutzbeauftragter	data controller
Deutsche Bundesbank	German Federal Bank
Diensterfindung	employment invention
Eigenhändler	appointed dealer
Eigentumsvorbehalt	title retention (conditional transfer of property title)
Einigungsstelle	conciliation board
Einkommensteuer	personal income tax
einstweilige Vergügungen	interlocutory injunctions
Einwohnermeldeamt	residents' registration office
Entscheidung	decision (court or authority)
Erbschaftsteuer	inheritance and gift tax
Erla	decree
Finanzgerichte	tax courts
Firma	either firm name or company
freie Erfindung	free invention
Friedenspflicht	duty to observe waiting period before striking
Gebrauchsmuster	registered design or utility patent
Generalvollmacht	general power of representation
Genußschein	participating certificate
Geschäftsführer	managing director
Geschäftsanteile	GmbH shares
Geschmacksmuster	design patent
Gesellschaft mit beschränkter Haftung (GmbH)	limited liability company
Gesetz	law, act or code
Gewerbesteuer	trade tax
Grundsätze Ordnungsmäßiger Buchführung	proper accounting principles
Handelsvertreter	commercial agent
Händler	distributor or dealer
Handlungsvollmacht	power of attorney or commercial signing right
in Gründung (i.Gr.)	'being established' (added to company name when not yet registered)
Industrie- und Handelskammer	Chamber of Commerce
Kaufmann	merchant or businessman
Kaution	deposit (security)
Kommanditgesellschaft (KG)	limited partnership
Kommanditgesellschaft auf Aktien (KGaA)	limited partnership on stock
Kommissionär	agent
Kommissionsagent	commission merchant
Korperschaftsteuer	corporation tax
Krankengeld	sickness benefit
Landesarbeitsamt	State Labour Office

GLOSSARY

Landesarbeitsgericht	higher Labour Court
Landgerichte	regional courts
Leitende Angestellte	executives
Lohnsteuerkarte	wage withholding tax card
Makler	broker
Massenentlassung	mass dismissal
Oberlandesgericht	court of appeal
offene Handelsgesellschaft (oHG)	general partnership
ordentliche Gerichte	ordinary courts
Organschaft	integrated group relief
partialische Darlehen	participating loans
Pauschbesteuerung	lump sum taxation regime
Prokurist	senior employee authorised to act as signatory
Provision	commission (agents' remuneration, etc.)
Rechtsanwalt	attorney-at-law
Regionalen Förderungsprogramm	regional promotion programme
Richtlinien	administrative guidelines
Schönheitsreparaturen	decorative repairs (clause in a lease)
Sozialgerichte	courts for social matters
Sozialplan	severance compensation plan
Überweisung	money transfer order
Umsatzsteuer	value added tax
Urkundsprozeß	documentary proceedings
Urlaubsentgelt	vacation pay
Urteil	judgment (court)
Vermögensteuer	wealth tax
Verordnung	regulation
Versicherungskarte	employee's insurance card
Vertragshändler	authorised or appointed dealer
Vertrieb	distribution
Verwaltungsgerichte	administrative courts
Vollmacht	power of attorney (proxy)
Vorstand	board of management
Warenzeichen	trademark
wichtiger Grund	important reason, cause (in cases of notice of termination forthwith or dismissal with immediate effect)
Wirtschaftsprüfer	public accountant
Zeugnis	performance review or testimonial (for employees)

1 Sales Conditions and Consumer Protection

INTRODUCTION

¶101   General outline

The German economy is a free market economy with basic economic rights set forth even in the Constitution (*Grundgesetz* of 23 May 1949). Whereas it is debatable whether such basic rights as personal freedom (art. 2(2)), or the right to choose a trade, occupation or profession (art. 12) and property (art. 14) do in fact prescribe the free market economy as the only workable economy in line with the Constitution, there is no doubt that the German legislator has wide discretion to set boundaries within which German entrepreneurs may exercise their basic freedom of trade and freedom of contract. The Federal Parliament has in fact made use of such discretion but the business law resulting from this can still be described as particularly liberal.

IMPORT AND EXPORT RESTRICTIONS

¶102   Foreign trade in general

According to s. 1 of the German Foreign Trade Act of April 1961 (last amended on 6 October 1980) (*Außenwirtschaftsgesetz*: AWG), foreign trade is generally free. Germany is also a party to the General Agreement on Tariffs and Trade (GATT) of 30 October 1947, which recognised the need to reduce to a minimum restrictions and formalities in the import and export of goods. In fact, it has been repeatedly emphasised that Germany is one of the world's most liberal trading nations. Yet, like any other state, Germany must also to a certain extent regulate and restrict her trade with foreign countries. The main instruments in that area are customs duties, which are discussed in Chapter 2. Other governmental measures include prohibitions and restrictions providing for the protection of Germany's market organisation, specific industries, public health and public order. Such measures are outlined below.

Usually, a distinction is drawn between foreign trade regulations on the one hand and non-commercial regulations on the other. Non-commercial regulations serve purposes that are not directly related to international trade, but rather to other public interests such as public health, safety, the protection of the environment and so-called public order. This distinction is maintained in the following paragraphs.

¶103   Non-commercial regulations

With the exception of goods covered by foreign trade legislation, all goods which are subject to import or export regulations by virtue of specific statutes are listed in the section 'Other Regulations' under the code 'SV' in the 'Compiled Regulations – Federal Revenue Administration' (*Vorschriftensammlung Bundesfinanzverwaltung*). Within this section, the various restrictions and prohibitions are divided into the following groups:

(1) *Protection of public order (SV 0200 et seq.)*

The regulations listed here include the Act on the Control of Weapons for Military Purposes and the Weapons Act, the Explosives Act, the Nuclear Act and the Ordinance for Protection against Radiation. Reference is also made to several provisions of the Penal Code banning the import of publications, audio or video recordings, illustrations or presentations with cruel, violent, pornographic or unconstitutional contents.

(2) *Protection of the environment (SV 0400 et seq.)*

Regulations in this area include the Waste Disposal Act and the Ordinance on the Import of Waste Materials (requiring an authorisation for the import of waste products), the Fuel Lead Act (banning the import of Otto fuels for car engines with more than 0.15 grams of lead compounds), and the DDT-Act (banning the import of DDT and DDT preparations).

(3) *Protection of human health (SV 0600 et seq.)*

A number of national and EEC regulations concern the import and export of meat and food products and drugs. The import of meat is governed by various sanitary regulations contained in the Meat Inspection Act and associated ordinances, and in the Implementation Act 'EEC Directive Fresh Meat' (governing imports from other Community member states). Imports of poultry must comply with the Poultry Hygiene Act and the Poultry Inspection Ordinance. The import of wine and certain other beverages is governed by Community regulations (reg. no. 816/70 and implementation regulations 1848/76 and 2115/76) establishing certain preconditions with respect to the production, marketing (labelling) and, in some cases, the distribution of the beverages in the country of origin. In addition, national regulations, among others contained in the Wine Act and Wine Ordinance, require official admittance of wine and certain other beverages by the customs authorities. Other important restrictions include the import of narcotics (import document issued by the Federal Health Office required) and medicaments (registration required).

(4) *Protection of animals (SV 0800 ff)*

Restrictions (prohibitions or licence requirements) for the protection of animals in Germany are contained in the Epizootics Act and various other ordinances dealing with specific species, which not only apply to transfers to, through or from Germany of live animals, but also to dead animals, parts of animals, animal products and other objects which may be carriers of infectious matter.

(5) *Protection of plants (SV 1000 et seq.)*

Under the Plant Protection Act the import of noxious animals (insects, parasites), plants and micro-organisms, or plants and objects carrying such organisms is regulated. Furthermore, the import of means for treating plants requires prior approval. Possible measures include strict prohibitions, compulsory decontaminations, health certificates, and compulsory or discretionary inspections. There are also specific regulations dealing with forest plants and seeds.

(6) *Protection of commerce and industry (SV 1200 et seq.)*

Germany applies the Madrid Agreement on the Suppression of False or Misleading Declarations of Origin of 21 March 1925. Therefore, goods bearing false statements on their origin, species, class or characteristic features may be confiscated officially or upon application when they are imported or exported.

There are also specific treaties between Germany and several countries on the protection of representations on the geographic origin of goods. Pursuant to s. 28 of the Trade-mark Act of 2 January 1968, foreign goods which unlawfully bear the name of a German firm or of a German place, or which unlawfully bear a trade-mark protected by the Trade-mark Act may be confiscated by the customs authorities upon the application of the person whose rights are infringed by the import of such goods.

(7) *Protection of cultural goods (SV 1400 et seq.)*

The export of German cultural objects registered in a specific directory is restricted by the Act for the Protection of German Cultural Goods Against Exodus of 18 June 1955.

¶103

(8) *Monopolies (SV 1600 et seq.)*

The Spirits Monopoly Act of 8 April 1922 establishes, *inter alia*, the monopoly of the Federal Monopoly Administration for the import of spirits, not including rum, arrak, cognac and liqueurs. No licence is required for imports from EEC member states and many other countries associated with the EEC. Furthermore, there is a general authorisation for the import of certain kinds of spirits if certain conditions are met (e.g. whisky in containers holding up to three litres). Also, the regulations on the labelling of imported spirit products (content in spirit, producer, etc.) must be adhered to.

(9) *Excise duty regulations (SV 1700 et seq.)*

Excise duty laws impose certain restrictions with respect to the packaging and labelling of, *inter alia*, tobacco and beer.

(10) *National market organisation (SV 1800 et seq.)*

Special importation procedures (compulsory tender to the Federal Institute for the Organisation of the Agricultural Market) apply under the Livestock and Meat Act of 21 March 1977 (governing the importation of sheep or sheep meat). It is not applied to goods originating from the free circulation within the EEC.

(11) *Other restrictions (SV 1900 et seq.)*

Other prohibitions or limitations include the mandatory description of crystal glass and the obligation to describe textiles (including the percentage of spinning materials used in compounds).

It should be noted that apart from the above regulations there are industrial standards which are not legally binding but are nevertheless highly important, . e.g. in the context of product liability. These include, in particular, the 'Regulations of the Federation of German Electrotechnicians and Electrical Engineers' (VDE regulations) and the 'DIN' standards, i.e. the industrial standards determined by the German Standardisation Committee.

¶104   Foreign trade regulations

(1) *Sources*

Since Germany is a member of the European Community (EEC), her foreign trade policy has become increasingly influenced by Community legislation. The Treaty of Rome of 25 March 1957, establishing the European Economic Community, not only provides for the creation of a common foreign trade for goods subject to market organisation (mainly agricultural products), but for all agricultural and industrial products as well. Therefore, German foreign trade law today is to a large extent based on Community measures and directives.

The main statutory sources of foreign trade export/import restrictions and regulations are:

(a) Foreign Trade Act of 28 April 1961, last amended on 6 October 1980 (BGBl. I 1961 p. 481, 1980 I, p. 1905);

(b) Foreign Trade Ordinance of 22 August 1961, last amended on 6 November 1984 (BGBl. 1984 I p. 1324);

(c) Import List (annex to the Foreign Trade Ordinance) in the version of the 63rd amendment ordinance of 22 December 1977, last amended by the 91 amendment ordinance (*Bundesanzeiger* no. 242 of 28 December 1984);

(d) Export List (commonly referred to as 'Cocom List') (annex to the Foreign Trade Ordinance) last amended on 6 August 1984, BGBl. I p. 1079.

In addition, there are various EC directives regulating exports and imports.

(2) *General restrictions under the Foreign Trade Act*

The second part of the Foreign Trade Act contains provisions that permit general restrictions on foreign trade. Four types of restrictions are permitted:

(a) *International treaties.* Foreign trade may be restricted if Germany is bound to impose restrictions under international treaties (s. 5 AWG). There are numerous treaties containing such obligations, in particular those related to the organisation of the EEC.

(b) *Harmful impacts from foreign economies.* Foreign trade activities having a harmful impact on the domestic economy may be restricted. Also, restrictions may be imposed to avoid negative effects resulting from conditions in a foreign economic territory that are incompatible with the liberal system of Germany: for example, permission may be required for the chartering of ships under the German flag by non-residents (ss. 44, 46 AWV). The former requirement for permission for the acquisition of licences in non-domestic films and international co-productions (s. 48 AWV) was abolished in 1982 (licences to and from non-residents and co-productions with non-residents need only be reported (s. 50a AWV)).

(c) *Harmful import of capital.* Former restrictions pursuant to the Cash Deposit Law of 1971 (as based on s. 6a AWG) have been abolished for the time being.

¶104

(d) *Security of foreign interests.*   On the basis of s. 7 AWG, the export of weapons and ammunition, as well as any documentation needed in order to manufacture such goods, may be restricted, and the export list (see below) contains a special section listing such goods.

(3) *Imports*

(a) *Industrial products (Import List)*   According to s. 10(1) AWG, the import of goods by residents is permitted without an import authorisation (licence) unless otherwise specified in the so-called Import List, which is more than 300 pages long and, in combination with the Lists of Countries, indicates whether a licence is required. The list has five columns. Goods are classified in columns 1 and 2 using the code numbers and descriptions used for foreign trade statistics and the common tariff descriptions of the customs tariff legislation (see below, Chapter 2: 'Tariffs'). Column 3 indicates the competent government department and Column 4 indicates import restrictions, if any. In Column 5 references are made to Community or national market organisation, to the possible requirement of a certificate or declaration of origin and to the Community or national surveillance over imports.

The general rule is that an import licence is only required if the Import List so specifies. This depends to a great extent on whether the country of purchase or origin is mentioned in country list C (state trading countries) or in country list A/B (other). In the latter case, almost all goods may be imported without a licence. The distinction between state trading countries and other countries is based on reg. (EEC) no. 925/79 of the Council of 8 May 1979, concerning the Common Regulation of Imports from State Trading Countries, and reg. (EEC) no. 926/79 of the Council of 8 May 1979, concerning the Common Regulation of Imports.

Special regulations (EEC and national) govern imports from Cuba and from the People's Republic of China.

It should be noted that unusual delivery periods, as specified in s. 22 AWV (e.g. delivery more than two years after the conclusion of the contract), require an authorisation even if no authorisation is required under the import list.

Certain goods listed in s. 32(1) AWV (such as books and graphics works up to DM 1,000, samples of goods for commercial trade worth up to DM 500, gifts worth up to DM 500, etc.) do not as a rule require an authorisation (facilitated procedure). Also, goods imported by non-residents to be sold at a fair are exempt from authorisation, if no authorisation would be required for their import by residents (s. 32(3) AWV).

Even if no authorisation is required, certain other formalities may be necessary. Goods marked with 'EE' or 'EEG' on the Import List require an import declaration for market surveillance purposes. Goods marked with 'V' or 'VE' require a certificate of origin or a declaration of origin, unless the goods originate from an EEC member state. The origin of goods and the country of origin are determined according to the respective definitions of customs legislation (see Chapter 2: 'Product Origin').

If an authorisation is required for industrial products, it must be applied for at the Federal Office for Commercial Business (*Bundesamt für gewerbliche Wirtschaft*). The authorisation must be applied for by the importer. In the absence of specific statutory restrictions (see above), the granting of authorisations is a matter of economic policy. Opportunities and conditions (e.g., import quotas) for obtaining an authorisation are, as a rule, announced in the Federal Gazette (*Bundesanzeiger*) in order to give anyone interested the chance to apply.

(b) *Agricultural imports*   All products marked with 'L' and with 'GMO' on the Import List (see above) are covered by Community import procedures pursuant to EEC reg. no. 3183/80, issued by the Commission on 3 December 1980, on Common Implementation Provisions for Import and Export Licences as well as Advance Fixing Certificates for Agricultural Products ('Licence Regulation'). Most of the individual regulations establishing a licence requirement are mentioned in the Licence Regulation.

Under these regulations a licence is required for various agricultural products (grain, beef, eggs, poultry, meat, milk and dairy products, etc.) entering the free circulation of the Federal Republic of Germany from third countries directly or via other EEC member states without having entered into free circulation there. This licence differs significantly from other licences under German foreign trade law. It establishes a duty to import the goods it has been obtained for. It will, as a rule, only be granted if security is deposited with the competent authority. This security is forfeited if the goods are not imported within the specified period of time (exceptions apply in cases of *force majeure*).

Procedural matters relating to the granting of licences are governed by the Act on the Implementation of Common Organisations of Markets of 31 August 1972 (BGB1. I 1617). According to the Act, licences are granted by the Federal Office for Agricultural Market Organisation (*Bundesamt für landwirtschaftliche Marktordnung*) or by the Federal Office for Food and Forestry (*Bundesamt für Ernährung und Forstwirtschaft*).

(4) *Exports*

(a) *Export list (Cocom)*   Annex AL to the Foreign Trade Ordinance contains a list of all goods subject to foreign trade restrictions on exports. The statutory bases of these restrictions are ss. 5–8 AWG.

¶104

The Export List does not impose prohibitions, but authorisation requirements. All goods requiring authorisation are classified by a four-digit code number. The Federal Office for Commercial Business (*Bundesamt für gewerbliche Wirtschaft*) has issued a reference list to the code numbers used for foreign trade statistics (seven digits) which is part of the German Official Customs Tariff code numbers (nine digits).

Restrictions determined by the Coordination Committee for West-East Trade (Cocom) (which includes NATO members and Japan, but not Spain and Iceland) are incorporated into the Export List and thereby become binding in Germany. The so-called Cocom-list of goods and documents with a strategic importance was revised substantially during negotiations in the summer of 1984. In particular, these revisions concern the export of electronic products. In view of the introduction of a more detailed procedure, the processing of applications is taking much longer.

Applications must be addressed to the Federal Office for Commercial Business (*Bundesamt für Gewerbliche Wirtschaft*).

(b) *Agricultural exports*   The export of certain agricultural products to non-EEC member states requires an export licence as set out in EEC reg. no. 3183/80, which also covers the import of such products. The same particulars concerning the import of agricultural products, as described above, also apply to the export of agricultural products.

(5) *Imports/exports without authorisation*

Legal transactions requiring authorisation are void under s. 31 of the Foreign Trade Act if effected without authorisation. It is, however, possible to rectify this by obtaining permission subsequently. Nevertheless, it is advisable and usual to enter into agreements on exports or imports that contain an express condition that such permission must be obtained.

Violation of export or import restrictions established under or pursuant to the Foreign Trade Act may be subject to a fine of up to DM 500,000. Under certain circumstances (e.g., if such violations endanger the security of the Federal Republic of Germany), there may even be a penalty of up to three years' imprisonment. Further, the goods in question may be confiscated.

Unless an import or export authorisation explicitly requires it, the seller of goods is not obliged to advise the buyer of possible restrictions concerning a re-export of the goods by the buyer to third countries.

¶105   Capital transfer

Currently, there are no substantive restrictions on the transfer of money to and from Germany, but only certain reporting obligations.

¶105

According to ss. 22, 23 AWG, certain transactions (e.g., the acquisition of real property, of bills of exchange, etc.) between residents and non-residents may be restricted in order to such public interests as, for example, the German balance of payments, and in order to avoid harmful impact on the German capital market.

Sections 55 et seq. AWG establish reporting requirements with respect to investments by residents abroad and by non-residents in Germany. The investments covered by these regulations include the establishment or the acquisition of enterprises, branches or permanent establishments, the acquisition of rights (e.g., shares) in an enterprise, the transfer of business assets or contributions to such enterprises, and the granting of loans etc., if such investments exceed DM 20,000 per calendar year (not applicable to the liquidation or dissolution of certain investments). Banks will normally remind the parties concerned of such reporting duties, the report being made on forms issued by the German Federal Bank.

Apart from these reporting duties, ss. 59 et seq. AWV establish an obligation to report money transfers between residents and non-residents under certain circumstances. These reports are usually made together with the instruction to the bank to carry through such transfers. Furthermore, residents (except banks) must report their financial claims or debts *vis-à-vis* non-residents to the Central Bank of the states (*Länder*) they reside in (*Landeszentralbank*) if the amounts involved exceed DM 500,000 at the end of a calendar month. Resident financial institutions are required to report pursuant to s. 69 AWV.

¶106 Recognition of foreign restrictions on exports, imports and exchange

It should be noted that German courts in some instances recognise foreign import or export restrictions. For instance, sales agreements that violate US export restrictions may be held void by a German court if made with the intention to circumvene such restrictions (see, e.g., Decision of the Federal Court of 21 December 1960, NJW 1961, 822). No clear rules have been formulated on this matter, however.

The recognition of foreign trade restrictions is in some instances governed by international treaties. For instance, Art. VIII, s. 2b of the Treaty of Bretton Woods (Treaty on the International Monetary Fund, BGBl. II 1952, 637/728) provides that 'exchange contracts which involve the currency of any member and which are contrary to the exchange control regulations of that member maintained or imposed consistently with this Agreement shall be unenforceable in the territories of any member'. The term 'exchange contract' has been interpreted broadly by German courts and thus may include payment claims resulting from sales agreements, commercial agency agreements, etc. (see, e.g., Decision of the Federal Court of 17 February 1971, NJW 1971, 983).

Contracts violating foreign restrictions on exchange contracts are not considered void by German courts, but may not be enforced by bringing an action in Germany.

APPLICABILITY OF GERMAN LAW

¶107   Conflicts of law

Legal transactions between parties of different countries (such as sales between a German buyer/importer and a foreign seller/exporter, but including distribution, employment or licence agreements) raise the question of which law governs the contractual relationship. As the law of contract is federal law in Germany, conflicts of law do not arise in entirely domestic transactions.

If a transaction involves foreign elements, contractual provisions on the applicable law may be crucial. Differences between the legal systems involved (e.g. mandatory regulations) often call for an express choice of law to be made. The applicable law may also have particular economic impact. For instance, a disclaimer of liability which may be possible under the chosen law will reduce the need for insurance coverage; the reduction of warranty periods may allow the purchase price to be reduced; the possibility of providing for security or floating charges would reduce financial risks, etc. Without knowing which system of law will apply it will remain doubtful whether a given contract clause may be enforceable.

¶108   General rules

(1) *Express choice of law*

A contractual relationship is generally governed by the system of law chosen by the parties ('law of the contract'). German courts will recognise an express choice of law by the parties unless the subject-matter is clearly domestic with no foreign elements.

Foreign elements that commonly constitute an international contract include such factors as the different nationalities and/or domiciles of the parties and transactions across the border. There are no precise *rules* as to which elements constitute an international contract, but German courts are usually reluctant to disregard an express choice of law unless such choice is arbitrary, and only motivated by the desire to evade German law.

Express stipulations concerning the law of the contract are usually only part of an agreement. From a legal point of view, however, the choice of law by the parties constitutes a separate contract and the validity of the choice of law is not necessarily affected by the invalidity of the main agreement.

It should be emphasised that there is, under German law, a unique distinction between the creation of mutual obligations by a contract on the one hand and the performance of such obligations on the other. For instance, the transfer of title to goods is a legal transaction that must be strictly separated from the underlying sales agreement. The same distinction is made by German conflict of law rules. The creation of contractual relations is governed by the principles outlined in this section while the creation of property interests in goods (*dingliche Rechte*) is, as a general rule, governed by the laws of the place where such goods are located (*lex rei sitae*).

(2) *Absence of express choice*

In the absence of an express stipulation on the applicable law, the question arises of whether there was an implied (tacit) choice of law. All underlying circumstances which resulted in the conclusion of the contract and its implementation may have to be considered in order to determine whether there was factual consent on which system of law is supposed to govern the contract. The existence of an implied choice of law may be evidenced by the express choice of a court or an arbitrator, express agreement of a place of performance or references to particular rules or customs of a specific legal system.

If no express or implied choice of law can be found, the governing law could be based on a so-called 'hypothetical choice of law.' Despite this somewhat misleading term, the silent intention of each party is not a factor in determining the hypothetical choice of law. Rather, this concept involves an evaluation of the conflicting interests of the parties in order to determine the legal system with which the transaction has the closest connection. In this context, German courts frequently use the term 'centre of the contract', which approach is similar to the determination of the 'proper law of the contract' in common-law jurisdictions. In fact, there is no clear distinction between the implied choice of law concept outlined above and the hypothetical choice of law, since the factors relied on in both tests are virtually identical.

(3) *Location*

If it is impossible to determine the applicable law on the basis of either of the approaches outlined above, German courts will look to the location of the obligation in issue. This may result in the division of the agreement as different obligations may have different places of performance. Therefore, the place of performance of that obligation which characterises the contract is likely to be regarded as the decisive factor in the tests outlined above so that the entire contractual relationship may be governed by the laws of one jurisdiction. (For example, a distribution agreement which goes beyond a simple long-term buying and selling arrangement would, under this theory, be subject to the law of the distributor, whereas a simple sales transaction may be subject to different laws depending on the obligation in question.)

It should be emphasised that the law governing a contract does not necessarily apply to all the issues raised by that contract. For instance, the capacity of a person to contract, and questions related to agency and representation may be subject to the law of the nationality or domicile, even when different from the law that characterises the contract. Also, as mentioned above, the law of the contract does not govern the transfer of ownership in goods or other movables or immovables which are treated in a different country at the time of the transaction (see further under 'Standard Terms' below).

¶109   Uniform laws

Germany adopted the Hague Uniform Law on International Sales of Movables in 1974 (BGBl. 1973 I 856, 1973 II 885; 1974 II 146). This Law has also been adopted by Belgium, Gambia, Israel, Italy, Luxembourg, the Netherlands, San Marino and the United Kingdom.

The Law contains specific provisions regarding the obligations of buyer and seller resulting from an international sales contract including, in particular, the consequences of a breach of contract. It does not contain provisions on the formation and validity of a contract nor does it apply to the transfer of ownership.

In Germany, the Law applies only if the parties have their company headquarters or habitual residences in different member states, provided that any one of the following preconditions is met:

(1) the parties stipulate that the goods shall be shipped from one state to the other;

(2) offer and acceptance occur in different states;

(3) the goods must be delivered to a state other than that in which offer and acceptance occurred.

Germany has adopted the Hague Uniform Law on the Formation of International Sale of Goods Contracts (BGBl 1973 I 868, 1973 II 885, 919; 1974 II 148), which applies under basically the same preconditions as the Uniform Sales Law. This Law contains specific rules on the formation of international sales agreements.

¶109

The parties to an international sales agreement may stipulate that neither of these two Laws shall apply to their contract. This is a frequent occurrence, as the parties do not want to have their contract governed by a relatively unknown set of rules. Furthermore, sellers often feel that the Uniform Laws are less favorable than German civil and commercial law. In this context it should be noted, however, that the simple choice of German law will not exclude the Hague Uniform Sales Laws as they are an integral part of German law. For the avoidance of doubt, an express exclusion of the Hague Uniform Sales Laws would be required.

¶110   Restrictions on the choice of law in standard business agreements

Choice of law clauses in standard business conditions or standard agreements ('fine print') are subject to specific restrictions pursuant to the Law on General Terms of Business of 9 December 1976 (*Gesetz zur Regelung des Rechts der Allgemeinen Geschäftsbedingungen*: AGBG).

This law establishes different standards depending on whether general terms of business are used *vis-à-vis* a merchant (*Kaufmann*), which includes companies and public entities, or non-merchants, which includes professions.

Under s. 10 no. 8 AGBG, a standard clause providing for the applicability of foreign law is void if there is no legitimate reason for such choice. Thus, one or more foreign factors that usually are sufficient to support the validity of an individual choice of law stipulation do not automatically suffice to justify a standard choice of law clause. The interests of the party using the general terms of business in providing for the applicability of a foreign legal system must outweigh the interest which the domestic party, as a rule, has in the application of German law. Using these principles, it will not normally suffice for a German company to refer to a foreign law simply because its parent company (whose products it distributes) is a foreign company.

If a standard contract is so governed by foreign law, s. 12 AGBG nevertheless provides that the provisions of the AGBG must be taken into consideration if:

(1) the contract was concluded on the basis of a public offer, of public advertising or similar business activities conducted by the user within Germany; and

(2) the other party had its domicile or habitual residence within Germany when making the contract and if the relevant statements were made within Germany.

'Consideration' of German law does not mean that German law must be applied. Rather, it means that provisions of the foreign law which govern the contract are superseded by the standard established in the AGBG if such provisions fail to provide protection for private consumers that is equal to the protection established by the AGBG (see 'Choice of forum' at ¶111 below).

Sections 10 no. 8, 12, 24 AGBG are not applicable if general terms of business are used *vis-à-vis* merchants. Thus, with regard to merchants, the general rules apply without modification.

¶111   Choice of forum

Choice of law clauses are commonly combined with provisions concerning the competent court. The validity of such stipulations depends on the parties (merchants or non-merchants), on the court chosen by the parties and on the nature of the stipulation (standard or individual contract).

(1) *Contracts with merchants*

If both parties are merchants, stipulations on which court shall be competent are generally given effect (s. 38(1) Civil Procedure Code) irrespective of whether standard clauses or individual stipulations are concerned. There is no requirement that such stipulations must be in writing.

Germany is a member state of the EEC Convention on Judicial Competence and on the Enforcement of Judgements in Civil and Commercial Matters of 27 September 1968. This Convention has also been adopted in Belgium, France, Italy, Luxembourg and the Netherlands. Furthermore, a revised version of the Convention has been signed but not yet ratified by the original member states and by Denmark, Ireland and the UK.

Article 17 of the Convention deals with choice of court clauses and supersedes s. 38 of the Civil Procedure Code. It provides that the parties to a contract may, if at least one of the parties resides in the territory of a member state, agree on the exclusive jurisdiction of the courts of one of the member states. The stipulation must be made in writing or in another form that is common in international commercial practice. It is irrelevant whether such stipulation is contained in standard terms or was specifically agreed upon.

(2) *Contracts with non-merchants*

Pursuant to s. 38 of the German Civil Procedural Code, choice of law stipulations between non-merchants are generally void. The most important exception regards cases where a German court would not otherwise have jurisdiction over one of the parties (i.e. where it does not have its registered office or company headquarters in Germany), in which case the choice of forum must be agreed in writing.

The applicability of art. 17 of the EEC Convention (see above) is not limited to commercial transactions. Thus, a venue clause covered by this Convention is generally valid irrespective of whether the parties are merchants or non-merchants.

It should be noted that art. 15 of the revised version of the EEC Convention (not yet in force) will considerably restrict the application of art. 17 in consumer transactions.

In addition to the above restrictions, there is strong authority for the view that choice of court clauses in standard contracts will be considered valid only if preconditions are fulfilled similar to those set forth in s. 10 no. 8 AGBG (see 'Restrictions on the choice of law in standard business agreements' at ¶110 above).

(3) *Exclusive or non-exclusive venue*

The parties may agree to a particular court to the exclusion of, or in addition to, those courts which would otherwise have jurisdiction. Where the parties leave this open, courts tend, in international matters, to interpret a venue clause as exclusive, which is what the European Convention prescribes (see art. 17). A warning must be added, however: such exclusivity would be absolute in that it would apply even where it may be obvious that the final decision cannot be enforced (e.g. for lack of reciprocity: Federal Court decision of 2 February 1971, NJW 71 p. 985).

FORMAL REQUIREMENTS

¶112   Overview

As a general rule, German law imposes no formal requirements on the validity of contracts. Thus, oral agreements are generally valid. Despite the general validity of oral agreements it is advisable and, in commercial dealings, common practice to execute agreements in writing since it may otherwise be difficult to prove the terms of the agreement in case of a dispute.

(1) *Written contracts*

Those contracts that must be in writing in order to be valid are specified in the Civil Code and other statutes. The more important requirements cover:

- (a) leases of land for longer than one year (s. 566 Civil Code);
- (b) guarantees of collectibility (s. 766 Civil Code);
- (c) promises and acknowledgements of debt (s. 780 et seq. Civil Code);
- (d) instalment contracts with non-merchants (s. 1a Hire and Purchase Act); and

(e) certain cartel law agreements, including agreements establishing exclusiveness or similar restrictions on competition (s. 34 Antitrust Law).

German courts are rather inflexible in determining whether the written-form requirement is met in any given case (s. 126 Civil Code). In principle, all agreed provisions must form part of one uniform deed and such writing requirements apply to the entire agreement, including any attachments, amendments and subsequent modifications. Such a deed must be signed by the parties in person at the end of the deed (a telegram or telex would not be sufficient).

(2) *Notarisation*

Certain transactions are only valid if executed before a notary. In particular, contracts for the sale of land and for the creation of certain interests in land (e.g. mortgages), and certain corporate law transactions (e.g. establishment of a limited liability company (GmbH) and assignment of shares in a GmbH) must be notarised.

To what extent notarisation may occur in front of a foreign notary, is debatable. The Federal Court has held, however, that the amendment of the articles of a GmbH may be notarised in front of a Zurich (Switzerland) Notar who is said to be the equivalent of a German Notar (BGH 80, p. 76; same OLG Frankfurt DB 1981, p. 1456 with respect to the assignment of GmbH shares).

An agreement which lacks the required notarial form will itself become valid through subsequent valid performance, e.g. where the change of ownership is actually entered in the land register or the transfer of shares is notarised.

STANDARD TERMS

¶113   Law in general

Business transactions in Germany are to a large extent based on standardised contracts (printed contract forms, fine print, etc.). In order to establish protection for private consumers against the unfavourable clauses frequently present in such standardised contracts, the 'Law on General Terms of Business' was enacted in 1977 (*Gesetz zur Regelung des Rechts der Allgemeinen Geschaftsbedingungen:* AGBG). Even though the main purpose of this Act is to protect private consumers, it also is of considerable importance in commercial dealings between merchants (see also 'Restrictions on the choice of law in standard business agreements' at ¶110 above).

¶113

¶114   Scope of standard terms law

The AGBG draws a distinction between general terms of business and 'individual stipulations'. Generally speaking, the test is whether a contract clause is the result of prior negotiations by the parties or, alternatively, whether it was drafted by one party for use in several contracts and imposed by that party upon the other party on the basis of 'take it or leave it'. Thus, the term 'general terms of business' as defined in the AGBG applies to contract clauses that one of the parties ('the user') introduces as a condition for the conclusion of a contract. Such clauses are 'general' if they were drafted by the user as a basis for a multitude of contracts, i.e. if they were not specifically drafted for the actual agreement in question.

The AGBG does not fully apply to general terms of business used *vis-à-vis* a merchant (*Kaufmann*) or public entity. The term 'merchant' includes any person engaging in a 'commercial business' as defined in s. 1 of the Commercial Code. Among others, resalers, manufacturers, insurers, banks, freight companies, commercial agents and brokers are considered merchants. Moreover, any other business extensive enough to require commercially organised business operations constitutes a 'commercial business' if the firm name has been registered in the commercial register (s. 2 Commercial Code). All provisions applicable to merchants are also applicable to corporations and commercial partnerships (s. 5 Commercial Code).

It should be noted that certain professions (physicians, lawyers, architects, etc.) do not constitute a 'commercial business'. Thus, the members of such professions are non-merchants.

¶115   Applicability of standard terms

Pursuant to s. 2 AGBG, general terms of business become part of a contract if, at the time of formation of the contract, the user:

(1) expressly referred to such terms;

(2) provided the other party with a reasonable opportunity to become aware of the contents of such terms; and

(3) the other party has consented to the application of the terms.

In order to avoid doubts on these issues, general terms of business are commonly printed on the reverse side of offers, orders, order acknowledgements, invoices, etc. If this is done, however, the user must unequivocally refer to the general terms of business on the face of such forms. Also, a reference to general terms of business after the formation of the contract (e.g. on invoices only) will not normally suffice.

Even though s. 2 AGBG does not apply to transactions between merchants, consent on the applicability of one or the other party's general terms of business is also required in commercial dealings.

Frequently both parties refer to their respective general terms of business ('battle of forms'). In such cases there is consent only to the extent that the parties' respective general terms of business do not differ from each other, but none of the other clauses will become part of the contract. Until recently the courts applied the terms of the party that was the last to refer to its terms (theory of the 'last word').

¶116   General concepts

The AGBG establishes several general rules on the interpretation and validity of general terms of business that apply irrespective of whether the parties are merchants or non-merchants:

(1) clauses that are so uncommon under the given circumstances that the other party could not reasonably anticipate them (so called 'surprising clauses') do not become part of the contract (s. 3 AGBG);

(2) individual stipulations have priority over general terms of business (s. 4 AGBG);

(3) ambiguous clauses shall be interpreted to the disadvantage of the user (s. 5 AGBG);

(4) to the extent that one or more clauses did not become part of a given contract or are void, the contract is governed by statutory law, unless this would result in an undue burden for one or other of the parties, in which case the entire contract is void (s. 6 AGBG).

¶117   Void clauses

The AGBG is based on the general concept of unconscionability. It basically restates prior case law. Sections 10 and 11 AGBG contain a list of 'typical' clauses that are declared void by the Act. Any clauses not coming within the scope of these specific provisions are governed by the general rule embodied in s. 9 AGBG, according to which clauses are void if they impose an undue burden upon the other party against good faith. If there is doubt, there is a presumption of an undue burden if a clause is incompatible with the basic concept of statutory law, or restricts the obligations or duties inherent to the given contract to such an extent that it would jeopardise the object of the contract. This general rule is also applicable in commercial and non-commercial transactions. The specific restrictions set out in ss. 10 and 11 AGBG only apply to standard terms used in relation to non-merchants. In commercial transactions, however, the same clauses will in many instances be held void pursuant to s. 9 AGBG. Thus, ss. 9 and 10 AGBG cannot be disregarded in commercial transactions.

The following is a survey of the more important clauses that are void pursuant to ss. 10 or 11 AGBG:

(1) *Performance period.* The user may not reserve for himself an un-reasonably long or insufficiently defined period for accepting or rejecting an offer or for performing an obligation. For instance, if the customer can reasonably expect a delivery within one or two weeks, the user cannot rely on clauses like 'the product will be delivered within 90 days of the date the order has been accepted,' or 'delivery will be made as soon as possible'. The same would generally apply in commercial transactions.

(2) *Period of grace.* The user may not provide for an unreasonably long period of grace for his performance after it has become due. Thus, if the user is in default in performing his obligations, the customer must be left with the right to set a final performance deadline and to cancel the agreement thereafter. The user only has the right to define a reasonable length for such a period of grace (in common consumer transactions usually not more than two weeks). The same general rule applies in commercial transactions.

(3) *Price increase.* Section 11, no. 1 AGBG prohibits clauses providing for an increase in the agreed prices for goods to be delivered or other obligations to be performed within four months of the conclusion of the contract. This prohibition is also applied to cases in which, instead of a specific price, the user claims payment of the prices set out in his current price list at the time of delivery or performance. Even if delivery or performance is to occur later than four months after the conclusion of the contract, any clause allowing the user in his sole discretion to increase prices would be void pursuant to s. 9 ABGB. Only clauses setting out specific circumstances that may result in price increases (for instance, increases in the cost of certain materials used) will be valid. Furthermore, the customer must be granted a right to cancel the agreement in case the price increase is substantially higher than the increase in the general cost of living.

In commercial transactions, these restrictions only apply to a lesser degree. In particular, the four months' prohibition on any price increases does not apply.

(4) *Right to set-off.* The user may not cut off the other party's right to set off claims against the user that are undisputed or that have been determined by a final judgment against the user. This prohibition also applies in commercial transactions.

¶117

(5) *Right to reminder.* Pursuant to s. 11, no. 4 AGBG, the user claiming damages for late or non-performance may not rely on a clause that relieves him from the statutory requirements to: (a) address a reminder to the other party before holding that party in default; and (b) set a final performance deadline before being entitled to cancel the contract. The former restriction is, for instance, of importance where the user is owed debts that do not become due on a specific calendar date, as he generally may not claim damages caused by late payment without having reminded the debtor to pay after the payment was due. The latter restriction confirms the statutory requirement of a final performance-reminder before the user is entitled to cancel a contract because of the debtor's late-performance. By contrast to the former restriction, it also applies in commercial transactions.

(6) *Penalties.* Standard clauses that entitle the user to impose penalties or to claim liquidated damages are void if:

(a) the liquidated amount exceeds the amount of damages reasonably foreseeable; or

(b) they deprive the other party of the right to prove that, in a given case, there was no damage or that the actual damage was substantially lower than the liquidated amount.

Similar restrictions apply in commercial transactions.

(7) *Liability.* Any exclusion or limitation of liability resulting from intentional or grossly negligent acts of the user is void pursuant to s. 11, no. 7 AGBG. German general terms of business commonly contain a clause limiting the user's liability for damages to damages caused by intentional or grossly negligent acts.

(8) *Warranties.* Section 11, no. 10 AGBG deals in detail with warranty obligations, in particular with warranty obligations in sales transactions. The term 'warranty' as used in German statutes applies, generally speaking, to the customer's rights upon the delivery of defective goods. Depending on the type of contract in question, the German Civil Code distinguishes the following warranty rights: rescission of a contract (i.e. to release both parties from further obligations and to restore them to the positions which they were in before the contract was made); reduction of the remuneration; rectification (cure, replacement); and (where express representations have been violated) damages. The following warranty-restrictions are void in contracts for the supply of newly manufactured goods or services:

• Exclusion and reference to third parties: The user may not refer the other party to warranty claims against third parties while excluding any warranty obligations against the user.

¶117

- Restriction to the obligation to cure: The user may not restrict his warranty obligations to the obligation to cure or replace without also expressly granting the other party the right to rescind or to claim a reduction of the remuneration if the user fails to cure or to replace.

- The user may not hold the other party liable for the costs and expenses caused by the cure, in particular costs of transportation, labour and materials.

- Conditional refusal of performance of warranty obligations: The user may not make the cure of a defect or the replacement conditional on the prior payment of the full remuneration or of an unreasonably large part of the remuneration.

- With respect to latent defects, the user may not impose on the other party a duty to give notice of such defects within deadlines that are shorter than the statutory warranty period, which is six months for the sale of goods.

- The statutory warranty periods (normally six months upon delivery) must not be reduced.

(9) *Representations.*   The user's liability for express warranties or representations, including liability for damages, must not be limited.

To draft valid terms and conditions now requires its own expertise, and the case law applying the AGBG to all kinds of standard provisions is rapidly expanding.

RETENTION OF TITLE

¶118   General concept

German law strictly differentiates between the creation of contractual rights and duties on the one hand (law of obligations) and their performance on the other hand (law of property). Thus, the seller's obligation to transfer the title in goods to the buyer must be distinguished from the actual transfer of title making the buyer the new owner of the goods. The transfer of title is effected by the specific consent of the parties in addition to the underlying contract and physical transfer of possession or its equivalent. In the absence of a specific stipulation to the contrary, the consent to the transfer of title is usually found to be implied in the delivery of goods.

If the purchase price is not received on or before delivery, the seller will in effect advance unsecured credit to the buyer. The German Civil Code therefore expressly recognises the validity of so-called 'reservation of ownership' clauses in sales agreements. According to s. 455 of the Civil Code, if the seller retains title in the goods until payment of the purchase price, ownership is normally transferred to the buyer under the condition precedent that the purchase price is fully paid. Furthermore, the seller is entitled to rescind the contract if the buyer is in default with the payment of the purchase price. On the basis of a reservation of ownership, the seller has the right to demand a return of the goods if the buyer is in default of payment, including in the case of bankruptcy. Also, the buyer generally does not have the right to transfer ownership in the goods to third persons without the seller's consent as long as the reservation of ownership is in force. In spite of this, there is, however, the risk of a transfer by the buyer to a bona-fide purchaser pursuant to ss. 932 et seq. of the Civil Code which cannot be avoided by a title retention clause.

¶119   Common types of clauses

In response to the diverse interests of buyer and seller in commercial sales, several types of reservation of ownership (title retention) clauses have become common practice. The more important types include:

(1) *Simple reservation of ownership.*   If a simple reservation of ownership clause is used, the acquisition of a full property interest by the buyer is dependent on the full payment of the purchase price for the goods as discussed under 'General concept' at ¶118 above. This type of clause is used in consumer transactions if there is no risk of a resale of the goods.

(2) *Authorisation for resales and assignment of future claims.*   If the purchaser buys the goods in order to resell them to third parties, it is often agreed that the buyer shall be authorised to resell the goods without disclosing the seller's property interest, but only on the basis of a second reservation of ownership clause. In addition, the buyer's future payment claims against third parties resulting from such resales are usually assigned to the seller. The buyer is then authorised to collect such claims without disclosing the assignment as long as he does not default in performing his obligations to the seller. Upon default the seller may disclose the assignment and claim direct payment from the buyer's customer.

(3) *Accession.*   If the goods are used by the buyer for the production of a new product, it will usually be agreed that the seller's property in the goods will be replaced by a property share in the new product. This stipulation will usually be combined with an assignment clause of the type described above concerning a sale of the new product.

(4) *Current account.*   If the seller's payment claims against the buyer are not settled individually for each delivery, but rather at regular intervals on the basis of current accounts, reservation of ownership clauses usually provide that the

seller retains the ownership in the goods until the account has been fully settled. This clause has proved helpful in general where the seller is likely to make more than isolated sales to a given customer.

(5) *Affiliated enterprises.*   If the seller is a member of a group of affiliated companies, there may be a reservation of ownership clause that does not only secure the seller's payment claims, but also payment claims of the entire group.

¶120   Restrictions

The general validity of the above and similar clauses has been confirmed in many instances by German courts. Yet, details of such clauses must be drafted with care in order to avoid the possibility that they will be held void due to the specific circumstances in a given case. For instance, it must always be possible to identify the goods subject to a reservation of ownership clause, which may be difficult if large quantities are delivered on the basis of a continuing business relationship. Further, the title retention would be ineffective where the value of the collateral unreasonably exceeds the secured debt. The validity of reservation of ownership clauses is not specifically restricted by the Law on General Terms of Business (AGBG) (see 'General concept' at ¶118 above). However, details such as the clause in favour of affiliated enterprises may be held void because they are 'surprising' or unfair.

It should be noted that, by contrast with other legal systems, a reservation of ownership must not be registered under German law, nor are there any other formal requirements. It has proved to be a most effective instrument for securing sellers' payment claims and replaces most other collateral available under German law.

PRODUCT LIABILITY

¶121   US v German law

The term 'product liability' was initially developed under United States law. In the US the predominant rule is that of strict liability. The manufacturer will normally be held liable without proof of his negligence being demanded, if one of his products has caused damage to a customer. Even the damage to the supplied article itself and pure financial losses have been held to be recoverable under the strict liability doctrine. The burden of proof of the claimant is not clear, even with respect to the existence of a defect. In effect, the manufacturer can be considered as 'insurer against damages caused by the use of its products'.

German courts have, to date, not departed from the fundamental principle of their legal system, namely that – with some statutorily determined exceptions – liability implies fault. They protect the consumer by imposing on manufacturers not only high duties of care with respect to the quality of their products, but also the burden of proof that they did not negligently fail to meet those strict requirements.

The product liability rules were implemented into the existing statutory concept of contractual and tort claims. Some authorities believe the protection of the consumer not to be satisfactorily effected by these means, however. Amendments have been made, therefore, particularly at the European level, which have resulted in a directive of the EEC Council aimed at the harmonisation of the product liability laws of the member countries (see 'New legislative initiatives' at ¶129 below).

It should be noted that German courts tend to be more reluctant to award high compensation than US courts (see 'Assessments of compensation' at ¶127 below).

The apparently reduced exposure of a manufacturer in Germany as compared with other countries (including the United States) has not only substantive but also procedural and practical reasons. One reason may be that Germany prohibits contingency fees: an injured party must sue at its own risk. Moreover, the loser must reimburse the winner's legal fees and court costs, such fees and costs depending upon the amount of damage claimed (see Chapter 13: 'Litigation in Civil Courts' at ¶1304 et seq.).

¶122   Violation of duties of care and protection

Product liability in Germany is in essence liability under tort law.

By far the most important basis for product liability claims is s. 823(1) of the Civil Code ('BGB'). It provides that compensation may be awarded if a person intentionally or negligently causes a wrongful violation of the specifically protected 'absolute rights' of another person, such as health, life and property.

(1) *Manufacturer*

The tortfeasor in such a case may be the manufacturer. A manufacturer is held to be under a duty to ensure that every reasonable effort has been made to render the products which are 'brought into commerce' safe, i.e. to avoid defects as far as may reasonably be expected. If it does not perform this duty it acts unlawfully and may be held liable as a tortfeasor for damages caused thereby.

A manufacturer is anyone who produces an article, even if it only consists in assembling prefabricated parts. In this latter case both the producer of the parts and the assembler are to be considered manufacturers, and each of them is responsible for its share of the manufacturing process. The assembler, however, cannot discharge its obligations by sharing the production with a third party.

Distributors only have restricted obligations to examine supplied products if they have reason to doubt that the products are in perfect condition. As opposed to the attempts of some authorities to treat an importer as a manufacturer (at least, if it 'brings into commerce' the articles under its own name) the Federal Court has ruled (NJW 1980, 1219) that an importer has in principle only the duties of a distributor. The case concerned the importation of a product from another EEC country, but the court indicated that the result might be different if articles were imported from undeveloped countries with lower standards of quality.

(2) Defect

Case law has developed three typical groups of product defects:

(a) *Defective construction.*   The standard of safety of a product has to comply with the minimum safety requirements imposed at any one time. This is not the case if, e.g. reasonable consumer protection devices are missing, the materials used do not have the solidity which the consumer can reasonably expect, the use of an article is unnecessarily complicated, or even if the construction itself induces the customer to a dangerous use contrary to the instructions. The manufacturer is not liable for risks not perceptible in the construction phase using reasonable care and attention (so-called 'development risk'). However, as soon as such risk become obvious, the manufacturer may be obligated to modify the construction, instruct the consumers appropriately and eventually recall already delivered products.

(b) *Defective fabrication.*   The manufacturing process must be organised and supervised in a manner such that, under the current state of technology, individual defects are eliminated as far as possible. If certain risks cannot be excluded, adequate quality control must be provided.

(c) *Insufficient instruction.*   If the nature of a product implies certain risks which cannot be eliminated, the manufacturer has a duty to warn the consumer. Such instructions must be clear and simple, which means above all in the language of the consumer. The Federal Court stated (17 March 1981, BGHZ 80, 186) that this duty exists even if the product itself is not dangerous but is ineffective under certain circumstances and the consumer, relying on the effectiveness, does not use another device to avoid damages.

(3) Violation of duties

The defect must be caused by the violation of the duty of care of the manufacturer. Most of these duties have already been mentioned, such as the obligation

¶122

to organise, supervise and control production as well as to clearly inform and warn the consumer. Another important duty involves monitoring products 'brought into commerce' for defects which appear only after distribution has commenced.

(4) *Fault*

As discussed above, liability implies at least negligence in the violation of certain duties. This includes insufficient organisation. In case of manufacturing defects the question is whether or not the defect was inevitable in spite of sufficient control and supervising devices.

(5) *Shifting the burden of proof*

Generally, German procedural rules impose on the plaintiff the burden to prove all facts supporting his claim. As a centre of the product liability doctrine, the Federal Court has partly shifted this burden to the manufacturer. It has been well established case law since 1969 that, if an injured person shows that recoverable damage was caused by a defective product, it is for the manufacturer to make representations and prove that it was not his fault that caused the defect. The court realises that, due to modern, complicated plant organisation, it is impossible for the injured individual to produce evidence in this respect. It is only the manufacturer, if anyone, who has the necessary insight and information.

As far as insufficient instructions are concerned, the burden of proof even includes the question whether or not the consumer had used the product correctly, if a proper instruction had been given. In other cases, prima facie rules are applied in favour of the plaintiff as to the question of causality between defect and damage.

This jurisprudence moves product liability in the direction of strict liability because, under normal circumstances, it will be difficult for the manufacturer to discharge his burden of proof. On the other hand, case-law has further refined this doctrine. More recently, the Federal Court ruled that in the case of an allegedly insufficient instruction, before the manufacturer needs to discharge his burden of proof, the plaintiff must prove that the scientific or technological information given was complex enough to give rise to the obligation of the manufacturer to give additional warnings or instructions (BGH 80, 186).

(6) *Recoverable damages*

Not all kinds of damages are recoverable under this scheme; only those resulting from a violation of a so-called 'absolute right', such as life, health or

¶122

property. This means that purely financial losses are not recoverable, such as profit reductions due to a failure of the product as opposed to a loss due to reduced working hours on account of illness caused by a defective product.

Damage to the defective product itself is generally not acknowledged as a property violation, unless the damage clearly exceeds the amount by which the defect itself devalues the product from the time of the purchase. According to a recent ruling of the Federal Court it must be determined from an economical viewpoint whether or not the defect makes the device practically valueless in its entirety from the beginning or not (NJW 1983, 810). This was denied and, therefore, the manufacturer held liable, e.g. when defective tyres (NJW 1978, 2241, 2242) or a defective accelerator pedal (NJW 1983, 811) caused the destruction of the entire car.

¶ 123   Violation of a protective regulation

A second route to recovery is s. 823(2) BGB which provides for compensation if the statutory law designed to protect the consumer is negligently or intentionally violated. In this respect the *Gerätesicherheits-Gesetz* (Equipment Safety Act) of 24 June 1968 is of particular importance. It provides that a manufacturer or importer of mechanical tools, machines or other work equipment, as well as of household appliances, toys and sports equipment must not bring those goods onto the German market unless they are in such a condition that operators, users and even third parties are protected against risks to their life and health.

The manufacturing standards to be met are the generally recognised rules of engineering as well as existing accident prevention regulations. Alternative production techniques are permissible, if equally safe conditions can be guaranteed.

The *Gerätesicherheits-Gesetz* only covers injuries to life or health and does not permit recovery of economic losses or property damages.

The manufacturer or importer acts negligently if he can foresee that his product will not meet the requirements of the *Gerätesicherheits-Gesetz*. It is not necessary for the injured user to show that the manufacturer could have foreseen that his product could lead to the injury.

If the plaintiff can show a violation of the *Gerätesicherheits-Gesetz*, it is for the manufacturer or importer to prove that he is not at fault (BGH, NJW 1969, 269, 274).

An importer does not necessarily have the same duties as a manufacturer. However, he must inspect the imported goods to ensure compliance with the recognised rules of engineering and the accident prevention regulations (BGH, NJW 1980, 1219).

¶124   Liability for wrongful acts of employees

The initial statutory remedy for recovering damages resulting from defective products was s. 831 BGB, imposing on a manufacturer/employer liability for damages caused by wrongful acts of employees, unless the employer could exculpate himself by showing that he did not negligently select, supervise or equip the employee or that the damage was unavoidable even if he had done so.

Technically, it is the fault of the manufacturer himself, and not that of the employee, which is the basis of the liability. Thus, in complex and decentralised manufacturing units courts have held it to be sufficient that the employer only proves that he did not negligently select and supervise the higher ranking supervisory staff responsible for the further delegation of duties in their respective departments.

Although case-law already imposes the burden of proof on the manufacturer where the plaintiff shows a defective product without any additional representation as to wrongful behaviour of the employee, and although it has also increased the requirements of proof during the last two decades, large corporations with sophisticated personnel testing and training programmes usually should be able to satisfy this duty.

For this reason, s. 831 BGB lost its importance for product liability claims and was more or less replaced by the concepts discussed above ('Violation of duties of care and protection'; 'Violation of a protective regulation').

¶125   Strict liability in drug cases

Since 1976, the new Drug Law (*Arzneimittelgesetz*) of 24 August 1976 provides for the strict liability of a drug manufacturer if damage is caused by the harmful effects of a drug or by insufficient instructions based on current medical and scientific knowledge (ss. 84–94). The maximum compensation is DM 500,000 or an annual pension of DM 30,000 in the event of the injury or death of one individual and DM 200,000,000 or an annual pension of DM 12,000,000, if several individuals are concerned. No compensation for pain and suffering is available.

¶126   Contractual liability

Unless the manufacturer sells its products directly to the consumer (which certainly is the exception in modern, multiple-level distribution schemes), contractual claims are perceptible only as a result of explicit warranties of the manufacturer. As a rule, warranties are restricted to the repair or substitution of the product which does not meet the warranty, and does not extend to consequential damages. However, the interpretation of the warranty in individual cases may result in finding that the warranty was intended to include consequential damages, such as loss of time or profit, as well as physical injuries (BGH, NJW 1981, 2249). If such interpretation is made, no fault of the manufacturer will have to be shown, which means that a kind of strict liability is acknowledged in those cases. On the other hand, the contractual relationship may also enable the manufacturer/seller to restrict or exclude its liability. However, liability restrictions or exclusions are not acknowledged if they appear in general terms and conditions (see 'Void clauses' at ¶117 above).

¶127   Assessments of compensation

Under s. 249 BGB, compensation means restoration of the condition which would exist without the wrongful act. An injured person must be in neither a worse nor in a better position than he would have been if the wrongful act had not occurred. Thus, no punitive and no exemplary damages are acknowledged. Compensation for pain and suffering is explicitly provided for in s. 847 BGB, but such compensation is usually calculated more conservatively than, for example, in the US. Loss of support is only recoverable to the extent that the deceased was legally liable to support the plaintiff. Moreover, German law requires the plaintiff to undertake all reasonable measures to reduce the amount of damages. For example, in a wrongful death action, a widow may be required to obtain employment in order to reduce a lost support claim, if she can be expected to do so under the given circumstances. Certain collateral sources of payment reduce the amount of any damages; e.g., the pension claim of a widow is reduced by the support provided by her new husband in case of a remarriage. No compensation is made for the loss of consortium or pre-accident pain and suffering.

¶128   Insurability

A question of immense practical importance is to what extent the product liability risk on the German market may be insured. The scope of this chapter does not permit detailed discussion of this question, but matters to be considered include whether to cover the worldwide production and distribution with a uniform insurance policy effective at the domicile of the parent company or the headquarters of a combine, or whether to rely on domestic insurances in each individual market.

The first alternative certainly has its advantages. Close relations between the manufacturer and its general insurer simplify communication and formalities.

The insurer should be aware of the specific needs of its client. The accumulated demand of the insured producer usually guarantees advantageous premiums.

On the other hand there are certain risks involved with activities on the German market which may not be covered by a foreign policy, such as the aforementioned liability for express warranties or the recourse to social security agencies in cases of personal injury or wrongful death cases.

Moreover, the generally lower exposure to risk of a manufacturer under the German concept of damage compensation might result in lower rates than a US insurer accustomed to US compensation awards would charge.

Insurance experts tend to recommend, as a general rule, a combination of a domestic insurance focused on the special requirements of the German market with an umbrella insurance of the parent company covering (as a so-called 'catastrophe-layer') risks of worldwide production exceeding the domestic coverage.

In any event, it should be noted that exposure on the German market may not automatically and entirely be covered by a general worldwide insurance policy. The particular needs and requirements of the respective manufacturer and its product line should be taken into consideration in order to establish appropriate, tailor-made insurance coverage for commercial activities on the German market.

¶ 129   New legislative initiatives

New developments have been initiated at European level. On 27 January 1977, the European Council presented the 'European Convention on Products Liability in the Regard to Personal Injury and Death' (European treaty series no. 91), which has since been signed by Belgium, France, Luxembourg and Austria.

Independently thereof, the Council of the European Community released on 25 July 1985 the 'Directive Providing a Harmonisation of the Statutory and Administrative Provisions of the Member Countries concerning the Liability for Defective Products' (*Richtlinie des Rates zur Angleichung der Rechts- und Verwaltungsvorschriften der Mitgliedstaaten über die Haftung für fehlerhafte Produkte*) (OJ 1985 L 210, p. 29). The new Directive, which is to be incorporated into the domestic laws of the member countries by 30 July 1988, establishes strict liability of the manufacturer and importer for personal and property damage caused by defects of its products. 'Manufacturer' includes everybody who participates in the production process, irrespective of whether the final product is produced or only a part thereof. The 'importer' is the person or firm who imports goods into the EEC. Several participants shall be jointly and severally liable.

A product is considered defective, it if does not provide the safety reasonably expectable. The plaintiff must prove the damage and the defect as well as the causal relation between the two. There is a deductible amount to be borne by the plaintiff of 500 European Currency Units (ECU), which are approximately DM 1,075.

The manufacturer may discharge its liability if it proves that:

(1) it did not bring the defective device onto the market; or

(2) the defect did not exist when the product was brought onto the market;

(3) the defect is the result of complying with mandatory legal requirements;

(4) the defect could not be detected using knowledge or technology available at the time when the product was brought into commerce (which means that so-called development defects are excluded from strict liability); or

(5) it was only responsible for part of the product and the defect is related to the construction of the final product into which that part was integrated, or to instructions of the manufacturer of the final product.

Any comparative negligence of the injured party may reduce or eliminate the manufacturer's liability.

The Directive does not affect the laws of the member states concerning compensation for pain and suffering or claims based on express or implied warranties. Member countries may, within certain bounds, also establish strict liability for development defects or limit the total liability of a manufacturer for wrongful death and personal injury damages caused by the same product to the amount of at least 70,000,000 ECU.

DATA PROTECTION

¶130   Scope of legislation

The Federal Republic of Germany was one of the first countries to enact national data protection legislation, the '*Gesetz zum Schutz vor Mißbrauch personenbezogener Daten bei der Datenverarbeitung BDSG*' of 27 January 1977. Furthermore, on 13 March 1985 Germany ratified the Council of Europe Convention for the Protection of Individuals with Regard to Automatic Processing of Personal Data of 28 January 1981.

The BDSG has as its expressed object the adequate protection of privacy (s. 1(1)), but only information on natural persons is protected by statute (s. 1(1) and (2)). The law distinguishes between data processing by public and by private entities, and only the latter will be covered by the provisions discussed below.

'Data processing' includes all data related operations, but not the mere collection of personal data (s. 1(2)). In consequence, data protection will start when personal data are stored. The BDSG is not limited to automatic files, but also to data processing with conventional methods. However, simple storing of personal data in conventional files which are not meant for transmission to third parties would escape BDSG (s. 1(2)).

The law distinguishes between data processing for the purposes of the private entity itself (so-called 'auxiliary activities,' ss. 22–30) and data operations as a main business objective of a company (ss. 31–40). In both cases the processing of personal data is only permissible if the data subject has consented thereto or if it is expressly allowed by law, which may be the BDSG or any other statutory provision (s. 3 BDSG). Consent must be given by the data subject in writing, except where another form is appropriate because of special circumstances. In the absence of such consent data processing may only be considered as 'lawful' under the BDSG in prescribed circumstances, which involve the careful evaluation and balancing of the conflicting interests of the data processing company and the private data owner. As general and vague as the wording of the BDSG may be, it is strictly applied by the courts and commented upon in great detail by legal writers.

¶131   Data processing as 'auxiliary activity'

(1) *Storage*

Section 23 BDSG allows a private company or an individual to store personal data:

(1) either within the scope of the purpose of a contract or a quasi-contractual relationship of trust with the individual concerned, or where the storage is required to serve a legitimate interest of the storing party, provided always that there are no reasons to believe that the storage will affect the legitimate interests of the individual concerned; or

(2) if the data are stored by non-automatic means, provided that the data are derived directly from generally accessible sources.

Serving the 'purposes of a contractual relationship' between data processor and data subject includes, for example, the storage of data on the credit standing of a borrower by a lender.

'Legitimate interests of the data processor' do not need to be provided by law, but have been held by the Federal Court to include commercial interests (BGH, NJW 1984, p. 1886; BGH, NJW 1984, p. 1887; BGH, NJW 1984, p. 1889). For instance, the storage of data necessary to solicit new customers could constitute such an interest as the increase of customers is generally a legitimate business concern. However, the storing party has to weigh its interest against the concerns of the individual. A general evaluation will be sufficient in this context unless a specific reason against the storage becomes apparent. Whether such 'reason' exists, will primarily depend on the nature of the personal data stored. Data commonly available, such as name, address or profession, normally will not meet objections, while data concerning the individual's religion, political affiliations or health will usually be considered unsuitable for storage. 'Generally accessible sources' includes telephone directories.

(2) *Transmission*

Personal data may be disclosed (transmitted) to third parties under s. 24 BDSG:

(1) either within the scope of the purpose of a contract or a quasi-contractual relationship of trust with the individual, or if the transmission is required to serve legitimate interests of the transmitting entity, of a third party or of the general public; or

(2) if only a list of personal data is transmitted which is confined to names, titles or academic degrees, birth dates, professions or designations of branch or business, addresses and telephone numbers (so-called 'list privilege');

provided always that there are no reasons to believe that the transmission will affect the legitimate interests of the individual concerned.

Legitimate interests of the data processor have to be weighed against those of the data subject as in the case of storage. However, unlike s. 23, the legitimate interests of the data processor may be replaced by those of a third party or of the general public. Hence, a generalised evaluation of both interests will not be sufficient. Rather, each individual case must be carefully scrutinised. For example, while the disclosure of personal data for promotional purposes may in principle be regarded as within the legitimate interests of the recipient, such interest must be balanced against the legitimate interest of the data subject not to receive unsolicited advertising materials, and in the end such disclosure would be considered illegal. The interest in a transmission requires particular justification if the information was supplied for a specific (contractual) purpose, but was then transmitted to a third party for a different purpose. In such cases the consent of the data subject is considered mandatory.

As a result, the 'legitimate interest' alternative of s. 24 will offer a sufficient basis for the transmission only in exceptional cases.

¶131

The 'list privilege' will be available only if the transmission is confined to the six categories of data expressly named. The evaluation of mutual interests is also required here, but a general consideration of both will be sufficient.

(3) *Modification*

Section 25 BDSG allows the modification of personal data either within the scope of the purpose of the contract or a quasi-contractual relationship of trust with the individual concerned, or if the modification is required to serve a legitimate interest of the storing party, provided always that there are no reasons to believe that the modification will affect the legitimate interests of the individual concerned.

'Modification' is defined as including any alternation or transformation of the content (s. 2(2) no. 3). Even the correction of an address would be considered as 'modification'.

¶132   Data processing as business objective

Companies which have data processing as their business objective are treated more favourably by the BDSG than those for which it is an auxiliary activity. Apparently personal data are considered to be less at risk in the first case. Such companies are required to file with the local supervisory authorities (s. 39).

Storage is generally permitted if no reason exists to believe that the legitimate interests of the individual concerned will be affected by such storage or if the data are derived directly from generally accessible sources (s. 32(1)).

Transmission is permissible if the interest of the receiving party can be demonstrated or if only lists of limited personal data of members of a group (restricted to the name, title, address and a description of the affiliation of the individual to such group) are to be transmitted, provided again that no reason exists for the transmitting company to believe that such transmission will affect the legitimate interest of the individual concerned (s. 32).

Modification is permitted unless the legitimate interests of the individual concerned will be affected (s. 33).

¶133   Right of access

A key element of German data protection law is the data subject's right of access to his personal data, which includes the right:

(1) to be informed immediately when personal data concerning him/her are stored unless he/she learns of the storage by other means (ss. 24(1) and 34(1));

(2) to be informed of all details of the personal data stored concerning him and to learn the persons to whom and establishments to which such data are regularly communicated (s. 26(2) and s. 34(2)); and

(3) to challenge the relevancy and accuracy of such data, and to require correction or even destruction of the stored data (ss. 27 and 35).

Companies and individuals which use automatic (e.g. computerised) methods to process data on individuals where such data processing is an auxiliary activity, and which regularly employ at least five persons to handle such processing, must name a 'data controller' (*Datenschutzbeauftragter*). The data controller shall be responsible for ensuring compliance with the BDSG (ss. 28, 29 and 38).

The supervisory authorities are entitled to request information on data processing performed by a private entity and to have access to the data processor's premises and files if suspicion of any infringment of the law exists. The authorities must not disclose any data so inspected to any other public authority.

¶134 Trans-border data flow

The BDSG does not directly address the question of to what extent a trans-border data flow between private enterprises is permissible, and no Federal Court decisions are yet available. Following the prevailing view in legal literature, however, the restrictions applicable to data processing in Germany must be applied at least as strictly to the transmission of personal data across the German borders. Even transmission between affiliated companies is considered as a disclosure of personal data to a third party in the sense of ss. 24 and 32(2). Hence, the legality of a trans-border transmission of personal data will depend upon an evaluation of the mutual interests concerned, unless alternative justification can be derived from the purpose of a contract existing with the data subject.

In evaluating such interests, all major commentaries concur that the interests of the individual will be particularly affected if his data are transmitted to a jurisdiction which does not have equally strict data protection legislation. Consequently, whether the transmission of personal data to a foreign country will be allowed under German law, depends on an analysis of the data protection legislation of such country.

The criteria for a comparison with the German law include:

(1) the existence and enforceability of the right of access for the individual;

(2) the right to request correction and/or destruction of incorrect or inappropriate data; and

(3) the right to refuse disclosure of personal data to public authorities by the data processor.

Using these criteria France, for example, is generally considered to have an equivalent legislation to the BDSG. If no such equivalent legislation exists, and trans-border transmission cannot be justified by contractual purposes, it would be legal only with the consent of the individual concerned.

¶135 Sanctions against unlawful data processing

The failure to inform a data subject when personal data concerning him or her are first stored, and other comparable offences, is subject to a fine of up to DM 50,000 (s. 42). Illegal transmission or modification of personal data is subject to imprisonment or administrative fines of unlimited amounts (s. 41).

In addition, the injured party has a claim in tort for damages in line with the German Civil Code. A draft amendment to the BDSG under discussion at this time even provides for strict liability of the data processor.

2 Importing into Germany (Customs)

SOURCES OF CUSTOMS LAW

¶201 General outline

The customs law applicable in the Federal Republic of Germany has three main sources: national legislation, European Community legislation and international treaties. National customs legislation is based on the Customs Act of 14 June 1961, extensively amended in 1970 (with a last amendment in 1980), which was designed to synchronise it with the Foreign Trade Act of 1970. The Customs Act and supplementary legislation and regulations include customs duties as well as prohibitions and restrictions on the movement of goods for the protection of the German economy, public health, agriculture, the environment and public order.

As a member of the European Community, Germany is also subject to the Common Customs Tariff (CCT) legislation of the Community. Such legislation governs tariffs on all goods imported into member states of the Community from outside, including special regulations concerning associate states and certain other preferentially treated states, and bans tariffs on intra-Community trade. Community measures also include numerous regulations and directives harmonising Community Law in areas other than tariffs.

Germany is party to numerous international, mostly multilateral, agreements concerning customs, such as the International Convention on the Simplification of Customs Formalities, and the General Agreement on Tariffs and Trade (GATT). She is also a member of the Customs Co-operation Council (CCC, formerly the Brussels Customs Council), and party to the two agreements served by it, the Nomenclature for the Classification of Goods in Customs Tariffs (CCCN) and the Convention on the Valuation of Goods for Customs Purposes.

DIFFERENT CUSTOMS TREATMENTS

¶202   Community customs treatment

Goods which have been cleared for free circulation in a member state of the European Community may enter Germany free of customs duties or charges that have an equivalent effect. The only exceptions are 'monetary compensating amounts' in the agricultural area, collected in order to balance currency fluctuation disparities that disrupt the common price level sought for various commodities, and the differential duties of the European Coal and Steel Community, levied as a form of anti-dumping duty on various products from countries selling at a low price. Intra-community goods require documentation showing evidence of the right to preferential tariff treatment. However, postal traffic and private passenger traffic do not require such documentation.

¶203   Tariff preferences for developing countries

(1) *General tariff preferences*

Since 1 July 1971, the European Community member states have been granting general, nondiscriminatory and nonreciprocal tariff preferences to (presently) 148 independent countries and dependent territories. For those states that also receive a regional tariff preference (see below), the more favorable treatment under the respective regulations is applied.

These Community preferences, which are revised annually, provide for exemption from duties for all semi-finished and finished industrial goods imported within the tariff quota or tariff ceiling on the volume of imports from these developing countries (excluding the countries and territories also receiving regional preferences), plus five per cent of the import quota from the other countries in certain reference years. A tariff quota is applied only to so-called 'sensitive products', the duty-exempt import of which is restricted by volume for each EEC member state (the total EEC quota being divided up among the members). For other goods, the ceilings for the entire EEC are applied without allocation by member states. 'Quasi-sensitive' goods, the excessive import of which would endanger the economies of the member states, are subject to a stricter control procedure than other goods.

There is an additional *per country* limitation, according to which an individual developing country may alone be responsible for only 50 per cent of the entire ceiling amount duty free. For certain goods this per country 'buffer' is reduced to 30 per cent, and other special rates exist for certain goods from particularly competitive developing countries. However, no limitation is placed on quasi-sensitive and non-sensitive manufactured goods from the 28 least developed countries.

To receive a tariff preference, it is necessary to present a proper certificate of origin issued by one of the authorised offices in the developing countries.

(2) *Regional customs tariff preferences*

The EEC also grants preferential treatment for goods from countries with which it has concluded an association, free trade co-operation, or other preferential treatment convention. A reciprocal preference is granted on the basis of a customs union applicable to goods coming from free circulation in the countries of the EEC and Turkey. All other regional preferences apply exclusively to goods originating in the subject country. Regulations on origin, and documentary evidence thereof, are specified in each agreement.

(3) *German Democratic Republic*

It should be noted that the German Democratic Republic (East Germany) is *not* considered foreign customs territory within the meaning of the Customs Act. Goods traffic with the German Democratic Republic is supervised by the customs administration but no customs duties are collected. Such trade is governed by the Protocol on German-German Trade and Connected Matters.

(4) *Miscellaneous preferences*

A preferential tariff may be granted for goods from any source, that are determined by the EEC to be in insufficient supply in the Community. A 'tariff quota' for such goods is established, and the quantity or value of goods imported under this quota receives the preferential rate. Additional imports receive the normal tariff rate.

A preferential tariff is also given to certain goods according to the use to which the goods are put. Such treatment is regulated by a Community procedure pursuant to EEC reg. no. 1535/77. Application in writing is required, and upon authorisation a permit will be issued. The goods will be cleared for free circulation, with the condition that they are actually used as stipulated otherwise an amount will be due to customs.

Certain goods, especially agricultural products, have variable tariff rates according to season.

Tariff reductions are granted under s. 26 of the Customs Act for goods produced in foreign customs territories but following domestic 'designs', including drawings, plans, manuscripts, clothes patterns, models, etc. This tariff treatment must be approved in advance by customs. In these cases, the basis for assessing the dutiable value will not be the full value of the goods but only

¶203

the cost of production, including delivery, packing, and accessories costs and an appropriate profit. This tariff reduction requires the prior approval of the customs authorities.

CUSTOMS PROCEDURE

¶204   Obligations of the foreign exporter

(1) *General*

Both the Customs Act and the Foreign Trade Act impose obligations on the importer and on the person liable to pay duty, who may be different parties. The foreign exporter thus has no statutory obligations unless he acts also as the importer or person liable to pay duty, which is usually not the case. However, for smoother transactions, and to help his German trading partner, the foreign exporter should present proper documents for customs clearance and should observe the statutory requirements concerning quality and specifications of goods to be imported.

It should be noted that customs clearance does not indicate that the product complies with all legal requirements for admission onto the German market. Other legislation concerning the purity and contents of foods, the safety specifications of industrial products, etc., must be complied with independently (see Chapter 1 — 'Import and Export Restrictions' at ¶102 et seq.).

In general there are no marking requirements for packages, except that false declarations of origin and abuse of registered trademarks are unlawful. Furthermore, the origin, purity, and certain other data are required to be declared for certain food and agricultural products in order to protect the consumer.

(2) *Documentation*

For goods delivered against payment and on which customs duties are payable, the written customs declaration submitted by the person liable to pay the duties (see 'Customs declaration' at ¶207 below) must be accompanied by an invoice in duplicate. Unlike many countries, Germany imposes no strict requirements as to the contents of the invoice. Thus compliance with the customary standards in international trade should suffice, provided, of course, that the names and addresses of the seller and buyer, a precise description of the goods and their quantity, price and terms of delivery and payment are included. Under the Foreign Trade Act the invoice must also show the country of purchase and country of origin of the goods.

¶204

A separate certificate or declaration of origin is required under foreign trade law for only a few commodities. In general, origin may be significant for preferential treatment under the customs laws. Unless the presentation of a formal certificate of origin is specifically prescribed, proof of origin by invoices, correspondence or other written documents is sufficient. The requirements pertaining to certificates of origin are contained in the International Agreement on the Simplification of Customs Formalities of 3 November 1923. The common definition of the EEC is applicable to the origin of goods (see 'Product Origin' at ¶217 below).

Furthermore, various EEC regulations provide specific standards for certificates of origin with respect to certain types of goods. Certificates of origin of a special nature are the 'movement certificates' that serve as proof of eligibility for preferential treatment for goods from associated countries or other countries with whom a treaty for preferential treatment has been concluded. The treaties themselves set the requirements for such movement certificates. Corresponding rules apply under Community legislation with respect to proof of origin from the developing countries.

¶205   Presentation of goods

Goods transported by road and inland waterways may only be imported via approved routes and during working hours of the customs offices. Ocean shipping is also confined to approved routes. Maritime and air traffic must use officially stipulated docking places and airports. Imported goods become subject to customs control at the moment they cross the border and must be presented to the customs office at the customs frontier without delay. However, with the approval of the customs office at the airport of entry, goods transported by air may be presented at any other airport customs office in Germany. A special rule applies to railway freight traffic in that presentation at the border is not required.

Presentation normally occurs at the point of destination unless there are restrictions on the movement of the particular goods across the border. In the case of postal traffic, the Federal Postal Administration is responsible for presentation of the goods and it may choose the place of presentation of the goods. The Postal Administration is entitled to carry out customs clearance itself unless the consignee has reserved that right to himself. Smaller, inexpensive packages and certain other items sent by post do not require customs clearance.

The person responsible for presentation of the goods is the person who brought them into the territory, namely the driver, ship's master, or pilot, or the railway or postal administration. In commercial transport, the goods are usually put at the disposal of the customs authorities by presenting the documents accompanying the goods, particularly the waybills. In the case of tourist traffic, it is generally sufficient to appear with the goods at the place of presentation. Unless presentation is immediately followed by customs treatment, the dutiable goods must be taken into official custody. The duration of custody is restricted to the period for filing a valid customs application, i.e. 15 days in general and 45 days if presentation is made immediately after transport by sea.

¶206 Customs application

Customs treatment cannot be effected unless customs clearance is applied for. The applicant is the person entitled to dispose of the goods and liable to pay duty, but the customs office does not examine the right of disposal and ownership. The applicant determines the type of customs treatment to be adopted by this entry for clearance, but only legally admissible treatment may be selected. The application must be filed within 15 days of presentation (45 days in the case of presentation immediately after ocean shipment) and may be modified or withdrawn. It should also be noted that import clearance often must also be applied for with customs clearance, pursuant to foreign trade legislation.

¶207 Customs declaration

In addition to the application for clearance, the person liable to pay duty must declare the goods, stating the characteristics relevant for the customs treatment and the nine-digit code number of the German Official Customs Tariff. If necessary the help of the customs office is available. The customs office can simplify the declaration for regularly imported goods, but complete summaries of the simplified entries must be submitted monthly (see 'Customs treatment without clearance' at ¶210 below).

Statements on the value of goods may only be made by one who is the buyer or consignee of the goods and a resident in any EEC customs territory, which person may or may not be the applicant. If there is no such buyer or consignee, the obligation to declare the customs value passes to the foreign non-EEC supplier, but a domestic authorised person may act on his behalf. The customs declaration and declaration of customs value are tax declarations within the meaning of the German tax regulations, and therefore must be correct and complete to the best of the declarant's knowledge and belief.

The declaration of customs value under EEC reg. no. 1496/80 of 11 June 1980 (which contains a questionnaire) has been incorporated into the relevant German forms. A commentary of the Commission of the Community and a leaflet issued by the German Customs Administration are helpful in completing these forms. It is required in particular to declare any special relationships or arrangements existing between buyer and seller that benefit the seller without being reflected in the invoice price, and the declarant must exercise special skill and care in assessing and properly completing the customs forms. False declarations of value are subject to penal proceedings.

For goods supplied against payment, the customs declaration must be accompanied by the invoice plus one duplicate. Upon request by the customs office, the purchase contract and any other documents relevant to assessing value must be submitted.

¶208   Customs value – transaction value

Under reg. no. 1224/80, which came into force on 1 July 1980, the Community took the first step towards implementing the customs valuation system agreed upon by the GATT member states in the Tokyo Round of GATT discussions. The new system represents a fundamental deviation from the hitherto so-called 'normal price' concept. It will take time to work out all of the details with additional legislation, but the basic system is as follows.

Five methods of determining the value of an imported article are provided in order of preference, each subsequent method being referred to only when the customs value cannot be determined using the previous one.

According to the first method the customs value will be the actual 'transaction value', i.e. the actual price for the imported goods, usually the invoice price. Four conditions must be met, however, before this method may be used:

(1) no limitations on the use of the goods by the buyer must exist, unless they are set by law, have no essential effect on the value of the goods, or merely limit the geographical area where the goods may be resold;

(2) no conditions must exist or further services with relation to the transaction be rendered the value of which cannot be determined and thereby calculated into the transaction value;

(3) no proceeds from later transfers or from use of the goods may be paid to the seller unless they can be calculated into the transaction; and

(4) no affiliation must exist between buyer and seller, or if they are affiliated, such relationship must not have any effect on the transaction value.

With respect to the requirement in (4) above, the regulation makes it clear that affiliation alone does not rule out the actual price, provided that the relationship has not in any way influenced the price. If the customs office believes that the relationship has had an effect on the price, it must state its reasons for so believing and allow the importer the opportunity to support the correctness of the price using evidence of sales of the same or similar goods between unrelated parties.

The regulation also specifies in great detail the costs and services paid for or rendered between the parties as part of the transaction price. In general, all costs with respect to the sale and delivery of the goods to the place of entry into the Community customs territory must be included in the value of the goods, except for taxes and customs duties paid on their sale or import.

If any of the conditions for the use of the first method are not met, then the second method is prescribed. This involves the use of a previously accepted transaction value for the same type of goods sold for import into the Community at roughly the same point in time, unless the prevailing conditions as spelled out by the regulation are different.

If no transaction involving the same type of goods is available, then the next method is to use a previously accepted transaction involving a similar type of goods sold for import into the Community.

Only in the fourth method is it prescribed that the customs value must correspond to the sales price within the Community, after import, of the same goods, the same type of goods, or a similar type of goods between an unrelated buyer and seller. The added costs such as taxes, customs duties, and insurance and transportation after import will be deducted. If the goods have been processed after import, the increase in value due to processing will also be deducted. The domestic sale which is closest in time to the import of the goods is to be used.

The fifth method derives the customs value from the production costs of the goods, plus an appropriate amount for profit and for all additional costs such as insurance and transportation to the point of entry into Community customs territory. The costs to be included are specified in detail in the regulation. The importer may choose to have the fifth method applied before the fourth.

If none of these five methods is available, other measures may be used in accordance with art. 7 of the GATT Agreement and the general provisions of the Agreement for implementing art. 7 entered into thereunder.

The importer may apply for a ruling of the customs authorities as to methods to be used for the valuation of the imported goods.

¶209   Clearance for home use

Customs treatment may include placement under special customs procedure, export, conversion under customs supervision, or even destruction. But with goods meant for domestic use, the norm is clearance for home use through exemption from duties or through customs clearance.

The customs authorities are free to examine the goods or to ask for further information.

Duty-free goods that are not subject to import turnover tax, other excise taxes, agricultural levies, or other import charges will be released by the customs authorities. The person concerned will be notified verbally.

For any other goods, the customs duty and other import charges are calculated and claimed from the person liable therefor by notice of assessment. Normally such notice of assessment is also verbal, but receipts and deferment notices are given in writing. Appeals against customs duty notifications must be lodged within one month. The customs authorities are entitled to modify a customs notice within the period of limitation (usually one year), and may issue a preliminary notice of assessment until final examination is carried out and the final assessment is ascertained.

Upon publication of the notice of duties or upon earlier release of dutiable goods, the customs debt becomes due and payable. On application by the customs debtor, payment may be deferred interest free to the fifteenth day of the month following the month the debt became due, if security is given. Deferment against payment of interest is only possible when immediate collection of duties would represent special hardship to the debtor and where ultimate collection is not jeopardised.

As soon as customs duty has been paid or deferred, the customs office releases the goods. The goods may be released earlier if the customs debtor appears reliable and no further examination of the goods is necessary.

¶210   Customs treatment without clearance

Under s. 40(1) of the Customs Act and the relevant regulations, it is possible to enter dutiable goods into free circulation without customs clearance in order to facilitate customs handling either following a presentation of the goods or under exemption from presentation:

(a) Following presentation, treatment without clearance is possible upon importation, after customs transit and after storage of the dutiable goods. The required authorisation from the responsible office will be issued if the goods can be described so clearly that they do not need to be inspected in order to fix the tariff classification or the import turnover tax, or in order to determine special features such as import restrictions.

(b) Customs treatment without clearance for goods without presentation is much rarer and applies only to bulk goods transported outside customs routes to avoid unreasonable detours, and to liquids and gases in pipelines. The same conditions must be observed as in treatment without clearance for goods that are presented, and the same regulations apply to declaration, registration, keeping of accounts and payment.

¶211   Refund of customs duties

There are a number of situations in which duty paid goods are later re-exported without being used, such as rejection by the importer for breach of contract, delivery by mistake, etc. Duties may be refunded if the requirements set forth in EEC reg. no. 1430/79 are met. In general, the goods must not have been used in EEC customs territory; they must be re-exported under customs control within a deadline set by the tax office of no more than two months after customs clearance, and the amount refunded must be more than 10 ECU. Also, the import turnover tax may be refunded in such cases unless the applicant is in a position to deduct such tax from any other import turnover tax levy (see 'Special Import Duties' below) so that refunding would be unnecessary. Finally, re-mission of duties or other import charges may also be possible on grounds of equity.

¶212   Customs ruling

The customs offices will give non-binding verbal or written information on tariff classification and other customs matters. In addition, application may be made for binding information on the subheading under which goods will be classified. This information protects the applicant for a period of three months from assessment of a higher rate of charges than is indicated by the information, if the applicant can prove that he imported the relevant goods in reliance on that information. Furthermore, information may become invalid due to material changes of the nomenclature, of the General Regulations on Tariff Classification, and of the explanations of the customs tariff, and at the latest on the expiration of six years from its issuance. Each of five Regional Finance Offices (as set forth in ss. 28 to 31 General Customs Regulations) is responsible for the issuance of binding information for certain chapters of the customs tariff, so that uniform classification is possible without the need for constant contact between offices.

TARIFFS

¶213   German Official Customs Tariff

Germany, like the other member states of the Community, applies the 'Common Customs Tariff of the EEC' ('CCT'). It is supplemented by the 'German Partial Customs Tariff'. Both tariffs are combined in the 'German Official Customs Tariff'. These tariffs are based on the Brussels Tariff Nomenclature, which is used by over 130 countries and customs territories and which requires the

classification of any imported commodity under one heading or subheaɑ.
the tariff nomenclature before the applicable tariff rate can be applied.

The CCT is issued annually by EEC regulation and covers both industr.
goods and agricultural products, as well as the customs duties applicable to
goods subject to the Euratom Treaty. The duties relating to ECSC goods are
fixed by the various national customs tariffs of member states, but they are also
listed in the CCT for convenience. The CCT also indicates agricultural goods
that receive agricultural levies instead of or in addition to import duties, and
certain processed agricultural products that receive additional specific 'variable
component' charges. The CCT includes rules for interpretation of the nomenclature and certain other special regulations as well.

The German Partial Customs Tariff fills gaps left by the CCT and contains
those tariff measures that are still within German national statutory competence. This tariff is revised annually by ordinance and is subject to continuous
modification. It contains the preferential duties for ECSC products, the customs
regulations on goods originating from associated overseas countries and territories, suspended national tariffs and tariff quotas, and the anti-dumping duties
to be levied along with some rules of application.

The German Official Customs Tariff ('GOCT') comprises all Community
and national customs tariff regulations and gives a general survey of all other
statutory fields relevant to imports.

SPECIAL IMPORT DUTIES

¶214   Import turnover tax

The importation of objects into Germany is also subject to German import
turnover tax, which is one part of the German value added tax ('VAT') system.

Under the VAT system, a tax is imposed on every kind of transfer of goods or
services. The tax is included in the price to the transferee, and the transferor is
liable to remit this amount to the government. However, one who qualifies as a
commercial or professional 'entrepreneur' may first deduct as 'input tax' (or
pretax) the amount of tax he himself has paid on any domestic deliveries.
Basically, the same applies as regards the import turnover tax which normally
appears as a transitory item and not as a cost factor on the balance sheets of an
entrepreneur (for further details see Chapter 5 – 'Value Added Tax').

Importation is subject to the same tax rate as domestic transactions. However,
a number of goods may be imported tax free (especially those that receive non-
tariff exemption from duties), and others such as foodstuffs receive a reduced
rate of tax. The tax rates are indicated in the GOCT (see 'Tariffs' above).

Goods from East Germany and goods imported from abroad into free zones are not subject to import turnover tax.

Import turnover tax is classified as an excise tax, and therefore the relevant regulations of the German Revenue Code apply. However, it is also an import charge under the Customs Act and subject (with some exceptions) to the regulations on customs duties. As an import charge, the tax is collected from the importer of the goods by customs when the goods are cleared for home use (see ¶209 above).

The amount of the tax is calculated on the basis of the dutiable value of the goods plus the customs duty to be paid, any other excise tax due, and the cost of transport to the first domestic destination. In inter-Community trade, however, the amount of tax is based on the payment amount rather than dutiable value, as in domestic trade.

In general, the entrepreneur deducts import turnover tax as input tax in the calendar month in which it was paid. This means that, if he has not immediately resold the goods and thus collected the amount from the transferee, he must pre-finance such import turnover tax. Alternatively he may apply for deferred payment of the tax in the same way as for deferred payment of custom duties (see 'Clearance for home use' at ¶209 above).

The foreign supplier may opt to be the entrepreneur liable to pay the import turnover tax, and this may be to his advantage. For instance, if the sum of the input taxes due on domestic deliveries which he receives and of his import turnover tax payments exceeds the amount payable on his own deliveries, he would be entitled to claim repayment of the surplus.

¶215   Other excise taxes

Other excise taxes are collected on the production and importation of certain goods, such as spirits, tobacco products, coffee, etc. These excise taxes are specified in the GOCT.

¶216   Agricultural charges

Under the EEC Treaty the agricultural markets of the member states are gradually integrated into a common market through the medium of market organisations for the individual product sections. For protection of the Community interests agricultural levies are instituted to bridge world market prices that are lower than Community prices. At the same time Community exporters are granted refunds to allow them to sell at the world market price. If, on the other hand, the Community price is lower, export levies may be fixed to avoid shortages on the Community market.

Levies and refunds are the same in all member states and are established by EEC regulation. They appear in the Common Customs Tariff (included in the German Official Customs Tariff). Where market organisations have not been created, the regular customs duties of the Common Customs Tariff are applied. Regular customs regulations apply except where EEC Regulations, the German Levy Imposition Act, or the German Law on the Implementation of Common Market Organisations contain different provisions.

In the case of fruit, vegetables, and unprocessed coffee, the invoice price will be replaced by 'standard average values' as determined by the EEC Commission and German Federal Customs Administration upon application by the person liable to pay the duty as the basis for the relevant charges. It should finally be noted that EEC customs value regulations also apply to charges on Euratom and ECSC commodities.

PRODUCT ORIGIN

¶217   Country of origin

EEC reg. no. 802/68 on the common definition of the origin of goods is applicable in the member states and defines the country of origin as the country where the goods were extracted or produced. Difficulties arise where several countries have participated in the manufacture of a product. The general principle is that the country of origin is where the last essential manufacturing process has been carried out by an industrial enterprise. Other increases in value or customs clearance by a foreign country have no bearing on origin.

There is no general rule as to the type of activity which would result in a change of the country of origin of the commodity; rather, a case by case approach is taken. In principle, sorting and repacking will not suffice, but assembly from component parts may be an origin-defining process.

There are a number of additional EEC regulations containing specific rules of origin for certain goods, for example textile goods. The form and issue of certificates of origin are also regulated by EEC regulation (see 'Obligations of the foreign exporter' at ¶204 above).

Various preferential trade agreements of the EEC and unilateral tariff preferences for developing countries contain special provisions concerning origin, all of which are based on a particular model with individual adaptations. The model is similar to the general system discussed above, except that the requirements for sufficient processing to create a change in origin vary significantly.

PROCESSING AND CONVERSION

¶218   Active and passive processing

Active, or inward, processing is defined as the importation of goods into Germany for processing and re-exportation. In general, no customs duties or import turnover tax will be levied on such goods upon their importation. This rule does not apply, however, to goods re-exported to other EEC states; they are entered for home use and subsequently transported duty-free to the other member state. Processing in this context means any economically significant working or transformation of goods, including repair and assembly, and requires an increase in value.

The processor must apply for clearance of the dutiable goods at the competent customs office (normally the customs inland from the frontier). In addition, all processing operations require advance authorisation. Such authorisation will be granted for inward processing if certain economic and recording (proper accounting) conditions are fulfilled. Processing plants are subject to customs supervision.

There are two systems by which the identity of goods imported for processing is tracked:

(1) Under the first, the goods must be registered and identified upon re-export. Thus, only goods capable of being identified through one of several methods (e.g. serial numbers, special characteristics, precise descriptions) qualify for this kind of treatment, in which case they are treated as dutiable goods but duties are only paid at the time of re-export on waste matter that remains in Germany.

(2) Under the second system, the goods are imported duty-free and an equivalent volume of separate, compensating processed goods is exported. The processed goods may have been produced from any goods in free circulation, and may even have been exported before the duty-free unprocessed goods are imported. The compensating goods must be of similar description and quality, as specified by the guidelines issued by the Federal Ministry of Finance.

Deadlines are fixed for the exportation of the processed goods, and a customs debt comes into existence for all duty-free goods not exported by such deadline and for all by-products and waste remaining in Germany. If goods processed by inward processing subsequently enter free circulation through customs treatment, they are normally subject to the customs duties applicable to the processed goods, although under certain conditions the duties may be reduced to those applicable to the originally imported goods.

¶218

Passive, or outward, processing is defined as the exportation from Germany of goods for processing in another country followed by the reimportation of the processed goods. In general, the customs duties on the reimported goods will be reduced by the amount that would normally be levied on the import of the unprocessed goods involved; in other words, only the difference between the duties on the processed and unprocessed goods is due. Special regulations apply in those cases where the tariff rates for the processed goods are lower than for the unprocessed goods, and where tariff reductions are applicable to the unprocessed goods.

When goods with material defects are repaired under warranty free of charge by the foreign supplier, no customs duties are levied upon reimportation.

To receive the tariff advantage, it is necessary to file an application before exportation of the unprocessed goods. To receive authorisation, identification of the goods must be possible. In general, the same means of identification as in active processing apply. An identification certificate must be filed with German customs upon exportation of the unprocessed goods, and the foreign customs office uses such certificates later to confirm the identity of the re-exported goods. In repair procedures, it is possible to receive tariff advantages without prior authorisation if exportation is sufficiently proved.

Under foreign trade legislation, reimportation after outward processing is treated in the same way as regular importation of the processed goods.

BONDED AREAS

¶219   Free ports

The activities of the free ports of Germany consist of shipbuilding and storage, processing and transhipment of goods in foreign trade. In general, goods may be traded and shipped in free ports without customs restrictions, except for trade in ship provisions and certain other items. The free ports are separate from German customs territory, and the movement of persons and goods across this frontier is controlled.

Subject to certain conditions, domestic goods may be admitted for storage in a free port. Conversion is permissible to the same extent as within customs territory. Processing of dutiable goods from third countries is governed by the regulations on inward processing (see 'Processing and Conversion' above), and processing of domestic goods may also be authorised.

¶220   Bonded warehouses

Another way to store imported goods customs free as goods in transit, or to postpone customs for imported goods designed for the German market is the use of bonded warehouses which may be public or private. Public bonded warehouses are under the control of the customs authorities, whereas private ones may be under the joint or exclusive control of the importer or other private company. The establishment of a private bonded warehouse will be authorised only if (among other things) the authorities consider that there is a valid reason for allowing it (s. 42 et seq. Customs Act and s. 88 et seq. Customs Regulations). The warehouse must meet high safety standards and entry into and withdrawal of goods from such warehouses require particular accounting practices and monthly filings with the authorities. The maximum storage period is five years. Goods removed for free circulation will be subject to rates in effect at the time of removal, but based on the value at the time of entry.

CUSTOMS EXEMPTIONS

¶221   Scope

Customs exemptions are available only for goods which:

    (1)   are in free circulation in a Community member state;

    (2)   are imported from a non-EEC country, but are tariff exempted by the customs tariff regulations (see 'Tariffs' above), in sectors of trade where human, cultural, political, or similar interests are of primary significance and commercial interests are of little importance;

    (3)   are exempted by the Customs Act.

Such goods are subject neither to customs duties nor to charges of equivalent effect, except for the import turnover tax, the monetary compensating amounts in the agricultural area and the differential duties of the ECSC. Non-tariff exemptions also exist in the trade of commercial items when no real transfer from one national economy to another is effected. Examples of such exemptions include samples and models, coffins, inherited property, objects for German official purposes, goods for members of diplomatic corps, etc.

3 Commercial Intermediaries

INTRODUCTION

¶301 Choice of intermediary

If a foreign company is of the opinion that simply exporting into Germany, on the one hand, or establishing itself there through an employed representative, a branch or subsidiary, on the other hand, is not suitable, it may choose to sell in Germany via an intermediary. The choice of the distribution system will (inter alia) depend on the degree of control to be exercised and the liabilities to be assumed.

(1) *Distinctions*

Although a commercial agent is still a self-employed businessman, he sells in the name of his principal whose instructions he has to follow. A distributor, on the other hand, is subject to less control and normally shields the foreign exporter to a far greater extent against risks of customer or other parties' claims as he buys, imports and sells in his own name.

The term 'commercial agent' is used as a translation of *Handelsvertreter* and the term 'distributor' (or dealer) as a translation of *Händler*, but it is important not to associate those terms too closely with their meanings under English or American law. When applying German law to an English language representation, agency, distribution, dealership or similar agreement a German court would not look to the title, but to the details of the agreement in order to determine which type of law should apply if the agreement is silent on a particular question or conflicts with mandatory German law.

In Germany, the basic rule of freedom of contract prevails. However, since there are special statutory provisions protecting the commercial agent, but not normally the distributor, the distinctions are important.

(2) *Applicable law*

Freedom of contract, within certain limits, also covers the question of applicable law, and a foreign exporter and his German intermediary may agree that their agreement should be subject to the law of the exporter. Quite often, however, the parties are silent on this issue. German courts would, in such a case, tend to apply German law as the basis of the relationship would be in Germany, unless the relationship is very casual and approximates that of a simple buying and selling situation.

Even where the parties agree to apply a foreign law certain aspects of German law, such as the retention or passing of title (security interest) and provisions of antitrust law, must be observed.

COMMERCIAL AGENTS

¶302   Main sources of law

German statutory law of commercial agents is as old as the German Commercial Code (*Handelsgesetzbuch*: HGB) of 1897. The current law was established by the Act of 6 August 1953, which reformed ss. 84 to 92c HGB. These provisions are supplemented by ss. 611 et seq. of the German Civil Code (*Bürgerliches Gesetzbuch*: BGB) relating to service contracts and by ss. 675, 663 et seq. relating to mandates. In addition, case law and commercial customs have had a considerable influence on the interpretation and development of German agency law.

In general, German agency law protects the agent's rather than the principal's interest. Accordingly, most provisions of this law are mandatory. Abrogation of these mandatory provisions is, however, allowed where the agent has no place of business in the Federal Republic of Germany (s. 92c HGB).

To the extent that an agency relationship is based, under German law, on a standardised agreement, the Law on Standard Terms and Conditions of 9 December 1976 (*Gesetz zur Regelung des Rechts der Allgemeinen Geschäftsbedingungen*: AGBGB) will apply. The main purpose of the law is to protect the other party against unusual or unfair provisions contained in agreements which had not been genuinely negotiated, but which had rather been presented on the basis of 'take it or leave it'. Such provisions will automatically be void (see Chapter 1, ¶113 for further details).

¶303   Basic principles of German agency law

(1) *Definition*

Pursuant to s. 84 HGB, the commercial agent (*Handelsvertreter*) is defined as a self-employed businessman who is permanently entrusted to arrange or close transactions on behalf of, in the name of, and on account of one or more principals. In order to qualify as an agent, a businessman must be in a position to organise his business activities freely and independently. If these requirements are not fulfilled, he may qualify as an employee.

A further distinction has to be made between an agent and a commission merchant (*Kommissionär* or *Kommissionsagent*) who acts in his own name but for a principal in areas where the principal wishes to remain unknown. Commission merchant contracts are subject to special statutory rules (s. 383 et seq. HGB) and are of little practical significance outside the trading of artistic works and antiques and the trading of securities by banks.

A person or entity who is not permanently engaged for a principal is usually considered as a broker (*Makler*) and not as an agent, and special statutory rules apply (ss. 652 et seq. BGB and ss. 93 et seq. HGB).

(2) *Agency agreement*

The agency agreement may be entered into verbally or may even be implied. However, under German law each party is entitled to have the agreement incorporated into a written document. Furthermore, certain special arrangements such as exclusivity or an agent's guarantee of customer performance (*delcredere*) require written form.

The appointing of an exclusive agent for a certain geographical area is, in principle, permissible both under German and European cartel law (for details see Chapter 10, ¶1009 ('(2) *Commercial agents*')).

(3) *Duties of the agent*

Pursuant to s. 86 HGB the agent must actively solicit or conclude transactions on behalf of his principal. In doing so he must act in the interests of the principal, which includes a basic confidentiality obligation and a prohibition on competition. He must visit existing and new customers as often as necessary for the acquisition of new and the maintenance of existing business.

According to s. 86, para. 2 HGB and s. 666 BGB the agent must supply the principal with the required information relating to his activities, and in particular those relating to the arrangement and closing of transactions.

As mentioned, the agent must follow all reasonable instructions of the principal, in particular as regards statements to be made with respect to the qualities of the contractual products, their price and other terms and conditions. Pursuant to s. 86, para. 3 HGB, he has the general duty to apply the diligence of a respectable businessman. Further or more detailed obligations are normally listed in the individual agreement.

(4) *Principal's duties*

The principal's duty is basically one of support. Pursuant to s. 86a HGB, he must supply the agent with the required promotion material, such as samples, drawings, price lists, prospectus and sales conditions, etc. and give him all relevant information. In particular, the principal has to inform the agent immediately of the acceptance or rejection of a transaction. According to s. 86a HGB, the principal has the mandatory obligation to inform the agent in advance when it is likely that he will only be able to sell in substantially reduced quantities, compared with what the agent was entitled to expect in the circumstances.

It follows from s. 86a that the principal is generally free to accept or reject offered transactions at his sole discretion. The obligation to inform the agent of the impending scarcity of goods has been extended by the Federal Supreme Court (see BGH Vol. 26, p. 167), to include an impending reduction of the quality of goods.

(5) *Commission*

Under s. 87, para. 1 HGB, the agent has a commission claim with respect to all transactions made during the term of the agency agreement, provided such transactions are concluded as a result of the agent's efforts or as repeat orders of customers recruited earlier by the agent. If the agent has exclusive rights for a certain area, his commission claim includes all transactions made with customers of this area, even if the agent has not contributed to these transactions (s. 87, para. 2 HGB). Pursuant to s. 87, para. 3 HGB, the agent is further entitled to claim commission with respect to transactions effected within a reasonable time after the termination of the agency agreement if he has arranged them or contributed considerably to its closing.

According to s. 87a HGB, the commission claim comes into existence as soon and insofar as the principal has executed the transaction. If this provision is modified by means of contractual arrangements, the agent acquires a mandatory claim to advance payments which are due on the last day of the month following the execution by the principal. Independently of such a contractual arrangement, the agent's commission claim comes into existence as soon as, and insofar as, the customer has made payment.

The commission claim becomes void if it is established that no payment can be obtained from the customer and any commission received must be paid back. However, the agent is entitled to a commission claim even if the principal does not execute the transaction as agreed, even if reasonably able to do so (s. 87a, para. 3 and 5 HGB).

According to s. 87a, para. 4 and 5 HGB and to s. 87c, para. 1 HGB, the commission is due on the last day of the month in which the statement of accounts is due, which is generally the following month. By means of contractual agreements, this date can be postponed, but not later than to the third month following the transaction.

Principal and agent are basically free to fix the amount or percentage of the commission. In the absence of a contractual arrangement, s. 87b, para. 1 HGB gives the agent the right to claim the commission at the rate commonly paid in the respective industry. Unless otherwise agreed, the amount of the commission is to be based on the price to be paid by the customer including deductions for cash payments, incidental charges, taxes, customs and other costs which are not separately billed to the customer.

According to s. 87c, para. 3 HGB, the agent has a right to full information about all circumstances and facts related to his commission claim.

Unless otherwise agreed, or consistent with the commercial usages, the agent's expenses are not reimbursed (s. 87d HGB).

Under s. 88a, para. 1 HGB, the agent has a statutory lien on the promotion materials received from the principal. Section 88a, para. 2 HGB, provides that this mandatory statutory lien continues to exist after the termination of the agency agreement, but only with respect to commission and reimbursed claims and not, for instance, with respect to compensation or damage claims.

The statute of limitation with respect to all claims resulting from the agency agreement is four years as of the end of the year in which these claims became due (s. 88 HGB).

(6) *Termination of agreement*

An agency agreement is usually entered into for an indefinite period of time, and s. 89 HGB provides that such an agency agreement can be terminated during the first three years with six weeks' notice prior to the end of calendar month. The notice may be reduced to a minimum term of one month. After three years of agency the six weeks' term is extended to three months. The notice period must always be the same for both parties, otherwise the longer period applies for both.

A unilateral change of contractual territory or products cannot normally be interpreted as a partial termination. It will rather be necessary to combine the termination of the entire agreement with the offer of a modified new one.

Both parties, pursuant to s. 89a HGB, are entitled to terminate the agency agreement forthwith for cause, and the terminating party has a damage compensation claim if the termination is caused by fault of the other party.

The law does not prescribe any form of termination but the terminating party will have to prove receipt of notice of termination by the other party. Quite often written termination is stipulated in the agreement in which case oral termination would be invalid.

(7) *Compensation for termination*

According to s. 89b, para. 1 HGB, the agent has a right to claim compensation after termination of the agency agreement if and insofar as:

¶303

(a) the principal continues to enjoy substantial advantage from his relationship with customers solicited by the agent;

(b) the agent loses commission claims by reason of the termination of the agreement; and

(c) equity calls for compensation considering all the circumstances of the case.

Such a claim is not meant as compensation for any loss of investment or other damage suffered by the agent, nor is it to be likened to severance pay under labour law. It is rather additional remuneration for the agent's services, it being considered inequitable to allow him any commissions earned during his service but to leave any future business (goodwill) resulting from his activities uncompensated.

The determination of the amount of the termination compensation requires a precise analysis of the structure of the agent's business both at the beginning and at the end of the agreement in order to find out what the principal's gain and the agent's loss would be. Section 89b, para. 2 HGB provides for a maximum amounting to the yearly average commission of the agent during the last five years or his shorter actual service as agent.

Pursuant to s. 89b, para. 3 HGB, no compensation can be claimed if the agent terminates the agreement, unless termination was caused by the principal or unless a continuation of the service cannot be expected from the agent considering his age or ill health. According to this section, the compensation claim is further excluded if the principal terminates the agency agreement for cause for which the agent is responsible.

Compensation has to be claimed within three months after the termination of the agreement, but this may be done orally and without specifying the amount.

Special rules apply to compensation claims of insurance agents.

The right to claim for termination compensation is absolute and can be abrogated only upon or simultaneously with effective termination of the agreement, except that where the agent is active abroad with no domestic branch, or in the case of a shipping agent, both parties may agree differently or exclude such compensation entirely (s. 92c HGB).

The agent's claim for termination compensation has been held not to be part of German public policy (BGH NJW 1961, p. 1061). A foreign principal may thus avoid it by agreeing on foreign law as part of the agency agreement, provided, of course, that such foreign law does not in turn provide for similar compensation.

(8) Secrecy and non-competition

Section 90 HGB imposes on the agent a secrecy obligation during the term of the agency agreement, and thereafter with respect to trade and business secrets received or learned by him as a result of his contractual activities. Facts are secrets only if:

(a) they are known to only a limited number of persons; and

(b) the principal has made it clear that they are to be treated as secrets.

According to s. 90a HGB, contractual restrictions on the business activities of the agent for the time after termination of the agency agreement must be made in writing and not exceed two years after the end of the agency agreement. The agreement must also provide for the principal's contractual obligation to pay reasonable compensation. A non-competition clause without compensation would still be valid, but the agent could claim such compensation as a matter of law. According to s. 90a, para. 2 HGB, the agent is prevented from claiming the agreed compensation if the principal terminates the agreement because of the fault of the agent. If the agent terminates the agreement because of the fault of the principal, he can withdraw from the non-competition clause by written statement within one month after the termination of the agency agreement (s. 90a, para. 3 HGB).

The amount of compensation for non-competition is not defined. Section 90a only states that it must be reasonable. It is necessary to consider what the agent loses by not competing, but also what the principal gains. Normally, the average commission should form the upper limit and other income, such as compensation for termination or proceeds from a new agency, is not to be deducted as a rule.

Diverging contractual provisions to the detriment of the agent are invalid, but the principal may, during the life of the agreement, terminate the non-competition obligation by giving six months advance notice in writing.

INDEPENDENT DISTRIBUTORS (DEALERS)

¶304 Main sources of law

Unlike commercial agents, independent distributors are not, at least not directly, subject to codified law. Rather, the relationship is widely subject to the freedom of contract. In essence the relationship is that of a buyer and seller, and consequently subject to the general provisions of German law of sales (ss. 433 et seq. BGB and ss. 373 et seq. HGB).

Where both parties are located in certain different countries, i.e. Germany on the one hand and Belgium, Gambia, England, Italy, Luxembourg, Netherlands, San Marino or Israel, the so-called Uniform Sales Laws will apply. These are national, i.e. German laws based on the Hague Conventions for the

Uniform Law on International Sales of Goods, and Uniform Law on the Formation of Contracts for the International Sale of Goods of 1 July 1964. Conversely, the uniform UN sales law (Vienna UNCITRAL Convention of 11 April 1980) has been signed, but not yet adopted by the Federal Republic of Germany.

Even though the dealer buys and sells in his own name, his contract may be very like that of a commercial agent. Consequently, depending on the degree of similarity, German courts increasingly apply the protective provisions of commercial agency law to independent distributors (see below). On the other hand, dealers carrying the full commercial risk qualify as independent enterprises and their agreements are thus fully subject to the restrictions provided for by German, and possibly EEC, antitrust laws, i.e. in particular ss. 15 and 18 of the German law against restraints of competition (*Gesetz gegen Wettbewerbsbeschraenkungen*: GWB) and the EEC Commission Regulations 1983/83 and 1984/83 of 22 June 1983, on the Application of art. 85(3) of the EEC Treaty to Categories of Exclusive Distribution Agreements and Exclusive Purchasing Agreements (Block Exemption of Exclusive Distribution).

Finally, as in the case of commercial agency agreements, dealer agreements will be subject to the Standard Terms Law (AGBG) to the extent that they are based on a preformulated text and not genuinely negotiated between the parties. In particular, the restrictions on warranties and liabilities of the supplier under a standard dealer or similar agreement risk being void and should therefore be screened under the AGBG to make sure that their wording does not in the end do more harm than good. However, the provisions of the Standard Terms Law may be disregarded where both parties are merchants (which should always be so in the case of an international distribution agreement) and the agreement is subject to foreign law. Hence, an express choice of law clause is of significance.

¶305   Basic principles of German distribution law

(1) '*Distributors*'

As already mentioned above, the distributor is not defined by statutory law, but rather developed by case law and legal theory on the basis of individual contracts. A distributor is generally defined as a person or entity who consistently buys from a certain supplier and sells merchandise in its own name and on its own account (see, for example, BGH BB 1970, p. 1458). In practice, various terms are used for distributors (dealers), the most common of which are *Vertragshändler* or *Eigenhändler*, or in English, 'authorised' or 'appointed' dealers (note that under German law there would be little, if any, difference between a dealer and a distributor, and in the following text both are used as synonyms). It should be noted that the analogous application of the rules of commercial agency law does not depend on which term is used, but rather on the degree of similarity of the distributor relationship with the agency.

Apart from buying and selling in one's own name, the main feature of a dealer is a long-term relationship which requires the dealer to have regard to the interests of the manufacturer in whose distribution system the dealer is integrated.

A distributor may have sub-distributors (dealers), and such sub-distribution agreements would have the same features as in the case of a one-tier distribution system.

Sometimes the manufacturer reserves certain customers for direct supply by himself. Where the dealer is nevertheless required to include such reserved customers in his general promotional and other activities, such as advertising and servicing, he may be promised commission on direct sales. In such cases the distributor would act in a dual capacity: commercial agent with respect to direct sales and distributor with respect to his own customers.

A special kind of a dealer agreement is a franchise agreement, according to which the franchisor authorises the franchisee, usually against a franchise fee, to distribute certain goods or services using a given name, as well as commercial and technical know-how, and observing certain organisational and advertising policies where the franchisor is often required to grant sales assistance and is entitled to exercise some control over the activities of the franchisee (BAG BB 1979, p. 325).

Another more recent example of a distribution agreement is an OEM (original equipment manufacturer) agreement which has an additional feature in that either the distributor resells the contractual product after it is made part of his own product, or value is added to the product by the distributor prior to resale.

(2) *Appointment of distributors*

As in the case of an agency, a written contract is not required in order to confer the status of a distributor. However, the imposition of certain restrictions and the granting of exclusivity do require written agreement (ss. 18, 34 GWB). Furthermore, it follows from the absence of directly applicable statutory law that even casual distribution agreements are usually in writing.

The distribution agreement, which is a long-term, basic agreement between the manufacturer (supplier) and the distributor (dealer), must be distinguished from the individual sales contract or purchase order governing the sale of and acquisition of title to the individual product or spare part. This leaves some flexibility as to whether most sales terms, in particular the price, should be

¶305

provided for within the distribution agreement or as part of the individual purchase agreement. Quite often they are part of the supplier's general terms and conditions which would be attached to the distribution agreement.

(3) *Duties of distributors*

In the absence of specific statutory provisions, the distributor's obligations are determined by contract. To the extent the contract is silent, certain duties may be implied. The basic duty is to serve the manufacturer's interest to an extent which will depend on the circumstances. Basically, the distributor must actively promote the sale of the contractual products and inform the manufacturer regularly and/or when the need arises on his activities and on the development of the market. He must not violate trade and business secrets of the manufacturer.

A violation of local laws by the distributor, such as the Law against Unfair Competition (*Gesetz gegen den unlauteren Wettbewerb*: UWG), would normally also constitute a violation of the distribution agreement at least insofar as the manufacturer himself or his reputation would be affected. Typical contractual obligations require the distributor to communicate the names and addresses of his customers to the supplier, but such an obligation is particularly dangerous in view of an analogous application of commercial agency law (see below).

Minimum quantities of goods to be ordered are usually agreed where the distribution agreement provides for exclusivity on a long-term basis; not achieving such agreed minimum purchases would entitle the manufacturer to terminate the agreement prematurely, unless he shares in the responsibility for not achieving such quantities.

(4) *Manufacturer's duties*

In the absence of specific contractual obligations, such duties are implied from the nature of the relationship or derived from explicit obligations of the distributor. Like all parties to long-term agreements, the manufacturer must have regard to the interests of the distributor. This includes a basic duty to keep the distributor informed.

If the distributor is subject to certain minimum requirements, the manufacturer is under a duty to supply. Otherwise he is free to reject or delay orders, unless not supplying would constitute an arbitrary action or a violation of a dominant position within the meaning of antitrust law (s. 26, para. 2 GWB). Where the distributor is required to provide for after-sales service, the manufacturer must supply spare parts.

¶305

(5) *Sales and resale prices and terms*

The counterpart to the commission of a commercial agent is the mark-up of the distributor, i.e. the difference between his sales and resale price, or the distributor's discount in the case of recommended retail prices.

In principle the manufacturer is free to quote his prices and also unilaterally to change sales prices and recommended retail prices. However, a manufacturer who is in a dominant position within the meaning of antitrust law must not discriminate. Furthermore, where a precise discount from the recommended retail price has been agreed, such discount must continue to be applied in the case of price changes.

German antitrust law prohibits a manufacturer from determining resale prices and terms, except in the case of books (ss. 15, 16 GWB). This provision not only prohibits resale price maintenance, it has been interpreted as preventing the manufacturer from promising favourable prices to the distributor (BGH, Vol. 80, p. 43). How this prohibition can be reconciled with contractual minimum requirements is still not quite clear (a dealer would be excused for not having ordered agreed minimum quantities where his customers prefer to buy from other sources who get better prices from the manufacturer).

German antitrust law also prohibits any economic, social or other pressure on the distributor to adhere to recommended resale prices (s. 38a GWB). The term 'pressure' is broadly defined by the German authorities.

While it is permitted by German antitrust law to restrict the distributor in the use of products, the allocation of potential customers, and to prescribe other restrictions, unless expressly prohibited by the Federal Cartel Office (s. 18 GWB), it follows from the above prohibition under s. 15 that the manufacturer must not impose warranty terms on the distributor for use in relation to the distributor's own customers (OLG Frankfurt WuW 1483). On the other hand, the manufacturer may require the distributor generally to provide for after-sales service, including repair services, provided that the manufacturer does not insist that these services are included in the resale terms of the product.

(6) *Exclusivity*

Distributors and dealers are often allocated a certain sales territory, combined with the promise that they will be the manufacturer's sole sales intermediary in such territory. In return, the distributor undertakes not to carry competitive products. How strictly the manufacturer may be required to protect the distributor's exclusivity varies. Most such restrictions would be legal under German law, unless and until prohibited by the Federal Cartel Office (s. 18 GWB). Under EEC law (if applicable – see Chapter 10, ¶1010), however, they would be legal only within the narrow scope of Group Exemption No. 1983/83, legalising distribution agreements where the manufacturer agrees to supply only the distributor within the territory, and the distributor agrees not to carry competitive products, to buy contractual products only from the manufacturer and not to solicit customers, establish branches or maintain a stock of inventory outside the territory. Furthermore, the agreement must not contain any other restrictions than the obligations of the distributor:

(a) to carry the full product programme or to commit himself to minimum purchases;

(b) to sell the products under prescribed trademarks or prescribed packaging;

(c) to provide for sales promotion, in particular advertising, establishing a distribution network or a stock or inventory, providing for after-sales and warranty services, and only using qualified or trained personnel.

In particular there must be no restriction as to customers (legal under German law) and resale prices and terms (also illegal under German law). The sales promotion obligation mentioned under (c) could be seen as providing for so-called selective distribution where the reseller may be forbidden to supply to unsuitable dealers if the entire network is based on so-called objective criteria of a qualitative nature relating to the professional qualifications of the owner of the business or the staff, or the suitability of the business premises, particularly if such criteria are actually applied in a non-discriminatory manner.

Further details are given in Chapter 10 (¶1001 et seq.), but it should be noted that exclusive distribution agreements with other restrictions, or restrictions of the following nature, require individual clearance with the Commission:

(a) *Competing companies.* In the case of agreements between competing manufacturers (the term being defined to include a company whose affiliate manufactures identical or equivalent goods), if the exclusive distribution is:

(i) reciprocal;

(ii) non-reciprocal, but one of the parties, including all its affiliate companies, has annual sales exceeding 100 million ECU.

(b) *Absolute territorial protection.*

(i) if no alternative sources of supply are available to the consumer, i.e. the manufacturer does not even offer to supply products on request to final users;

(ii) if it is made difficult for retailers or consumers to be supplied by dealers outside the territory, in particular through the use of industrial property rights.

(7) *Termination*

Normally, an agreement provides for specific notice periods. Otherwise, German law requires reasonable notice. Such a term needs to be interpreted in the light of the circumstances of each case, the statutory notice periods applying to commercial agents being useful guidelines, i.e. six weeks prior to the end of a calendar quarter or, if the agreement had lasted three years or longer, three months.

In the case of termination, the important question is whether the distributor can claim some kind of compensation. In answering such a question, the starting point ought to be that making use of normal notice provisions does not constitute any infringement and thus does not call for any compensation. However, the distributor may rely on s. 89b HGB if his relationship is sufficiently analogous to that of a commercial agent, and the Federal Court has held this to be so in certain circumstances in its well-known 1977 decision (BGH, Vol. 68, p. 34).

The circumstances in which the distributor *will* be able to rely on s. 89b HGB in this manner are as follows:

(a) A special skeleton or appointed dealer agreement integrates the dealer into the manufacturer's distribution system, which to a large extent requires him to perform functions which normally would be expected of a commercial agent. This would, as a rule, include the allocation of a particular sales territory, a duty to actively promote the products, and other duties which are typical for a commercial agent.

(b) The dealer must be contractually bound, either during the term of the agreement or at the time of termination, to advise the manufacturer of his customers, so that the manufacturer may without further difficulties continue the relationship with such customers after termination of the distributorship.

Of course, the requirement referred to under (a) above does not necessarily include an exclusive sale. This would be only one (although very typical) indication. Others include detailed provisions regarding co-operation with the manufacturer's own sales force, minimum stock, minimum purchases, non-competition clauses, recommended retail prices, instructions as to the premises, personnel and advertising.

The requirement in (b) above has recently been diminished, and is now satisfied where, for example, a manufacturer of automobiles obtains customer data by receiving sales notification cards on the occasion of the individual car registrations. Even where such a requirement is not spelled out in a written agreement, the courts, where customer data have actually been provided to the manufacturer, may find an oral agreement to so advise the manufacturer. Some sources believe that this requirement may eventually be completely replaced by the mere fact that the manufacturer is actually in a position to continue to use the dealer's customers, even if only on the basis of the reputation of the brand, as in the automobile industry (*Sogwirkung der Marke*). For the time being, however, if a manufacturer wants to avoid liability for termination compensation, no requirement regarding the transmission of customer data from the dealer should be included, either in writing or orally.

The amount of the termination compensation in the case of a dealer is calculated on the basis of such estimated sales commissions as would be normal in the industry considering the agreed activities of the dealer.

4 Forms of Doing Business

BRANCH

¶401 Introduction

Acting through dealers, representatives or commercial agents may not, or may no longer, be the right answer to the challenge and chances of the German market, and a foreign company may feel better off after having established its own presence in Germany. Unless the activities to be carried out through or from such local presence are to be of a merely preparatory or auxiliary nature, as defined by tax law, the company must decide between two basic alternatives: organising a local presence as a branch operation or as a subsidiary.

A modification of the above two alternatives would be the acquisition of an existing business or the establishment of a joint venture, either by acquiring part of an existing company (see below) or by agreeing to establish a new company with another party by forming a closed corporation (GmbH – see below) or a civil or commercial partnership.

¶402 Branch or subsidiary

A branch, in contrast to a subsidiary, is not a separate legal entity distinct from the parent company. Thus, although it may have extensive facilities within Germany, it is not incorporated there. The branch itself has no rights or obligations, but derives them from the status of the head office. Consequently, the branch may not enter into agreements with the head office of the parent company (loan or licence agreements, for example) and may sue or be sued only through the parent company, but its local presence may subject the foreign company to local jurisdiction.

Apart from commercial considerations prevailing in industries such as banking, insurance or shipping, tax considerations often play a major role in deciding between the two alternatives.

(1) *Taxation*

The long-term, obvious tax advantage of a subsidiary has been significantly reduced as a result of the German corporate income tax reform of 1976. Branch operations are subject to corporate income tax at a rate of 50 per cent, which is lower than the 56 per cent tax rate for retained profits of a subsidiary. As is discussed in more detail in Chapter 5, the tax rate for distributed profits of subsidiaries, however, is reduced to 36 per cent plus a withholding tax of 25 per cent (which is, in turn, reduced to 15 per cent under most German tax treaties with industrialised nations). Hence, if the subsidiary distributes its entire profits, the corporate income tax burden will be slightly lower than the 50 per cent tax burden of a branch operation, if the tax treatment of the dividends in the country of the parent company is disregarded.

The comparison is further complicated by the fact that a subsidiary will seldom be able to distribute its entire profits. Also, the definitions of income and business expenses may not be the same in the case of a subsidiary or a branch. Inter-company charges within a group of affiliated companies are, as a rule, recognised as proper business expenses of the German subsidiary if they reflect arm's length standards and are based on a written agreement. Such charges can include interest on loans, royalties for licences of patents, know-how or other intangible rights, as well as remuneration for administrative services. There may even be a cost-sharing agreement for research activities or for administrative services. In the case of a branch operation, however, the deduction of such charges by the head office is severely restricted. Interest on loans granted by the head office to its German branch is deductible only if it can be established that the head office borrowed the funds merely for channelling them into the German branch and only to the extent that the foreign head office actually paid interest on such funds. On the other hand, a branch can deduct as business expenses an appropriate part of the general and administrative over-heads of the head office.

A favourable characteristic of branches is that their losses are normally immediately deductible for tax purposes by the foreign head office, whereas the carry-forward period for losses of a German subsidiary is limited to five years (they may be carried back two years). Thus, the branch may have significant initial advantages where operating losses are anticipated for an extended period of operations. However, if for one reason or another the foreign head office should at a later stage wish to reorganise its German branch operation into a subsidiary, the branch will be subject to German corporate income tax on the excess of the fair market value of its assets, including goodwill, over the book value at the time of the reorganisation.

(2) Cost

Contrary to what might be expected, the formation of a branch will usually not be any less cost and time consuming than the establishment of a subsidiary in the form of a GmbH. Where the articles of a GmbH do not include unusual

¶402

provisions, it should normally be possible to establish it within six weeks, depending on the workload of the commercial registrar. The paper work involved with the registration of a branch often results in a much more burdensome and usually longer procedure.

(3) *Other aspects*

Among non-tax aspects, the most obvious advantage of a subsidiary is that the liability of the foreign company is limited to its participation in the local subsidiary company, whereas in the case of a branch the parent is liable to the full extent of its assets for claims arising out of judgments rendered against the branch. It should be noted that protection available to a foreign corporation through the so-called *ultra vires* doctrine would under German law not normally apply in the case of its local branch. Furthermore, the intangible value of a German firm, as opposed to a branch of a foreign company, should not be overlooked. Finally, a branch may have difficulties in dealing with parties such as landlords or lessors, and encounter problems in securing telephone lines, telex listings, or in opening bank accounts, at least where the branch had not been entered into the local commercial register (see 'Setting up a branch' at ¶403 below). On the other hand, a branch will not, or only to a lesser degree, be affected by co-determination (see Chapter 9) or the new accounting and reporting (disclosure) requirements (Chapter 6).

¶403   Setting up a branch

Up to 30 September 1984 the setting up of a German branch by a foreign corporation required the prior approval of the Ministry of Economics of the German State in which the corporation intended to start its German operations; operations being widely defined. As from 1 October 1984, however, this requirement (which did not apply to branches of EEC countries anyway) was abolished in its entirety.

(1) *Filing with trade and tax offices*

According to s. 14 of the Trade Law (*Gewerbeordnung* of 21 June 1869: GewO), whoever starts the independent operation of a trade or business or the operation of a dependent or independent branch, must notify the local trade office. Failure to carry out the required notification may result in a fine. The purpose of notification is to enable the authorities to determine whether a special licence is required.

Under tax law, the commencement of a branch operation must be filed with the local tax office for the purpose of obtaining a tax number (s. 138 General Tax Law: *Abgabeordnung*).

Where the opening of operations coincides with entry into the commercial register (see below), the trade and tax offices will automatically be informed, and will remind the branch manager of his filing duties by providing him with their standard filing forms.

Notifications are also required where a branch office is moved or where the type of business is altered or expanded compared with the business initially filed, or where the business is closed.

(2) *Licences*

In principle, the commencement of a business is free in Germany and not subject to an official licence. A number of businesses require a licence, however, which will be granted as a matter of law, provided the applicant can show himself to be trustworthy (not subject to criminal prosecution) and/or possessed of the necessary education, training or experience. In the case of branch, trustworthiness and/or experience etc. must be present within the local branch (branch manager) rather than the foreign headquarters. The most important types of licensed businesses are the following:

- banks (s. 1 *Kreditwesengesetz*);

- brokers and agents for real estate, houses, apartments and offices, credits, investment or mutual funds, land and building developments (s. 34c GewO);

- correspondence ('learn-by-mail') schools (s. 12 *Fernunterrichtsschutzgesetz*);

- drugstores (s. 1(2) *Gesetz über das Apothekenwesen*);

- gambling (s. 83c,d GewO);

- security (s. 34a GewO);

- handicraft (s. 1 *Handwerksordnung*). (Note: Handicraft, based on long traditions, is broadly defined. For example, product maintenance beyond normal warranty services requires entry in the handicraft roll as a *Meister* or equivalent qualification);

- hospitals (s. 30 GewO);

- insurance (s. 5(1) *Versicherungsaufsichtsgesetz*);

- leasing of personnel (art. 1, s. 1 *Arbeitnehmerüberlassungsgesetz*). (Note: Private employment agencies are illegal in Germany);

- lottery (*Rennwett- und Lotteriegesetz*);

¶403

- mining (s. 6 *Bergbaugesetz*);
- pharmaceuticals (manufacture and trading) (s. 13 *Arzneimittelgesetz*);
- restaurants, bars, hotels and pensions (s. 2 *Gaststättengesetz*);
- traffic with merchandise (truck carriers), persons (taxicab or bus) and air traffic (ss. 8 and 80 *Güterkraftverkehrsgesetz*, s. 2 *Personenbeförderungsgesetz* and ss. 2,6 and 20 *Luftverkehrsgesetz*).

(3) *Stationery*

Any foreign corporation with an office in Germany, even if not registered as referred to below, must only use stationery in their local office which shows the place and country of the registered head office and the name (including one fully-written first name) of its legal representatives (board members) (s. 15b(2) Trade Law). (In practice, it is acceptable if not all, but only some of the board members are named.) Technically, branch offices of companies of other EEC Member States are exempted from this obligation, but their national legislation is supposed to make similar provision.

(4) *Registration*

A registered branch may have its own company name consisting of the company name of the (parent) company and a distinguishing addition. It may also have a *Prokurist* (signing clerk) whose powers may be registered as being limited to the affairs of the branch.

(a) *Commercial register.* The commercial register is carried by the local court. In Germany it is a public record which means, for instance, that if a manager who has been dismissed and recalled is still registered, he has the power to commit the company *vis-à-vis* third parties because a fact requiring registration but not registered and published can not be asserted against a third party acting in good faith (s. 15 HGB).

Certain material which must be given to the commercial registrar (e.g. names of shareholders, financial statements) is also open for public inspection, but it cannot be relied on as being correct and the good faith of third parties is not protected.

(b) *Conditions.* Not every branch qualifies for registration. Inclusion in the commercial register is a requirement and a privilege for so-called separate or independent branches (s. 13 German Commercial Code, *Handelsgesetzbuch* of 10 May 1897 HGB). In this sense the term 'branch' is narrower than the term 'permanent establishment' (*Betriebsstätte*) under tax law. A branch is considered independent where it can conceivably continue its business even after the closing of the entire head office operation. Facilities for the mere carrying

¶403

out of auxiliary activities such as warehousing, research or liaisoning, would thus not qualify for registration. It is rather required that the branch:

(1) has its own or leased premises with certain assets, bank account and separate book-keeping; and

(2) is represented by a responsible manager who, although internally subject to reporting and instructions, has the power to commit the branch (simple signing rights according to s. 54 HGB).

(c) *Documentation.* The application for registration must be signed by all authorised officers of the company in front of a public notary, and the signature of the notary requires legalisation by the German consulate. Consular legalisation may be replaced by attaching a so-called *Apostille* as provided by the Hague Convention of 5 October 1961, inter alia, in the following countries: Austria, Japan, Netherlands, Luxembourg, Portugal, United Kingdom, USA, Spain. No legalisation is prescribed under bilateral treaties with France and Italy and special rules apply under a treaty with Switzerland.

The application must include: the corporate name of the company and place of registration; the purpose of the company; the number of unpaid shares and their nominal amounts; the make-up of the board; and the form of publications of company notices. It must be accompanied by the memorandum and articles of association, and proof of valid existence of the company by an official excerpt of a company register, certificate of incorporation or equivalent. All such papers require notarisation, legalisation (as above), and translation into German by a sworn interpreter. If the foreign company corresponds to a German stock corporation, i.e. if its shares are freely negotiable, and if the application is made within two years of incorporation, further detailed information is required (see ss. 44(2), 40(1) Stock Corporation Law: AktG). If the business requires a licence as mentioned above, such licence must also be attached.

(d) *Costs.* Notarial fees and registration costs, including costs of publication, depend on the estimated assessment value of the local branch in proportion to the capital of the parent company and the required publication space (i.e. information on the parent company including, in particular, names of all directors who may commit the company), and in the case of a small sales office would range between DM 1–2,000. In addition, 1 per cent capital transaction tax will be due on any capital contributions, except where the parent company is a corporation of another EEC country (s. 2(1) No. 6 KVStG) (see Chapter 5, ¶554).

(e) *Publication.* Before ordering registration, the court will also investigate whether the company name is not similar to another name already registered

¶403

by the same court. The filing and all subsequent notifications, including any change within the board of the parent company, which need to be filed, will be published in the Federal Gazette and at least one other designated newspaper.

LIMITED LIABILITY COMPANY (GmbH)

¶404 General outline

Due to the flexibility offered under German law, the closed corporation (limited liability company – *Gesellschaft mit beschränkter Haftung*: GmbH) is particularly popular in Germany. There were, at the end of 1984, 324,773 GmbHs with a stated capital of DM 129,306 million, compared with approximately 2,000 stock corporations. Also the overwhelming majority of German subsidiaries of foreign corporations are GmbHs rather than AGs (*Aktiengesellschaft*, or public stock corporation), or other forms of companies discussed under ¶417 et seq. below. The reasons for this include the fact that the setting up of a GmbH is much simpler and its statutes can be more specifically tailored to the requirements of the shareholder(s). Incorporation in Germany (or acquisition of a German company) is not subject to Government control or authorisation, with the exception of merger control (see Chapter 10). However, if the purpose of a GmbH includes an activity which requires a licence as stated under 'Setting up a branch' at ¶403 above, the licence must be obtained before the GmbH can be registered.

¶405 Corporate law

The law concerning the different types of companies is codified either as part of the commercial code (HGB) or in the form of special laws such as the GmbH Law (*Gesetz betreffend die Gesellschaften mit beschränkter Haftung GmbHG*) of 20 April 1892, as amended last on 12 December 1985. It provides for a legal entity separate from its shareholders who may be individuals, partnerships or corporations, and whose liability is limited to the amount of their subscription to the stated equity capital. As a legal entity, the GmbH may enter into contracts, may acquire land and buildings and thus will have its own rights and obligations. Represented by and acting through its managing director(s), it may sue in its own name and be sued. One of the main objectives of the GmbH Law is to safeguard the contribution and preservation of the company's stated capital.

¶406   Incorporation

The GmbH enters into existence as a legal entity upon registration in the commercial register carried by the local courts (see ¶403 above).

(1) *Capital*

One of the objectives of the GmbH Law is to ensure that the minimum stated capital is paid in and is at the free disposal of the management, and that once paid in the capital must not at any later stage be paid back to the shareholder(s), neither as declared nor as disguised dividends or otherwise.

(2) *Articles*

The company may have as few as one shareholder. Its articles of association (statutes) must at least contain the name and registered seat of the company, a purpose clause, the amount of the stated capital and the amount subscribed by any of the shareholders. The capital must be fully subscribed; the concepts of 'authorised capital' and 'issued capital' are unknown in the case of the GmbH. The law sets forth numerous voluntary provisions which, in order to be enforceable, must form part of the articles (e.g., assessability of shares, obligation of shareholders to make contributions other than payment of capital, representation of the company by less than all managing directors acting jointly – see below). The life of the company may be indefinite. There is no requirement that the managing director(s) be a German citizen or resident.

(3) *Notarisation of articles*

The establishment of a GmbH takes place before a *Notar* (in Germany, a fully trained legal professional who is required to advise the parties on the legal significance of the documentation and act impartially). Traditionally, there had to be at least two shareholders initially subscribing to the shares. Since 1980, however, it suffices if only one incorporator subscribes to the share(s), and this has become common practice when foreign parent companies incorporate a fully-owned subsidiary.

As a prerequisite to registration, satisfactory evidence must be provided that the shareholders subscribing to the shares exist and that the persons representing them are properly authorised to do so. Where such a shareholder is a corporation itself, this is normally done through a certified excerpt of the commercial register in which the shareholder (parent company) is registered.

Where no such official register exists (e.g. in the US), or where it does not disclose and/or prove the representative's (director's) authority (e.g. the register of companies in the UK), it is at the discretion of the judge of the commercial register what proof of the above facts is admissible instead. It has become more or less standard practice in such cases, however, to have a power of attorney executed by an authorised officer of the parent company. Such representative's signature must be made in front of a public notary whose own signature needs to be legalised. In addition, the secretary (clerk) of the US corporation (whose signature must also be notarised) or the public notary (if considered equivalent to a German *Notar*) must certify that:

   (a) the articles of association, by-laws and resolutions of the board of directors are known to him;

   (b) according to such corporate documents the shareholder-corporation is duly incorporated and established under the laws of the state of the incorporation; and

   (c) the person who executed the power of attorney was authorised to do so in his sole capacity.

Such an excerpt of the company register or a certificate enables the director(s) (or such document plus power of attorney will authorise his (their) representative) to notarise the articles of association (statutes) of the future subsidiary GmbH and, as part of a shareholders' resolution, to appoint the initial managing director(s) (*Geschäftsführer*).

(4) Application for registration

A GmbH comes into existence only by registration. Registration is effected by the commercial register which is carried by the local court of the place where the company will have its registered office. The application for registration must be signed in notarised form by all managing directors. Normally, this takes place at the same time the articles are notarised (see above). The application must include:

   (a) a statement whether the managing directors are authorised single or joint representation;

   (b) an assurance that they are not legally prohibited from acting as managing director(s) and that they have not been sentenced for criminal bankruptcy or similar crimes within the last five years, and that they have been instructed by the Notar of their duty to make full disclosure;

   (c) an assurance of the managing directors that the agreed share capital has been contributed (normally an excerpt of the bank account of a German bank will be required);

   (d) the full business address of the company (registered office, domicile);

   (e) a shareholders' list signed by the managing directors (no notarisation required), setting forth the name and address of each shareholder and the amount of his capital contribution;

   (f) any required licence and information on the supervisory board, if any has been created.

¶406

(5) *Costs and time of registration*

Notarial fees and registration costs depend on the amount of the stated capital and the space needed for publication of the company name and information on the business purpose (object), representation (managing directors) and, if applicable, contributions in kind and the supervisory board. In the case of a 'simple' GmbH with a stated capital of DM 50,000 the fees of the German Notar would amount to approximately DM 600, the court fees to about DM 200 plus approximately DM 250 for publication. Sometimes the court asks for advance payment of such costs. In addition, a one-time 1 per cent capital contribution tax will be due.

The time of registration depends on the workload of the court. Normally, about six weeks will lapse between filing and registration. The procedure may be significantly more time-consuming if the judge should detect any anomalies and give the incorporator(s) time to remedy them. As the court normally asks the chamber of industry for its opinion on the proposed company name, it will thus expedite the procedure if the name is cleared with the chamber prior to notarisation.

(6) *Stationery, publication*

As in the case of a branch, the law prescribes certain information to be printed on the company's stationery, i.e. place of registration and registry court, registration number, names (including one fully-written first name) of all managing directors and of the chairman of the supervisory board, if any.

The registration and other important business of the company will be published. Unless the articles provide for further or other company papers, publication will occur in the Federal Gazette and one other newspaper as determined by the commercial register.

¶407   Pre-registration activities

The GmbH starts to exist only upon registration. However, it is often difficult, if not impossible, to postpone any and all transactions until such date. This raises the question of liability of managing directors and shareholders for pre-registration activities, which is one of the most controversial issues of the GmbH Law being based, after all, on the principle that the stated equity capital is to be preserved. Two stages must be distinguished: notarisation (incorporation) and registration.

(1) *Pre-notarisation activities*

Prior to the notarisation of the articles, the proposed company's shareholders are regarded as partners of a partnership under civil law. Such partners are jointly and severally liable for any obligation resulting from such partnership activities, and such liability will not be affected by subsequent notarisation of the articles and/or registration (Federal Court Decision of 26 October 1981, NJW 1982, 932). Managing directors, even when acting within their authority, will also be jointly and severally liable unless the relevant agreement with the third parties clearly provides otherwise.

(2) *Activities between incorporation and registration*

After the articles have been adopted, a pre-incorporation company is deemed to have come into existence, to which the provisions of the GmbH Law and the articles will apply, except where inconsistent with the fact that the company is not yet registered. Normally this is made clear by adding to the firm name 'i.Gr.' (*in Gründung*: 'being established'). The incorporators are liable for obligations resulting from activities between incorporation and registration, but such liability is limited to the amount of the subscribed capital (Federal Court Decision of 16 March 1983 BGHZ 80, 82). If the incorporators do not pursue registration, then according to the prevailing view their liability may even be unlimited (Federal Court Decision of 9 March 1981, BGHZ 80/129, 142).

According to s. 11(2) GmbHG, whoever acts in the name of the GmbH prior to registration (managing director) will be personally liable, but upon registration such liability will be automatically assumed by the GmbH. Of course, the other parties may expressly waive such liability, even prior to registration.

(3) *Pre-registration losses*

Upon registration, all commitments, even those resulting from prenotarisation activities, automatically pass over to the GmbH by operation of law. However, as mentioned, it is a fundamental principle of German GmbH Law that the stated amount of the capital is present at the date of registration, except for normal incorporation costs. Consequently, any losses resulting from pre-registration activities would remain a liability of the shareholders (parent company) (*Differenzhaftung*). It does not make any difference to the shareholders' obligation to make good such losses whether they were incurred in the normal course of business or as the result of any type of mismanagement. The liability exists for five years and in cases of bankruptcy will be enforced by the receiver.

Thus, where the capital is spent prior to registration or is committed to be spent for the acquisition of the business of another company, and it later turns out that at the date of registration the value of such business was less than the stated capital, the shareholder(s) will have to pay the difference.

¶407

¶408   Company name

The German law of company names is stricter than that of other countries and the principles of this law are virtually sacrosanct. The names of GmbHs must derive either from the name of a shareholder or the purpose of the company, and in neither case tend to deceive the public.

If the name is derived from a shareholder (parent company), then both names must be identical, except that additions like 'Ltd' or 'plc' may be deleted. Also, parts of a shareholder name which would be misleading in the case of the subsidiary (e.g., 'Bank' when the GmbH does not have a banking licence) must be deleted from the name, provided that the balance can still be recognised as a name. Geographical indications such as '(*Deutschland*)' may be added if this serves to distinguish the GmbH from affiliate companies with the same name in other geographical areas.

If the name is derived from the purpose of the company, then it must correctly reflect such purpose as shown by the purpose clause of the articles. For example, where the purpose is the distribution (*Vertrieb*) of electronic products, the firm name can not just be *Elektronik*, because this would indicate manufacture of electronic products. In order to be able to distinguish a given *Elektronik-Vertriebs GmbH*, some other addition will be required, thus resulting in *XYZ Elektronik-Vertriebs GmbH* as the company name.

¶409   Capital, shares, liability

(1) *Minimum capital*

With effect from 1 January 1981, the minimum capital (equity) of a GmbH was increased from DM 20,000 to DM 50,000. The minimum contributions must be one-quarter of the stated capital, but no less than DM 25,000. However, if the GmbH is established by only one shareholder, then he must post security such as a bank guarantee covering the non paid-in part of the capital. In practice, this requirement normally causes a parent company to make full payment.

(2) *Contributions in kind*

Contributions may be made in kind, but this must be expressly stated in the articles and a report on the valuation procedure must be attached (s. 5(4) GmbHG). If the contribution takes the form of an existing business, then a statement of the last two years' profits and losses must be attached. In practice, any type of non-cash contribution is normally substantiated by adding audited statements in order to avoid complications such as an audit by an expert appointed by the chamber of commerce.

Registration may be refused by the court, or shareholders be held fully liable if the value of the contribution fails to match the face value at both the dates of filing for registration and of registration (Federal Court Decision of 9 March 1981 BGH 80, 136 et seq.). For this and certain technical reasons, where the contribution consists of a going concern (assets and liabilities of another company) a merger is normally preferred (see ¶416 below).

(3) Capital shares, liability

The stated capital consists of *Geschäftsanteile* (GmbH shares), which are not negotiable. Certificates are seldom issued and do not have the significance of stock certificates. 'Share' is a term combining all rights and obligations of a shareholder. The amount is indicated in German Marks and must be divisible by 100 and amount to no less than DM 500. The aggregate of all shares must equal the amount of the stated share capital. GmbH shares are non-assessible except where provided in the articles.

Assignment of shares requires a notarised deed. Although the assignee may use his shareholder rights only upon due filing of the assignment with the company, and the managing directors must in January of each year submit a correct list of shareholders to the commercial register, there is no share register, and in the case of a previous transfer to another assignee, the good faith of the second assignee is not protected, except by damage claims against the assignor.

The articles may provide for all kinds of binding restrictions on the assignment of shares, including a shareholders' resolution or rights of first refusal of the shareholders.

In principle, shareholders are liable only up to the amount of the share capital subscribed. However, they are jointly and severally liable until full payment of all capital shares, and this includes the situation where cash payments or other advantages may have been made which were in fact not made out of distributable profits (dividends) but must be considered as a repayment of capital. In such case one shareholder's liability is not limited to the face amount of his share, but may extend up to the full amount of the entire stated capital (subject, of course, to recourse against the relevant fellow shareholder).

According to a recent decision of the Federal Court (16 September 1985, NJW 1986, p. 188), a parent company could be held liable by creditors of a bankrupt subsidiary GmbH if the latter had prior to bankruptcy been organised as a mere branch operation. The court found this to be the case where the managing director did not in fact enjoy any decision making power, but was subject to continuous instructions on individual transactions to the benefit of the parent but to the detriment of the subsidiary and its creditors, which was inconceivable for a 'responsible manager of an independent GmbH.'

¶409

(4) *Financing*

In addition to making capital contributions as a shareholder, a parent company may, of course, enter into any kind of transaction as between unrelated parties. This includes financing through shareholder loans. The GmbH Law does not impose any debt/equity ratio. However, with effect from 1 January 1981, the legislator has written into the GmbH Law court decisions which treated the question whether certain shareholder loans should be treated like capital in the case of bankruptcy. According to the new s. 32a GmbHG, a shareholder loan cannot be claimed back if it was granted at a time when the shareholder, applying normal business principles, would instead have contributed capital. The test is whether the company would have been able to obtain the loan at market conditions from an unrelated third party.

Under tax law interest charges of a parent company will be recognised as a proper business expense if the loan was based on a written agreement providing for arm's length terms.

If a third party such as a bank in lieu of the shareholder grants the loan, but with the shareholder providing for a guarantee or other security, then in the case of bankruptcy such third party must first enforce the guarantee or other security before turning to the bankrupt company for repayment. Under s. 32b GmbH Law, the company has a direct claim against the shareholder where a secured shareholder loan has been paid back within one year before bankruptcy.

The above provisions of the GmbH Law apply *mutatis mutandi* with respect to other transactions which have the same economic objective as a shareholder loan or security.

In recent years the effects of taxation have caused companies to consider further alternatives to equity and to outright loan financing. Aside from participating loans (*partialische Darlehen*) and loans with variable interest rates, silent partnerships and participating certificates (*Genußscheine*) have become popular.

In its atypical form (*atypische stille Gesellschaft*) a silent participation arrangement is treated like a partnership for income tax purposes. In its typical form the silent participant is entitled to a share in the profits of the GmbH, whereas participation in its losses is usually excluded. In the latter case the portion of the profits payable to the silent partner constitutes a proper business expense for corporate income tax (not for trade tax) purposes, but the distribution is still subject to dividend withholding tax. A major advantage over loans is that such payments only need to be made in profitable years and may be considerably higher than ordinary interest charges.

A participating certificate (*Genußschein*) issued by a German corporation entitles the holder to any kind of financial benefit from the company but does

¶409

not carry membership rights, e.g. voting rights. This means that if it entitles the holder to a share in the profits as well as in the liquidation proceeds, it can be compared to non-voting preferred stock. If the holder is not entitled to such a share in profits and liquidation proceeds, the certificates can be treated as debts and payments thereunder as business expenses.

It is not necessary for capital contributions to increase the stated capital. Informal contributions would equally increase the value of the share participation and leave the company with some flexibility regarding later (re-)distributions. They are used in particular where the company's profit and loss situation is such that an interest bearing loan or other alternatives may not seem viable. An informal contribution would constitute an income item for financial reporting purposes (commercial balance sheet), but for tax purposes it would be treated as tax free income. It would attract capital contribution tax, but if it sought to eliminate any overindebtedness only half the normal rate would be applicable. Such contributions can be made in cash or in kind (e.g. by way of waiver of a shareholder's loan).

¶410 Management

(1) *Managing directors*

The GmbH is represented *vis-à-vis* third parties by one or several *Geschaefts-fuehrer* (managing directors). They are appointed and recalled by the shareholders' meeting and need neither be German citizens nor residents. However, foreigners from non-EEC countries who intend to exercise their functions actively in Germany will be required to obtain a residence permit with permission to engage in self-employed business (see Chapter 14).

The authority of managing directors to commit the company cannot be limited with respect to third parties, except that where more than one managing director is appointed, they may be registered as joint signatories, in which case only the signatures of two managing directors or one managing director and a *Prokurist* (signing clerk) are necessary to commit the company. This is common practice in the case of domestic companies of a certain size.

In order to avoid conflict of interests, German law prohibits anybody to act on both sides of a transaction, unless specifically authorised to do so (prohibition of self-contracting: s. 181 BGB). According to s. 35(4) of the GmbH Law, such prohibition is also applicable in the case of a fully-owned subsidiary GmbH, and any exemption must be provided for in the articles and entered into the commercial register.

Apart from his position under corporate law, a managing director normally is, but does not need to be, an employee of the company and his rights and obligations are usually spelled out in a written service agreement. Whereas his position as an organ of the company may be terminated any time by the shareholders' meeting, his service agreement, in the absence of cause, can be terminated only by observing the notice period prescribed by the agreement or statutory law. However, although an employee he does not enjoy the protection provided by labour law, such as protection against unfair dismissal (see Chapter 9), and no compensation needs to be agreed for a non-competition clause (Federal Court Decision of 26 March 1984, BGH 91, 1).

(2) Prokura, Handlungsvollmacht

Apart from managing directors, other signatories authorised to represent the company are the so-called *Prokurists* and *Handlungsbevollmaechtigte*. A *Prokurist* will be registered as such in the commercial register and is authorised to perform any kind of business transaction, except for the disposal and encumbrance of land. In fact, his authority is almost as broad as that of a managing director, although his title indicates a more junior status and he is not an organ of the company.

A *Handlungsvollmacht* (power of attorney or commercial signing right) is not registered and would have to be given informally subject to the following kinds of restriction:

(a) if given without restriction the authority includes all transactions of the company's kind of business, except transactions involving real estate, bills of exchange, and loans and litigation, unless such statutory restriction is expressly removed. In no case, however, must a managing director authorise any other person (not even another managing director) to act in his place;

(b) where the authority is generally restricted, the restriction must be according to kinds of business. In order to protect bona fide third parties, 'where a person is authorised to undertake a certain kind of transaction, his power of attorney extends to all transactions which normally relate to the undertaking of such transaction' (s. 54 HGB). Other limitations of such commercial authority would affect a third party only where they were known or should have been known, except that;

(c) a power of attorney may validly be limited to an individual transaction.

(3) Restrictions on management

As mentioned above, a managing director's outside authority cannot be limited. Internally, i.e. *vis-à-vis* the company, his authority is usually limited by the articles or his employment agreement. As a rule this is done by specifying those business transactions which will be considered as outside the normal course of business and which will thus require approval of the shareholders'

¶410

meeting (parent company). Without such prior approval the managing director will be liable to the company for damages and for immediate termination. His acts will nevertheless commit the company, unless the respective third party knew or had reason to know that the managing director was acting outside his authority to the detriment of the company (Federal Court Decision of 28 February 1966, NJW 1966, 1911).

The shareholders are at liberty to relieve any managing director from restrictions, either generally or selectively. On the other hand, managing directors are bound to follow shareholder resolutions such as company policies or guidelines, or instructions on a specific transaction unless the articles (or the employment agreement) provide otherwise.

¶411   Duties and liability of the directors

Managing directors are liable for damages resulting from any violation of their duties, including the basic duty to manage the company with the diligence of an ordinary businessman (s. 43 GmbHG), and any duties spelled out in the articles, the employment agreement or shareholder resolutions. Apart from the violation of such a general obligation, personal and even criminal liability may result from violation of the following duties:

(1) to notify the shareholders when the losses of the company reach half the amount of its stated capital (s. 84 GmbHG);

(2) not to repay capital (ss. 30(1), 43(3) GmbHG);

(3) to declare bankruptcy without delay after illiquidity or overindebtedness (s. 64 GmbHG) (see 'Capital increase, liquidation and bankruptcy' at ¶415 below);

(4) to file tax returns, withhold dividends and wages tax and social security contributions (s. 69 AO of the General Tax Code and applicable social security laws);

(5) not to disclose company secrets (s. 85 GmbHG).

Repayment of capital within the meaning of (2) is not limited to cash (dividends), but includes any granting of benefits to a shareholder, whereby the net assets of the company would fall below the value of the stated capital.

¶412   Shareholders' meeting

The company's main body is the shareholders' meeting. As a rule, it decides the following issues:

(1) the appointment and dismissal, as well as the employment and termination of managing directors;

(2) instructions to and supervision of the management;

(3) approval of the annual financial statements and distribution of profits;

(4) amendment of the articles, including increases of capital.

Unless the articles prescribe otherwise, the shareholders' meeting makes decisions by a majority of the votes cast, except that amendments to the articles of association require a majority of no less than three-quarters. Resolutions must be passed at meetings, except where all shareholders agree to take a resolution in writing.

According to s. 47, para. (4) GmbH Law, a shareholder cannot vote on resolutions concerning his discharge from liabilities or on transactions or litigation between him and the company. A shareholder may, however, vote for his appointment or against his recall as managing director (except for cause), and a sole shareholder is not subject to any such voting restriction.

GmbH Law does not prescribe the need to keep official minute books, except as regards resolutions of a fully-owned subsidiary GmbH which shall be made part of written minutes to be signed by the shareholder (or the legal representative of the parent company, as the case may be) (s. 48(3) GmbHG).

¶413   Supervisory board

Unless the company employs more than 500 employees (or the company is a management company of a mutual fund (see s. 4 KAGG)), the establishment of a supervisory board is at the discretion of the shareholders. Such optional board may be created by the articles or the articles may authorise its appointment by the shareholders' meeting.

(1) *Supervisory functions*

In the case of an optional board, the details are left to the discretion of the shareholders, but some basic principles must be complied with. These include the two-tier system of German corporate law according to which:

(a) a managing director cannot be a member of the board; and

(b) the board cannot be given management functions.

While it is possible and usual to specify that certain transactions require prior board approval, it is not possible to make provision for a certain type of business to be managed by the board itself. For example, accounting and preparation of annual financial statements are genuine functions of the managing directors.

In addition to the right and duty to supervise the management, certain typical shareholder functions, such as the authority to appoint and to recall the managing directors, may be assigned to the board. On the other hand, since it

¶413

is reasonable for the outside world to assume that a company with a supervisory board is more carefully controlled, it is not permitted to provide for a supervisory board which does not undertake any basic supervisory functions.

The creation of a supervisory board, as well as any change of membership, must be published in the company papers (see 'Incorporation' at ¶406 above). Furthermore, the name of the chairman must be printed on the stationery of the company.

Unless the articles provide otherwise, the duties and liabilities of board members are similar to those of a supervisory board of a public stock corporation, and these include personal liability for violation of their supervisory duties.

Because of the above restrictions, shareholders often prefer to elect a less formal advisory board or a shareholders' committee.

(2) *Mandatory board – functions*

If the company employs more than 500 employees one-third of the members of the supervisory board must be labour representatives. If the company operates in the coal and steel industry and employs more than 1,000 employees, one half of the board members must be labour representatives. The same applies to any GmbH which alone or including its subsidiaries employs more than 2,000 employees. In this last category half of the labour representatives must be employees of the company and the other half union representatives. They must be allocated proportionally to groups of blue-collar, white-collar, and key staff (executive) employees.

In the case of such a mandatory supervisory board, the statutory provisions relating to the supervisory board of a stock operation must be strictly adhered to. The functions must include the exclusive right to appoint and recall managing directors.

Detailed statutory provisions and case law seek to resolve conflicts between the labour and shareholder representatives within the supervisory board, and between the right of the shareholders' meeting to give instructions to the management and the mandatory functions of the supervisory board. For example, to avoid a tie, the law prescribes that the vote of the chairman (who is either elected by a two-thirds majority or by the shareholder representatives within the board) will be counted twice if a majority resolution cannot be reached.

¶414   Annual statements, disclosure

(1) *Fiscal year.*   The fiscal year of a GmbH is the calendar year, unless the articles provide otherwise. While the shareholders are initially free to determine the fiscal year at their discretion, provided it does not exceed 12

months, any subsequent change deviating from the calendar year requires the approval of the tax authorities. Such approval is normally given if the fiscal year is changed in order to comply with the fiscal year of the parent company.

(2) *Financial statements.* The managing directors are responsible for ensuring that the books of the company are kept in accordance with sound accounting principles. They must also prepare the annual balance sheet and the profit and loss statements within three or six months, depending on the size of the company (see '*Disclosure*' at (3) below). According to the recent amendment of s. 29, the distribution or reserving of profits is to be left to a resolution of the shareholders' meeting (majority), except where the articles provide otherwise.

Further changes have been made with regard to annual financial statements by the Fourth EEC Directive of 25 July 1978, which has been translated into German law (see Chapter 6 for further details). As from 1 January 1986, a note must be attached to the financial statement which, *inter alia*, lists the remuneration, advances and credits of managing directors, securities given to creditors, financial commitments not shown on the balance sheet (such as leases or pension commitments), allocating sales according to divisions and markets, and share participations exceeding 20 per cent.

The business report must include the expected development of the company and state any significant events after the closing of the fiscal year and make statements on research and development activities.

(3) *Disclosure.* Under the previous law (*Publizitätsgesetz* of 15 August 1969), only very large companies were required to disclose their financial statements. 'Very large' was defined as comprising companies which met any two of the following criteria:

(a) balance sheet total exceeding DM 125,000,0000;

(b) annual sales exceeding DM 250,000,000; or

(c) at least 5,000 employees.

Under the new amendment following the Fourth EEC Directive there are, as of 1 January 1986, three sizes of corporations (including stock corporations).

Approximately 90 per cent of all the 350,000 GmbHs are *small corporations.* A corporation is small if it has a balance sheet total of up to DM 3.9 million, sales of up to DM 8 million, or no more than 50 employees (two of these three criteria must be met).

Such small corporations (excluding partnerships) must draw up their financial statements within six months of the fiscal year end, and the balance sheet and the business report must be submitted to the commercial register within 12 months. Statements concerning affiliated companies and profit distribution must also be attached.

¶414

These financial statements do not need to be audited, but they must refer to the commercial register in which they have been deposited, which information must also be published in the Federal Gazette.

A company is *medium-sized* when it fulfils two of the following criteria: a balance sheet total between DM 3.9 and 15.5 million, annual sales between DM 8 and 32 million, and 51 to 250 employees.

A medium-sized company must prepare its financial statements within three months. These statements must be more detailed than those of a small corporation and must be audited. The financial statements plus the annexes and the business report must be submitted to the commercial registrar within nine months and a reference to the relevant commercial register must also be published.

Large corporations are those companies with a balance sheet total exceeding DM 15.5 million, annual sales of DM 32 million or more and/or at least 250 employees. A corporation will always be deemed large if its stock is quoted on a stock exchange within the EEC or admitted to authorised or general trading. A large corporation must prepare extended annual statements including annexes and a business report within three months, have them audited and publish them in the Federal Gazette within nine months. (See s. 267 HGB (Commercial Code).)

Starting in 1990, all corporations with domestic and foreign subsidiaries must also prepare a world-wide consolidated balance sheet and business report.

¶415   Capital increase, liquidation and bankruptcy

(1) *Increase of capital*

Any increase or decrease of the stated capital of a company requires an amendment of the articles of association. The procedure involved is almost the same as that used when establishing the company. However, in addition to a notarised shareholders' resolution (which requires a three-quarters majority) notarised filing of the amendment by all managing directors and registration is required. It should be noted that any subscription to new shares (including any power of attorney) requires notarisation.

The shareholders' resolution must set forth details such as the amount of the increase, the number and amount of new shares, the identities of the persons admitted for subscription and the proposed manner of providing for the new capital.

In principle, all existing shareholders have a subscription right in proportion to their existing shares. The capital can be contributed in cash, in kind or by transforming open reserves. In the last case, the law requires that such reserves are shown either on the last preceding annual balance sheet or on an interim balance sheet, either of which must be audited, and the date of which must not precede the filing of the capital increase by more than seven months (ss. 3, 4 KapErhG).

The principle that the capital must be fully contributed and preserved prohibits a shareholder offsetting the company's claim for cash payment against his claim for repayment of a shareholders' loan (s. 19(2) No. 2 GmbH Law). The company, in turn, must only declare such a set-off if the shareholder's claim is due, undisputed and liquid in the sense that the company is neither overindebted nor would it be insolvent if it had to pay the loan. Similar problems arise where a contribution in kind consists of converting a shareholder's loan into capital because the full realisable value of such loan claim would have to be proven to the court. The prohibition against offsetting claims is broadly interpreted and would include the formal paying-in of capital by and subsequent repayment of a loan to the same shareholder or parent company. Of course, the shareholder could waive any shareholder loan and this would indirectly increase the value of the share, but would not result in an increase of the stated capital (see 'Capital, shares, liability – (4) *Financing*' at ¶409 above).

It should be noted that any shareholder is liable not only for the capital contributions owed by him, but also for those owed by other shareholders in connection with the same or a preceding capital increase or the establishment of the company (see 'Capital, shares, liability – (3) *Capital shares, liability*' at ¶409 above)).

(2) *Liquidation*

The shareholders may at any time, by no less than a three-quarters majority, resolve the dissolution of the company (s. 60(1) No. 2 GmbH Law). The adoption of such resolution will not cause the company to disappear immediately, but rather it will change its purpose. The company may thereafter only engage in activities to facilitate the final dissolution, i.e. payment of creditors, sale or distribution of assets. Such activities are carried out by a liquidator appointed by the shareholders, who could be the former managing director or any person replacing him. He must apply for registration of the dissolution and of his appointment, and the dissolution must be published in the Federal Gazette at three different times with a notice to all creditors to make their claims.

Furthermore, the liquidator has to prepare a balance sheet both at the commencement of the liquidation, then for each following year until the end of the liquidation procedure (s. 71 GmbH Law). The assets of the company may only be distributed twelve months after the third publication in the Federal Gazette, provided all liabilities of the company have been settled. Upon such

¶415

distribution, the liquidator will file for de-registration of the GmbH from the commercial register.

The law prescribes that the files of the company must be kept by a shareholder or another person for a period of ten years after completion of the dissolution.

Even after de-registration, the company will automatically revive if it turns out that there are still assets. In such a case, the court will appoint a liquidator for final liquidation.

(3) *Insolvency, bankruptcy*

The law provides for bankruptcy if a GmbH is either unable to pay all or part of its current debts due to lack of liquid funds (illiquidity), or if its liabilities exceed its assets, both being valued at their current fair market values (s. 61(1) GmbH Law).

Bankruptcy procedures start only upon application, but any creditor may file such application. Managing directors of a GmbH must apply for bankruptcy proceedings without delay, but in any case no later than three weeks after insolvency occurs or overindebtedness is evident. Where such overindebtedness does not appear on the annual balance sheet, but other factors would warn a prudent director that it may exist, the managing directors must proceed with all due diligence to establish the company's position. Late filing may result in both personal and criminal liability. Personal liability would include the obligation to guarantee payments made by the company after bankruptcy should have been declared, except for payments which even a diligent businessman would have made.

The balance sheet for the determination of liability does not have to include subordinated liabilities. Subordination requires a valid statement according to which the payment can be claimed only out of balance sheet profits after all other creditors have been fully satisfied. Capital replacing loans which have not been expressly subordinated must be considered as liabilities, although this question is controversial.

Upon application, the bankruptcy court will be in control of the proceedings. The court will appoint an expert to determine whether the assets justify the opening of bankruptcy proceedings and if so appoint a receiver in bankruptcy (*Konkursverwalter*), who will be the legal representative of the bankrupt company.

As an alternative to bankruptcy, the managing director may apply for a court settlement, which procedure is designed to provide for the reorganisation and survival of the company. The ultimate decision will lie with the creditors in this case, but the law provides for precise majority rules.

¶415

¶416 Mergers and acquisitions

Mergers and acquisitions are discussed in the context of the GmbH because in practice most cases involve a GmbH, although the law applies equally to other forms of companies.

Take-over bids are not accorded separate statutory treatment under German law. Rather, they are covered by the law of contract or specific merger provisions. In addition, non-binding guidelines would commit a company when making a bid for publicly quoted stock to promise to increase ('improve') the bid if it should later offer a higher price to third parties (*LS Ubernahme-angebote* of 31 January 1979).

(1) *Acquisitions*

The acquisition of the business of another company can be effected either by the purchase of the share capital or of the assets. Tax considerations will play a major part in deciding which method to adopt.

The seller may prefer a share deal, provided the business is incorporated, because a sale is simple and would not leave the seller with residual liabilities and the burden of liquidating the company. The purchase price which is paid to private shareholders may qualify for a privileged tax rate for capital gains.

Conversely, the buyer of all the shares in a company will also inherit its less desirable characteristics. The company will have to continue its book values and depreciation methods. Furthermore, the buyer may have to deal with several shareholders/sellers.

Under an assets deal the buyer may be able to allocate all or most of the purchase price, including liabilities assumed to depreciable assets. The excess will have to be shown as goodwill which, from 1987 on, can be depreciated for commercial purposes over the four years following the year of acquisition and for tax purposes, in practice, over 15 years. If he prefers to operate the new business as a separate entity, the buyer may establish a subsidiary GmbH to act as the buyer. If he acquires all the assets of the seller he will also assume all liabilities by virtue of general civil or commercial law. All employment contracts will automatically pass over, except where employees exercise their right to refuse (s. 613a BGB).

The acquisition agreement does not need to be in a specific form except where real estate or shares in a GmbH are involved, in which case the entire agreement must be notarised. In addition, both parties are normally well advised to insist on a detailed agreement as German statutory and case law, in the case of a sale and acquisition of a business, often does not deal adequately with issues such as precontractual duties, transfer of title, misrepresentation, warranties (see Federal Court Decision of 18 March 1977, NJW 77, p. 1538) and deadlines. (Unless a time-scale is formally agreed, the Statute of Limitations will impose a period of only six months (s. 477 BGB).)

Acquisitions of companies, even if involving a foreign buyer, do not require any exchange control or other government approval, except that the acquisition may be subject to merger control (see Chapter 10).

(2) Mergers

Since 1 January 1981, a statutory merger of one GmbH into another has become possible under ss. 19 to 32 of the law on capital increases (KapErhG). This means that during the merger all of the assets of the merging company transfer through operation of the law to the surviving GmbH, and that the shareholders of the merging company become shareholders of the surviving GmbH. The requirements for such merger include:

(a) the final balance sheet of the merging company – The date of such balance sheet must not precede the filing with the commercial register by more than eight months. The balance sheet is the basis for the transfer of the assets;

(b) a merger agreement between the two GmbHs which must provide for the nominal values of the new shares to be issued by the surviving GmbH to the shareholders of the merging company;

(c) shareholder resolutions of both companies with three-quarters majority (the resolutions must be unanimous if the shares of the surviving company are not fully paid-in);

(d) the filing of the merger by all managing directors of each company with each of the relevant commercial registers.

No gain or loss will be realised to the merging company as a result of the merger which is effected at book value. The merging entity, however, has the option of recognising a gain up to the fair market value of its assets as required to use an accumulated loss carry-forward, because no such loss carry-forward can be transferred to the surviving company. For a further discussion of the tax consequences of a merger, see Chapter 5.

A GmbH may also be merged into a stock corporation (s. 355 AktG) or a limited partnership with a stock corporation as general partner (KGaA s. 356 AktG). It may further be reorganised into a partnership (ss. 3–14 UmwG), a limited partnership (ss. 20–24 UmwG) or merged into its shareholder (ss. 24 and 15 UmwG).

OTHER COMPANY FORMS

¶417　Introduction

The law dealing with branches of foreign companies and with limited liability companies is only a fraction of the total body of German company law. However, it is certainly the most important part from the point of view of a foreign party. For this reason, the foregoing paragraphs have discussed this aspect of the law in some detail, whereas the following only summarise the other types of companies which may exist under German law.

¶418　Stock corporation (AG)

The stock corporation (*Aktiengesellschaft*: AG) is a legal entity the shares of which are, in general, freely negotiable. From an economic point of view, its importance lies in its ability to attract capital contributions from the stock market. This has been the main reason for various well-known, family-owned enterprises such as Nixdorf, Porsche or Springer going public in 1984/85 after the conversion of their sole proprietorships or family-partnerships into an AG. 'Going public', however, is not nearly as commonplace yet as it is in other countries. There were 2,141 AGs in 1980 with a total stated equity capital of DM 92 billion, which increased to 2,182 AGs by the end of 1984 with a stated equity capital of DM 161 billion.

(1) *Corporate law*

The provisions of the stock corporation law (*Aktiengesetz*: AktG) of 6 September 1965, which significantly revised the preceding law of 1937 (in turn preceded by relevant provisions within the Commercial Code) consist of 410 sections (compared to only 85 sections of the GmbH law). They are mandatory to a much greater extent, and offer far less flexibility. The purpose is to protect the general public, in particular investors, since the AG is designed for large enterprises with an indefinite number of private stockholders.

(2) *Shares (stock)*

The membership of the corporation is documented by stock certificates. One of the most important differences to a GmbH is that the stock in the AG is freely transferable, i.e. no notarisation is required. It is possible, however, to provide in the articles of association (statutes) that the stock may only be transferred with the consent of the corporation (so-called *vinkulierte Aktien*), and this is done mainly where the former family-owners want to keep control or at least a major influence over the corporation or in crucial industries where outside or foreign control is not considered desirable by the present owners.

(3) Incorporation

The establishment of an AG takes place before a German notary. By contrast to a GmbH there needs to be at least five incorporators subscribing to the stock in the AG. They appoint the first supervisory board which, in turn, appoints the first board of management. Such appointments need to be recorded in notarised deeds. A formation report must include details such as a statement whether any incorporator has become a member of either board, the contribution made and remuneration or other benefits agreed, if any.

The AG comes into existence as a legal entity upon entry in the commercial register. The application for registration must be signed by all incorporators, all members of the board of management and all members of the supervisory board. All underlying documents, including the articles, must be attached.

The articles must at least set forth the name and registered seat of the corporation, its purpose, the amount of the stated capital, the par values, various classes (preferred or common), number of shares allocatable to each class (if there is more than one class), registered shares or shares issued to bearer, and the number of board members.

No stock certificates must be issued before registration. If a public offer is considered, banks normally act as initial stock holders, bearing all risks and responsibilities.

All persons involved in the formation are responsible, to varying extents, but the law does not provide that the stock capital must be reasonable in relation to the purpose of the corporation.

(4) Board of management

There is a strict division of responsibilities between the board of management (*Vorstand*) and the supervisory board (*Aufsichtsrat*) and no person can be a member of both (two-tier system).

The board of management is responsible for managing the business and for representing the corporation *vis-à-vis* third parties. Such authority must not be limited. Internally, it is possible to provide for certain kinds of (but not individual) transactions which require the approval of the supervisory board or even the stock general meeting. Transactions entered into in violation thereof are nevertheless valid and binding on the AG, but the board of management will be liable to the corporation for damages. If there is more than one member of the board of management, they represent the company jointly unless the

¶418

articles provide otherwise. Normally, an AG is represented by two signatories which may include *prokurists* (see 'Management' at ¶410 above). The members of the board of management are appointed by the supervisory board normally for a period of five years. Their internal position is much stronger than that of managing directors of a GmbH. They may be recalled only for cause, but such cause would include a vote of no-confidence of the general meeting 'unless the confidence has been withdrawn for obviously arbitrary reasons' (s. 84(3) AG Law).

The board members are responsible for damages caused by mismanagement and breach of duty, unless they acted on a valid resolution of the stockholders' meeting (s. 93 AG Law). The management is not subject to individual influence except as explained below ('*Affiliation*').

(5) *Supervisory board*
The main functions of the supervisory board are the appointment of the board of management, supervision of the management (excluding individual instructions), approval of the financial statements as prepared by the management and approval of certain transactions expressly reserved (see '*Board of management*' at (4) above). Depending on the size of the corporation, the supervisory board has between three and 21 members, some of whom must be labour representatives (see 'Supervisory board' at ¶413 above).

(6) *General meeting*
The general meeting is responsible for the election and removal of its representatives within the supervisory board, the appointment of the auditors, decisions on the appropriation of profits (as the latter is determined by the management and supervisory board) and the amendments of the articles including capital increases. Except in the last case resolutions require a simple majority.

Normally only stockholders who have deposited their shares with a notary or a bank at least ten days before the meeting are entitled to participate and vote. It is customary for small stockholders to grant written proxies to their banks.

Every individual stockholder has a right of information from the board of management, and stockholders representing at least 5 per cent of the stock capital may demand that a general meeting be convened. Stockholders representing 10 per cent or more may demand that the court decides whether the auditors should be replaced or that special auditors (*Sonderprüfer*) be appointed in order to investigate a gross violation of the law or the articles (s. 142(2) AG Law).

(7) *Affiliation*
Affiliation including a subsidiary relationship is subject to detailed provisions in order to protect outside stockholders and creditors. The acquisition of one quarter of the stock of an AG by another company must be notified (s. 20 AG

¶418

Law). The board of management must annually issue a report on its relationship to affiliated companies (s. 312 AG Law). Anyone who intentionally uses his influence on an AG to its detriment is personally liable unless such influence is exercised by the vote of the general meeting or is based on a control agreement (s. 117 and 317 AG Law). Such control agreement (*Beherrschungsvertrag*) must, *inter alia*, provide for an assumption of the losses of the AG by the parent company and for reasonable compensation to outside stockholders.

¶419 Civil partnership

The characteristic of a partnership is that it lacks legal personality. Where two or more natural or legal persons join in order to pursue a trade or business according to the meaning of s. 1(2) HGB, there is a commercial partnership subject to the provisions of the commercial code. Conversely, where no such trade or business is pursued, the partnership constitutes a civil partnership subject to the provisions of the civil code. This does not mean, however, that the civil partnership is insignificant for business purposes. Civil partnerships, on the contrary, are used for many purposes, such as a one-off construction deal where a major construction job is beyond the capacity of each of its members (so-called *Arbeitsgemeinschaft* or ARGE), underwriting and placement (*Konsortium*), joint research and development of companies with supplementing capacities, or vote binding or security pooling. It is typical for these kinds of arrangements that long-term, joint commercial organisations are not required or desired.

A civil partnership must act, sue and be sued by listing all its members. Some civil partnerships such as law firms, accounting firms or construction partnerships do in fact use a joint firm name, which practice is permissible as long as it does not cause third parties to believe they are dealing with a commercial company.

(1) *Formation*

The formation of a civil partnership requires an agreement which does not need to be in writing, although this is certainly advisable. Contractual freedom is virtually unrestricted and most provisions of the civil code apply only to the extent that the partners have not agreed differently.

(2) *Rights and obligations of the partners*

The rights of the partners are mainly to manage the partnership business, to vote in the partners' meetings and to participate in the profits and the liquidation proceeds. Unless it is agreed that their rights be in proportion to their individual contributions, each partner will enjoy the same rights. They must act for the good of the partnership, and owe the same degree of care as exercised in their own business (s. 708 BGB).

(3) *Management and representation*

Unless the partnership agreement provides differently, the partners manage the affairs of the partnership jointly and may only represent the partnership *vis-à-vis* third parties jointly, i.e. all partners acting together. In cases of urgency, however, each partner may act individually. The partnership may agree to have one or more managing partners or grant power of attorney to a third party, but they cannot delegate full management functions to an outside manager. The liability of the partnership for acts of a managing partner or such third party, either within or outside their authority, follows normal agency principles, including the principle of apparent authority. In theory, it would thus be possible to restrict the authority to represent to the assets of the partnership, but the crucial question would then be to what extent this restriction must be made known to the creditor. This question is controversial and cannot be answered in a generalised way.

(4) *Assets*

A partnership may have assets of its own. In such case the title will be held by all partners jointly (*Gesamthand*) and such ownership is not fractionally shared. No partner may dispose of his share nor may a debtor of the partnership set off a claim which he has against a single partner against the claim which belongs to the partnership property (s. 719 BGB).

(5) *Liability*

All partners are jointly and severally liable for obligations resulting from transactions which have been executed in the name of the partners. Such liability extends to the partnership's as well as the individual's assets, unless it has been otherwise agreed with the relevant third party creditor.

The partner who commits a tort is liable, but according to the prevailing view the other partners would not share such liability.

Claims against the partnership may be enforced against the partnership as well as the individual partner. Creditors are not required first to try to collect from the partnership, but enforcement of a claim against the assets of the partnership requires judgment against all of the partners.

¶420　Commercial partnerships (oHG and KG)

The commercial code recognises two types of commercial partnerships: the general partnership (*offene Handelsgesellschaft*: oHG) with two or more general partners with unlimited liability and the limited partnership (*Kommanditgesellschaft*: KG) with at least one general partner and at least one partner who is liable only to the amount of his agreed contribution.

The rules governing commercial partnerships are included in the commercial code (HGB) and primarily deal with the general partnership (s. 105 et seq. HGB), but are also applicable to the limited partnership unless modified by certain provisions (ss. 161 et seq. HGB). In practice, however, most commercial partnerships are limited partnerships and relatively few consist only of general partners. It is recognised that not only natural persons may be general partners, but also legal entities such as a GmbH, which by definition is only subject to limited liability. As a result of this there are many commercial partnerships with no party in fact subject to unlimited liability (so-called 'GmbH & Co.').

(1) *Formation*

A commercial partnership may only be established for the purpose of running a business within the meaning of s. 1 HGB (type of business) and s. 2 HGB (size), which excludes the activities of artists, scientists and the liberal professions. Furthermore, the nature and size of the business must be such as to require a commercial organisation, including book-keeping and accounting. Consequently, small merchants are excluded from forming a commercial partnership, and where a business declines the partnership will no longer be a commercial, but a civil partnership even if still registered. The same is true for joint ventures established only for a single transaction.

The formation of a partnership requires an agreement which may be oral, and the partnership must be filed in the commercial register in notarised form. The application must include the name (including one first name), occupation and residence of each partner (in the case of a limited partner, the amount of his contribution), as well as the firm name and domicile (registered office) of the partnership and the date of commencement of business. Specimen signatures of the partners with signing rights must be attached.

The limitation of liability of limited partners requires registration (s. 176 HGB). In order to exclude risks a limited partner should make his joining a partnership subject to the condition of registration (Federal Court Decision of 21 March 1983, NJW 83, 2259).

(2) *Firm name*

As mentioned under 'Company name' at ¶408 above, German law on such names is particularly strict. A new partnership must form its name by using the name of at least one general partner and an addition indicating a partnership

¶420

(e.g. '& Co.', 'KG'). Descriptive additions are admissible, but must be neither misleading nor confusing. A partnership may continue to use the firm name of an acquired business, but if no general partner is a natural person, then the firm name is required to indicate limited liability (i.e. normally 'GmbH & Co.KG'). Finally, the firm name must not be similar to an existing firm name within the same court district.

(3) Management and representation

Each of the general partners is authorised to represent the partnership *vis-à-vis* third parties, and such authorities may not be limited otherwise than by registering that a general partner is excluded from representation or that the partnership is represented only by two general partners signing together.

Internally, however, the partnership agreement may provide that prior approval is required, e.g. for transactions which exceed the usual scope of the partnership's business. Ignoring such restrictions would only affect a third party who knew, or had reason to know, of such restrictions (Federal Court Decision of 10 December 1980, DB 81, 840).

A commercial partnership may grant signing rights (*Prokura* or *Handlungs-vollmacht* – see 'Management' at ¶410 above) to other persons, including limited partners.

The law provides for a prohibition on competition for general partners (s. 112 HGB) but not for limited partners (see Chapter 10).

(4) Liability

All general partners are subject to direct and unlimited liability. This means that a third party creditor is not required first to sue the partnership or to sue partners in proportion to their interest in the partnership. In practice, the creditor will sue the partnership and the partners at the same time in order to be able to execute the same decision against either. Internally, a partner who has had to satisfy the creditor will have a proportional claim for reimbursement against the other partners.

In contrast, a limited partner is liable only to the extent that his registered contribution has not been paid in or has been repaid, provided he is duly registered as a limited partner when the partnership commences or the entry to the partnership takes effect. Repayment of the registered contribution would occur in a situation where limited partners receive more profits than the partnership has actually made.

In view of the personal liability of the general partners a commercial partnership must declare bankruptcy only in the case of insolvency, and not in the case of overindebtedness like a GmbH.

¶420

(5) *GmbH & Co.KG*

A GmbH & Co.KG is a limited partnership with a GmbH as the only general partner. In this case representation and management of the partnership rests in the GmbH (in effect in the latter's managing director(s)).

The commercial code has been amended with effect from 1 January 1981 in order to provide for restrictions applicable to limited liability companies to also apply in the case of commercial partnerships with no natural person as a general partner (GmbH & Co. or GmbH & Co.KG).

Such provisions include:

(a) stationery;

(b) capital replacing loans; and

(c) overindebtedness.

(6) *Assets and shares*

As in the case of the civil partnership, the assets of the partnership are jointly, but not severally, owned (*Gesamthand* – 'Civil partnership' at ¶419 above).

The partner's interest is not evidenced by any certificate, but rather expressed through the so-called 'capital account', which is an accounting figure representing a partner's interest in the partnership's assets and profits in relation to the interests of the other partners.

Subject to the provisions of the partnership agreement, a partnership interest may be assigned, but *vis-à-vis* creditors such assignment approximates a withdrawal of the assignor (he continues to be liable for any liabilities which have so far arisen) and entry of the assignee into the partnership (he will assume existing liabilities). The assignee of a limited partnership interest may be subject to unlimited liability if the assignment is effected prior to entry in the commercial register (s. 176 HGB).

¶421   Silent partnership

The term 'silent partnership' refers to the fact that it does not need to be disclosed. Colloquially speaking, it is a legal arrangement combining elements of a loan with those of a commercial partnership. It is similar to a loan in that the partner does not share ownership in the partnership assets: it is similar to a limited partnership in that the limited partner shares the profits of the business and his risk is limited to the amount of the contribution, and that *vis-à-vis* the principal his rights correspond to those of a limited partner (s. 338 HGB). In the case of bankruptcy, however, his position is the same as any outside creditor.

For tax purposes, a typical silent partnership is treated like a loan and the silent partner's shares of the profits will be taxed as income from capital and not as business income.

In order for its profits to qualify as business income the silent partnership must be structured so that the silent partner also participates in losses, any increase or decrease of the value of the assets (hidden reserves), and perhaps to some extent in the management. A foreign, typical silent partner would thereby create a permanent establishment in Germany and be fully exposed to German taxes. For this reason the foreign investor would normally prefer a typical silent partnership if a share in a GmbH was not possible or desirable.

¶422   Limited partnership on stock (KGaA)

The limited partnership on stock (*Kommanditgesellschaft auf Aktien*: KGaA) is a corporate form rarely used in Germany. It combines the partnerships with the AG insofar as it consists of normal stockholders (holding stock certificates) and one or more natural persons with unlimited liability who replace the board of management and are the general partners (s. 272 AG Law). Whether a legal entity such as GmbH may be general partner of a KGaA is a controversial question (left open in the Federal Court Decision of 25 February 1982, BGH 83, 122, 133). The KGaA form has regained a certain popularity after the introduction of the Co-determination Law of 1976.

5 Taxation

OUTLINE OF THE TAX SYSTEM

¶501 Principal taxes

The Federal Republic of Germany has a very complex tax system, with many different taxes. Most of these are imposed by the Federal authorities and the States (*die Länder*) and the municipalities have only a very limited taxing authority.

The most important taxes for foreign entities and individuals investing in the Federal Republic of Germany are:

- the income tax imposed on individuals (*Einkommensteuer*) and on corporations (*Körperschaftsteuer*);
- the wealth tax (*Vermögensteuer*);
- the trade tax (*Gewerbesteuer*);
- the value added tax (*Umsatzsteuer*);
- the inheritance and gift tax (*Erbschaftsteuer*); and
- a number of transactional taxes such as the capital contributions tax, the stock exchange transfer tax and the real estate transfer tax.

The foregoing taxes are not regulated in a single comprehensive tax statute but in specific tax statutes which include the following:

- the income tax act (*Einkommensteuergesetz*: EStG);
- the corporate income tax act (*Körperschaftsteuergesetz*: KStG);
- the wealth tax act (*Vermögensteuergesetz*: VStG);
- the trade tax act (*Gewerbesteuergesetz*: GewStG);
- the value added tax act (*Umsatzsteuergesetz*: UStG);
- the inheritance tax act (*Erbschaftsteuergesetz*: ErbStG).

These particular tax statutes are supplemented by ordinances promulgated by the Federal Ministry of Finance, which include detailed rules implementing the particular tax law (*Durchführungsverordnungen*), as well as by administrative regulations (*Richtlinien*) and decrees (*Erlasse*). Furthermore, court

decisions have become an important source of tax law. Decisions of the Federal
Tax Court are reported, *inter alia*, in the official reporter of the *Bundesfinanzhof* (BFH). Selected tax court decisions are published in *Entscheidungen
der Finanzgerichte* (EFG).

All of the above-named specific tax laws are regulated by Federal law, but
they are administered by state tax offices. In order to assure uniform application
of such laws nationwide, regulations are issued by the Federal Ministry of
Finance, and the state tax experts for particular taxes meet periodically to
discuss and resolve open questions.

Most taxes are assessed by the local state tax office on the basis of tax returns
filed by the taxpayer, and the deficiency is payable within 30 days of the receipt
of the assessment notice by the taxpayer. The filing of an administrative protest
(*Einspruch*) does not defer the obligation to pay the tax unless a stay of
execution (*Aussetzung der Vollziehung*) is granted by the tax office or a tax
court. If the administrative protest is rejected, the taxpayer may file suit at the
local tax court, and a tax court decision can be appealed to the highest German
tax court, the *Bundesfinanzhof* (BFH).

INCOME TAX – RESIDENT INDIVIDUALS

¶502   Scope of taxation

Income tax applies to resident individuals and it extends to their worldwide
income irrespective of whether this income is derived from domestic or from
foreign sources, unless a tax treaty provides for the exemption of a specific item
of income.

¶503   'Residence' defined

An individual is considered to be a resident if he maintains his domicile or his
habitual abode in Germany. 'Domicile' is defined as the place where the
individual maintains a residence under circumstances which indicate that he
will retain and use it not merely temporarily (s. 8 AO). If these requirements
are not met, the individual can still be regarded as a German resident provided
he is physically present in Germany under circumstances indicating that his stay
will not be a merely temporary one. A habitual abode is irrefutably presumed
to exist if the individual's stay in Germany exceeds six months, and this six-
months test does not have to be met in a calendar year; the six-month period is
extended to one year if the presence in Germany merely serves the purpose of
visiting friends and relatives or is intended for recreation or rehabilitation

purposes, or for other similar, private purposes (s. 9 AO). A taxpayer can be a resident of more than one country, but he can maintain only one habitual abode.

¶504   Categories of gross income

The consolidated amount of income from the following categories is included in gross income:

- agriculture and forestry;
- income from a trade or business;
- compensation for independent personal services;
- remuneration for services as an employee or worker;
- income from capital investments;
- income from the rental of real property, of units of personal property as well as royalties; and
- certain miscellaneous items of income (i.e. short-term capital gains, annuities and other periodic or recurrent income).

Other items of income such as gifts, inheritances and lottery gains are not taxable.

¶505   Determination of net income

Net income from agriculture and forestry, business or independent personal services is determined by deducting business expenses from gross receipts (s. 2(2)(1) EStG). Sole proprietors and commercial partnerships which are obliged to maintain proper accounting records under commercial law have to maintain such records for tax purposes as well and report their income on an accrual basis (s. 140 AO). Businessmen and farmers may use a financial year which deviates from the calendar year (s. 4(a) EStG).

Conversely, net income from employment, investment of capital, rentals and income from certain miscellaneous sources is determined on a cash basis per calendar year by deducting from each item of gross income so-called 'income related expenses' (*Werbungskosten*) which are incurred by the taxpayer in order to gain, protect or to retain the source of such income (s. 2(2)(2) EStG). The taxpayer may either itemise such expenses or use standard allowances which, in the case of income from employment, amount to DM 564.

If an employee elects to itemise his income-related expenses, the single most important item may be his commuting expenses. If he uses public transport, he can claim his actual expenditures. If he uses a private car, the allowance is limited to DM 0.36 per kilometre for the distance between home and office for one trip per day. Thus, if an employee lives 20 kilometres away from his place of work, he may deduct DM 7.20 per working day.

(1) *Business income*

Business income includes all income which is generated by an individual as the owner of a sole proprietorship or as a partner in a partnership (and this includes salaries, interests, rentals or other remuneration paid to him by the partnership), the sale or closing of an unincorporated business or a separate part thereof, and the sale of a partner's interest in a partnership (ss. 15, 16 EStG). The sale of shares in a corporation by an individual who owns more than 25 per cent of the corporation's shares of stock is similarly deemed to constitute business income, and the share interest is determined by reference to the entitlement to dividends and liquidation proceeds and not to voting rights (s. 17 EStG). Business income also includes other items of income (such as interest, dividends, rental income) to the extent that such income, or the assets from which it is generated, is properly attributable to the business activity.

Business expenses are allowable as deductions, and they include, *inter alia*, financial charges, wages and social charges and insurance premiums, as well as depreciation allowances and provisions for bad debts. For a more detailed discussion see 'Allowable business expenses' at ¶514.

(2) *Income from dependent services*

The term 'income from employment' encompasses the total cash remuneration, as well as all other benefits of a monetary value, which an employer grants in connection with the employment such as salaries, wages, bonuses, housing allowances, foreign service allowances, educational allowances or income tax equalisation allowances. Benefits under stock option plans are deemed realised at the time of the exercise of the option. On the other hand, service-connected moving expenses, travel allowances and other specific expenditures incurred on behalf of the employer can be reimbursed (or advanced) by the employer and they do not constitute income from employment.

In the case of employment income, income tax normally is collected by way of withholding at source, but this tax is fully creditable against the ultimate income tax.

Foreign employers are obligated to withhold wage taxes of their employees who are performing services in Germany if the employer maintains a 'permanent establishment' or a 'permanent representative' in Germany as such terms are defined in domestic law (Tax Court Düsseldorf of 6 November 1984, EFG 1985, 618).

¶505

(3) *Income from independent services*

Income from independent services includes income from professional activities and other independent activities, i.e. as an executor of an estate or a member of the supervisory board of a corporation.

In determining the net income from professional services, the taxpayer may deduct his business expenses plus a general allowance of 5 per cent of his receipts but not more than DM 1,200 per annum (s. 18(4) EStG).

(4) *Rental income*

Rental income includes all compensation for the leasing of realty, of units of personal property and for licensing intangible artistic or industrial property rights or know-how. It also includes imputed income from the use of one's own residence to the value of 1 per cent per annum of the assessed tax value of the property (s. 21, 21(a) EStG).

(5) *Income from capital investment*

Interest income is fully taxable irrespective of whether the underlying debt is represented by a security instrument or not, and where a withholding tax is levied, this tax is creditable against the final income tax. Dividends paid in cash or in kind are fully taxable as well. If distributed by a resident corporation, the cash distribution (or its cash value in the case of dividends in kind) has to be grossed-up by the 36 per cent corporate income tax as well as by the withholding tax which is normally levied at the rate of 25 per cent. In this context, the term 'dividend' includes constructive dividends as well as stock dividends. However, stock dividends can be received tax free by the shareholder if they are granted in accordance with the provisions of a special statute, the *Gesetz über steuerrechtliche Maßnahmen bei Erhöhung des Nennkapitals aus Gesellschaftsmitteln und bei Überlassung eigener Aktien* of 10 October 1967, as amended. The provisions of this statute also exempt foreign stock dividends if the procedure under foreign corporate law corresponds to the procedure of declaring a stock dividend under German law.

There is a general allowance of DM 300 per year, or of DM 600 in the case of husband and wife who file a joint return (s. 20(4) EStG). In addition, the taxpayer may claim a standard allowance of DM 100 (200 for spouses filing a joint return) (s. 9(a)(1)(2) EStG).

(6) *Capital gains*

While capital gains realised upon the sale of shares in a corporation in which the taxpayer holds an interest of more than 25 per cent constitute business income (see (1) above), capital gains realised upon the sale of other securities

¶505

are taxable only if the securities are sold prior to their acquisition (short sales) or within six months of their acquisition. Capital gains from the sale of real estate are taxable if the land is resold within two years.

Such short-term capital gains are taxed at ordinary tax rates. If shares in a corporation are sold within six months of their acquisition by a taxpayer who holds an interest of more than 25 per cent in such corporation, then the rules for short-term capital gains apply. Short-term losses can be deducted only from short-term capital gains realised in the same taxable year. A net short-term capital gain is exempt from income tax if it does not reach the amount of DM 1,000 during the taxable year.

¶506   Net income computation

Once the taxpayer has determined his net income from the various categories of income, he can consolidate and even them out. This means that, in principle, losses incurred in one or more categories of gross income can be used to reduce other items of income realised during the same calendar year (s. 2(3) EStG). Nevertheless, this principle is not applicable in a number of instances, in particular:

- if a limited partner's loss from an interest in a partnership exceeds the amount of his contributions to the partnership – Such losses can be carried forward indefinitely and used to offset future profits realised by the limited partner from such partnership only (s. 15(a) EStG). Similar rules apply to silent participations (s. 20(1)(4) EStG);

- losses incurred in a treaty jurisdiction if profits from such activity would have been exempt from German income tax under a tax treaty – This applies, e.g., to losses incurred in a permanent establishment maintained by the taxpayer in a treaty jurisdiction. In this instance relief may be obtained, however, under s. 2 AIG (see ¶524).

- if foreign losses are not excluded from deduction by operation of a tax treaty, certain items of losses enumerated in s. 2(a)(1) EStG cannot be used as an offset against other income – Instead they can be carried forward for seven years and used to offset subsequent profits of the same kind realised in the same foreign jurisdiction. Such losses include losses from foreign agricultural installations, from a permanent establishment which does not engage in an active business, from silent participations in a foreign enterprise or a participating loan granted to a foreign enterprise, or from the letting of immovable property or from units of movable assets situated in a foreign jurisdiction.

In order to compute net taxable income, the total gross income arrived at may be further reduced by the following expenditures and deductions:

(1) *Special expenses*

Unlike *Werbungskosten*, special expenses (*Sonderausgaben*) are not income related expenses. They cover personal or family expenses and are deductible as a matter of social or economic policy. Special expenses may be itemised if they exceed the standard special expense allowance which amounts to DM 570 per annum in the case of a single taxpayer and to DM 1,140 per annum for taxpayers who file a joint return.

As a general rule, only church taxes and costs incurred by having the income tax return prepared by a professional tax adviser can be fully deducted. Premiums paid with respect to life, health, accident or third party liability insurances, as well as social security dues and payments made to building and loan associations, can be deducted up to a ceiling that depends on the taxpayer's family status.

Special expenses also include charitable contributions and dues and contributions paid to political parties. They can be deducted up to 5 per cent of total gross income or 2 per cent of total sales and total payroll. So far as contributions for scientific and specifically recognized cultural purposes are concerned, the ceiling is increased to 10 per cent of total gross income (s. 10(6) EStG). So far as political contributions are concerned, also see s. 34(g) EStG.

(2) *Loss carryforward – loss carryback*

Up to a maximum of DM 10 million a loss incurred in one year may be carried back to the two preceding years and a remaining loss can be carried forward for the following five years (s. 10(d) EStG).

(3) *Hardship allowances*

If, under specific circumstances, an individual incurs personal expenses due to an extraordinary, unusually burdensome hardship (*außergewöhnliche Belastungen*), he may be granted a specific allowance. In order to qualify, the expenses must exceed a certain percentage of the person's income. For example, relief may be granted in cases where an accident or a sudden illness leads to extraordinary medical or hospital bills which are not covered by health insurance (s. 33–33(c) EStG).

¶507   Methods of assessment

(1) *Individual or joint returns*

An individual who receives no income from employment during the taxable year must file a return if his income from all other sources (such as income from capital investments) during that year was in excess of DM 4,836, or DM 9,672 in the case of a married couple filing joint returns. A joint return may be filed only if both husband and wife are residents of Germany and if they are not permanently separated (s. 26(1) EStG).

An employee must file an income tax return if his annual income from employment and other sources exceeds DM 24,000. If his income is DM 24,000 or less he must file a return if:

(a) his total income other than employment income (for which income tax was withheld) amounts to more than DM 800 in the taxable year; or

(b) if he receives salaries or wages from several employers exceeding DM 18,000, or DM 36,000 in the case of a married couple entitled to file a joint return.

If an employee is not required to file a return, his income tax liability is satisfied by payment of the withholding tax. The taxpayer may, however, use a special procedure (*Jahreslohnsteuerausgleich*) and request a refund of taxes withheld by the employer in excess of his individual income tax liability.

Income tax returns usually have to be filed no later than 31 May of the year following the taxable year (s. 149(2) AO). However, if the return is prepared by a tax adviser, general and special filing extensions may be and are usually granted (s. 109 AO).

The filing of the income tax return does not have to be accompanied by a payment of the taxes due. Taxes due are payable within one month after the taxpayer receives the notice of assessment.

(2) *Estimated advance payments*

The taxpayer must make quarterly advance payments of income tax on 10 March, 10 June, 10 September and 10 December of each year. The payments are fixed by the local tax office on the basis of the previous tax assessment unless substantial increases or reductions of the net taxable income are anticipated.

A taxpayer who starts business operations or who takes up an activity which involves the rendering of independent personal services is under the obligation to notify the local tax office thereof within one month (s. 138(3) AO). The tax office will request the taxpayer to fill out a form which, among other things, asks for the estimated profits in order to permit the tax office to fix advance payments of tax.

(3) *Income tax rates*

The progressive income tax rates presently start at income in excess of DM 4,536. They begin at slightly less than 22 per cent and reach a maximum of 56

¶507

per cent for taxable income which exceeds DM 130,031 per annum (for a husband and wife who file a joint return these amounts are doubled).

¶508   Double taxation relief

(1) *Unilateral relief*

In the absence of a tax treaty which provides for an exemption of a particular item of income from German income tax, resident individuals have to include in their taxable income all items of income derived from whatever sources. Nevertheless, foreign income taxes paid with respect to foreign source income may be taken into consideration when determining the German income tax deficiency.

Foreign income taxes which correspond to the German income tax levied on items of income from sources within such foreign state are creditable against the German income tax payable with respect to the same income. The creditable foreign income taxes may not exceed the German tax payable with respect to such income and this maximum is computed by dividing the total German income tax payable by the ratio which the income from sources within the particular foreign state bears to the total taxable income (s. 34(c)(1) EStG).

Instead of claiming the foreign tax credit, the taxpayer may elect to deduct the foreign income taxes paid from his income taxable in Germany (s. 34(c)(2) EStG). Where foreign income taxes do not correspond to the German income tax, or where the foreign taxes are not levied in the state of the source of the income, the foreign income tax may be deducted only from the taxpayer's income taxable in Germany; no tax credit against the German income tax is available (s. 34(c)(3) EStG).

(2) *Tax treaties*

Germany has entered into income tax treaties with most industrial countries as well as with a significant number of developing countries. Most of the tax treaties exempt certain items of foreign source income from German tax: they all provide for a tax credit if foreign source income is not exempt from German income tax, and some of the treaties with developing countries contain tax sparing provisions.

The extent to which income from sources within the other treaty state may be excluded from German tax varies from treaty to treaty. Under the US-German tax treaty, for example, a German resident may exclude from his gross income industrial or commercial revenues from a permanent establishment located in the United States or income from real estate situated in the United States.

However, to prevent a taxpayer from benefiting from reduced tax rates both in Germany and in the other treaty states, Germany reserved the right to take into account in the determination of its rate of tax for the items of income which remain taxable in Germany the items of income excluded under the treaty (*Progressionsvorbehalt*) (s. 32(b) EStG).

If an item of income is exempt from German income tax by operation of a treaty, then expenses incurred in connection which that income cannot be deducted either. However, if such expenses lead to a loss, such loss will also be taken into account in determining the German tax bracket for the individual's taxable income.

If no double taxation treaty applies or if a specific item of income is not covered by such treaty, the foreign source income is included in the German resident's income, but German tax law provides for a credit with respect to such income (s. 34(c)(6) EStG).

Instead of a credit the taxpayer can also choose to have the foreign tax deducted from his overall income.

Some treaties, especially those with developing countries, contain tax-sparing provisions according to which fictitious foreign withholding taxes on dividends, interest and/or royalties are creditable against the German income tax.

¶509   Special tax status for immigrants

Individuals who move to Germany and become subject to German income taxation on a worldwide basis may apply for relief under the so-called *Pauschbesteuerung* or lump sum taxation regime. This may be granted for up to ten years following the move to Germany; in practice, it is granted for an initial term of up to three years with the possibility of one or more renewals of two years each. It may exclude a part or all of the foreign source income, it may exclude foreign source income for purposes of determining the applicable tax rate with respect to German source income, and it may authorise (otherwise not permissible) deductions of insurance premiums paid to foreign insurance companies not engaged in business in Germany. The application must be filed with the local tax office which, internally, will seek the approval of the State Ministry of Finance with the concurrence of the Federal Ministry of Finance. The application will be granted if the taxpayer's move to Germany is considered beneficial to Germany. In determining whether this requirement is met, the tax authorities will consider cultural, scientific or economic aspects. Thus, scientists, artists and persons with specific technical know-how may have a chance of securing such preferential status. Guidelines for this procedure were last published in 1978 (see StEK s. 31 No. 18). Special rules apply to foreign journalists who move to Germany (StEK para. 31; EStG No. 25).

CORPORATE INCOME TAX – RESIDENT CORPORATIONS

¶510 Outline of corporate income tax system

(1) *Mechanism of the imputation system*

At company level, the general tax rate amounts to 56 per cent of the corporation's taxable income, subject, however, to a refund of 20 per cent of the tax paid with respect to dividend distributions. This means that out of a total taxable income of DM 100 the corporation can pay a cash dividend of DM 64 if the withholding tax and the trade tax are disregarded. The shareholder, in turn, has to gross-up the cash dividend of DM 64 by the remaining corporate income tax of DM 36 and to include in his taxable income a dividend of DM 100; against the income tax due he can credit the DM 36 corporate income taxes paid by the corporation.

The mechanism can be illustrated as follows (excluding trade tax and withholding tax):

		Taxes paid
Income before corporate income tax	100	
56% corporate income tax	(56)	56
	44	
Reduction of corporate income tax assuming full distribution	20	(20)
Available for maximum distribution	64	36
Shareholder includes in his income:		
cash distribution	64	
imputation tax credit ($^{9}/_{16} \times 64$)	36	
taxable income	100	
Shareholder's individual income tax (an individual tax rate of 40% is assumed)	40	
Shareholder credit or refund (see above)	(36)	
	4	4
Overall taxes paid		40

This shows that in the ideal situation the corporate income tax as well as the individual income tax of resident individual shareholders are integrated. The corporate income tax can be completely credited against the individual income tax of the shareholder and distributed corporate income ultimately will bear only the income tax at the rate applicable to the individual shareholder. Moreover, as there is no time limit for the refund of the 20 percentage points corporate income tax at company level and for the credit at the shareholder's level, the system works not only for current dividend distributions. At the liquidation of the company at the latest, the tax burden at company level will be transformed into the tax burden applicable to the shareholder. Nevertheless, as long as the corporate income is distributed to German resident corporations and remains in corporate solution, it remains subject to corporation income tax at the rate of 56 per cent.

(2) *Tracing of income*

Eligible shareholders are entitled to the credit of 36 per cent corporate income tax against the income tax payable by them if they meet the formal requirements for the credit; they do not have to establish that the 36 per cent tax was assessed and paid at the company level. Instead, the distributing corporation has to pay the 36 per cent tax at the latest at the time a dividend is distributed. This means that dividends paid out of profits which were taxed at the regular 56 per cent rate will entitle the corporation to a refund of 20 percentage points. On the other hand, the corporation will have to pay a 36 per cent compensatory tax (*Erhöhungsbetrag*) upon distributions which have been made out of tax-exempt or otherwise untaxed items of income. For that purpose, fully taxed profits are deemed to be distributed first, items of income taxed at the rate of 36 per cent follow, and finally so far untaxed items of income are deemed distributed in the following order:

(a) tax exempt items of foreign source income realised in fiscal years which ended after 31 December 1976;

(b) other tax exempt items of income which are not covered by items (c) or (d), below; losses which can be carried forward are deducted from this item which, as a result, may become negative; subsequent profits offset by the loss carryforward are added to such items;

(c) equity available for distribution generated in fiscal years which ended on or before 31 December 1976 and;

(d) contributions to capital effected in a fiscal year which ended after 31 December 1976; if tax free income included in this item is distributed it attracts neither the 36 per cent compensatory tax nor a withholding tax.

The various available net equity accounts have to be computed on separate forms outside the corporation's accounting system.

(3) *Status of non-resident corporate and individual shareholders*

Non-resident corporate or individual shareholders are not included in the imputation system as they are not eligible for the credit or refund of the

¶510

corporate income tax imposed at the corporate level. However, they can apply for a refund of the 36 per cent corporate income tax levied with respect to dividend distributions deemed to have been made out of tax exempt foreign source income realised under the present tax system, or out of items of available net equity built up under the former corporate income tax system which applied to fiscal years which ended on or before 31 December 1976. The amount refundable is, however, subject to withholding tax at the rate of 25 per cent or a lower treaty rate.

In order to mitigate the combined German tax burden of trade tax, corporate income tax and withholding tax on dividends paid to non-resident shareholders, the German Ministry of Finance offered to all treaty states a general reduction of the German withholding tax from 25 per cent to 15 per cent. This was accepted by Canada and Switzerland but most other treaty states still wait for the outcome of the discussions for a revision of the United States-German tax treaty. Pending such outcome, the German Ministry of Finance waived the application of the reinvestment clause of Art. 6(3) of the US-German tax treaty with respect to all re-investments effected after 31 December 1980. Furthermore, it has been reported that, under the protocol to the French Treaty of 11 July 1985, French resident portfolio shareholders of German corporations will receive an indirect imputation credit of 10 per cent of the dividend.

¶511 Worldwide income of resident corporations

A resident corporation is subject to German corporate income tax with respect to its worldwide income unless a tax treaty exempts particular items of income from German taxation. A corporation qualifies as a resident if it maintains either its statutory seat or its actual principal place of business within Germany. Since corporations organised under German law have to maintain both their statutory seat and their actual principal place of business within Germany, they always qualify as resident corporations. On the other hand, a foreign corporation may qualify as resident if it transfers its actual principal place of business to Germany. It should be noted, however, that a decree by the Hamburg tax authorities of 15 January 1985 (RIW 1985, 253) held that a UK non-resident company which maintained its principal place of management in Germany could not be recognised as a corporate taxpayer for German income tax purposes.

¶512   Accrual method of accounting

(1) *General*

German corporations are required by commercial law to maintain books of account and to prepare regular financial statements in accordance with generally recognised accounting principles. Such books of account and financial statements will be definitive for tax purposes too, unless specific adjustments are required by tax law. This means, in the first place, that corporations report their income on the basis of the accrual method of accounting. It means, further, that certain conformity requirements have to be observed, i.e. that in setting up the financial statements for corporate purposes, the tax consequences have to be taken into account. For instance, depreciation allowances can be claimed for tax purposes only if the same or higher depreciation allowances are used for financial reporting purposes. On the other hand, tax law restricts the options available to the corporation under generally recognised accounting principles where such rules would permit the corporation to understate its profits and thus to reduce its taxable income.

(2) *Basic accounting rules*

Under the accrual system of accounting, prepaid items of income can be deferred to the financial year to which they relate, whereas in the case of prepaid expenses only such part of the expenses can be currently recognised which is properly eligible to the current fiscal year. Furthermore, since German financial accounting principles look to the protection of the corporation's creditors, they permit the recognition of unrealised losses whereas unrealised gains cannot be recognised. For a more detailed discussion of accounting aspects, see Chapter 6.

(3) *Taxable year*

The corporation's taxable income is computed on the basis of its fiscal year, which may or may not be identical with the calendar year. A change to a fiscal year which deviates from the calendar year requires the consent of the local tax authorities. If the books are kept on a fiscal year deviating from the calendar year, the taxable income is computed for the fiscal year which ends during the particular calendar year (s. 7(4) KStG).

¶513   Determination of gross income

(1) *General*

By definition, a resident corporation is engaged in a business activity and, as a consequence, all its income constitutes ordinary business income irrespective of whether it consists of dividends, rentals, royalties, capital gains or ordinary operating income (s. 8(2) KStG).

(2) *Dividend income*

As a general rule, dividends received with respect to shares in domestic or foreign corporations constitute income which is taxable at ordinary tax rates. The same applies to constructive dividends. Nevertheless, the following exceptions should be noted:

(a) *Intercorporate dividends exclusion under a tax treaty.*   Under most German tax treaties resident corporations may exclude from their taxable income dividends received from subsidiary corporations in the other treaty state, provided the German corporation holds an interest of at least 10 per cent in the foreign corporation (s. 26(7) KStG). However, if a distribution of a dividend by the resident corporation is deemed to have been made out of such exempt foreign dividends, the compensatory tax of 36 per cent will have to be paid (see ¶510).

(b) *Dividends received from developing countries' subsidiaries.*   Even without a tax treaty, dividends received from a subsidiary in a developing country can be received free from German corporate income tax: there is a deemed indirect foreign tax credit which equals the German tax which would be payable in the absence of the foreign tax credit (s. 26(3) KStG).

(c) *Integrated group relief (Organschaft).*   If a domestic corporation is integrated with another domestic corporation from a financial, organisational and economic point of view, and if a profit and loss absorption agreement is concluded between the two corporations, then the taxable income or loss of the subordinated corporation is attributed directly to the controlling corporation. Under the profit and loss absorption agreement, which has to be concluded for an initial fixed term of at least five years, the controlled corporation assumes the obligation to transfer all its profits to the controlling corporation which is committed to make good any losses which the controlled corporation may incur during the term of the agreement. While German tax law does not permit the filing of consolidated tax returns, the integrated group relief achieves similar results because it permits a consolidation of profits and losses of the subordinated and of the controlling corporation. This relief is important, in particular, if the controlled corporation incurs losses; if it is profitable, a consolidation can also be obtained under the imputation system if the controlled corporation distributes its income to the controlling corporation.

(d) *Constructive dividends.*   If a corporation has effected a constructive dividend in a fiscal year, its taxable income will be increased for such fiscal year. The constructive dividend is furthermore deemed to be distributed out of the

¶513

net 'available equity' at the close of the fiscal year ending during which the distribution of the constructive dividend occurred (s. 28(2) KStG).

At the level of the corporation which receives the constructive dividend, it is includable in taxable income if and when it can be accrued on its books. In this context, a controlling corporation can report as income the dividend which its domestic subsidiary will distribute to it during the next year out of its current year income if the financial statements of the subsidiary are adopted prior to the finalisation of the audit of the financial statements of the controlling corporation and if at such time at least a dividend proposal exists (BGHZ 65, 230; BFH decision of 12 April 1980, BStBl. 1980 II 702).

(e) *Interim dividends.* A GmbH (not an *Aktiengesellschaft*) can declare an interim dividend out of current income of the fiscal year if this is authorised by its charter and if certain other requirements are met. For the purposes of the corporate income tax of the distributing corporation, this interim dividend is deemed to be distributed out of 'net available equity' at the close of the fiscal year during which the interim dividend is declared.

(3) *Capital gains*

It is a general rule that all capital gains realised by the corporation are includable in its taxable income as ordinary income. Nevertheless, some exclusions are available.

(a) *Rollover for involuntary gains.* Involuntary capital gains such as fire damages covered by insurance proceeds are not taxable if a replacement asset is acquired in the same fiscal year in which the gain is realised. The replacement asset must perform the same business functions as the original asset. If the replacement is not made in the same year, the gain may be put in a tax free reserve; nevertheless, the gain becomes taxable if the replacement asset is not ordered within one year from the end of the fiscal year in which the reserve was formed (or within two years for immovable assets) (s. 35(2) EStR).

(b) *Voluntary conversions.* 80 per cent of a capital gain realised on the sale of certain fixed assets (100 per cent if real estate or buildings are sold) can be rolled over tax free if certain replacement assets are acquired in the fiscal year of the sale or within a specified period of time thereafter. Eligible assets include real estate, buildings, ships, shares of stock in a corporation, and depreciable movable assets with a useful life of at least 25 years. The assets disposed of must have been held by the corporation for more than six years prior to the sale (s. 6(b) EStG).

(4) *Exclusions from income*

(a) *Contributions to capital.* Contributions to capital (whether declared or constructive in nature) constitute income for financial reporting purposes but

¶513

not for tax purposes. As a result, they reduce or eliminate a loss carryforward for financial reporting purposes but leave a net operating loss carryforward for tax purposes unaffected.

(b) *Rehabilitation gains.* If creditors forego part or all of their loans to a corporation such remittance does not create taxable income to the corporation provided the transaction is entered into for the express purpose of restoring the corporation to a sound financial position and provided it is capable of reaching such result (s. 3(66) EStG).

¶514 Allowable business expenses

A corporation generally can deduct all expenses incurred by it in conducting its business operations irrespective of whether they are necessary, appropriate, customary or useful. However, in the case of related parties such expenses will be very closely scrutinised by the tax authorities as to whether they meet arm's length standards. Additionally, certain expenditures (such as organisational expenses incurred in connection with the organisation and incorporation of the taxpayer) are deductible, whereas other expenses (such as income taxes, wealth taxes, fines and half of the remuneration paid to members of a supervisory board) are specifically disallowed, and others such as business gifts are deductible only up to certain amounts (s. 10 KStG; s. 4(5)(1) EStG).

(1) *Rental payments*

Current rental payments for the premises of a business are deductible. Prepayments of rent are only deductible in the financial years to which they relate. Payment of finder's fees to real estate agents and leasehold improvements have to be capitalised and amortised over the term of the tenancy. In the case of financial leases, there are regulations which determine whether a particular lease will be recognised as a lease or whether it constitutes an instalment sale and has to be treated as such. For full payout leases of movable assets, see BdF letter of 19 April 1971, BStBl. 1981 I 264; full payout leases of immovable assets, BdF letter of 21 March 1972, BStBl. 1972 I 188; and for non-payout leasing arrangements, BMF letter of 22 December 1975, BB 1976, 72.

(2) *Salaries*

Salaries and other compensation for services of employees and former employees are allowed as business expenses. Restrictions apply with regard to compensation paid to a shareholder for his services as an employee of the corporation. To the extent such compensation is excessive, it is considered a constructive dividend distribution to such shareholder.

(3) *Pension reserves*

An employer can choose between deducting pension payments when payable or setting up a reserve for future pension commitments. When setting up a pension reserve, the present discounted value of future pension costs is computed by using an interest rate of 6 per cent per annum (s. 6(a) EStG). Furthermore, the pension reserve must be actuarially computed and the employer's commitment towards the employee must be in writing. However, a pension reserve need not be funded: the amounts so reserved may be used for general corporate purposes of the employer. Major corporations may set up separate pension funds which are subject to insurance regulation and which have to be funded. Another alternative for backing up pension commitments, used, in particular, by smaller companies, is to buy insurance.

(4) *Interest*

Interest on loans or debts incurred by a corporation is generally a deductible business expense unless – from an economic point of view – the loan or debts are directly related to tax free income (s. 3(c) EStG). Interest on shareholders' loans may be disallowed if such loans in reality represent a contribution to capital. This might be true, for instance, in the case of an illiquid company if a reasonable and prudent businessman would have made a contribution to capital instead of granting a loan (s. 32(a) GmbHG). The same applies to the extent that interest rates exceed arm's length standards. An original issue discount and other costs incidental to the loan (brokerage fee, fees for administration etc.) must be capitalised and spread over the term of the loan.

(5) *Insurance premiums*

Business-related insurance premiums, such as premiums for property or damage insurances, are deductible business expenses. Reserves for self-insurance are not permissible.

(6) *Taxes*

Generally, taxes imposed on a particular object are deductible, whereas taxes imposed on the corporation as a person are not. Thus, the trade tax, excise taxes, property taxes and transfer taxes are deductible. On the other hand, the wealth tax and corporate income tax are not deductible (s. 10(2) KStG). Deductible taxes accrued but not yet paid may be shown in a tax reserve. Additions to tax and interest charges due to late payments are deductible if the underlying taxes are also deductible.

¶514

(7) *Bad debts*

Doubtful or uncollectable accounts receivable can either be written off directly or indirectly through a reserve.

(8) *Casualty losses*

Losses from casualties or acts of God are deductible business expenses.

(9) *Costs of repairs and maintenance costs*

It is rather difficult to draw a line between expenditures necessary for the proper upkeep of a building (*Erhaltungsaufwand*) and expenditures necessary for the construction of a building (*Herstellungsaufwand*). The first applies to expenses incurred without changing the character of the asset and which occur at more or less regular intervals in about the same amounts; they are currently deductible. The latter applies to major repairs which then have to be capitalised and thus increase the cost basis of the respective asset.

(10) *Depreciation*

Depreciation allowances are deductible for the owner of depreciable fixed tangible or intangible assets with a useful life in excess of one year. Deduction of depreciation allowances is mandatory and may not be intentionally shifted to reduce profits in subsequent taxable years. However, if the taxpayer inadvertently claims depreciation allowances which are too low, this may be remedied by spreading the adjusted basis over the remaining useful life of the asset.

Depreciation allowances are based on the costs of acquisition or manufacture of the depreciable asset. The costs of manufacture have to be distinguished from the expenses for the proper upkeep of an asset. Immovable assets can, as a rule, be depreciated only by using the straight-line method. For buildings which were completed after 31 December 1924, usually a useful life of 50 years is assumed, while for buildings for which the application for the construction permit was filed after 31 March 1985, a useful life of 25 years will be recognised. In the latter case, the taxpayer can elect to claim a 10 per cent depreciation allowance during the year of completion or acquisition and the subsequent three years, 5 per cent during the three years next following and 2.5 per cent during the remaining 18 years (s. 7(5) EStG). Goodwill acquired in a fiscal year which starts after 31 December 1986 can be depreciated over 15 years by using the straight-line method; goodwill acquired before such fiscal year will be treated as if it had been acquired as of the beginning of the first fiscal year which starts after 1 December 1986 (s. 7(1)(3) EStG). In the case of movable fixed assets, on the other hand, the following three methods are available: straight-line, three times declining balance with a maximum rate of 30 per cent, and the unit of production method (s. 7(2) EstG).

A change from the declining balance to the straight-line method is permissible but not vice versa. The depreciation allowances have to be computed so that the costs of acquisition or construction of the depreciable assets are depreciated over the useful life of such assets. Scrap value needs to be taken into account only if substantial, as in cases of very heavy or very valuable materials.

(11) *Intercorporate charges*

Management fees, rentals and royalties charged by a foreign parent to its German subsidiary will be recognised as deductible business expenses to the extent that they are reasonable, meet arm's length standards and have been agreed upon in writing in advance. Intercorporate charges exceeding such standards will be disallowed and treated as constructive dividends. For further details, see ¶523 ('(1) *Adjustment of inter-company charges*') below.

(12) *Entertainment expenses*

Expenses for business entertainment are deductible if they are appropriate and if their amount and business purpose is established on a specific form (s. 4(5)(2) EStG).

(13) *Travel expenses*

Travel expenses (including meals and lodging) are deductible if incurred exclusively or almost exclusively for bona fide business purposes and if reasonable in amount.

(14) *Loss carryover*

Net operating losses may be carried back for two years, and to the extent that they exceed DM 10 million or cannot be deducted in the two preceding years they can be carried forward for five years. This even applies for foreign losses of a resident taxpayer unless the foreign income to which they relate is exempt from German income tax by operation of a tax treaty. In the latter case the foreign losses may be taken into account in determining the applicable tax rate and, if the provisions of the Foreign Investment Tax Act apply, they may be deducted subject to recapture unless the provisions of s. 2(a) EStG prevent this.

The right to the loss carryover or the loss carryforward is not transferable to another taxpayer but a set-off with profits of another taxpayer may be possible under an *Organschaft* arrangement (see at ¶513 (2)(c), *supra*).

¶514

¶515   Liquidation, reorganisation

(1) *Liquidation of a corporation*

The liquidation of a corporation may produce taxable income to the corporation as well as to its shareholders.

The corporation's gain is computed by determining the difference between its financial statements as of the beginning of the fiscal year in which the dissolution occurs and the financial statements at the end of the liquidation. The financial statements have to show the fair market value of the corporation's property distributable to its shareholders after payment of all debts and liabilities. The taxable period of liquidation may not exceed three years. Net operating losses incurred during the five preceding years and not used as a set-off against taxable income in previous years can be taken into account when computing the corporation's taxable liquidation gain.

The liquidation proceeds received by the shareholder constitute taxable dividends to the extent that they are deemed distributed out of equity available for distribution exclusive of contributions to capital effected in fiscal years which ended after 31 December 1976 (s. 17(4) EStG). Only a distribution in excess of such amounts will qualify as a capital gain or as liquidation proceeds proper, and if the cost of the shares is higher, a capital loss will result which, depending on the tax status of the shareholder, may or may not be used to offset the dividend income or other items of income.

(2) *Statutory mergers and reorganisations*

Generally, a transferor corporation realises a gain or loss when substantially all of the assets and liabilities of a resident corporation are transferred to another resident corporation in a statutory merger or reorganisation. A net operating loss of the final taxable period or a loss carryforward from the five preceding fiscal years can be used to offset a reorganisation gain. However, a tax attribute such as a net operating loss or a reorganisation loss incurred by the transferor cannot be transferred to the transferee. The amount of the gain of the transferor is the excess of the consideration received in the transfer over the book value of the assets transferred as shown on the transferor's balance sheet at the close of the fiscal year preceding the transfer.

The following types of reorganisations can be effected free from corporate income tax, provided the basis of the transferor's assets is carried over to the transferee:

(a) the statutory merger of a stock corporation (*Aktiengesellschaft*: AG) into another stock corporation, of a GmbH into another GmbH, or of a GmbH into an AG or vice versa;

(b) the statutory merger of several AGs into a newly-formed AG or of two GmbHs into a newly organised GmbH;

(c) the 'upstream' merger of an AG or a GmbH into its parent domestic corporation;

(d) the transfer of an entire business or a separable part thereof to a resident corporation in exchange for newly issued shares of stock in the transferee corporation;

(e) the transfer of a 100 per cent interest in a domestic or a foreign corporation by a resident taxpayer to a resident corporation in exchange for the transferee corporation's stock.

This tax free status may, nevertheless, be disadvantageous if the transferor corporation has a substantial amount of net available equity. This amount cannot be recognised as a distribution (and, therefore, does not carry with it the corporate tax credit to the shareholder) but has to be carried over to the transferee corporation. Therefore, and because of the very complex provisions of the Reorganisation Tax Act, the income tax and the transfer tax consequences have to be considered carefully in every particular case.

(3) *Redemptions*

If a corporation redeems a part of the shares of stock issued by it in the context of a formal reduction of its share capital, the payment to the shareholders will qualify as a return of capital and not as dividend income unless available net equity (with the exception of available net equity of the 04 category) is deemed distributed.

¶516   Assessment procedure

Corporate income tax returns accompanied by financial statements, auditors' reports (if available), and shareholders' resolutions concerning financial statements and the distribution of dividends have to be filed by resident corporations by 31 May of the year following the close of the taxable year (s. 49(1) KStG). Extensions may be granted upon application (s. 109 AO).

As in the case of individual taxpayers, resident corporations must effect quarterly advance payments of corporate income tax on 10 March, 10 June, 10 September and 10 December of each year. The filing of the annual return does not have to be accompanied by a payment of the remaining tax due. If the total tax assessed for the taxable year exceeds the advance payments made for the respective taxable year, the excess is payable within one month after the receipt of the assessment notice by the corporation.

Large businesses are audited at least every three years (ss. 193 et seq. AO). Usually, the corporate taxpayer receives an advance notice of the date of the audit. The purpose of such audit is the determination of the tax matters of the corporation which the auditor is required to examine whether they are advantageous or disadvantageous to the taxpayer. At the end of the audit, the taxpayer receives a copy of the auditor's report and at a final meeting between taxpayer, auditor and local tax office disputes regarding factual matters and the interpretation thereof can often be settled. While settlements as to matters of law are not permissible, questions of fact can be settled amicably, and such a settlement is binding (BFH decision of 11 December 1984, BStBl. 1985 II 354). In addition, the taxpayer can ask for a ruling concerning the future tax treatment of matters covered in the auditor's report (ss. 204 et seq. AO).

¶517   Double taxation relief

(1) *Unilateral relief*

(a) *Direct foreign tax credit.*   In the absence of a tax treaty, income derived from foreign sources must be included in the resident taxpayer's income, but foreign income taxes assessed and paid may be credited against the German income tax due with respect to such income and up to the part of German tax otherwise payable which corresponds to the ratio which the foreign source income bears to worldwide income as computed for German tax purposes.

The tax credit is only available if no tax treaty applies or if a specific item of income is not covered by such a treaty. Furthermore, the foreign source income has to be derived from one of the following sources:

- agriculture and forestry operated in the foreign state;
- income derived from a foreign permanent establishment or a foreign representative;
- income derived from independent services rendered or used in the foreign state;
- income derived from the sale of goods which form part of the fixed assets of a business and are located in the foreign state, or shares in a corporation which maintains its principal place of business or its statutory seat in such foreign state;
- income from capital investments, provided the debtor resides or has his principal place of business or his statutory seat in the foreign state, or the capital investment is secured by foreign real estate situated in the foreign country which imposes the tax;

- income from the leasing of real estate or of movable property forming an economic unit if it is located in a foreign state or if rights to use it have been granted in a foreign state; and

- certain other items of income (s. 34(d) EStG).

The foreign income tax only qualifies for the tax credit if it corresponds to German income tax. This is true if it directly relates to the taxation of income. The method of taxation (assessment, withholding, lump sum taxation) is irrelevant. Annex 10 to the Income Tax Regulations contains a list of foreign income taxes which have been recognised as creditable.

(b) *Indirect foreign tax credit.* In addition, if certain requirements are met, resident corporations may claim an indirect foreign tax credit for foreign corporate income taxes paid by a foreign subsidiary against German corporate income taxes which are imposed on dividends distributed by such subsidiary corporation. This indirect foreign tax credit will be granted only upon application (s. 26(2) KStG).

If the subsidiary has its principal place of business and its statutory seat in a developing country, and if the requirements of the Developing Countries Tax Act (which has been repealed but still is relevant in this context) are met, then it is presumed that the creditable amount of foreign tax equals the amount of German tax which would become payable with regard to such dividends (s. 26(3) KStG).

(c) *Deduction of foreign income taxes.* As an alternative, the corporation may choose to deduct the foreign taxes paid from its taxable income. This may be advantageous especially if the resident corporation is operating with losses or if the foreign taxes are disproportionately high (e.g., very high withholding taxes imposed on gross income).

(d) *Shipping income.* Instead of claiming a credit for or a deduction of foreign income taxes, the taxpayer can apply for the assessment of a flat rate of 28 per cent so far as income from the operation of ships in international transportation is concerned (s. 26(6)(4) KStG).

(e) *Other relief.* The highest tax authorities of the states may – with the consent of the Federal Ministry of Finance – partially or totally waive German income tax payable with regard to foreign source income if this is necessary because of economic considerations.

(2) *Tax treaties*

Germany has entered into an extensive network of income tax treaties with all West European countries and with many other countries including Argentina, Australia, Brazil, Canada, Egypt, Hungary, India, Indonesia, Iran, the Ivory

Coast, Israel, Jamaica, Japan, Kenya, Liberia, Malaysia, Mauritius, Morocco, New Zealand, Pakistan, the Philippines, Poland, Rumania, Singapore, South Africa, South Korea, Sri Lanka, Thailand, Trinidad and Tobago, Tunisia, USSR, the United States and Zambia. Further, treaties are being negotiated, have been initialled or are awaiting ratification with Bulgaria, China, Ecuador, Yugoslavia and Turkey.

German tax treaties by tradition allocated particular items of income either to the country of source or the country of the taxpayers' domicile and exempted such income from taxation in the other state. Nevertheless, since the fifties, the tax credit method has been increasingly adopted as well. Accordingly, certain items of foreign source income are exempt from the German corporate income tax, whereas foreign taxes imposed on other sources of income may be creditable against the German corporate income tax on such foreign income.

This concept of the German income tax treaties generally means that the tax exemption method applies for business income from a permanent establishment in the other state, for income from immovable properties situated there, and from independent and dependent personal services rendered in the other contracting state.

The tax credit method, on the other hand, generally applies for income from capital investments including interest and dividends, and for royalty income.

(a) *Income from a foreign permanent establishment.*   Most treaties contain a very detailed definition of 'permanent establishment' because the business income of a German corporation can be taxed in the other treaty state only if it maintains a permanent establishment in such state and only to the extent that such income is properly attributable to the activities of such permanent establishment. Most of the treaties follow the definition of art. 5 of the OECD Draft Conventions of 1963/1977.

Business profits which include interest, dividends, royalties, and capital gains attributable to the activity of such a foreign permanent establishment are as a rule exempt from German income taxation and may be taxed in the state where the permanent establishment is maintained. As a consequence, losses incurred in a foreign permanent establishment cannot be used to offset taxable income from other sources. As an exception to this rule, the corporation may exercise an option to deduct losses from an active business conducted in the permanent establishment but such deduction is subject to recapture if the corporation subsequently realises profits in the foreign permanent establishment, unless it can establish that, under the laws of the foreign state, a carryover of the losses to another financial year is not available to it (ss. 2, 5 AIG).

Regional (i.e. European) headquarters activities which are conducted in Germany by a foreign entity, will be considered to constitute a permanent

¶517

establishment for the foreign entity but, as a rule, the tax authorities will accept a 5–10 per cent mark-up on the expenses incurred in such activities as proper taxable income for German corporate income taxes. Moreover, this also applies if such headquarters activities are performed by a German corporate entity.

Dividends, interest or royalties paid by a third country subsidiary to a foreign parent company will not be deemed effectively connected with the activities of the headquarters operations merely because the headquarters advised and guided the management of the third country subsidiary. See Decree of 24 August 1984, DB 1984, 1849.

(b) *Income from capital investments.*   Interest paid by a debtor residing in the other contracting state is exempt from income taxation in such other state under most treaties unless the income is attributable to a permanent establishment of the German creditor in such other state.

Dividends distributed by a corporation of a treaty state are usually subject to withholding tax in such other state at a reduced rate. They must be included in the resident shareholder's income, but the withholding tax imposed by the foreign state is creditable against the German tax. However, under most German treaties, dividends received by a German corporation which holds at least 10 per cent of the voting shares of the foreign corporation are able to be excluded from taxable income in Germany. This is true for the treaties with Argentina, Canada, Denmark, Finland, France, India, Iceland, Ireland, Ivory Coast, Kenya, Luxembourg (with the exception of dividends paid by Luxembourg holding companies), Malaysia, the Netherlands, New Zealand, Norway, Pakistan, Portugal, Sweden, the United Kingdom and the United States, and for the draft agreements with Ecuador and Turkey. Under the Swiss-German treaty the exclusion is available only if the Swiss subsidiary engages exclusively or almost exclusively in certain business activities which are specified in s. 8(1) and (2) of the Foreign Tax Law (*Außensteuergesetz*: AStG.).

(c) *Royalty income.*   Income from royalties paid by a licensee in a treaty state for the use of intangible property rights is generally exempt from tax in such treaty state but has to be included in the resident licensor's taxable income.

(d) *Capital gains derived from the sale of movable property.*   Capital gains derived from the sale of movable property not attributable to a permanent establishment maintained in the other treaty state are, as a rule, taxable only in Germany.

(e) *Income not specifically dealt with in a treaty.*   Under some treaties, items of income not specifically dealt with in such treaties and derived by a resident of one of the countries can be taxed only in the territory where the recipient is domiciled. This means, in the first instance, that items of income from sources in third countries can be taxed only in the country of residence. However, such

¶517

provisions may also cover income from sources within the other contracting state. Thus, for example, rentals paid by a UK company to a German corporation with respect to tangible personal property are taxable only in Germany.

INCOME TAXATION OF NON-RESIDENT INDIVIDUALS AND CORPORATIONS

¶518 Scope of taxation

Non-resident individuals or corporations are subject to German income or corporate income taxes only with respect to certain items of income derived from German sources.

¶519 German-source income

German-source income of non-resident individuals or corporations is defined as including the following items:

(1) *Business profits*

The term 'business profits' includes all items of income which are generated through the activities of a German permanent establishment or a German permanent representative and includes, *inter alia*, capital gains from the sale of more than 1 per cent of the shares of a domestic corporation, provided the seller owns or owned an interest of more than 25 per cent in such corporation at any time in the five years prior to the sale. Even without a permanent establishment or a permanent representative, income realised by professional sportsmen or by artistes from their participation in sports or artistic events in Germany can be taxed as business income from German sources. In the case of non-resident corporations, the presumption that a domestic corporation generates business profits only is not applied. This means, for example, that rental income from the leasing of an apartment house situated in Germany does not qualify as business income unless the renting activity amounts to a continued business activity and that in the absence of a permanent establishment or a permanent representative such income can be taxed as rental income.

(2) *Income from employment*

Under internal German tax law income from employment is considered German-source income if the services are or were rendered, or if they are or were utilised in Germany. Utilisation within Germany is very roughly interpreted to include services rendered abroad to a domestic employer, although this rule is being interpreted more and more restrictively; it was held by the Tax Court Hamburg on 6 July 1983 that services rendered by ground personnel of a German airline in the Bahamas were not utilised in Germany (EFG 1984, 124).

(3) *Income from independent services*

The income of self-employed professionals and of similar independent persons is similarly deemed to be derived from German sources if the services are or were either rendered or utilised within Germany. As to the concept of utilisation see '*Income from employment*' at (2) above; this may cause problems, if, for instance, a non-resident attorney prepares documents for submission to a German court or a German public authority. (See *Herrmann/Heuer/Raupach, Einkommensteuer- und Körperschaftsteuergesetz*, annotation 27(a) to s. 49 EStG.)

(4) *Income from capital investment*

This category of income includes, in particular, dividends paid by domestic corporations, the profit share of a non-resident, typical silent participant in a domestic enterprise, as well as interest paid with respect to a loan which is secured by German real estate or by a ship flying the German flag or which is represented by certain domestic negotiable instruments. Other interest paid by domestic parties to non-resident individuals or corporations is not taxable. This means that interest paid in respect of simple loans granted by a tax haven company does not attract German withholding tax and, therefore, treaty protection is not required.

(5) *Rental income*

This category includes rentals from the leasing of real estate situated in Germany, of units of personal property situated in Germany and royalties from the licensing of intangible artistic or industrial rights which are registered in a German register or used in a domestic permanent establishment.

(6) *Capital gains*

Capital gains derived from the sale of real estate situated in Germany which does not form part of a German permanent establishment are fully taxable at ordinary tax rates unless the seller observes a holding period of more than two years; in the latter case the capital gain will not be taxed. Capital gains from the sale of securities issued by domestic corporations are not taxable irrespective of the holding period observed.

¶519

¶520 Assessment procedures

Withholding tax or assessment

The German income tax with respect to dividends, interest and royalties, as well as certain rental charges, is withheld at source at the rate of 25 per cent or a lower treaty rate. For such items of income an assessment is neither necessary nor possible unless the income forms part of another category of income which is taxed by way of assessment. Other items of income are assessed in a way similar to that described above for resident taxpayers. Business expenses or other income-related expenses may be deductible only to the extent that they are economically connected with specific items of taxable German-source income (s. 50(5) EStG). A loss carryforward is similarly available insofar as the losses in question are economically connected with taxable German-source income and can be established on the basis of records maintained in Germany (s. 50(1)(3) EStG).

In the case of non-resident individuals (except for non-resident employees), special expenses and expenses caused by extraordinary hardship and family allowances are not available (s. 50(1), (4) EStG).

Tax rate

In the case of non-resident individuals, the tax rate for taxable income which is not subject to withholding tax is determined under the normal rates schedule for resident individuals with a minimum tax rate of 25 per cent (s. 50(3) EStG).

The tax rate for non-resident corporations for income derived from German sources which is taxed by way of assessment and not by withholding amounts to 50 per cent.

¶521 Double taxation relief

Non-resident individuals or corporate taxpayers may avail themselves of the provisions of the German tax treaty with the country of their residence. As a general rule, such treaties adopt the following pattern:

(1) *Business profits*

All German tax treaties confine the German jurisdiction to impose income taxes on business profits to those which are generated by a non-resident individual or corporate taxpayer through the operation of a permanent establishment located in Germany. However, the treaty definition of 'permanent establishment' is narrower than the definition of 'permanent establishment and permanent representative' under internal German tax law. Insofar as non-resident individuals participate in sports or artistic events in Germany, some treaties authorise taxation in Germany under provisions which correspond to art. 17 of the OECD Draft Conventions of 1963/1977.

(2) *Dividends*

Most German tax treaties reduce the withholding tax on dividends paid to non-resident individuals or corporate investors to 15 per cent, unless a foreign parent company holds an interest of at least 25 per cent in the German corporation in which case Germany retains the right to impose withholding tax up to a rate of 25 per cent. In all cases, the payer corporation is obliged first to retain the withholding tax at the regular rate of 25 per cent subject to a claim for refund.

As a consequence of the introduction of the imputation system of corporate income taxation in 1977, the German Government offered its treaty partners a general reduction of German withholding tax to 15 per cent. Although a few countries such as Switzerland and Canada have accepted this reduction, most of the other treaty states wait for the outcome of the negotiations on a revision of the US-German tax treaty. Under this treaty, the German tax administration unilaterally waived the application of art. 6(3) with respect to amounts deemed reinvested after 31 December 1980. Furthermore, under a protocol to the treaty with France initialled on 11 July 1985, Germany apparently agreed to grant to French portfolio investors in German corporations an indirect imputation credit of 10 per cent of the dividend. A similar provision apparently is being discussed in the negotiations on a revision of the treaty with Italy.

(3) *Income from employment*

While all tax treaties permit Germany to tax remuneration paid with respect to employment services rendered in Germany, there is usually an exemption for services rendered by employees residing in the other treaty state who work in Germany for a period of less than 183 days per year if their salaries are paid and borne by an employer residing in their home country (under some treaties, the exemption is available if the employer is not a German resident).

(4) *Income from independent services*

If independent services are performed or used in Germany, then income of a non-resident individual derived from such services is deemed income from German sources. Most treaties, however, limit the taxation of such services. Some treaties apply the same rules as for income from dependent services, according to which such income is exempt from German taxation if the presence of the (dependent) employees in Germany did not exceed 183 days during a calendar year and if the remuneration is paid by or on behalf of a person who is

¶521

not a German resident. Other treaties permit taxation in Germany only if the individual maintains a fixed base in Germany in the context of his services.

(5) *Interest and royalties*

As a general rule royalties and interest payments are exempt from German withholding tax if paid to a resident of a treaty state, unless such interest or royalties are properly attributable to a German permanent establishment of the payee.

SPECIAL INCOME-TAX-RELATED STATUTES

¶522   Introduction

The following is a summary of some of the statutes designed to supplement the Income Tax Act with regard to international transactions but which may also affect such other taxes as the wealth tax or the inheritance tax.

¶523   Foreign tax law (Außensteuergesetz)

(1) *Adjustment of inter-company charges*

Section 1 AStG provides that a taxpayer's income may be adjusted upward to an arm's length compensation if it should be determined that it was reduced as the result of international business dealings with related parties to a price below the compensation which would have been agreed upon between unrelated parties. Taxpayers will be deemed to be related if one of them owns an interest of at least 25 per cent in the other, if he directly or indirectly can exercise a controlling influence over the other, if a third person holds such interests or can exercise such an influence with respect to both taxpayers or if one of them or the third person is otherwise in a position to exercise such an influence.

While s. 1 AStG docs not itself list any specific criteria or tests which should be used in determining the proper arm's length compensation, administrative regulations (so-called Administrative Principles), dated 23 February 1983, contain a fairly comprehensive set of rules for the determination of transfer prices, for interest rates for loans, and service charges for inter-company services (including royalties), as well as for the sharing of costs of research and administrative service centres (BStBl. 1983 I 218).

(2) *Special tax status of German citizens who move to a low tax jurisdiction*

Sections 2 to 5 AStG introduced a special tax regime for German citizens who move to a low tax jurisdiction. If they retain significant economic ties with

Germany they remain subject to German income tax for a period of 10 years following their move abroad with respect to more items of income than normal non-resident individuals and at tax rates which take into account their worldwide income. Sections 3 and 4 AStG extend such rules to the wealth tax and to the inheritance tax.

Section 5 AStG tries to frustrate efforts to avoid the impact of these provisions by interposing a foreign base company.

(3) *Imputed capital gain on interest in a domestic corporation*

If an individual who has been a German resident for at least ten years and who holds an interest of at least 25 per cent in a German corporation moves abroad, he will be deemed to have realised a capital gain as if he had sold his interest in the German corporation. Such imputed capital gain equals the amount by which the fair market value of such shares exceeds their cost basis. The gain will be taxed at half the normal tax rate, and if the taxpayer subsequently does sell his interest, his actual gain will be reduced by the amount of the gain previously imputed to him.

Such taxation of the imputed capital gain is not prevented under a tax treaty, but some treaties (such as the treaties with Switzerland and Canada) contain specific provisions to cover such cases and to eliminate double taxation.

(4) *Attribution of base company income to resident taxpayer*

The Foreign Tax Law, ss. 7 to 14, imposes rules which were modelled on the provisions of Subpart F of the US Internal Revenue Code. According to these sections of the Foreign Tax Law, foreign base company income is attributed directly to the German individual or corporate shareholders. A foreign entity qualifies as a foreign base company if German corporate or individual shareholders own more than 50 per cent of the shares or voting rights, or if they otherwise can control the foreign entity and if the foreign entity is subject to low level taxation in the jurisdiction in which the principal place of business or its statutory seat is located.

The definition of 'foreign base company income' includes all items of income with the exception of certain items specifically laid down in s. 8(1) and (2) AStG. Such 'good' items of income which are not attributed to the German shareholders include, *inter alia*, manufacturing income, income from agriculture and income from banking or insurance activities, whereas sales, service and rental income can qualify as 'good' only within very strict boundaries. Dividend income will be attributed unless it is received by a holding company from an active subsidiary organised in the same country as the holding company or from an active third country subsidiary, but only if the interest in such third country subsidiary is held in the economic context of the holding company's business activities.

(5) *Foreign family foundations*

Under s. 15 AStG, both the income and the net worth of a family foundation which maintains its principal place of management or its statutory seat outside Germany are attributed to the founder if he is a resident and subject to worldwide German income taxation, or, if this should not be the case, to the resident persons who are entitled to the income or to the liquidation proceeds of the foundation; the attribution is made in proportion to their shares in the income of the liquidation proceeds.

For the purposes of s. 15 AStG, the term 'family foundation' has been defined as a foundation in which the founder or his descendants are entitled to more than 50 per cent of the income or of the liquidation proceeds. Conglomerations of property and incorporated or unincorporated associations are treated like foundations.

¶524   Statute on foreign investment by German industry

The statute regarding tax incentives in the context of foreign investments by German industry (*Auslandsinvestitionsgesetz*: AIG) includes provisions which may be of particular interest.

(1) *Tax-free transfer of assets abroad*

If assets are transferred to a foreign permanent establishment of a resident taxpayer, and if the income therefrom is exempt from German income or corporate income taxation by operation of a tax treaty, then this normally is considered a taxable transfer in which a gain is realised if the going concern value of the asset exceeds its adjusted basis. Nevertheless, under s. 1 AIG, such gain may be deferred by setting up a reserve which has to be dissolved at an annual rate of at least 20 per cent beginning with the fifth financial year following the year in which it was set up.

(2) *Losses incurred in foreign permanent establishment*

If under a tax treaty the income of a foreign permanent establishment is exempt from German income tax, corresponding losses are not deductible either. Under s. 2 AIG, the taxpayer has the option to deduct such losses from his taxable income in Germany provided the permanent establishment engages in an active business as defined in s. 5 AIG. Furthermore, such deduction is

subject to recoupment if the foreign permanent establishment should subsequently generate profits corresponding to the losses initially deducted. No
recoupment is required where the state in which the permanent establishment
is maintained does not permit a loss carryforward to non-resident taxpayers.

(3) *Tax-free reserve for losses incurred by a foreign subsidiary corporation*

When acquiring 50 per cent or more of the shares of a foreign corporation or 25
per cent or more of the shares of a corporation which has its statutory seat and
principal place of business in a developing country, a taxpayer can set up a
reserve in the year of the acquisition or in the following four years up to the
amount of the pro rata losses allocatable to the share interest in the foreign
corporation but not exceeding the tax basis of the shares held in such foreign
corporation. The reserve must be dissolved under certain circumstances, at the
latest at the close of the fifth fiscal year following the year in which the reserve
was set up.

¶525   Rollover treatment for capital gains from the sale of shares in a corporation

Under s. 6(b) EStG, resident taxpayers who dispose of shares in domestic or
foreign corporations and who acquire shares in a foreign corporation can
deduct 80 per cent of the gain derived from the sale from the cost of the newly-
acquired shares in the foreign corporation, provided that the foreign corporation conducts exclusively or almost exclusively an active business as defined in s. 6(b)(1) EStG, that the participation in the foreign corporation
represents an interest of at least 25 per cent in its capital and is held in the
economic context of an active business conducted by the resident taxpayer,
and, further, that the Federal Ministry of Economics, with the concurrence of
the Federal Ministry of Finance, the Federal Ministry of Labour and the
competent state government, certifies that the acquisition of the shares in the
foreign corporation is beneficial to the German economy and is capable of
improving the business structure of an industry or to serve the aim of a
spreading of share ownership among the public. In addition, the resident
taxpayer must have observed a holding period of at least six years prior to the
disposal of the shares in the domestic or foreign corporation.

¶526   Special provisions for investments in developing countries

For special provisions for investments in developing countries under the Developing Countries Tax Act (*Entwicklungsländersteuergesetz: EntwlStG*)
(which was repealed with effect from 1 January 1982), see ¶517 (1)(b) *supra*.

WEALTH TAX (VERMÖGENSTEUER)

¶527   Scope of taxation

Wealth tax is imposed on the net assets of individuals, corporations and other entities as of 1 January of each year. Since for wealth tax purposes partnerships are not considered taxable entities, their partners are taxed on their respective shares of the partnership's net assets. Resident taxpayers are taxed on worldwide assets while non-residents are taxed only on certain assets located in Germany.

The values of the taxable assets are established under the Valuation Act (*Bewertungsgesetz*) for business assets. The financial statement prepared for income tax purposes will be definitive subject to certain adjustments. The following adjustments require specific attention:

(1)   Real estate is not valued at cost but at specific tax values which, in most cases, are significantly lower than the fair market value of the real estate.

(2)   Securities traded on a stock exchange are valued at their quoted value even if it exceeds their costs: this unrealised appreciation is included in the basis for computing the wealth tax. Shares in unlisted corporations are valued at their fair market value in accordance with extensive regulations which take into account both the asset value and the earning power (so-called 'Stuttgart valuation formula').

(3)   Low-cost fixed assets (up to DM 800 per asset) which are fully depreciable in the year of acquisition for income tax purposes have to be included at an averaged value.

¶528   Taxability of resident individuals

In the case of resident individuals the worldwide net assets serve as the tax base. The annual rate amounts to 0.5 per cent. Before applying the tax rate, the tax base is reduced by the following personal allowances: DM 70,000 each for the taxpayer, his wife and each child under the age of 18 (under certain circumstances the exemption may be available also for children up to the age of 27). Additional personal exemptions of up to DM 50,000 are granted to elderly taxpayers who meet certain requirements (s. 6 Wealth Tax Act (*Vermögensteuergesetz*: VStG)).

¶529   Resident corporations

Resident corporations are taxed on their total net assets provided their value amounts to at least DM 20,000. Unpaid parts of contributions to capital must be shown as accounts receivable at their nominal value unless the corporation does not intend to request payment (s. 11(1) Wealth Tax Regulations (*Vermögensteuer-Richtlinien*: VStR)). The annual tax rate amounts to 0.6 per cent (s. 10(2) VStG).

In order to avoid multiple taxation for groups of resident corporations, a corporate shareholder may exclude from its taxable assets the value of shares in another resident corporation, provided it has held a direct interest in such resident corporation of at least 10 per cent for an uninterrupted period of at least 12 months prior to the close of its fiscal year. A similar exclusion is available with respect to shares in a foreign corporation, provided such foreign corporation generates exclusively or almost exclusively active income as defined in s. 8(1) or (2) AStG; in particular, income from agriculture or manufacturing or income from certain banking and insurance activities (s. 102 Valuation Act (*Bewertungsgesetz*: BewG)). The existence of such exclusions explains share transfers which are effected at the logical second between the end of the transferor's fiscal year and the beginning of the fiscal year of the transferee if it is assumed that both are on the same fiscal year (so-called midnight transfers).

In the determination of the net taxable assets, the first DM 125,000 of the value of business assets is excludable, and of the rest only 75 per cent are taken into account (s. 117(a) BewG).

¶530   Non-resident individuals and corporations

Non-resident individuals and corporations are subject to limited tax liability with respect to their domestic assets if the value thereof amounts to DM 20,000 or more. Domestic assets include:

(1)   domestic agricultural and forestry assets;

(2)   domestic real estate;

(3)   domestic business assets – this term comprises the assets which serve a trade or business operated in Germany if a permanent establishment is maintained or a permanent representative has been appointed, and it also includes interests in domestic partnerships;

(4)   shares in a resident corporation if the shareholder directly or indirectly owns an interest of at least 10 per cent in the corporation's stated equity capital;

(5)   inventions and petty patents which are not covered by (3) above, but are entered in a domestic public register, such as the patent roll;

(6)   assets which are not covered by (1), (2) or (5), if they have been let for use in a domestic enterprise, and in particular, if they have been leased to a domestic enterprise;

(7) mortgages and other claims or rights, if they are directly or indirectly secured by domestic real estate, equivalent rights, or ships which fly the German flag, with the exception of bonds and debentures which are represented by negotiable securities;

(8) the interest of a silent partner in a domestic enterprise and the claim of a creditor of a participating loan, if the debtor maintains his domicile, principal place of management or statutory seat in Germany; and

(9) rights to use the property listed in (1) to (8) above.

In determining the taxable net worth, only such debts and other liabilities which are economically connected with domestic property can be deducted.

As in the case of resident taxpayers, the tax rate is 0.6 per cent. for non-resident corporations and 0.5 per cent. for non-resident individuals.

¶531   Method of assessment

Even though the wealth tax is an annual tax it is, in principle, assessed once every three years only on the basis of the net worth at the beginning of such period. Subsequent changes of net worth can lead to interim adjustments if certain minimum changes are exceeded (ss. 16, 17 VStG).

The tax is payable in four quarterly instalments on 10 February, 10 May, 10 August and 10 November of each calendar year; if the annual tax liability does not exceed DM 500 it has to be paid in one instalment on 10 November of each year (s. 21(2) VStG).

¶532   Special status for individuals who move to Germany

Individuals who move to Germany and thus become subject to wealth tax with respect to their worldwide net assets, may be granted special tax relief during the first ten years of their residence in Germany (s. 13 VStG). The circumstances under which such relief is granted are substantially the same as those outlined at ¶509 above for income tax purposes.

TRADE TAX (GEWERBESTEUER)

¶533   Scope of trade tax

The trade tax is governed by Federal law but assessed and collected by the municipalities. This tax is imposed on all business activities exercised in Germany regardless of whether they are incorporated or whether they are domestic or foreign, provided they maintain a permanent establishment in Germany. Thus, a partnership is a separate taxpayer for purposes of the trade tax if it engages in a business activity.

The trade tax does not apply to independent personal services, agriculture, capital investments, rental of realty and licensing income unless such activities have a commercial character. Domestic, as well as foreign, corporations will, however, be irrefutably presumed to be engaged in a business activity for purposes of the trade tax (BFH decision of 28 July 1982, BStBl. 1983 II 77; 23 European Taxation 5 (1983) 192).

In the case of partnerships, it is presumed that their income and net worth constitute trade income and trade assets for purposes of the tax, but this presumption can be overridden (s. 2(2) Trade Tax Act (*Gewerbesteuergesetz*: GewStG)). However, a partnership organised for one particular venture (in particular, a construction project) will not be considered to be engaged in a business activity if its duration is not expected to exceed three years (s. 2(a) GewStG).

If a domestic corporation is integrated into another domestic enterprise from a financial, organisational and economic point of view (*Organschaft*), then the subordinated corporation is treated as a mere permanent establishment of the controlling enterprise (s. 2(2) GewStG).

The trade tax is based on two factors, namely trade profits and trade capital. For trade profits the basic rate is 5 per cent, whereas for trade capital is it 0.2 per cent. If a municipal multiplier of the trade tax on trade profits and capital of 450 per cent is applied, the resulting tax rate is 22.5 per cent on trade profits and 0.9 per cent on trade capital.

The trade tax is a deductible business expense for corporate and individual income tax purposes. Furthermore, in determining profits for trade tax purposes, the trade tax itself can be deducted. As a result, the actual tax rate may be only about half of its nominal rate. The trade tax income component may also qualify as an income tax for purposes of the direct or indirect foreign tax credit in the country of the foreign parent corporation. This is true, for instance, for US taxpayers.

¶534   Trade tax on trade income

Trade income is determined on the basis of the taxable income as determined for corporate or individual income tax purposes subject to certain adjustments.

Gains from the sale of a business and expenses incurred in organising a business are not taken into account for the purposes of the trade tax which is imposed only on the business itself as a going concern.

(1) *Additions*

The taxable income as determined for income tax purposes is adjusted for trade tax purposes by the following additions:

(a) 50 per cent interest paid or accrued with respect to long-term indebtedness. Long-term indebtedness is indebtedness economically connected with the organisation, acquisition or expansion of the business, or which has a term in excess of 12 months. Open account indebtedness may be considered long-term if in fact it remains outstanding for more than 12 months;

(b) annuities and other recurrent payments and permanent burdens connected with the organisation or acquisition of a business (unless the payments are subject to the trade tax on trade profits in the hands of the recipient);

(c) profit distributions paid to silent participants unless the recipient is subject to trade tax;

(d) the distributive share of the profits of a general partner of a partnership limited by shares;

(e) one-half of the rental charges incurred for the use of movable business assets unless such rent is included in the lessor's trade income subject to trade tax. However, even if 50 per cent of the rent is included in the lessor's trade income, one-half of the rent has to be added if the object of the lease is an entire business (or a separable part thereof) and if the annual rent exceeds DM 250,000; and

(f) the distributive share in the losses of a domestic or foreign partnership.

(2) *Exclusions*

From taxable income computed for income tax purposes, the following items must be specifically excluded:

(a) 1.2 per cent of the assessed value of real property situated in Germany – instead the taxpayer may elect to exclude the income from the management and use of real property provided the taxpayer manages exclusively real properties owned by it or real properties and securities investments owned by it;

(b) the distributive share of profits as a partner in a domestic or foreign partnership if such distributive share was included in calculating taxable income;

(c) rentals or royalties received for the use of movable trade assets to the extent that the lessee or licensee is required to add the rental income or royalties under (1) (e) above;

(d) dividends received from a domestic taxable corporate entity in which the taxpayer held an interest of at least 10 per cent at the beginning of the taxable year – a similar exclusion applies under certain circumstances to dividends received from foreign subsidiary corporations which generate exclusively or almost exclusively active income as defined in s. 8(1)–(6) or 8(2) AStG;

(e) profits realised through a foreign permanent establishment of the tax-payer.

¶535   Net operating loss carryforward

Net operating losses can be carried forward to the succeeding five taxable years (s. 10(a) GewStG).

¶536   Capital component

The trade capital component equals the assessed value of the business as computed for wealth tax purposes, adjusted by certain additions and exclusions:

(1) *Additions*

Additions to the assessed value of the business are, in particular:

(a) 50 per cent of the principal of long-term indebtedness as well as indebtedness incurred in the organisation, acquisition or expansion of the business;

(b) the going concern value of movable assets used in the business but owned by a partner or a third party which are not included in the assessed value of the business. Movable assets leased and included in the assessed value of the lessor for trade tax purposes must only be included if the lease covers an entire business or a separable part thereof and if the total value of the assets leased and located in the same municipality exceeds DM 2,500,000.

(2) *Exclusions*

The assessed value of the business is reduced by the value of an interest in a domestic or foreign partnership or limited partnership if the taxpayer is deemed to be a co-entrepreneur of such partnership. Under certain circumstances, interests in foreign corporations may be similarily excluded. The assessed value of the business for wealth tax purposes is similarly decreased by the assessed value of real estate if included in the assets value of the business. The value of capital allocatable to a foreign permanent establishment is not taken into account when computing the trade capital component.

¶537   Assessment of trade tax

Trade tax returns are reviewed by the local state tax office together with the income and wealth tax returns, and the Federal base rates of trade income and trade capital are determined by the state tax offices. These rates are communicated to the competent municipality which then applies the municipal multiplier fixed by the municipality for the taxable year, computes the trade tax due and issues the deficiency notice to the taxpayer. Any excess of the amount assessed over advance tax payments is payable within one month of receipt of the deficiency notice. Advance payments of trade tax are fixed by the municipal tax office on the basis of previous assessments and they are payable in equal quarterly instalments on 15 February, 15 May, 15 August and 15 November of each calendar year.

INHERITANCE TAX (ERBSCHAFTSTEUER)

¶538   Overview

Contrary to what its name might suggest, the inheritance tax law not only covers transfers by reason of death but *inter vivos* gifts as well. There is basically no differentiation between *inter vivos* gifts and transfers by reason of death.

Gifts effected within the last ten years prior to the date on which the deceased died will be included in the inheritance tax return at the value which was attributed to them at the time the gift was perfected, and the tax on such prior gifts which would have been payable at the time of the death will be creditable against the inheritance tax (s. 14 Inheritance Tax Act (*Erbschaftsteuergesetz*: ErbStG)).

As an inheritance tax, it is not imposed upon the estate as such but upon the beneficial share of each individual beneficiary or donee. For this reason, the tax status of an inheritance or gift depends on whether the deceased/donor or the particular beneficiary are German residents and whether the assets belonging to the estate or the gift are situated in Germany. To a limited degree, the citizenship held by the deceased or donor is of importance, too.

¶539   Estates of residents

If the deceased was a German resident at the time of death, then his entire estate is subject to inheritance tax regardless of his citizenship, the residence of the beneficiary and the location of the assets which belong to the estate. The same rules apply with respect to decedents who gave up their German residence within the five years preceding their death.

For purposes of determining the taxable estate, the gross estate may be reduced by debts incurred by the deceased as well as by general expenses of administering the estate, such as funeral expenses and legacies.

The surviving spouse may claim a personal exemption of DM 250,000 plus an additional exemption of DM 250,000 towards which the capitalised value of tax-exempt pensions will be credited. Children can claim a personal exemption of DM 90,000 plus an additional exemption ranging from DM 10,000 to DM 50,000 towards which the value of tax-exempt pension rights will also be credited.

Foreign estate or inheritance taxes assessed with respect to items of property situated in the respective foreign jurisdiction are allowable as a credit against the German inheritance tax unless the foreign tax liability arose five years or more prior to the German tax liability. The foreign *situs* of assets is determined in accordance with the provisions of s. 121 of the Valuation Act. This means, in particular, that securities owned by the deceased will be deemed situated at his last residence irrespective of where the issuer is situated or where the certificates are deposited, unless the deceased owned a share interest of at least 10 per cent in a corporation in which case the shares are deemed situated in the jurisdiction in which the corporation maintains its statutory seat or its actual principal place of management (s. 121(2)(4) BewG).

¶540   Estates of non-residents

If the decedent was not a resident of Germany at the time of his death and had not given up his residence within the five years preceding his death, the inheritance tax is imposed only to the extent that the estate or part of it transfers to a resident beneficiary, or with respect to assets which are deemed situated within Germany under s. 121 of the Valuation Act or with respect to rights to use such assets.

(1) *Resident beneficiary*

If the beneficiary is a resident, the beneficial share in the estate is determined as in the case of a resident decedent's estate.

(2) *German situs assets*

If neither the deceased nor the beneficiary were German residents at the date of death, then only assets situated in Germany attract the tax. Such assets include:

(a) property situated in Germany and used in domestic agriculture or forestry;

(b) real property situated in Germany;

(c) assets forming part of the business assets of a German permanent establishment or a permanent representative;

(d) shares of stock in a domestic corporation if the decedent held, directly or indirectly, a share of at least 10 per cent in the capital of the corporation; if only a part of such a share interest is transferred as a gift then further transfers of the remaining shares within 10 years will be deemed taxable even if the remaining shares should represent less than a 10 per cent interest in the corporation (s. 2(1)(3) ErbStG).

(e) patents and registered designs (*Gebrauchsmuster*) not included in (c) above, if entered into a German public register;

(f) personal property not included in (a), (b) or (e) above, which is leased to a domestic business enterprise;

(g) mortgages, land charges and debts which are secured directly or indirectly by German real estate or by ships flying the German flag; loans which are represented by negotiable bond certificates are, however, not considered property even if they are secured by German real estate;

(h) the interest of a non-resident silent participant in a domestic enterprise;

(i) rights to use one of the above-named assets.

If neither the deceased nor the beneficiary were residents of Germany at the time of death, then only such debts can be deducted which are economically connected with such domestic property.

¶541 Tax rates

The tax rates depend on the value of the bencficial share of each individual beneficiary and the degree of kinship between the deceased (donor) and the beneficiary (donee), irrespective of whether the deceased or the beneficiary are or were German residents.

The beneficiaries are classified in four categories of taxpayers depending on the degree of kinship, and they are taxed at the rates shown which depend on the value of their respective net taxable beneficial shares (ss. 15, 19 ErbStG)):

- *Class I*: the surviving spouse and children: 3 per cent to 35 per cent;

- *Class II*: descendants of the decedent's children, as well as (in the case of transfer by reason of death) parents and ancestors: 6 per cent to 50 per cent;

- *Class III*: parents and other ancestors (in the case of *inter vivos* gifts), brothers and sisters and their children, sons in law and daughters in law, parents in law and the divorced surviving spouse: 11 per cent to 65 per cent; and

- *Class IV*: all other beneficiaries: 20 per cent to 70 per cent.

¶542   Assessment procedure

In the case of transfers by reason of death, the beneficiary is required to notify the local tax office of the transfer within three months of receiving notice of such transfer (s. 30(1) ErbStG). In the case of an *inter vivos* gift, both the donor and the donee are required to notify the tax office. No notice is required if the will of the deceased is probated by a German court or notary or if the gift contract is notarised by a German notary (s. 30(3) ErbStG).

Upon receipt of the notice, the tax office forwards the appropriate forms which normally have to be filed within one month of their receipt, although extensions are granted. The tax office reviews the returns and issues a deficiency notice, and the amount of the inheritance tax so assessed has to be paid within thirty days of the receipt of the deficiency notice.

There is no procedure comparable to a US transfer certificate but insurance companies and banks have to notify the tax office if they learn of the death of one of their former customers and they must forward a list of the assets which they are holding in his name to the tax office. If they effect payments prior to the payment of the inheritance tax they may be personally liable for the payment of the tax up to the amount of money so transferred (s. 20(6) ErbStG). For this reason, banks and insurance companies insist on the submission to them of a confirmation from the tax office to the effect that either the inheritance tax has been paid or that no inheritance tax is due. An executor may similarly be exposed to personal liability if he fails to pay the inheritance tax.

¶543   Double taxation relief

(1) *Unilateral relief*

The inheritance tax does not permit the exclusion of assets situated abroad from taxation in Germany merely because they are subject to estate or inheritance tax in the jurisdiction where they are situated. However, foreign inheritance or estate taxes will be eligible for a tax credit against the German inheritance tax due if either the deceased (donor) or the beneficiary (donee) were or are German residents at the time at which the tax liability arose, provided the assets concerned were situated in such foreign jurisdiction under the tests of the German law. Furthermore, such credit is available only where the German inheritance tax liability arises no later than five years after the date on which the foreign tax liability arose. This five years' limitation is of importance, especially so far as testamentary trusts are concerned, since the taxable event is deferred until the trust is dissolved if a trust is interposed (s. 9(1)(1)(a) ErbStG).

(2) Impact of tax treaties

Germany has concluded death tax treaties with Austria, Sweden, Greece, Switzerland and Israel, and a treaty with the US is signed but not yet ratified. The treaty with the United States of America is unique in that it will apply to transfers by reason of death as well as to *inter vivos* gifts; the other estate tax treaties do not apply to gift taxes. The treaty with Israel is applicable only to the estates of decedents who died before 1 April 1981, as Israel repealed its estate duty as of that date.

While the treaties with Greece and Sweden apply only with regard to the estates of decedents who were citizens of one of the two contracting states, the treaties with Austria and Switzerland apply if the deceased at the time of his death was domiciled in either one or in both of the contracting states.

Under the treaty with Switzerland, the estate of a deceased domiciled in either Germany or Switzerland is exempt from duties in the other country except where the estate comprises immovable property located within that other country; such immovable property is then, in turn, exempt in the country of domicile.

The treaties with Austria and Sweden do not go that far. Immovable assets as well as assets which form part of the business assets of a permanent establishment are taxed only in the contracting state where the immovable assets or the permanent establishment are located. All other items of property are exclusively taxed in the country in which the deceased had a domicile at the time of his death. The OECD Draft Convention of 1966 pertaining to death duties adopts the same solution as far as the exemption method is concerned.

Unlike the German inheritance tax, such tax treaties accord importance only to the domicile of the deceased and the *situs* of certain items of property. The residence of the heir or of other beneficiaries is immaterial. Nevertheless, the applicable tax rate will be determined on the basis of the total enrichment of the resident beneficiaries in order to preserve the progressive rate structure.

Another material difference between the conventions and internal German inheritance tax law concerns the deduction of debts, in particular, if neither the

¶543

deceased nor the beneficiary is a German resident. In this case, only such debts are deductible which are economically connected with taxable assets. Under the convention with Switzerland such part of the remaining so-called 'general debts' will be deductible in Germany as corresponds to that part of the estate which Germany is authorised to tax.

VALUE ADDED TAX (UMSATZSTEUER)

¶544   Scope of taxation

The value added tax (VAT) replaced the former cascading system of general sales tax in 1968 and its latest version dates from 1 January 1980, on which date German value added tax was brought into line with the Sixth EC VAT Directive.

The value added tax seeks to tax the consumer only, and for this reason taxable transactions between entrepreneurs do not present an actual tax cost to the parties: the entrepreneur who sells merchandise in a taxable transaction to another entrepreneur has to charge separately on his invoice the net sales price and the applicable VAT charge. The entrepreneur who purchases the merchandise may use such input value added tax charged to him as a credit against VAT charged by him on his outgoing invoices. By this mechanism, the tax ultimately is shifted to the final consumer.

¶545   Taxpayer

For the purposes of the value added tax, the taxpayer (i.e. the entrepreneur) is any person who engages in business activities in his own name with third parties. This concept covers all commercial entities such as stock corporations (*Aktiengesellschaften*), closely held corporations (*GmbHs*), general partnerships, limited partnerships and other incorporated businesses, and sole proprietorships and independent professionals, whether foreign or domestic, provided they effect taxable transactions within Germany.

¶546   Taxable transactions

Value added tax is imposed on taxable transactions which are divided into five categories:

(1) *Supply of goods*

The supply of tangible goods is considered to take place at the time and the place at which the authority to dispose of the goods in one's own name is transferred to the purchaser or a third party nominated by him (s. 3(1) Value Added Tax Act (*Umsatzsteuergesetz*: UStG)). If the goods are shipped to the purchaser or, at his direction, to a third party, the delivery is deemed to be effected at the time and the place at which the goods are handed to the forwarding agent, the mail, the railroad, a shipping agent or another intermediary. However, if tangible goods are shipped into Germany in the course of the transaction and if the seller, or his nominee, owe the importation VAT payable upon the importation into Germany, then the delivery is deemed to be effected within Germany (s. 3(8) UStG). Similar rules apply if tangible goods are exported from Germany to another Member State of the EC and if the German exporter or his nominee owe the value added importation tax in the other EC country.

(2) *Supply of services within Germany*

Services supplied for a consideration are held to be taxable if effected within Germany. As a general rule, services are deemed to be supplied at the place where the entrepreneur who performs the services conducts his business; if the services are performed in a foreign permanent establishment of the entrepreneur they are deemed to be supplied outside Germany (s. 3(a)(1) UStG). There are, however, a substantial number of exceptions to this general rule:

(a) Services directly relating to real estate are deemed supplied at the *situs* of the real estate (s. 3(a)(2)(1) UStG).

(b) Transportation services are deemed supplied at the place where they are effected. If only part of the transportation is effected within Germany, only that part of the consideration attracts German value added tax (s. 3(a)(2)(2) UStG).

(c) The following categories of services are deemed supplied at the place where the services are exclusively or mainly performed –

(i) services of an artistic, scientific, educational, sportive, entertainment or similar character, including services rendered by the respective promoters;

(ii) forwarding, storage and other services which are usually connected with transportation services referred to in (b) above; and

(iii) work performed with respect to tangible personal assets where such assets were supplied by the other party to the entrepreneur, as well as services rendered in preparing opinions or appraisal regarding such services.

(d) The following categories of services are deemed supplied in the country in which the recipient of such services maintains his business: if the services are rendered to a foreign permanent establishment of the recipient, the location of such permanent establishment shall be applicable. If the recipient is not an entrepreneur and if he maintains his residence or principal place of business within the EC, then the general rule or the more specific rules discussed above remain applicable. The services covered by this provision include:

(i) the licensing, assignment or use of patents, copyrights, trademarks and similar intangible property rights;

(ii) services related to advertising and publicity work, including services rendered by advertising agencies and intermediaries;

(iii) the supply of advice of a legal, economic or technical nature, including, in particular, services rendered by attorneys at law, patent lawyers, tax lawyers, chartered public accountants and experts, as well as services rendered by engineers;

(iv) data processing services;

(v) the supply of information, including information on technical processes and know-how;

(vi) the leasing of personnel;

(vii) the letting of personal property, except for the letting of means of transportation; and

(viii) refraining (voluntarily or contractually) from engaging in whole or in part in a business or a professional activity (s. 3(a)(4) UStG).

(3) Importation of goods into Germany

As within the EC, the value added tax is intended to be imposed in the country of consumption rather than the country where the goods are manufactured. The exporter from one EC Member State can claim as a credit all VAT charged to him in connection with the manufacturing of the goods exported. The export proceeds do not attract VAT, but the physical importation of the goods into the other EC Member State attracts importation VAT in such state.

If the country of importation is Germany, the importation VAT is administered by the customs and excise offices and substantially the same rules as for custom duties apply. The importer who owes importation VAT can claim an extension of payment until the middle of the month following the importation, and he can claim the importation VAT paid or payable by him as a creditable input value added tax against his own VAT liability in the VAT information return for the month in which the goods were imported. As this information return must be filed by the tenth day of the month following the importation,

¶546

the importation value added tax, as a rule, can be claimed as a credit even prior to its payment (s. 16(2) UStG).

(4) *Withdrawal of goods for the entrepreneur's own use*

In this context a transaction is taxable if:

(a) an entrepreneur withdraws tangible goods serving his enterprise within Germany for purposes outside the scope of his enterprise;

(b) the entrepreneur uses physical goods serving his enterprise within Germany for purposes which are outside the scope of the enterprise; or

(c) the entrepreneur incurs expenditures within Germany which are disallowed as business expenses for the purposes of determining taxable income (s. 1(1)(2) UStG).

(5) *Constructive dividends*

The supply of goods or of services by a partnership to its partners or by a corporation to its shareholders, as well as to third parties affiliated with a partner or shareholder, is considered a taxable transaction if the recipient does not pay a consideration therefor. Typically, this covers constructive dividends by corporations. In this case, the market value of the goods or services supplied serves as the tax basis where no consideration is paid or where the actual consideration is lower than the market value (ss. 1(2)(3), 10(4)(1) UStG).

¶547 Exemptions

The Value Added Tax Act lists a catalogue of transactions within Germany which are exempt from value added tax. The most important of such exemptions are as follows (s. 4 UStG):

(1) the exportation of goods;

(2) the granting of loans, assumption of liabilities, guarantees and similar securities, the deposit or management of securities and similar banking transactions;

(3) transfers of securities, bonds, shares in closely held corporations and partnerships;

(4) transactions covered by the real estate transfer tax or the capital contributions' tax.

¶548 Method of assessment

Within ten days of the end of each calendar month (or the calendar quarter if the tax in the preceding year did not exceed DM 6,000), the entrepreneur is required to file an information return covering the calendar month and to pay the VAT due. In computing the VAT, the entrepreneur may deduct the creditable input value added tax charged to him on the supply of goods or services, or an importation VAT paid or payable by him, during the preceding month. If the entrepreneur prepays one-eleventh of the VAT paid in the prior year, he can be authorised to file the monthly information returns one month later (s. 46 et seq. UStDV).

After the close of the calendar year, the entrepreneur must prepare the annual VAT return together with his other annual tax returns. If the monthly payments made during the year do not reach the total value added tax liability for the year as computed by the entrepreneur in his annual return, the deficiency is payable within one month of the filing of the return. An excess of the payments made during the year over the final VAT liability will be refunded.

¶549   Value added tax withholding

A system of withholding applies with respect to the taxable supply of services effected by non-resident entrepreneurs to other entrepreneurs, and the recipient entrepreneur has to withhold proper value added tax except where the goods are exchanged for goods, where the non-resident entrepreneur maintains a permanent establishment or controls a subsidiary in Germany or where the services concern the transportation of persons only (s. 18(8) UStG).

Where the VAT is imposed by way of withholding, the entrepreneur who acts as the withholding agent is personally liable to pay the tax if he fails properly to withhold and pay the tax to the tax authorities.

¶550   Zero withholding

No VAT withholding is required in respect of taxable services rendered by a non-resident entrepreneur in instances where the non-resident entrepreneur who supplies the services does not charge German value added tax on his invoice to the recipient entrepreneur and where the recipient entrepreneur would be entitled to a full credit of such input value added tax.

¶551   Refund procedure

If a non-resident entrepreneur does not effect taxable transactions and does not maintain a permanent establishment within Germany, he may apply for a refund of German VAT charged to him; the same applies to value added tax charged to him in the context of taxable transactions where the tax was satisfied by way of withholding or was avoided under the rules of the zero withholding VAT regime. The application for a refund has to be filed within six months of the close of the calendar year. Together with the application, the non-resident entrepreneur must submit the original bills and importation documents as well as a confirmation by the tax authorities in his home country which shows that he has obtained a VAT registration number as an entrepreneur.

¶552 Tax rates

The regular tax rate amounts to 14 per cent but there is a preferential tax rate of 7 per cent for certain specified taxable transactions (s. 12 GewO).

OTHER TRANSACTIONAL TAXES

¶553 Introduction

While there are numerous transfer taxes, the following four taxes merit particular attention.

¶554 Capital contributions' tax (Gesellschaftsteuer)

The capital contributions' tax of 1 per cent is imposed on the transfer of cash or other assets to a German corporation in exchange for the issuance of shares of stock in such corporation. It also applies to open or constructive contributions to capital by a shareholder which are capable of increasing the value of its shares in the corporation. The tax is also imposed upon the infusion of fixed or working capital by a foreign corporation into its domestic branch.

A tax exemption is available in cases of certain corporate reorganisations and recapitalisations, and also for informal contributions to capital effected to reduce or eliminate an overindebtedness (s. 7(4) KVStG). This covers, in particular, the waiver of a sharcholder's loan if the company is overindebted.

The capital contributions' tax is a deductible expense of the corporation when determining taxable income for purposes of the corporate income tax.

¶555 Stock Exchange transfer tax (Börsenumsatzsteuer)

The Stock Exchange transfer tax is imposed at the regular rate of 0.25 per cent of the consideration or of the value of securities or of shares in a GmbH purchased or sold within Germany. The tax rate is reduced to 0.125 per cent if the transaction is effected abroad and if only one party to the transaction is a German resident. Transactions concluded by correspondence, cable or phone between a place within Germany and the place abroad are deemed to be effected abroad.

As a rule, the parties to the transaction are jointly and severally responsible for the payment of the tax.

¶556   Real estate transfer tax (Grunderwerbsteuer)

The real estate transfer tax is imposed on *inter vivos* transfers of title of real estate. Apart from the outright sale and transfer of real estate, it covers contributions of real estate to the capital of a corporation and the division of real property among co-owners, as well as the transfer or sale of all shares in a corporation which holds real estate situated in Germany (s. 1(3) GrEStG). This latter provision accounts for the quite frequent situation where 95 per cent to 98 per cent (but not all) of the shares issued by a corporation are sold.

The tax is levied at the rate of 2 per cent. The tax basis normally is the consideration paid, except where the taxable event is the acquisition of all shares in a corporation owning German real estate in which case the assessed tax value of such real estate forms the tax basis.

¶557   Tax on drafts and bills of exchange (Wechselsteuer)

The tax on drafts and promissory notes amounts to DM 0.15 for each DM 100 of the face value of the instrument. The tax is payable in the form of stamps by the issuer upon transfer of the instrument. The tax rate is reduced to one-half for drafts drawn abroad on a domestic drawee payable in Germany and for drafts and bills drawn in Germany on a foreign drawee and payable abroad. Promissory notes issued abroad, as well as bills issued abroad and drawn on a foreign drawee, are exempt from the tax if they are payable abroad.

6 Accounting and Auditing

SOURCES OF THE RULES

¶601 General overview

Until very recently, German accounting, auditing and publication rules were spread over a great many statutes. The Commercial Code (*Handelsgesetzbuch*: HGB) contained some basic rules which applied to all businesses irrespective of their legal structure, such as the rule that every businessman had to maintain books which showed his transactions and the financial position of the business in conformity with principles of proper accounting (s. 38 HGB). Such proper accounting principles (*Grundsätze Ordnungsmäßiger Buchführung*) provided that all transactions had to be recorded individually and chronologically, that the related accounting records and documents had to be maintained in Germany and that annual financial statements had to be prepared. These general rules applied to sole proprietorships and to partnerships, whereas the GmbH Code (*GmbH-Gesetz*: GmbHG) contained some specific rules applicable to GmbHs. The Stock Corporation Code (*Aktiengesetz*: AktG) contained the specific rules applicable to stock corporations which concern, in particular, the format of the balance sheet and profit and loss statement presentation, as well as valuation rules.

These accounting rules under the Commercial Code, the GmbH Code and the Stock Corporation Code also applied for tax purposes, which required a correlation between financial reporting and the tax reporting requirements (s. 140 General Tax Code (*Abgabenordnung*: AO)). However, since certain options available for tax purposes (in particular accelerated depreciation allowances) could be taken only if they had been claimed in the financial statements as well, there was also a reverse correlation between tax reporting and financial reporting.

While stock corporations had to have their financial statements audited and published irrespective of their size, auditing and publication requirements for sole proprietorships, partnerships and GmbHs were mandatory only for large enterprises which met, as of the close of three successive fiscal years, at least two of the following three tests:

- a balance sheet total for the annual balance sheet in excess of DM 125 million;

- total sales in the twelve-month period prior to the close of the fiscal year in excess of DM 240 million; or

- the enterprise employed over the twelve-month period prior to the close of the fiscal year an average of more than 5,000 persons.

In addition, there were (and still are) special rules for companies engaged in certain activities such as banks or insurance companies.

On 19 December 1985, a statute was written into law which implemented the Fourth, Seventh and Eighth Directives of the EC and achieved, in particular, a consolidation of most, if not all, statutory requirements concerning the accounting, auditing and publication of financial statements in the Commercial Code. This statute is referred to here as the Balance Sheet Directive Act (*Bilanzrichtlinien-Gesetz*: BiRiLiG).

¶602   Balance Sheet Directive Act

The Balance Sheet Directive Act introduced a new third chapter into the Commercial Code which contains, *inter alia*, subchapters covering:

(1) accounting for all businesses, irrespective of their legal structure (ss. 238–263 HGB);

(2) supplementary provisions for corporations (stock corporations, limited partnerships, limited by shares) and GmbHs (ss. 264–335 HGB) with the subheadings –

    (a) financial statements of the corporation and the management's report (ss. 264–289 HGB),

    (b) consolidated financial statements and group management's report (ss. 290–315 HGB),

    (c) auditing (ss. 316–324 HGB), and

    (d) disclosure, as well as publication requirements for the financial statements of corporations (ss. 325–330 HGB).

In addition, the statute requiring the auditing and publication of financial statements for large businesses remains applicable to sole proprietorships and partnerships.

In the context of the enactment of this new statute, the GmbH Code and the Stock Corporation Code were amended to eliminate duplication and possibly even discrepancies.

¶603   Effective date

While the Balance Sheet Directive Act generally entered into force on 1 January 1986, this does not apply to all provisions, and the following two exceptions merit specific attention:

(1) *Preparation of financial statements, auditing and disclosure*

The provisions regarding the preparation of financial statements, their audit and the companies' obligation to disclose their audited accounts to the public will be applicable for the first time for the first fiscal year beginning after 31 December 1986. They may be applied voluntarily to prior fiscal years but only if the new provisions are applied in their entirety (art. 23(1) *Einführungsgesetz zum Handelsgesetzbuch* or 'Statute to Introduce the Commercial Code': EGHGB). Companies which have not had their financial statements audited so far will have to have them audited starting with the first fiscal year after 31 December 1986 (art. 23(1) EGHGB).

(2) *Provisions regarding consolidated financial statements*

The new provisions regarding the preparation of consolidated financial statements, as well as their audit and publication, have to be applied for the first time to financial statements for the first fiscal year commencing after 31 December 1989. They may be applied voluntarily to prior fiscal years but only if the new provisions are applied in their entirety; nevertheless, parent companies which under prior law already had to prepare consolidated financial statements need not include foreign subsidiaries, use uniform valuation rules or the equity method of consolidation (art. 23(2) EGHGB).

ACCOUNTING, AUDITING AND PUBLICATION REQUIREMENTS UNDER THE BALANCE SHEET DIRECTIVE ACT

¶604   Introduction

The requirements imposed on corporations for the preparation of financial statements, their audit and their publication depend on the size of the corporation.

¶605   Classification of small, medium-sized and large corporations

Small corporations are corporations which do not meet two of the following three tests at the close of two successive financial years, namely:

- a balance sheet total (*Bilanzsumme*) of DM 3,900,000 after deduction of losses over equity shown on the assets side of the balance sheet;
- total net sales during the 12-month period prior to the end of the fiscal year of DM 8,000,000; or
- an average for the fiscal year of 50 workers or employees.

Medium-sized corporations are corporations which, as of the close of two successive fiscal years, exceed at least two of the foregoing tests but do not meet at least two of the three tests below, namely:

- a balance sheet total of DM 15,000,000 after deduction of losses over equity shown on the assets side of the balance sheet;
- total sales during the 12-month period preceding the close of the fiscal year of DM 32,000,000; or
- an annual average of 250 workers or employees.

A large corporation must meet at least two of the above three tests. A corporation will irrefutably be deemed to be a large corporation if shares or other securities issued by it are admitted to official trading or to the over-the-counter market on a stock exchange within the European Community, or if an application for such a listing has been filed (s. 267(3) HGB).

While normally the classification is based on the facts of two successive fiscal years, newly-organised corporations or corporations which result from a merger or other reorganisation will be classified as small, medium-sized or large on the basis of the facts as they present themselves at the end of the first fiscal year following the organisation, merger or other reorganisation (s. 267(4) HGB).

The average number of workers or employees is computed by dividing by four the total of the persons employed on 31 March, 30 June, 30 September and 31 December of the calendar year. The number of workers or employees has to include workers or employees employed abroad but does not include apprentices (s. 267(5) HGB).

¶606 Preparation of financial statements

The financial statements of a corporation comprise the balance sheet and the profit and loss statement, as well as an annex thereto (s. 242(3), 264(1) HGB). The financial statements must present a true and fair view of the corporation's assets, liabilities and financial position, including profits or losses. If, in particular circumstances, the financial statements should fail to provide such a true and fair view, then additional information must be provided in the annex (s. 264(2) HGB).

The balance sheet must be prepared in account form. A detailed list of required headings and items is included in s. 266(2) and (3) HGB. Nevertheless, small corporations may prepare a short-form balance sheet as described in s. 266(1), (2) HGB.

The profit and loss statement must be prepared in report form as described in further detail at ¶612. However, small and medium-sized corporations may consolidate certain items into one item; in particular they may avoid showing their total sales as a separate item (s. 276 HGB).

The mandatory contents of the annex are listed in ss. 284 and 285 HGB. Medium-sized corporations may omit, however, a breakdown of gross revenues as to lines of business and geographical markets (ss. 288(2), 285(4) HGB). Small corporations may, in addition, delete some of the information required to be disclosed by medium-sized and large corporations (s. 288(1) HGB).

¶607   Audit

While medium-sized and large corporations will have to have their financial statements audited prior to their ratification by the shareholders' meeting, small corporations are exempt from such obligation. This means that small stock corporations, which until now were required to have their financial statements audited irrespective of their size, will in future be able to avoid an audit. The audit has to be performed by an independent public accountant (*Wirtschaftsprüfer*) or by a CPA (Certified Public Accountant) company. Medium-sized corporations may also have their accounts audited by sworn accountants or by sworn accountants' companies (*Vereidigte Buchprüfer*) (s. 319(1) HGB).

¶608   Publication requirements

Large corporations must publish the audited financial statement together with the management's report, the report of the supervisory board and, if the proposal for the use of the profits and the resolution adopting it is not reflected in the financial statement, such proposal and resolution in the Federal Gazette (*Bundesanzeiger*). Subsequently, the publication in the Federal Gazette, together with the documentation listed above, must be filed with the Commercial Register Court in the place in which the registered seat of the corporation is located (s. 325(2) HGB).

Medium-sized corporations have to file the same documentation with the Commercial Register Court at the place where their statutory seat is registered within the nine months following the close of their financial year. As soon as practicable following such filing, the management of the corporation must publish a notice in the Federal Gazette which specifies the commercial register docket number and the Commercial Register Court to which the documentation was submitted (s. 325(1) HGB). Nevertheless, for the purposes of such submission, the medium-sized corporation may use a short-form balance sheet comparable to the one permissible for small corporations with certain adjustments listed in s. 327(1) HGB. If it elects to do so, then each shareholder can request that he be furnished at the shareholders' meeting with financial statements in the form required for large corporations (s. 131(1) AktG). For medium-sized corporations organized as GmbHs, the same disclosure requirements can be based on s. 51(a) GmbHG.

Small corporations have to file the balance sheet and any annex with the Commercial Register Court on or before the end of the twelfth month following the end of the fiscal year. If the balance sheet and the annex so submitted do not disclose the profits for the year, the proposal for the use of the profits or losses and the resolution regarding its use, then the proposal for the use of the profits as well as the resolution also have to be filed and the annual profits or losses must be stated. The annex need not contain notes regarding the profit and loss statement. See s. 326 HGB.

¶609   Planning considerations

The publication of financial statements and other information, which will be required henceforth for all corporations (even, and in particular, for small GmbHs which have not had to make such information public before), may cause problems with regard to suppliers, major customers or trade unions (e.g. if profits realised by the company are substantial). For this reason, some corporations may seek to avoid the disclosure and publication requirements, and some of the devices enabling them to do so are listed below.

(1) *Use of branch of foreign corporation*
The publication and disclosure requirements of ss. 325–330 HGB apply to domestic corporations only. Unless the branch is registered in the commercial register in Germany, branch operations of the foreign corporation remain subject to the accounting, financial reporting and disclosure requirements imposed by the laws of the jurisdiction in which the company maintains its principal place of management (Tax Court Cologne, decision of 14 October 1981, EFG 1982, 422). It is true that such a branch is required to maintain certain records for German tax purposes, and that such records have to be maintained in Germany if the branch wishes to claim a loss carryforward (ss. 141 AO; 50(1)(3) EStG). Nevertheless, these records are covered by the tax secrecy rules, and there is no statutory requirement that they be disclosed to third parties other than the tax authorities. Furthermore, a branch of a

foreign corporation is not covered by the provisions of ss. 290 et seq. and of s. 325(3) HGB for the preparation and publication of consolidated financial statements.

On this basis, a foreign corporation which wishes to operate in Germany may consider setting up a branch for that purpose. For a discussion of the pros and cons of a branch operation, see Chapter 4, ¶402.

The situation may be more complicated for foreign corporations which already operate in Germany via one or more German subsidiary corporations. Such German subsidiary corporations will be subject to the provisions of ss. 264 et seq. HGB.

The liquidation of an existing subsidiary corporation and the conversion of its business to a branch operation will cause problems. In particular, the liquidation will attract German corporate income tax on the amount of the liquidation gain which equals the amount by which the fair market values of the assets of the subsidiary exceed their book values (See Chapter 4, ¶412). The foreign corporation will have to take these tax costs into account in evaluating whether the conversion of its subsidiary into a branch operation is worthwhile or whether one of the two alternatives outlined below should be considered.

(2) *Use of a partnership structure*

Since a partnership is not affected by the auditing, disclosure and publication requirements imposed on corporations unless it qualifies as a large business under the special statute which requires the auditing and publication of financial statements of large businesses referred to at ¶601 and ¶602 above, a reorganisation of a corporation into a partnership may avoid the publication and disclosure obligations at least.

Such a reorganisation, in which all assets and liabilities of the subsidiary transfer *uno actu* and by operation of the law to the partnership and the subsidiary disappears, is possible under the Reorganisation Act (*Umwandlungsgesetz*: UmwG). Nevertheless, s. 1(2) UmwG prohibits reorganisation if a corporation is one of the (at least two) partners of the partnership. This rule prevents direct reorganisation into a GmbH & Co. KG, i.e. a limited partnership whose sole general partner is a GmbH which need not have substantial assets and which need not (and, as a rule, does not have to) make a contribution to the capital of the limited partnership. In order to circumvent this problem, certain structures are currently being explored in various publications, in particular the following:

(a) The partnership is organised with an individual as the sole general partner and such partner remains a general partner until after the reorganisation is registered with the commercial register. Thereafter, the individual may cease to be a partner or may convert his interest in the partnership to a limited partnership interest. This structure will, as a rule, not present a viable solution for corporate groups of companies.

(b) The partnership is organised as a two-tier GmbH & Co. KG. In this structure, the sole general partner of the GmbH & Co. KG into which the subsidiary is to be reorganised is a second GmbH & Co. KG. As this second GmbH & Co. KG is a partnership and not a corporation, this structure should not be covered by s. 1(2) UmwG and there are a number of authorities which suggest that such structure is permissible.

From a tax point of view, the income and trade tax status of the transferor subsidiary, of its shareholder(s) and the partners in the partnership, as well as transfer taxes, have to be taken into account. The transferee must set up a transfer balance sheet in which all assets (except for intangible property and goodwill developed by the subsidiary) are stepped up to their going concern values. Such reorganisation gain is not subject to corporate income tax but it attracts trade tax (ss. 4, 18(1) Reorganisation Tax Act – *Umwandlungssteuergesetz* (UmwStG)). If, in preparation of the reorganisation, the shares in the subsidiary are transferred to the partnership, this may lead to a capital gain at the shareholders' level but such gain is exempt from German income tax under most tax treaties. The partners of the partnership will, finally, recognise an ordinary gain in the amount by which the value of the assets of the subsidiary exceed the book value of the shares in the subsidiary on the books of the partnership (s. 5(5) UmwStG).

(3) *Transfer of business activities by leasing arrangements*

In using this devise the subsidiary leases its business and its fixed assets to a limited partnership in which the subsidiary may be a partner, or in which it may assume the function of the sole general partner. As the employment agreements transfer to the partnership by operation of s. 613(a) of the Civil Code unless an employee objects, and as the gross receipts of the subsidiary will be reduced to the amount of an arm's length rental, the subsidiary may thereafter qualify as a small corporation and thus will have to meet the reduced publicity requirements imposed on small corporations only.

From a tax point of view, it is imperative that the rent payable by the partnership should reflect arm's length standards, as too low a rent will give rise to a constructive dividend distribution. In particular, the rent has to include adequate compensation for intangibles (including goodwill) developed by the subsidiary. As the rent agreement may require the partnership to acquire replacement fixed assets, this method may be attractive if the subsidiary is to be phased out gradually. It may also be attractive for German subsidiaries of foreign corporations. Nevertheless, the tax and non-tax aspects of such a reorganization are complex and careful attention must be paid to the details of the particular case before a decision is taken.

PRESENTATION OF FINANCIAL STATEMENTS

¶610   Generally recognised accounting principles

(1) *General accounting rules*

Each corporation must record its transactions completely, correctly chronologically and in such an order so as to assure that a knowledgeable third party can obtain within a reasonable period of time an overview of the business transacted and the status of the enterprise. While the books and other records may be maintained in any living language, the financial statements (and this includes the balance sheet, the profit and loss statement and the annex (see ss. 242(3), 264(1) HGB)) must be prepared in German and expressed in Deutsche Mark (s. 244 HGB).

(2) *Inventories*

The opening and closing balance sheets have to be prepared on the basis of annual physical inventories. In the preparation of such inventory the kind, quantity and value of assets may be determined by using mathematical-statistical methods and samples. The physical inventory need not be taken on the date of the close of the financial year if the inventory is taken not more than three months prior to or two months following the close of the fiscal year and if the book-keeping permits reliable computations as of the end of the fiscal year (s. 241 HGB).

(3) *Valuation rules*

The valuation of assets and liabilities shown in the financial statements must comply with the following principles: the values shown in the opening balance sheet of the fiscal year have to be identical with the corresponding values in the year-end balance sheet of the prior fiscal year. For the purposes of the valuation it has to be assumed that the business activity will be continued unless this is not possible because of factual or legal reasons. Assets and debts must be valued individually, even though group valuations of tangible fixed assets, raw materials and consumables are permissible under s. 240(3) and (4) HGB. All valuations must be made by taking into account all predictable risks and losses which have arisen on or before the end of the fiscal year even if they have become known only after the end of the fiscal year. Nevertheless, profits can be taken into account only if they were realised on or before the end of the fiscal year. In applying these rules, the principle of consistency is to be applied (s. 252 HGB).

(4) *Fiscal year*

The fiscal year need not coincide with the calendar year but it must not exceed a period of 12 calendar months (s. 240(2) HGB).

¶611 Balance sheet presentation

(1) *Form and structure of balance sheet*

The Fourth EC Directive authorised the member states to elect either the account form of balance sheet presentation or a kind of report form. The German legislators elected the account form which had been used traditionally in Germany.

The balance sheet must be arranged in the inverse order of liquidity: fixed assets have to be shown at the top of the asset side of the balance sheet. This also means that on the liability side of the balance sheet equity capital comes first as it is permanently appropriated to the use of the enterprise.

(2) *Items of particular interest*

It is beyond the scope of this work to discuss all the individual items which are required to be shown in the balance sheet by law. Instead, the following paragraphs focus on such items as should be of particular interest to foreign direct investors who maintain a German subsidiary corporation.

(a) *Intangible fixed assets.* Section 248(1) HGB prohibits the capitalisation of organisational costs and costs incurred in order to secure equity capital. It further states that intangible fixed assets (as to financial fixed assets see (d) below) which have not been acquired for a consideration must not be capitalised. This provision implies that acquired intangible fixed assets have to be capitalised. For the purposes of the provision, intangible fixed assets include, *inter alia*, licences, concessions, intangible industrial property rights and advances paid in respect of such items. However, acquired goodwill may, but need not be, capitalised at the amount by which the purchase price for an enterprise acquired exceeds the total value of all individual assets of the enterprise less debts. The amount so capitalised as goodwill has to be amortised by annual depreciation allowances of at least one-quarter each in the subsequent fiscal years, but the corporation may also elect to amortise such capitalised goodwill over the years during which it will presumably be used (s. 255(4) HGB).

(b) *Tangible fixed assets.* Tangible fixed assets must be shown at their historical cost increased by subsequent costs, such as major repairs, and reduced by depreciation allowances and the basis of fixed assets disposed of and, finally, increased by subsequent recaptures of depreciation allowances if it is determined later that an extraordinary depreciation allowance taken earlier is no longer necessary. All such items have to be disclosed separately on the asset side of the balance sheet or in the annex to the balance sheet (s. 268(2) HGB).

Tangible fixed assets which are used up or which exhaust themselves over a period of time may be depreciated by regular depreciation allowances over their useful life. However, in the case of such fixed assets (as well as of other tangible fixed assets which are not amortisable by regular depreciation allowances (e.g. land)), if their value has decreased as a result of other extraordinary events, such as a change of economic situation or an early obsolescence for economical or technical reasons, then extraordinary depreciation allowances can be taken under s. 253(2)(3). HGB. If it should later be determined that this extraordinary depreciation is no longer necessary, then the amount must be recaptured (s. 280 HGB).

(c) *Start-up costs.* Start-up costs and costs of expansion of the business (but not organisational costs, see s. 248(1) HGB) can be capitalised under s. 269 HGB. This is meant to help the corporation if the start-up costs or the costs of an expansion are substantial. As such events may not immediately lead to the acquisition or manufacture of assets which may be capitalised under general accounting rules, the corporation might appear to be technically overindebted if it was unable to capitalise such start-up costs. However, if the corporation wishes to take advantage of this authorisation to capitalise start-up costs, it must explain this in the annex to the financial statements.

Such capitalised start-up and expansion costs have to be amortized by at least 25 per cent in the following fiscal years (s. 282 HGB). Furthermore, while such an item is capitalised, profits may be distributed only if after the distribution accumulated retained earnings and earned surplus less a net operating loss carryforward equal at least the capitalised amount (s. 269(2) HGB).

(d) *Financial fixed assets.* Financial fixed assets include, in particular, participations in other enterprises, i.e. shares in other corporations which are held to foster the business of the corporation by creating a permanent relationship with such other corporation. A 20 per cent interest in another corporation is refutably deemed to constitute such a participation (s. 271(1) HGB).

(e) *Current assets.* Current assets include such standard items as inventory and accounts receivable, but also include treasury shares and shares in

¶611

controlling companies or in companies which hold an interest in the corporation. Such shares must be shown as current assets irrespective of how long and for what purposes they are held by the corporation. A stock corporation may acquire its own shares or treasury shares only under certain circumstances set out in s. 71 AktG, and even then only up to maximum of 10 per cent of its stated equity capital, and while it holds treasury shares the voting rights in respect of such shares may not be exercised (s. 136(2) AktG).

A GmbH, too, may only acquire its own shares if it does not involve an invasion of its stated equity capital (s. 33(2) GmbHG). However, the corporation has to set up a special reserve for treasury shares on the liability side of its balance sheet in the same amount as the cost of such treasury shares (s. 272(4) HGB). This reserve is also required for shares in controlling corporations or in corporations which hold a majority interest in the corporation.

(f) *Equity capital.*   The first item at the top of the liability side of the balance sheet is the equity capital of the corporation. Under prior law, the stated equity capital had to be shown irrespective of whether it had been paid-up in full or not. That part of it which had not been paid-up was shown as a specific account receivable at the top of the assets side of the balance sheet.

Under the new law, the item of equity capital heading the liability side of the balance sheet is called 'equity capital subscribed to' (*Gezeichnetes Kapital*) in order to indicate clearly that this is the amount subscribed to by the shareholders only and not necessarily in the amount paid in. The part of the capital subscribed to which has neither been paid nor called in by the corporation may be either shown as an account receivable at the top of the asset side or it may be listed as a separate sub-item in the equity section of the balance sheet and deducted from the amount of the equity capital subscribed to (s. 272(1) HGB). If this latter presentation is chosen, the amount of the called but not yet paid-in equity capital has to be shown as an account receivable on the asset side. The equity capital subscribed to has to be shown at its par value (s. 283 HGB).

The law also distinguishes the items of paid-in surplus (*Kapitalrücklagen*) and earned surplus (*Gewinnrücklagen*). Paid-in surplus includes all amounts received by the corporation in the context of issuing shares or convertible bonds in excess of the par value of the shares or the nominal value of the convertible bonds, as well as all other contributions by shareholders which are not reflected in an increase of the corporation's stated equity capital. This should include, in particular, so-called constructive contributions to capital (see *Bundesratsdrucksache* 61/82, at p. 82). As a stock corporation is required to build up a statutory reserve of up to 10 per cent of its stated equity capital, the new law provides that the capital reserve or paid-in surplus will be added to such statutory reserve in order to determine whether the 10 per cent of stated equity capital has been reached already or even exceeded (s. 150(2) AktG).

At the end of the equity section in the balance sheet, the accumulated profit or loss carryforward and the profits or losses of the fiscal year as computed in the profit and loss statement are listed (s. 266(3) HGB). However, if accumulated losses should exceed all other items of equity capital, this amount will have to be shown at the bottom of the assets side of the balance sheet as an excess of losses over equity capital (s. 268(3) HGB).

(g) *Special tax equalisation reserve.* Reserves can, of course, be set up for contingent liabilities or for anticipated losses from pending transactions. Furthermore, reserves can be set up for the costs of repairs which were deferred but which will be made in the course of the following fiscal year (s. 249(1) HGB).

Nevertheless, there are some specific reserves which merit attention. One such reserve which has equity characteristics in part may be set up under ss. 247(3), 273 HGB. It relates to instances in which, because of the interrelationship of financial and tax reporting, special reserves permitted under tax law may be claimed only if they are set up for financial reporting purposes as well. This concerns, in particular, instances where tax law permits the setting-up of a reserve which has to be dissolved and restored to income in a later year or the use of accelerated depreciation allowances for tax purposes which exceed the amount of depreciation which would be claimed for financial reporting purposes. This reserve has the advantage of coordinating tax reporting and financial reporting. On the other hand, it has the disadvantage of sometimes distorting the income of the corporation for financial reporting purposes.

Another similar situation occurs where specific reserves are set up for tax purposes, irrespective of whether a similar reserve is set up or can be set up for financial reporting purposes as well. At the present time, there seems to be only one example of this, i.e. an inflation reserve permitted by s. 74 of the Income Tax Ordinance – *Einkommensteuerdurchführungsverordnung* (EStDV). Such a reserve can be set for a certain percentage of the costs of raw materials, consumables or semi-finished or finished goods if the price of such assets has increased by more than 10 per cent during the preceding fiscal year (s. 228(5)(1) Insurance Tax Regulations – *Einkommensteuerrichtlinien* (EStR)).

Such a reserve has to be shown in the tax balance sheet only, it may not be shown in the balance sheet for financial reporting purposes. However, the latent future tax burden which results from the dissolution of this kind of reserve must be recognised in a special reserve for future tax payments under s. 274 HGB.

¶611

(h) *Pension reserves.* Pension reserves are a very peculiar instrument for providing for future pensions which the corporation is committed to pay to its employees or workers upon their retirement. In order to induce German employers to provide certain retirement benefits to their workers and employees in addition to the state funds under the social security system, employers were permitted to deduct from their current income for income tax purposes contributions to the so-called pension reserve which were to be computed on the basis of actuarial tables by using an interest rate of, at present, 6 per cent per annum. However, the employers did not have to set up a like reserve for financial reporting purposes. They could instead elect to report the actual costs of pension payments when they were incurred. As the amounts put in the reserve and deducted for tax purposes do not have to be segregated or funded but can continue to be used in the business of the corporation, this provided (and still provides) a substantial liquidity benefit for the corporation.

The new law now provides that reserves for contingent liabilities must be set up, and this includes pension reserves (s. 249(1) HGB). Nevertheless, this provision is not mandatory if the employee has acquired vested pension rights before 1 January 1987, or if vested rights prior to such date are increased after 31 December 1986. However, if the corporation elects not to set up pension reserves for such prior commitments, the amount of the deficiency has to be specified in the annex to the financial statements (art. 28(2) EGHGB).

¶612   Profit and loss statement

The profit and loss statement must be prepared in report form, and the corporation may elect either one of the two models proposed in art. 23 and 25 of the Fourth Directive.

The model proposed by art. 23 classifies the costs according to their nature. It starts with sales less VAT, adds or deducts variations in stocks of finished goods and in work in process, adds other ordinary items of income and then deducts materials, labour costs, depreciation allowances and other ordinary deductions to arrive at what represents income from normal business activities. Furthermore, dividends and interest received and depreciation allowances claimed with respect to financial assets to arrive at profits (or losses) from ordinary business activities are included (s. 275(2) HGB). As this is the format which formerly was prescribed by s. 157 AktG, most of the corporations presumably will opt for it.

The alternative available is the so-called 'cost of sales' method which is regulated by s. 275(3) HGB and which reflects art. 25 of the Fourth Directive. It may be suitable for trading companies, in particular.

¶613   Annex to the balance sheet and the profit and loss statements

This annex is a new mandatory requirement which replaces the notes to the financial statements. It must include additional mandatory or voluntary information as listed in ss. 284 et seq. HGB.

As an example, s. 284(2)(2) HGB requires the annex to specify how items denominated in a foreign currency were translated into German Marks. For an export-orientated country like Germany the conversion of items denominated in a foreign currency has significant importance. Generally this conversion is made on an item by item basis and by using the principles of prudence and imparity (*Imparitätsprinzip*). This means that when a foreign currency item is first entered into the German books, the exchange rate at the time of the actual transaction applies. If no actual conversion of funds occurs, the medium exchange rate may be used even though the selling rate is predominantly used in practice.

In preparing the year-end financial statements, the valuation will be examined in order to avoid the recognition of unrealised currency gains and to make sure that unrealised currency losses are taken into account immediately. This means that accounts receivable which are payable in a foreign currency remain capitalised at the historical exchange rate even if the rate has changed, so that if these payments had been made at year-end a currency gain would have resulted. Conversely, accounts payable in a foreign currency can be increased if current exchange rates would require a higher amount in German Marks to satisfy this obligation.

The resulting exchange gains or losses have to be accounted for under miscellaneous income or miscellaneous expenses and, therefore, directly affect the profit and loss account of the corporation.

¶614   Auditors' certificate

Traditionally, certificates issued by German auditors only confirmed that the attached financial statements had been prepared in conformity with statutory requirements and with requirements imposed by the corporation's charter. In particular, the auditor's certificate did not address the financial situation of the company in general. Under the new law, the auditor's certificate has to confirm that the financial statements supply a true and fair view of the financial position of the company (s. 322(1) HGB).

In addition, the auditor is free to add comments which seem necessary to him in order to avoid a wrong or misleading impression regarding the scope and contents of his audits and importance of the certificate (s. 322(2) HGB).

¶615   Discrepancies between financial reporting and tax reporting

Section 5(1) Income Tax Act (*Einkommensteuergesetz*: EStG), requires businessmen (and this includes corporations) who have to prepare financial statements for financial reporting purposes to use such financial statements for tax reporting purposes as well. This means that the balance sheet prepared for financial reporting purposes is also applicable for income tax purposes, provided such balance sheet complies with the provisions of commercial law and does not violate a provision of tax law. In essence, therefore, financial statements for tax purposes are derived from the financial statement prepared for financial reporting purposes, and options available for financial reporting purposes have to be exercised in the financial statements for financial reporting purposes if they are to be claimed for tax purposes as well.

On the other hand, there are a number of tax benefits (such as accelerated depreciation allowances or roll-over of capital gains for voluntary or involuntary exchanges of assets by replacement assets) which can be claimed only if they are used for financial reporting purposes as well. This has led to the widespread practice of preparing the tax balance sheet first and developing the balance sheet for financial reporting purposes from such tax balance sheet. This means that there is not only a correlation between the commercial balance sheet and the tax balance sheet but also a reverse correlation between the tax balance sheet and the balance sheet prepared for financial reporting purposes.

Throughout the discussions which led to the adoption of the Fourth EC Directive, the German Government tried to retain this delicate interrelationship between financial reporting and tax reporting and it generally succeeded. In addition, in introducing the implementing German statute the Government tried to exercise elections in a way which would be neutral so far as tax revenue is concerned. While this succeeded generally, there are a number of instances in which tax status has changed as a result of the enactment of the Balance Sheet Directive Act. For the purposes of this introductory discussion, it should suffice to note the following aspects:

(1) *Capitalisation of start-up costs and costs of major expansions*

Start-up costs and costs for the expansion of the company's business may be capitalised under s. 269 HGB subject to a restriction on the distribution of dividends and, further, subject to depreciation of the amount capitalised over not more than the four subsequent fiscal years (s. 282 HGB). For tax purposes, however, this capitalisation is not permissible and the corresponding depreciation is not allowable as a business expense.

(2) *Amortisation of acquired goodwill*

Previously, acquired goodwill had to be capitalised at cost for both financial and tax reporting purposes. For financial reporting purposes, however, the amount capitalised then had to be amortised over not more than five fiscal years. Under the new s. 255(4) HGB such amount must be amortised over not more than four fiscal years unless the corporation elects to depreciate the goodwill over its anticipated useful life.

For tax purposes acquired goodwill was not amortisable at all by regular depreciation allowances. This has now changed. Under s. 7(1)(3) EStG, capitalised goodwill may be amortised over a useful life of 15 years starting with the fiscal year which begins after 31 December 1986; for the purposes of this provision, goodwill acquired prior to such fiscal year will be deemed to be acquired as of the beginning of such fiscal year. This means that there will be a discrepancy between financial reporting and tax reporting if the corporation elects to depreciate such goodwill over not more than four fiscal years for financial reporting purposes. Nevertheless, if it elects to treat the useful life of 15 years recognised for tax purposes as the anticipated useful life of the goodwill, then the goodwill may be depreciated over such 15 years period for financial reporting purposes as well and, in this case, there is complete correlation between the two reporting systems.

(3) *Interest charges as part of the cost basis of assets*

Under s. 255(3)(1) HGB, interest costs allocatable to the period of manufacture of goods may be treated as part of the costs of the goods. As this definition of manufacturing cost applies for tax reporting purposes as well, such interest charges can also be capitalised for tax purposes, while, so far, s. 33(7) of the Income Tax Regulations has permitted this treatment only in the case of long-term manufacturing processes in excess of one year.

(4) *Inventory valuation methods*

Section 256 HGB permits the use of inventory valuation methods such as FIFO (first-in, first-out) or LIFO (last-in, first-out) if they generally reflect accepted accounting principles. On the other hand, for tax purposes such methods may only be used if they are specifically permitted. One such instance concerns, for example, inventories of gold, silver, platinum or palladium as provided for under s. 74(a) Income Tax Ordinance (*Einkommensteuerdurchführungs-verordnung*: EStDV).

(5) *Recapture of tax-induced accelerated depreciation allowances*

Section 254(1) HGB permits the corporation to take into account extraordinary depreciation allowances which exceed the amount otherwise permissible for

¶615

financial reporting purposes if such depreciation allowances are permissible under tax law and, where tax law permits them, only if they are also claimed for financial reporting purposes (s. 279(2) HGB). This clearly is a case of a reverse correlation between the two reporting systems. However, under s. 280(1) HGB, the corporation must recapture such accelerated depreciation allowances less regular depreciation allowances for the time which has elapsed if in a subsequent fiscal year it is determined that the reasons for setting up the special accelerated depreciation no longer exist. In this context, s. 6(3) Income Tax Act was amended to provide that if such a recapture is effected under s. 280(1) HGB for financial reporting purposes it must be mirrored in the tax reporting system with the consequence that the corporation has to recognise a corresponding taxable gain.

CONSOLIDATED RETURNS

¶616 Introduction

Previously, consolidated returns had to be prepared if the German parent company was organised as a stock corporation or, if it was organised as a GmbH, if at least one stock corporation was included in the consolidation. Other groups of companies had to prepare consolidated financial statements if the group met certain tests as to size which are specified under s. 11 of the special statute referred to in ¶601 above. Furthermore, any consolidation did not need to include foreign subsidiaries.

The new law, which will be applicable to fiscal years which commence after 31 December 1989, considerably expands the obligation to prepare consolidated financial statements.

¶617 Current law

A domestic parent corporation will now be required to prepare consolidated financial statements if the balance sheet total, the sales and the average number of persons employed by the parent company itself, as well as of those subsidiaries which would have to be included in the consolidated financial statement, exceed certain amounts at the end of a fiscal year of the parent company and at the end of the preceding fiscal year. Such amounts are specified in s. 293(1) HGB.

If a consolidated financial statement has to be prepared, it must include the domestic parent company as well as the domestic and foreign subsidiaries which are under its uniform management and control and in which the parent company holds an interest of at least 20 per cent of the stated equity capital (ss. 290(1), 271(1) HGB).

A subsidiary has to be included in consolidated financial statements in any event if the parent company holds directly or indirectly the majority of the voting rights in the subsidiary, or if it is entitled to appoint or terminate the majority of the members of a board of directors, a board of managers or of a supervisory board and if the parent company simultaneously is a shareholder in such subsidiary, or if the parent company is entitled to exercise a controlling influence on the basis of a management agreement concluded with the enterprise or on the basis of the charter of such enterprise (s. 290(2) HGB). However, if the domestic parent company at the same time qualifies as the subsidiary of a parent company which maintains its registered seat in another Member State of the European Community, then it is relieved of the obligation to prepare a consolidated return if its parent company publishes consolidated financial statements which bear an auditor's certificate, provided such consolidated financial statements comply with German law and are published in the German language (s. 291(1) HGB).

The requirements which have to be met by such consolidated financial statements of the foreign parent company are listed in s. 291(1) HGB. Under s. 292 HGB, consolidated financial statements prepared by parent companies which maintain their registered seats outside the European Community will also be recognised in accordance with regulations to be promulgated by the Federal Ministry of Justice in concert with the Federal Ministries of Finance or Economic Affairs.

The consolidated financial statements consist of the consolidated balance sheet, the consolidated profit and loss statement and the consolidated annex (s. 297(1) HGB). Unless otherwise provided, the provisions governing the preparation of the financial statements for large corporations are applicable (s. 298(1) HGB). Nevertheless, the consolidated financial statements must present the assets, financial status and the profits of the enterprises consolidated as if such enterprises constituted one single enterprise, and this means that they also have to comply with the law in the country of the parent company (ss. 297(3), 300 HGB). In addition, the consolidated financial statements have to follow the valuation rules imposed by the law of the state of the parent company (s. 308(1) HGB). The consolidation itself has to follow the equity method as laid down by s. 301 HGB.

The consolidated financial statements have to be audited, as does the management's report on the state of the group, and both must be published in accordance with the provisions which apply to large corporations (s. 316(2), 325(3) HGB).

¶617

THE ACCOUNTING PROFESSION

¶618 Accountants and tax advisers

The German *Wirtschaftsprüfer* is comparable to a certified public accountant in the United States or to a chartered accountant in England so far as his education, professional qualifications and the scope of his services are concerned. A *Wirtschaftsprüfer* may practise as a sole practitioner, in partnership with other *Wirtschaftsprüfer*, tax advisers or lawyers or in a corporation of certified public accountants (*Wirtschaftsprüfergesellschaft*).

The second largest group of professional accounting advisers are the *Steuerberater* or tax advisers. These are university graduates who have to have three years' practical experience before they can submit to the examination for tax advisers. Tax advisers can perform basically all the functions of a certified public accountant except that they cannot audit a corporation where the audit is mandatory. However, since the number of companies which have to be audited was increased significantly under the new legislation, and as tax advisers traditionally advised smaller and medium-sized GmbHs, they were granted the option to become *Wirtschaftsprüfer* or sworn accountants (*Vereidigte Buchprüfer*), a profession which had almost died out but which has been given new life under the new law.

7 Banking and Finance

OVERVIEW OF BANKING IN GERMANY

¶701 Banking system

Germany has a qualified and very sophisticated banking system with a central bank and numerous national or regional banks, as well as foreign banks which operate through branches or subsidiaries in Germany.

Although there are specialised banks, German banks by tradition engage in a wide range of banking services. In addition to accepting deposits and savings accounts, they may grant commercial and private loans; they may act as brokers, underwriters for equity and debt securities; they may deal in foreign exchange and they may hold substantial equity interests in other companies. Foreign banks who maintain branch or subsidiary operations in Germany may also, to a lesser extent, offer such a wide range of banking services unless they are prohibited from doing so under restrictive legislation in their home country.

By tradition, German banks maintain branch offices on a regional or national basis, and all major German banks maintain branch operations, subsidiaries or representative offices in the major banking centres of the world.

BANKING REGULATION

¶702 Banking Act

Banks are subject to supervision by the Banking Supervisory Authority (*Bundesaufsichtsamt für das Kreditwesen*) in Berlin in co-operation with the German Federal Bank in Frankfurt. The Banking Supervisory Authority acts under the provisions of the Banking Act (*Gesetz über das Kreditwesen*: KWG) of 10 July 1961, as amended to date. The statute regulates in the first place the admission of banks to do business, the conduct of banking operations, and the information, investigation and intervention rights accorded to the Banking Supervisory Authority. With few exceptions, it applies to all banks, and it is supplemented by special statutes such as the Building and Loan Associations Act, the Investment Companies Act (*Gesetz über Kapitalanlagegesell-schaften*) or the Savings Bank Act.

¶703   Admission of banks

A partnership or a corporation which wishes to engage in banking activities as defined in s. 1(1) KWG needs a prior written licence from the Banking Supervisory Authority (s. 32(I) KWG). Sole proprietorships may not engage in a banking activity (s. 2(a) KWG).

Banking activities comprise the following, provided that the scope of business requires the maintenance of commercially equipped business installations (s. 1(1) KWG):

(1) the acceptance of funds from third parties as deposits, irrespective of whether the deposits bear interest or not;

(2) the extension of loans in the form of money or acceptance of notes;

(3) the purchase of notes or cheques (discount activities);

(4) the acquisition or sale of securities for other parties (brokerage);

(5) the deposit and administration of securities for other parties;

(6) transactions defined in s. 1 of the Investment Companies Act;

(7) the assumption of the obligation to purchase loans prior to their maturity;

(8) the assumption of guarantees, sureties and other warranties for other parties; and

(9) the execution of money transfers, including the clearing of money transfers between banks.

The licence can be restricted to particular kinds of banking activity or it can be granted subject to the reservation that certain requirements be observed. Nevertheless, a banking licence must be issued, as a rule, if:

(1) the financial funds required to engage in the banking activity are available within Germany, in particular in the form of equity capital; and

(2) the applicant has appointed at least two full-time managers who are qualified to manage a bank and who are considered reliable.

A person will generally be considered qualified to manage a bank if he has held a managerial position in a bank of comparable size and business for at least three years. German citizenship is not required but the Banking Supervisory Authority insists that the applicant must be sufficiently fluent in the German language.

If a corporation is formed to engage in a banking activity, it will not be registered in the commercial register and will not exist as a separate legal entity until the banking licence has been granted. The holder of a banking licence may use the word 'bank' as part of its firm name, a privilege which is not available to parties who do not hold such a licence unless the context is such that no-one could possibly imagine that a particular firm was engaged in a banking activity (ss. 39, 41 KWG).

¶704   Equity capital

Section 10(1) KWG stipulates that the bank must have sufficient equity capital to ensure that the bank can meet its obligations towards its creditors, but it does not stipulate the amount of equity capital which will be required. Instead, the Banking Act delegates the authority to fix such amounts to the Banking Supervisory Authority which has to issue guidelines in concert with the central bank.

While, for the purposes of organising a bank, an equity capital of DM 6,000,000 has generally been considered acceptable as a minimum during past years, the bank has to observe equity guidelines once it has started its operations. Such equity guidelines were promulgated by the Banking Supervisory Authority on 20 January 1969 and last amended on 16 January 1980. They can be summarised as follows:

Principle I: Total lendings and participations in other enterprises less reserves for bad debts or depreciation are not to exceed more than 18 times the equity capital.

Principle Ia: As at the end of each business day the difference between creditor and debitor positions in foreign currency and in precious metals must not exceed, irrespective of their maturities, 30 per cent of the equity capital.

¶705   Liquidity requirements

The liquidity requirements imposed on a bank are also contained in the equity guidelines of 20 January 1969, as amended, namely in the form of Principles II and III which may be summarised as follows:

Principle II: Long-term lendings and investments (participations in other enterprises, holdings of unlisted securities, land and buildings, furniture and equipment) are not to exceed the amount of long-term funds available to the bank, and such long-term funds are defined in detail in *Principle II*.

Principle III:　Short-term and medium-term lendings (up to four years term), as well as listed securities and shares in investment funds less reserves for bad debts or depreciation, are not to exceed financial funds available to the bank on short and medium terms as defined in detail in *Principle III*.

¶706　Supervision of lending activities

The bank must notify the German Federal Bank without undue delay of loans to a single creditor which exceed, alone or in the aggregate, 15 per cent of the bank's equity capital. The Banking Supervisory Authority has to be notified again if such a major loan is increased by more than 20 per cent of the amount of which the German Federal Bank already had been informed or if it exceeds 50 per cent of the bank's equity capital. The German Federal Bank relays such notifications to the Banking Supervisory Authority, together with its comments, if any.

Irrespective of the obligation to notify the German Federal Bank, a bank may not grant such major loans except on the basis of a unanimous decision of all managers of the bank. As a rule, such decision has to be taken prior to granting the loan; if this is not possible because of the urgency of the matter, then the decision has to be adopted thereafter without undue delay, and, in this case, the German Federal Bank and the Banking Supervisory Authority are to be notified within one month whether (and with what result) the decision has been taken.

Furthermore, no major credit may individually exceed 50 per cent of the equity capital of the bank, and all major credits in the aggregate may not exceed eight times the equity capital (s. 13 KWG). Similar rules apply to major loans granted by different members of groups of banks.

Loans to single borrowers which reach or exceed DM 1,000,000 at any time have to be notified to the German Federal Bank by the tenth day of February, April, June, August, October and December of each year. If the German Federal Bank is aware of the fact that one or more other bank granted similar loans worth DM 1,000,000 or more to the same borrower, then it will notify each of the banks concerned of the total amount of the borrowings and the number of banks concerned.

Finally, loans to managers of the bank, to members of the bank's supervisory board or to other related persons, as defined in s. 15(1) KWG, may not be granted except on the basis of a unanimous decision taken by all managers of the bank and only with the express consent of the supervisory board. Moreover, loans granted by the bank to members of its management or to its shareholders or partners have to be notified without undue delay to the German Federal Bank and to the Banking Supervisory Authority if the loan exceeds DM 250,000 in the case of individual borrowers, or 5 per cent of the bank's equity capital or more than DM 250,000 in the case of entities. If loans are granted in violation of s. 15 KWG, then the members of management who violate their obligations and the members of the supervisory board who are aware of the intended granting of a loan and who do not take proper action are personally, jointly and severally liable to the bank for the resulting damages. In the case of a claim against such persons, they have to establish that they did not act wilfully or negligently if they want to defend themselves successfully (s. 17(1) KWG). Such claims may even be raised by creditors of the bank if and to the extent that they are unable to collect from the bank (s. 17(2) KWG).

The bank has to compile and keep proper loan files for each borrower who owes the bank more than DM 100,000, and such files must include information on the economic and financial status of the borrower and, in particular, its financial statements (s. 18 KWG).

¶707 Enforcement of compliance by the Banking Supervisory Authority

The Banking Supervisory Authority has a multitude of means to enforce compliance with the foregoing restrictions imposed on banks. These include, apart from using moral persuasion, the following measures:

(1) requesting information and conducting investigations either directly or via special auditors;

(2) the approval or disapproval of the appointment of managers or requiring the recall of the appointment of a manager or issuing warnings in minor cases of non-compliance;

(3) the withdrawal and restriction of banking licences, in particular in cases where the security of deposits held by a bank is jeopardised and where this security cannot be restored by using other means. Such a danger for deposits is deemed to exist, in particular, if the bank incurs a loss of at least one half of its equity capital or if it incurs losses of more than 10 per cent of its equity capital in at least three consecutive fiscal years (s. 35(2)(4) KWG). If a banking licence is withdrawn, then the Banking Supervisory Authority can decide that the bank is to be liquidated. This decision has the same effect as a shareholders' resolution or partners' resolution to dissolve the bank. The decision will be submitted to the register court which will enter it into the commercial register (s. 38(1) KWG).

MONETARY POLICY

¶708   The German Federal Bank

The German Federal Bank (*Deutsche Bundesbank*) acts as the central bank within the German banking system. It is the:

(1) sole bank of issue in Germany;

(2) the bank which supplies refinancing, clearing and collection services for other banks; and

(3) it acts as bank for the Federal Government.

The German Federal Bank maintains its head office in Frankfurt; it has eleven regional head offices (*Landeszentralbanken*) in each of the ten states and in West Berlin. It is responsible for exercising monetary control of the banking system in accordance with the terms of the Federal Bank Act of 26 July 1957, as amended. While the Federal Government is the sole shareholder, the German Federal Bank is not bound to abide by instructions from the Federal Government; the provisions of the Banking Act do not apply to it and it enjoys a high degree of independence from the Federal Government (s. 12 Federal Bank Act).

It is responsible for regulating the supply of money and the availability of loans, and to that end it has been given, *inter alia*, the following *powers* (¶709 to ¶712 below).

¶709   Setting of discount rates and discount ceilings

From time to time the German Federal Bank sets the discount rate at which it is prepared to purchase from banks eligible bills of exchange, which must bear the signatures of at least three parties in financially sound condition and which mature within three months of the date of the purchase by the German Federal Bank. At the present time, this discount rate amounts to 3.5 per cent per annum (effective 7 March 1986).

In addition, semi-annually the German Federal Bank sets the ceilings for such discount transactions and it also sets ceilings for each individual bank within which that bank may sell eligible bills of exchange to the German Federal Bank.

¶710   Lombard limits

The Lombard rate at which the German Federal Bank is prepared to lend to banks on the basis of collateral (securities or certain other claims against public authorities) currently is set at 5.5 per cent per annum. In addition, the German Federal Bank sets an overall Lombard ceiling, as well as individual ceilings for each bank. Such Lombard loans are not granted for terms in excess of three months.

¶711   Open market operations

Within its open market operations, the German Federal Bank buys and sells on its own account treasury notes and non-interest bearing papers issued by the Federal Treasury and bonds issued by the Federal Treasury, the Federal Railroads or the Federal Mails. It buys and sells private discount papers with the *Privatdiskont-Aktiengesellschaft* acting as intermediary and also buys certain securities from banks under a repurchase arrangement which requires those banks to repurchase such securities at specified dates.

¶712   Minimum reserve requirements

Under the authority granted by s. 16 of the Federal Bank Act, the German Federal Bank promulgated minimum reserve regulations on 20 January 1983 which specify in detail the amount of non-interest bearing funds which each bank has to maintain with the German Federal Bank. On the basis of these regulations, the German Federal Bank publishes reserve rates which are subject to change from time to time. The present current rates have remained unchanged since 1 October 1982, but an amendment is currently under consideration.

In order to enable the German Federal Bank to fulfil its obligations, it may (and does) request under s. 19 of the Federal Bank Act a large number of statistical data and reports.

FOREIGN EXCHANGE CONTROLS

¶713   In general

At the present time, there are no foreign exchange controls which concern the free flow of money and capital from Germany or to Germany. Nevertheless, banks and private businesses are subject to a wide range of reporting requirements which are used for statistical purposes.

Under s. 6(a) Foreign Trade Act (*Aussenwirtschaftsgesetz*: AWG), resident parties may be required to deposit with the German Federal Bank on a non-interest bearing account a certain percentage of amounts borrowed from non-resident parties if the economic equilibrium is jeopardised by the inflow of funds from abroad. Currently this cash deposit rate is set at zero.

Furthermore, under s. 22(2) AWG, the Federal Government is authorised to restrict the public offering in Germany of bearer bonds which can be transferred by endorsement and which are issued by non-resident companies. Nevertheless, at the present time, the Federal Government has not made use of this authorisation.

BANKING STRUCTURE

¶714   Introduction

While various banks are increasingly offering the same types of loans and services, it is still usual and necessary to distinguish the different types of banks.

¶715   Commercial banks

Commercial banks are all-purpose banks which conduct almost all conceivable banking transactions and services. They are heavily engaged in short-term lending (loans with maturities of up to one year) and, to a more limited extent, medium-term lending (loans with a term of one to four years).

The big three commercial banks, Deutsche Bank, Dresdner Bank and Commerzbank, play a dominant role among commercial banks. All three of them have a nationwide branch network and they hold large equity interests in many German industries and act as proxies for many of the shareholders who have deposited their shares with them. The big three also account for a substantial share of Germany's international banking transactions and they maintain representative offices, branch operations and/or subsidiary banks in all major financial centres around the world.

¶716   Savings banks and their central giro-institutions

Savings banks, despite their original purpose of taking care of the savings of the working classes, have expanded their business to most fields of commercial banking. The savings banks are owned and guaranteed by municipalities or counties.

Although savings banks, and especially giro-institutions, are moving rapidly into many traditional spheres of commercial banking, there are still significant differences compared to commercial banks. Since the savings banks handle approximately 50 per cent of total savings deposits, they are the principal lenders of long-term funds mostly secured by mortgages. On the other hand, commercial banks are most important in the field of short-term financing.

The savings banks are subject to certain limitations in their activities. For example, they can extend loans only to borrowers residing in the municipality or county that owns and guarantees the particular savings bank, and this regional restriction is regaining increased importance. Furthermore, they are not allowed to buy shares on their own account, but they may acquire bearer bonds and trade in all types of securities. Their broker and dealer functions and their holdings in securities are of much less importance than those of commercial banks.

The eleven central giro-institutions were established either by the savings banks alone or jointly with the respective state government. The giro-institutions assist the savings banks where the latter need the support of a centralised body (for example, trading in securities and export financing). The interrelationship between the giro-institutions and the savings banks is reflected primarily in their inter-regional and nationwide system for clearing cheques and currency and handling transfers.

¶717   Credit co-operatives

The credit co-operatives serve mainly farmers, craftsmen and small businesses, and they are of limited importance to medium-sized or large businesses. However, their central institution, the *Deutsche Genossenschaftsbank* (DG-Bank), with bond issuing capacity, is an important player in long-term lending and foreign business.

¶718   Union banks

Union banks are basically represented by the *Bank für Gemeinwirtschaft* (BfG), an entity which belongs to the universal banks (commercial business) and which stresses its independence from the trade unions which are its ultimate shareholders via *Beteiligungsgesellschaft für Gemeinwirtschaft AG* (BGAG) which acts as the holding company for the trade unions' interests in private commercial institutions.

¶719   Postal cheque system

The postal giro and postal savings banks (*Postsparkassenämter* and *Postscheck-ämter*) are part of the organisation of the Federal Post Office service, and they accept deposits on cheque accounts and on savings accounts. They do not grant loans except small overdrafts. Deposits and withdrawals can be made in every post office.

¶720   Mortgage banks

Mortgage banks extend long-term loans which are secured by mortgages, as well as long-term loans to municipalities, states and the Federal Republic of Germany. They fund these loans through the issuance and sale of bonds secured by mortgage loans and loans to public authorities.

¶721   Special purpose banks

Among those banks in Germany with special functions are the *Industrie-Kreditbank AG – Deutsche Industriebank*, which primarily provides long- and medium-term financing to small and medium-sized business which do not have access to the capital market; and the *AKA Ausfuhrkredit-Gesellschaft mbH*, which provides medium- and long-term export financing; and *Kreditanstalt für Wiederaufbau*, which is a state-owned bank formed for the purpose of supplying West German industry with the loans necessary for its reconstruction after World War II. It extends long-term loans to small and medium-sized companies to finance capital expenditures, and it finances selected projects in developing countries.

¶722   Foreign banks

While German representative offices of foreign banks which do not engage in a banking business in Germany do not need a banking licence, such a licence is required for branch operations and German bank subsidiaries.

Initially, foreign banks set up branch operations in Germany in order to arrange for a direct Deutsche Mark clearing for their group and to support trade between their country of origin and Germany. However, they increasingly offered a wider range of banking services which finally led to extraordinary competition in this field.

As their business expanded, foreign banks also organised new German subsidiary banks or they acquired existing banks, and in such acquisitions tax considerations (availability of pre-existing net operating loss carryforwards) seem to have played a major role.

DEPOSITS AND LOANS

¶723   Types of deposits

There are three types of deposits; demand, time (or term) and savings deposits. There is no Government regulation as to maximum or minimum interest rates nor for charges to be set by the banks. This means that the terms and conditions of deposits and loans can be freely negotiated, and this field of banking is highly competitive. Saving deposits can be set up subject to the statutory minimum advance termination notice period of three months, or a longer period negotiated between the bank and the account holder of not less than six months' prior advance notice of withdrawals. Savings account holders with the statutory minimum advance notice period of three months may withdraw up to DM 2,000 during a 30-day period without prior notice. Savings certificates (*Sparbriefe*) which bear interest or which are issued at a deep discount (zero coupon savings certificates) have become important investment vehicles, and the admission of certificates of deposit, which presently is under consideration, may offer additional investment opportunities.

¶724   Money transfers

While payment by cheque (up to DM 400 per cheque guaranteed by Eurocheque card) has become more and more important, the predominant method of transferring money still is the money transfer order (*Überweisung*) where the account holder instructs his bank to transfer a specified amount to the account of another person with the same or another bank. Such money transfers can also be structured as standing orders for the periodic transfer of identical amounts to the same party (for instance, rental payments, insurance premiums, home mortgage interest) (*Dauerauftrag*).

Another method of transferring funds is the reversed money transfer (*Abbuchungsermächtigung*), under which the account holder authorises the recipient of the funds to request periodic payments from his account. This reversed money transfer is flexible as it permits the transfer of changing amounts, but for this same reason it is also more dangerous for the account holder. Nevertheless, the reverse money transfer itself will be reversed if the account holder so requests within six weeks of the withdrawal.

¶725   Types of loans

It is usual to distinguish short-term loans with a term of up to six months from medium-term loans with terms of up to four years, and from long-term loans with a maturity of more than four years.

¶725

(1) *Short-term loans*

In the order of their importance, the types of short-term loans are as follows:

(a) *Overdraft facilities.* The most common type of short-term loan in Germany is the overdraft facility. The borrower will usually take the loan only if and to the extent required from time to time. It is typical, therefore, for the degree of utilisation of overdraft facilities to show fluctuations. The borrower pays interest on the part of the loan that is actually used, and there may be a commitment fee on the unused portion of the facility.

While overdraft facilities are usually granted for a period of six months, they are prolonged as a matter of routine unless the financial position of the account holder has deteriorated. Overdraft facilities are usually secured by mortgages, security deposits, receivables or by guarantees. Due to large fluctuations of the interest rates, it has become usual for the bank to extend loans at rates which are valid until further notice only, in which case the rate can be adjusted according to the bank's costs of funds.

(b) *Trade bill discounts.* In Germany trade bill discounts are widely used because of the relatively high degree of security and liquidity that trade bills of exchange offer to lenders. In particular, trade bills of exchange can be redis-counted at the German Federal Bank if they carry at least three prime signa-tures and have a maturity of not more than three months.

Banks discount trade bills of exchange at a rate between 1 and 2 per cent above the Federal Bank's discount rate. The discount rates applied are lower for trade bills of exchange which can be discounted at the German Federal Bank than for other bills of exchange which are not eligible for rediscount.

(c) *Uncommitted money market facilities.* Uncommitted money market fa-cilities (*Nichtzugesagte Geldmarktlinien*) are regularly extended in unsecured form and the interest is calculated on a FIBOR plus basis ('Frankfurt Interbank Offered Rate').

(d) *Consumer purchase financing.* Instalment loans are granted under stan-dardised loan agreements at fixed interest rates and they provide for equal monthly repayment schedules. Because of the fixed term and fixed interest rates, they bear interest at rates well above the short-term rates (4–5 per cent higher) which provides a source of profits for retail business orientated banks.

(2) *Medium- and long-term loans*

(a) *Mortgage loans.* Mortgage loans are granted primarily by mortgage banks and savings banks; commercial banks grant mortgage loans for medium-term financing only.

¶725

Mortgage loans are secured by a lien which is registered in the land register. While a mortgage certificate can be issued, usually mortgages are created, assigned and lifted by registration in the land register only.

Mortgage loans can be granted for any term up to 30 years, although the usual term does not exceed 15 years. The amount of the mortgage loan granted by a savings bank is generally limited to 50 per cent of the appraised value of the real estate and, in the case of mortgage loans by mortgage banks, it is limited to 60 per cent of the appraised value.

Irrespective of the term of the mortgage loan, the interest rate payable may be fixed or flexible. Savings banks normally grant mortgage loans with flexible interest rates which may be changed by the bank at short notice. Mortgage banks, on the other hand, usually offer flexible rates or rates which are fixed for terms of five or ten years and which can be adjusted to the end of the period for which the interest rate is fixed.

(b) *Loans against receipt (Schuldscheindarlehen).* In the case of *Schuldscheindarlehen*, the loan is evidenced by a simple receipt in which the borrower, usually a prime company, acknowledges the receipt of a specified amount for a specified term, which is to bear interest at a specified rate which may be tied to the discount rate fixed by the German Federal Bank. Although the *Schuldscheindarlehen* usually is concluded between the bank and the borrower, banks usually place the loan with an insurance company or a pension fund, provided they are eligible by meeting certain balance sheet and security ratio conditions, and they determine how a particular *Schuldscheindarlehen* should be placed before they assume the commitment.

The *Schuldscheindarlehen* normally is represented by a simple receipt and not by promissory note, as an interest clause on a promissory note is disregarded under German law, promissory notes being by necessity discount papers. Secondly, there is a tax on bills of exchange and promissory notes (*Wechselsteuergesetz*: WStG) of DM 0.15 per DM 100 principal amount, which is levied on promissory notes but not on the simple acknowledgement of a debt. Furthermore, both lenders and borrowers can split the costs saved which could have been incurred in the case of the issuance of bonds.

(3) *Export financing*

Export financing is available in two versions, namely as loans to exporters (*Lieferantenkredite*) or loans to importers (*Bestellerkredite*). As a loan to the exporter or supplier has a negative effect on the supplier's balance sheet ratios, direct loans to the importer are the prevailing form of export financing. Both forms are eligible for coverage by the government export guarantee programme which is administered by *Hermes Kreditversicherungs-AG*. Unlike in various

¶725

other countries, this only covers country risks (transfer risks and other political risks) and commercial risks (i.e. insolvency of the importer or its failure to pay at maturity) without providing financing at subsidised rates.

Export financing at subsidised interest rates is provided by *Kreditanstalt für Wiederaufbau* (KfW) (in particular 'soft' loans at low interest rates and for long terms) and by *AKA-Ausfuhrkredit Gesellschaft mbH* (B-Plafond loans).

For loans not covered by *Hermes*, forfeit transactions have become very common, i.e. the sale of an export receivable without recourse to the previous lender and/or exporter.

(4) *Access to Euromarket*

Access to the Euromarket is restricted to banks with a presence outside the Federal Republic of Germany. This form of financing is offered at sometimes advantageous interest rates as Eurofunding is not subject to the minimum reserve requirements on deposits applicable in Germany.

NON-BANK SOURCES OF FINANCING

¶726   Insurance companies and pension funds

Insurance companies and pension funds are a major source of long-term funds, primarily in the form of *Schuldscheindarlehen* and mortgage loans (see ¶725 above).

¶727   Leasing

Leasing has become an established means of financing both for business purposes and for private purposes (in particular car leasing). While a leasing activity does not qualify as a banking activity, leasing companies not associated with a German bank are disadvantaged by discriminatory provisions as are non-resident lessors (s. 19 Trade Tax Ordinance (*Gewerbesteuerdurchführungsverordnung*: GewStDV)).

Generally, the leasing business is heavily tax-sensitive, and the terms of leasing agreements usually follow the tests accepted for tax purposes and laid down in a decree of 19 April 1971 (BStBl. 1971 I 264: full payment leasing of movable assets), a decree of 21 March 1972 (BStBl. 1972 I 181: full pay-out leasing of immovable assets), and a decree of 22 December 1974 (BB 1976, 72: non-full-payout leases of movable assets).

¶728   Factoring

Like leasing activities, factoring is not one of the banking activities defined under s. 1(1) of the Banking Act, as only the extension of loans, as opposed to the acquisition of already existing debts, constitutes a banking activity under s. 1(1)(2) of the Banking Act. Factoring is slowly growing in importance.

¶729   Venture capital financing

In recent years, venture capital has become an additional source of financing even though its contribution is still modest. Whilst some companies are controlled by or affiliated with banks, others are independent. Few of these venture capital companies view themselves as the provider of 'seed' money or start-up or first-stage financings; instead, they look more to companies that have already demonstrated the viability of their business but do not have access to the capital market.

On 12 December 1985, the Federal Government introduced a Bill to Parliament which will regulate venture capital companies (*Entwurf eines Gesetzes über Unternehmensbeteiligungsgesellschaften*: UBGG) (*Bundestagsdrucksache* X/4551). Under this Bill, venture capital companies may be organised only in the form of stock corporations with a stated equity capital of at least DM 2,000,000 which has to be paid-in in full. Such companies can invest their funds only in:

(1) shares which are neither listed nor admitted to the over-the-counter market on a German stock exchange or traded on another domestic organised market;

(2) shares which are acquired upon the exercise of subscription rights held by the company;

(3) shares in a GmbH;

(4) limited partnership interests;

(5) participations as a silent partner in enterprises whose shares are neither admitted to nor traded on the over-the-counter market of a domestic stock exchange nor traded on any other domestic organised market;

(6) subscription rights, provided the shares to which they related could have been acquired under (1) above; and

(7) shares which are issued to the company as stock dividends.

In order to qualify as a venture capital company under this Bill, the company has to commit itself, *inter alia*, to offer within eight years of its recognition as venture capital company at least three-quarters of the shares of the company to the public.

So far as the tax status of venture capital companies is concerned, the Bill is designed to treat the investor as if he had acquired the interest or participation in the target company directly and to eliminate tax-induced additional burdens. For this reason, the Bill proposes to eliminate additional wealth tax and trade tax burdens which would result from the interposition of the venture capital company between the investor and the target company. However, there are no special provisions for corporate income tax as it is fully integrated with the income tax at the shareholders' level anyway (see Chapter 5 – Taxation).

It is at this time not possible to state if and when the Bill will be enacted.

CAPITAL MARKET

¶730   Organisation of stock exchanges

There are stock exchanges in Frankfurt, Düsseldorf, Hamburg, Munich, Bremen, Hannover, Stuttgart and Berlin, the most important stock exchanges being those in Frankfurt and Düsseldorf. They are organised in accordance with the Stock Exchange Act (*Börsengesetz*) and function under charters and rules adopted by the respective stock exchange. An integration and co-ordination of the activities of the various stock exchanges is currently under review.

¶731   Trading on the stock exchange

Share prices on the stock exchanges are stipulated by state-appointed brokers (*amtliche Kursmakler*) who match buying and selling orders during the exchange session. Only banks or their representatives are admitted as members of the exchanges and are allowed to trade in officially listed shares.

Equity securities which are not listed on the stock exchange are traded in a semi-official market (*geregelter Freiverkehr*) within the stock exchange, but no official quotations are fixed.

Apart from these two markets, shares are traded through over-the-counter transactions (*ungeregelter Freiverkehr; Telephonverkehr*) mainly between banks and securities dealers.

¶732   Admission of shares in domestic corporations

The admission of securities to trading on a German stock exchange is regulated by the provisions of the Stock Exchange Act (*Börsengesetz*), as well as the rules and regulations of the respective stock exchange. The admission must be sponsored by a bank which is a member of such stock exchange, and it is effected on the basis of a prospectus. False or incomplete statements in such prospectuses may expose the issuer to claims for damages.

The prospectus must include, *inter alia*, information on the following:

- the history and corporate purpose of the company;
- the development, nominal value and classes of capital stock and their respective rates;
- substantial holdings of outside parties and references to inter-company agreements (in particular on controlling interests and profit and loss absorption agreements);
- members of management and a description of their functions;
- provisions of the articles of association which concern the convening of shareholders' meetings and voting rights of the shareholders;
- the publication of announcements to be made by the company;
- paying agents and depositories;
- appropriation of profits;
- the most recent financial statements of the company or, where applicable, consolidated financial statements dating back no more than 13 months. Should the balance sheet be older than nine months, a current financial statement and relevant data covering the current fiscal year has to be attached;
- explanations regarding all balance sheet items of substance, and, in the case of long-term liabilities, the average terms; an indication of any liabilities not shown on the balance sheet;
- substantial holdings in other companies;
- a description of business operations; and
- current business activities and prospects.

¶733   Admission of domestic bonds

Bonds must be in bearer form in order to be eligible for trading on a stock exchange, and the issuance of bearer bonds requires the prior approval of the Federal Minister of Finance (see s. 795 of the Civil Code (*Bürgerliches Gesetzbuch*: BGB) and the provisions of a specific statute promulgated thereunder). If approval is obtained, the listing procedure is similar to that for domestic equity securities. No approval under s. 795 BGB is required if foreign finance subsidiaries issue bonds which are guaranteed by the German parent companies.

¶734   Admission of foreign securities to trading on a German stock exchange

In principle, the admission of securities issued by foreign issuers is treated like the admission of domestic securities. Nevertheless, there are a few differences, and the most important difference relates to the marketability of the securities.

Because German stock corporations, as a rule, issue shares in bearer certificate form, registered shares issued by foreign corporations, as well as share certificates issued by foreign corporations which are not easily readable (such as Japanese securities certificates) must be made marketable in Germany by interposing a depository receipt issued by the *Deutsche Auslandskassenverein* (AKV) before such securities can be admitted to trading on a German stock exchange.

¶735   Activity of foreign brokers in Germany

Under s. I(1)(4) of the Banking Law, the acquisition and sale of securities for the account of another party qualifies as a banking activity. This means that foreign brokerage houses who wish to market securities traded on a foreign stock exchange will require a banking licence unless they can avoid engaging in a banking activity in a way which is considered covered by the Banking Law. In order to avoid such exposure, they have to act as a mere intermediary between the German customer and their foreign head office which merely transmits to the head office orders received from customers; they may not be involved in the execution of the transaction, and they merely transmit to the customer the confirmation and execution notice prepared by the head office abroad.

¶736   Domestic mutual funds

Domestic mutual funds are regulated by the Investment Companies Act (*Gesetz über Kapitalanlagegesellschaften*: KAGG). They are managed by a type of management company (*Kapitalanlagegesellschaft*) which can only be organised as a stock corporation (AG) or as a GmbH and which requires a banking licence under s. 1(1)(6) KWG. With the consent of the Banking Supervisory Authority, it can set up any number of separate funds which are unincorporated structures, and the certificates issued by the management company can stipulate that title to the assets of the fund (securities or real property) is held by the management in trust for the holders of the certificates or that the holders of certificates have an undivided co-ownership interest in the assets. The assets have to be kept segregated from the assets of the management company and from the assets of other funds managed by it, under the control of a custodian bank.

Domestic mutual funds must be fully open-ended and are subject to numerous investment restrictions. German resident investors must report income dividends as well as the net investment income retained by the fund, but capital gains realised by the fund are not taxed to the investor whether distributed or retained and irrespective of the holding period observed by the fund.

¶737   Foreign mutual funds

Mutual funds governed by the laws of a foreign jurisdiction are regulated by the Foreign Investment Fund Act or ForInvest Law (*Gesetz über den Vertrieb ausländischer Investmentanteile und über die Besteuerung der Erträge aus ausländischen Investmentanteilen*: AuslInvestmG) of 28 July 1969, as amended.

This statute covers two aspects, namely the registration of foreign funds with the Banking Supervisory Authority and the tax status of the fund's resident investors. The foreign mutual fund has to register with the Banking Supervisory Authority if it wishes to distribute its shares to the public in Germany. For this purpose, the foreign fund must submit to numerous restrictions and issue and publish German language prospectuses, annual and semi-annual reports, etc. In particular, the fund must stand ready to redeem its shares at their current net asset value, it may not invest in shares of other mutual funds and it has to appoint a custodian bank which controls the assets of the fund (s. 2 ForInvest Law).

German investors in the fund are treated like investors in a domestic fund if the foreign fund is registered with the Banking Supervisory Authority or if its shares are officially listed on a German stock exchange (s. 17 ForInvest Law). If these requirements are not met but the fund has appointed a German tax representative, then the fund's net investment income and its realised capital gains are taxed to the resident investors whether they are distributed or not (s. 18(1) ForInvest Law). If the fund does not appoint a German tax representative either, then the resident investor must report as taxable income not only actual distributions but also 90 per cent of the appreciation of the fund's shares during the calendar year (in any case not less than 10 per cent of the net asset value of the shares last determined during the calendar year: s. 18(3) ForInvest Law).

8 Investment Incentives

INTRODUCTION

¶801 Incentives in general

Domestic and foreign companies establishing new or modernising existing plants may be eligible for a variety of subsidies, particularly cash grants and subsidised loans. The main criteria of an investment project to qualify for incentives are:

(1) the number of new jobs;

(2) the amounts to be invested; and

(3) the geographic area.

In addition, incentives in the form of subsidised loans are available upon start-ups or enlargements of small businesses (so-called *Mittelstandsförderung*, 'promotion of small or medium-sized businesses').

Incentives are granted, *inter alia*, by the following German authorities:

(1) the Federal Ministry of Economics, especially for investments in areas in need of promotion, as well as for the promotion of small or medium-sized businesses;

(2) the Federal Ministry of Research and Technology for investments in qualifying research projects;

(3) the state governments for certain areas in need of promotion;

(4) the municipality, which may grant low utility rates and provide cheap land and free construction of road and rail connections;

(5) the West Berlin Government for investments in West Berlin.

Government grants are available only upon prior application, which must include detailed information. Such application must be made before the actual start of the investment project as subsequent financing is not possible.

INCENTIVES AT FEDERAL LEVEL

¶802   In general

Three major laws govern the Federal incentive programme: the *Investitionszu-lagengesetz* (Investment Allowances Act: InvZulG), the *Zonenrandförde-rungsgesetz* (law for promotion of areas next to Czechoslovakia and the German Democratic Republic), and the *Berlinförderungsgesetz* (West Berlin Promotion Act).

¶803   Investitionszulagengesetz

The InvZulG provides investment grants for investments in certain geographic areas or for certain types of investment.

(1) *Investments in areas in need of promotion*

Pursuant to s. 1 of InvZulG the *Investitionszulage* is available for investments in so-called 'areas in need of promotion' and consists of a non-repayable cash grant which amounts to 8.75 per cent of the costs of depreciable fixed movable and immovable assets. Such assets must be purchased for the purpose of setting up, extending, converting or streamlining manufacturing operations. The assets in question have to remain in the plant of the taxpayer for at least three years after the date of purchase or production.

The *Investitionszulage* amounts to 10 per cent in the case of investments in areas close to Czechoslovakia or the German Democratic Republic. It does not constitute income under German income tax and does not reduce the basis for depreciation allowances.

A formal application must be filed with the competent tax office within nine months of the close of the fiscal year in which the qualifying investment has been made. According to s. 1(1) of the InvZulG, the *Investitionszulage* is based upon a certificate which is issued by the Federal Ministry of Economics in consultation with the competent state authorities (in Munich, for example, the *Regierung von Oberbayern*). This certificate is granted if the investment is set up in a region in need of promotion, is worthy of promotion under aspects of national economy, and corresponds to the aims and principles of national planning.

In addition to such criteria and the number of job facilities, the amount of the investment and, in particular, the company's own funds are of significance. The administrative authorities tend to avoid subsidising projects which are ill-founded. An indication of a sound foundation is the company's own investment (*Eigenmittel*). This term is not identical with nominal capital or equity under

¶802

corporate law. Rather, it is a financial term of art and is meant to be distinguished from outside financing, in particular secured financing (loans granted on the basis of mortgages, collateral or passage of title to assets such as equipment and inventory). To a certain extent, loans of family members or affiliate companies would qualify as *Eigenmittel*, unless they were secured in a privileged way.

(2) *Investments in R & D facilities and/or in energy supply facilities*

Investments in research and development facilities qualify for a special *Investitionszulage* which amounts to up to 20 per cent for the initial DM 500,000 and to 7.5 per cent for amounts exceeding that level. Investment for certain energy supply devices, such as power plants or heating plants, qualify for an *Investitionszulage* of 7.5 per cent which – as opposed to any other type of *Investitionszulage* available at Federal level – may be granted in addition to the *Investitionszulage* for investments in areas in need of promotion or in R & D facilities.

In addition, the Federal Ministry of Research and Technology may grant investment cash subsidies of up to 50 per cent of the costs of an investment in the case of special research and development projects which benefit national interests.

¶804   Zonenrandförderungsgesetz

Under the *Zonenrandförderungsgesetz* investors in border areas next to West Germany's eastern border (which is generally in need of special promotion) are eligible for special, accelerated depreciation allowances of up to 50 per cent (movables) or 40 per cent (immovables) of the costs of acquisition or construction of fixed assets in the year of acquisition or construction and in the four subsequent years. Such tax advantages are available in addition to the 10 per cent *Investitionszulage* discussed at ¶803 above.

¶805   Berlinförderungsgesetz

A special *Investitionszulage* is available for investments in West Berlin. It amounts to 25 per cent of the total investments in movable fixed assets of production plants and 15 per cent for immovable assets of such plants. Investments for data processing or energy supply facilities qualify for an *Investitionszulage* of up to 25 per cent (movables) or 20 per cent (immovables) of the costs of acquisition or construction of fixed assets. In the case of investments in R & D facilities, cash grants for up to 40 per cent of the investment for the equipment are available for the initial DM 500,000 and 30 per cent of the amounts exceeding that level. In addition, there are favourable ERP-loans (European Recovery Programme) as well as special depreciation allowances of up to 75 per cent of the investment.

Further, corporate tax rates in West Berlin are lower than elsewhere in Germany; the same applies with regard to value added tax rates on sales from West Berlin to Germany.

Finally, the *Berlinförderungsgesetz* provides that employees working in West Berlin may opt for either an 8 per cent subsidy on their gross wages and salaries or for a 30 per cent reduction of personal income taxes.

¶806   Promotion of small and medium-sized businesses

The promotion of small and medium-sized businesses mainly consists of subsidised loans with, in principle, up to two years of grace. In order to qualify for such loans the applicant has to demonstrate professional experience as well as the proper foundation of his investment.

INCENTIVES AT STATE LEVEL

¶807   Regional Promotion Programme

Under the *Regionale Förderungsprogramm* (Regional Promotion Programme), incentives are available at state level for certain less-developed regions. Among those less-developed regions several sites, called *Schwerpunkt* sites, have been elected to receive most of the subsidies that are available at state level.

The subsidies available at state level are granted in addition to the Federal *Investitionszulage* (see ¶803 above) and are, in general, composed of either a cash grant (*Investitionszuschß*) or a subsidised loan (*zinsbegünstigtes Darlehen*). The amount of the cash grant (as well as the amount of the loan, its interest rate, and its maturity) depends on the type of investment (mere conversion, rationalisation of a manufacturing plant, extension of a plant, or establishment of a new plant) and the criteria indicated at ¶801 above, with special emphasis on the geographic area of the investment (i.e. whether a *Schwerpunkt* site or not).

¶808   Cash grants

As a rule, financial assistance in the form of cash grants is limited to between 10 and 20 per cent of the eligible cost of an investment (the Federal *Investitionszulage* of 8.75 per cent or 10 per cent, plus a cash grant of up to 10 per cent).

¶806

The eligible costs for the cash grant available at state level include the purchase price of the real estate for the construction of the plant.

The maximum assistance is available in the case of the establishment of a new plant and amounts to 25 per cent of the costs of the investment (Federal *Investitionszulage* of 10 per cent, plus a 15 per cent cash grant available at state level). The cash grant at state level, however, is not exempt from German income tax.

¶809 Subsidised loans

Financial assistance in the form of subsidised loans generally should not exceed 40 to 50 per cent of the eligible cost of an investment (including land, buildings and equipment). As a rule, such loans are granted at a rate of 3.5 per cent and for a term of up to 15 years; in exceptional cases up to 20 years (including up to three years of grace).

¶810 Other incentives

Other types of financial assistance include state guarantees in case the investor cannot provide adequate security acceptable to his bank, or employment incentives in the form of training grants.

9 Labour Law and Social Security

INTRODUCTION

¶901 Overview

In West Germany there is no unitary law governing the individual and collective aspects of employment. The large volume of labour legislation, regulations and case law notwithstanding, labour/management relations are primarily moulded by collective bargaining between trade unions and employers and, to some extent, by custom and tradition. Generally, collective agreements providing for remuneration, working conditions, work safety, and similar matters are setting standards beyond their scope of immediate application.

The regulation of employment conditions concerning employees' safety, health and welfare, and the implementation of laws with regard to work permits, fall under the domain of the Federal Ministry for Labour and Social Welfare and its counterparts at state level. The National Employment Office with state and regional agencies is a part of the Federal Ministry. The powers of this administration to ensure compliance with labour and welfare legislation are supplemented by labour representation at shop and board level. In the case of disputes, labour and management may avail themselves of the assistance of the Labour Courts.

INDIVIDUAL LABOUR RELATIONS

¶902 Statutory and contractual provisions

(1) *Sources and hierarchy of law*

An employment agreement is seen as a special form of service agreement which is regulated by the Civil Code ('BGB'). The provisions of the BGB are applicable to all types of employment relationships to the extent not supplanted by special legislation.

The Commercial Code ('HGB') covers the legal relationship between the commercial employer and the commercial employee (*Handlungsgehilfe*), as well as the provisions concerning commercial agents (*Handelsvertreter*). The provisions on the latter are not regarded as part of labour law and are dealt with separately under Chapter 3 on 'Commercial Intermediaries'.

Trade law ('GewO') is concerned with protective labour provisions, e.g. the obligations of the employer to provide a safe and healthy work place and certain restrictions on freedom of contract, which will be discussed later in connection with specific provisions of selected laws concerning, for instance, minimum wages, minimum notice periods, vacations etc.

It is characteristic of labour law that, in addition to the individual labour contract, there are some forms of collective agreements which apply to all workers on a national or regional basis, or at least to contracts concluded between members of the union and members of an employers' association, and which are superimposed on the individual labour contract.

Furthermore, since the legislators (as in most jurisdictions) cannot always keep up with development, case law has become an important source of labour law and special Labour Courts have been set up to provide for the reasonably fast and inexpensive settlement of disputes between workers and their employers. On the lower level, a professional judge is assisted by two laymen, one appointed by the employees' side and the other by the employers' side. There are nominal court fees; the employee usually can get free legal advice and assistance in court from his union and, at first instance, the employer has to bear the costs of his own counsel even if he should win the case.

Generally, the Labour Courts are sympathetically disposed toward employees, and the employee sues with the knowledge that he will get a speedy first hearing and that the court will listen attentively to his cause.

(2) *Written or oral contract*

In West Germany, there is no specific formal requirement for labour contracts, except for agreements with apprentices which have to be in writing or except for instances where a collective bargaining agreement imposes the obligation to reduce a labour agreement to writing. In these instances oral agreements will be considered void and unenforceable.

In all other instances, a labour contract concluded orally will be binding on both the employer and the worker, and where agreement on a specific aspect has not been reached or where an agreement on such aspect cannot be proved, the statutory minimum terms will be used to fill the gap. Thus, all workers and employees in West Germany have a contract to which the minimum standards imposed by statutes or developed in case law apply, unless there is an express provision which is more favourable to the worker or employee. It is nevertheless recommended that all such agreements should be put in writing, if only in order to be able to prove the contents of the agreement if a dispute should arise. In particular, if the parties want to provide for a trial period, reassignment or relocation, or a non-competition commitment (which provision would deviate from labour law), a written document would be required.

(3) International relations

For the regulations applying to alien employees (namely the requirements for a residence and work permit), see Chapter 14 on 'Personal Business'.

As restated by the Federal High Court for Labour Matters ('BAG'), as from February 1985 German law recognises the choice of a foreign law insofar as employment contracts are concerned, provided the employment has a substantial connection with the foreign law. This test would be met where, for example, the foreign law governs the registered place of the employer's corporation or the territory where the services have to be rendered. On the other hand, in the absence of an express choice of law clause, the German Labour Courts tend to apply German law whenever local personnel have been employed to work and have taken up residence in Germany, even if the employer is a foreign corporation.

¶903   Types of employees

(1) Salaried employees

Salaried employees (*Angestellte*) or 'white-collar' workers perform predominantly mental work (e.g. office employees) and their salary is usually paid by the month. They are often difficult to distinguish from *Arbeiter* (see below).

(2) Wage earners

Wage earners (*Arbeiter*) or 'blue-collar' workers are all employees who are not *Angestellte*. They are usually paid by the hour or week.

Apart from the form of remuneration, the distinction between salaried employees and wage earners is still significant with regard to the length of notice periods (s. 622 BGB), representation on the shop floor (s. 6 Shop Constitution Law: BetrVG), collective bargaining agreements and social security systems which are set up separately for *Arbeiter* ('RVO') and *Angestellte* ('AVG').

Advanced technologies and improved training programmes, however, constantly cause a proportionally higher demand for salaried employees than for wage earners. Those wage earners who are not yet promoted to the level of

Angestellte are eager to avail themselves of the social benefits and legal advantages the latter category may have. This trend is backed by case law which readily finds discriminatory aspects of statutes and regulations exclusively dealing with wage earners. In a more recent decision (1982) the Federal Constitutional Court held that, for example, the use of an age formula (25 years of age for salaried employees and 35 years of age for wage earners) as a criterion for extending notice periods depending on age *and* length of service is discriminatory against *Arbeiter* and, thus, null and void in that respect.

(3) *Executives*

A separate labour group is formed by management or supervisory employees or executives (*Leitende Angestellte*). This group, which has formed its own Association of Executives (*Union Leitender Angestellter*: ULA), covers 1.5 per cent of all employees.

For many years case law and legal scholars have discussed the concept of *Leitender Angestellter* and who should belong to the group, as there exists neither a statutory definition of the term nor is its meaning necessarily the same in every branch of the law. By definition of law it has only been made clear that officers of stock corporations (*Vorstand*) or companies with limited liability (*Geschäftsführer*) form the top of the group, which leaves a vast majority of borderline cases for definition by case law. As labour legislation protecting, for instance, employees against unfair dismissal or working overtime, or which grants representation on the shop floor, is not applicable to *Leitende Angestellte*, the proper distinction is a matter for major concern with regard to decisions required in day-to-day business.

As a starting point the qualification contained in s. 5(3) BetrVG may be used, according to which *Leitende Angestellte* must be either:

(a) authorised, at their sole discretion, to hire and fire; or

(b) granted a general power of representation (*Generalvollmacht*) or signing power (*Prokura*); or

(c) entrusted, due to their particular experience and knowledge, with management functions to be exercised essentially at their own discretion.

Where one of these tests is met it is possible to determine whether the scope of responsibility and power of the executive is, if not identical, at least substantially similar to the status of a corporate officer.

¶903

¶904 Employment contracts

(1) *Contract for a fixed term*

Labour law generally does not view fixed-term labour contracts favourably. For this reason such contracts are used under the following circumstances only:

(a) *Probation period.* At the beginning of a labour relationship, a probation period can be agreed upon for a fixed period of time, with the effect that at its end it is terminated automatically without the necessity of giving notice, unless a new and final labour contract is concluded for an indefinite period of time. During the term of the probation period, the agreement can normally be terminated by either party without that party being required to state a reason therefor and on short notice, i.e. one month to the end of a calendar month for employees and two weeks for workers.

Unless otherwise provided for in a collective bargaining agreement (they usually restrict the probation period to a maximum of three months), a probationary term of up to six months is considered as the legal maximum. After a term of six months the employees are protected by a special statute against unfair dismissals.

(b) *Special assignments.* Limited labour assignments will as a rule be recognised as a genuine reason for fixing a term. This will be the case, for instance, if someone is hired for a specific event, such as work on a trade fair, or the shooting of a motion picture or the preparation of a TV show.

The Labour Courts look with particular disfavour upon extensions of such contracts, especially in all instances where there are multiple consecutive extensions, as such actions suggest a scheme designed to avoid mandatory provisions for the protection of employees. A decision of the Federal High Court for Labour Matters ('BAG') of 1982 seems, however, to permit consecutive agreements for fixed terms in the case of employees of the German Public Radio and Television Stations.

(c) *Interim regulations.* With effect from 1 May 1985, the German Federal Parliament introduced the *Beschäftigungsförderungsgesetz* 1985 (Law on the Advancement of Employment 1985: BSchFG 1985) with the purpose of reducing the current unemployment rate (8.5 per cent). Under the new law (s. 1 BSchFG 1985) it is now possible, until 1 January 1990, to contract term employments without giving any justification, provided that:

(i) the employment term does not exceed 18 months or 24 months, if the employer established himself not more than six months ago, and if the employer does not employ more than 20 employees; and

(ii) such fixed-term employment is agreed only once with the same employee and cannot be extended; and

¶904

(iii) the employee is either newly hired by the employer or immediately upon completion of his vocational training with such employer, provided that unlimited employment is not available.

(2) *Contracts of indefinite duration*

Most employment agreements are concluded for an indefinite period of time and most of the protective legislation, collective bargaining agreements and case law are concerned with them.

(3) *Essence of contractual obligations*

The basic obligations of the parties under employment contracts are the employee's obligation to offer his services and to work diligently during working hours and the employer's duty to provide safe and healthy working conditions and to pay the salary and other agreed emoluments, such as vacation pay, Christmas bonuses, etc. The employee remains entitled to receive salary even if he should be prevented from performing his services by reasons which are in the employer's domain, even if they are beyond the employer's control, and even if such reasons are in the employee's domain but beyond his control. The most important case concerns the employee's sickness, which is dealt with under ¶912 below.

(4) *Assignment by operation of law*

The employment agreement survives the sale of the business in which the individual is employed. In such a case the provisions of s. 613a BGB apply as follows:

'(1) If a plant or a portion of a plant is transferred to another owner, the transferor assumes the rights and duties of the employment relationship existing at the time of the transfer.

(2) The transferor is jointly liable with the transferee for the obligations referred to in paragraph (1) to the extent that these exist prior to the time of transfer and are due prior to the expiration of one year from the date of transfer. If such obligations became due after the date of transfer, the transferor is liable only to the extent which corresponds to the portion which accrued prior to the date of transfer.

(3) Paragraph (2) is not applicable when a corporation ceases to exist, through merger or reorganization. Section 8 of the Reorganization Act in the version of November 6, 1969 shall remain unaffected.'

These provisions do not apply, of course, if only the shares in the employer corporation are sold to another party, as such a share transfer does not affect the corporation and its employment relationship with its employees as such. On the other hand, if there is a transfer of all the assets of a business or of a part thereof, then s. 613a BGB cannot be circumvented; it is a mandatory provision and the status of other arrangements between transferor and transferee regarding employment matters would be invalid and unenforceable. This concerns, for instance, an arrangement under which the transferor agrees to terminate the agreements with any workers and employees the transferee does not want to take over. The sale of a business is not recognised as sufficient cause for the termination of an employment agreement. The BAG has held that these rules apply in the case of the bankruptcy of the employer as well.

Furthermore, the reverse situation is also regulated. An agreement between transferor and transferee is valid but unenforceable if the transferor agrees not to hire specific workers or employees that the transferee wants to take over and where he is afraid that they might terminate their employment with him and return to the former owner (s. 75(f) HGB).

¶905   Termination

(1) *Procedure*

Notice of termination is an unilateral declaration given by one party with the intent to cancel the employment relationship from a certain date, which declaration has to be received by the other party. Prior to giving notice the shop council has to be notified of the employer's intention (see ¶915 below).

Unless agreed otherwise by contract, or unless provided in a collective bargaining agreement, notice of termination may be given verbally. As the notifying party has the burden of proof with regard to the time of receipt of notice, however, the statement should be made in the presence of a third person, or it should be formally handed over by having the other party sign the duplicate for receipt. Alternatively, the notice of termination may be served by a bailiff in accordance with the Civil Procedure Code ('ZPO'), or be communicated by registered mail. As a registered letter is considered as 'received' only when handed over to the addressee (and not upon notification by the post office of the letter waiting for collection) a faster mode of transmission (e.g. hand delivery) should be considered when time is of the essence.

The notice period begins on the day following receipt of the notice. In the case of a one-month notice period notice has to be given, i.e. received, on the last day of the preceeding month. In the case of a six weeks' notice period to the end of a calendar quarter, notice has to be received on 17 February (18 February respectively), 19 May, 19 August and 19 November.

If the last day of the notice period is a Saturday, Sunday or statutory legal holiday (which is determined by state law), notice has to be received on either of these days; receipt on one of the following days would be considered as late.

When giving notice corporate employers must be represented by their statutory legal representative (e.g. managing director) or an agent (e.g. personnel manager) generally or individually authorised for this function. Unless the person has express or apparent authority, he should be furnished with a power of attorney in writing (personally signed by the officer of the company), as verbal authorisation may be rejected as insufficient.

Statutory law requires information about the reasons for termination only in the case of extraordinary dismissals. The employer is generally considered to have the same duty in the case of ordinary notices in order to allow the employee to evaluate the chances of arguing the dismissal in the Labour Court.

(2) Regular notice

In principle, all employment agreements are subject to ordinary notice. The right to give notice of termination may be restricted by statutory law, individual contracts or collective bargaining agreements. In particular, the Law Concerning Protection against Unfair Dismissal ('KSchG') restricts the freedom of the employer very extensively: for the vast majority of employment relationships it seems safe to state that the employer has to observe not only the applicable notice period but also an additional element – in legal terms styled 'social justification' – in order to allow effective termination of employment.

(3) Statutory notice periods

Except in cases of 'severe cause' (*wichtiger Grund*) an employer may terminate a contract of unlimited duration only by giving advance notice. The minimum notice periods are now contained in s. 622 BGB, with the exception of:

   (a) maritime personnel (ss. 62 et seq. *Seemannsgesetz*);

   (b) long-term employed (ss. 1, 2 *Angestelltenkündigungsschutzgesetz*) and apprentices (s. 15(2) No. 2 *Berufsbildungsgesetz*).

Section 622 BGB draws a line between *Angestellte* (employees) and *Arbeiter* (workers), which is a significant example of the traditional distinction referred to at ¶903 above.

(a) *For employees.* Irrespective of age and term of employment, employees have to observe a notice period of six weeks before the end of a calendar quarter (s. 622(1) BGB).

For the employer the same minimum notice period is mandatory (s. 622(1) BGB); in cases where more than two employees (except apprentices) are employed, the notice period is extended as follows, it being understood that any term of service expiring prior to the date the employee reaches 25 years of age will not be counted:

¶905

Minimum term of service	Minimum age of employee	Length of notice to end of calendar quarter
5 years	30 years	3 months
8 years	30 years	3 months
	33 years	4 months
10 years	30 years	3 months
	33 years	4 months
	35 years	5 months
12 years	30 years	3 months
	33 years	4 months
	35 years	5 months
	37 years	6 months

It should be noted that such statutory extensions of the notice period work to the benefit of the employee. Thus, if the employment contract provides for a six weeks' notice period for both sides, the employee may rely thereon even after five years of service, while the employer will have to give three months notice before the end of a quarter if the employee is 30 years of age or older.

(b) *For workers.* The provisions regarding the giving of notice to or by workers are to be found in s. 622(2) BGB. Basically, the period for giving notice is two weeks, both for the employer and the worker. As with employees, the period of service in the same firm or plant extends the statutory period, although in the case of workers this applies only from the age of 35, as follows:

Minimum term of service	Minimum age of worker	Length of notice
5 years	40 years	1 month to the end of a month
10 years	45 years	2 months to the end of a month
20 years	55 years	3 months to the end of calendar quarter

These statutory periods can be extended or shortened by collective bargaining agreements which, it must be emphasised, play a major role in German industrial relations. Such shorter notice periods can be extended to non-union members in the same field if it is individually agreed upon by the parties (s. 622(3) BGB).

¶905

Although the age factors discussed above still apply, careful consideration must be given to the Constitutional Court Decision of 1982 (see ¶903). In Autumn 1985 the Social Democrats introduced a Bill in the Federal Parliament according to which the scheme of extended notice periods for employees will also be applicable to workers. Until the Federal Legislator has harmonised the divergent age levels for workers (35 years) and employees (25 years), it may be advisable to allow workers more favourable treatment in case of termination, i.e. to apply the longer notice periods relating to employees.

(4) *Contractual notice periods*

It is accepted that the provisions referred to above reflect the statutory minimum. The periods can be extended by individual agreement or, where applicable, by collective bargaining agreement. Of course, when an employment relationship is to be dissolved, both parties can agree on a shorter period.

A notice period shorter than the statutory minimum may be individually agreed upon if the employee is engaged (e.g. for temporary assistance) for a period of not more than three months (s. 622(4) BGB) or where the employment is entered into on a trial basis as explained at ¶904 above.

On the other hand, the parties may agree to have the notice period extended for both sides; the period for the employee, however, may be no longer than for the employer (s. 622(5) BGB), and in no case may the employee be bound for more than five years (s. 624 BGB).

(5) *Termination for cause*

Section 626(1) BGB provides that either party may terminate an employment contract without observing any period of notice if the other is responsible for a serious cause (*wichtiger Grund*):

> 'The employment relationship can be terminated by either party for cause without a notice period, if facts are present, by reason of which, with consideration of all the circumstances of the individual case and by weighing the interests of both contract parties, it cannot be expected of the party terminating that he continues the employment relationship to the end of the normal notice period or to the agreed end of the employment relationship.'

The law stipulates, however, that the contract may no longer be terminated when the act or omission giving rise to the dismissal has been known to the terminating party for more than two weeks prior to termination (s. 622(2) BGB). This period begins at the time the individual thereby entitled to give notice learns of the conclusive facts justifying the extraordinary notice.

'Conclusive knowledge' is deemed to be present if the facts are or, as a result of thorough investigation, have or may have become clear. Such investigation must start immediately after facts have come to light which raise suspicions

¶905

rendering the continuation of the employment until the end of the ordinary notice period difficult. Provided the relevant facts have been established, or the employee has admitted the charge, further investigation will not prevent the two-week period from running.

Where the extraordinary dismissal is based on a permanent and continuing breach of contract (e.g. unexcused absence), the period will run from the time the action causing the breach ceases. If notice is based on repeated breaches of contract, the period will commence upon the occurrence of the most recent breach, provided the charges are corresponding or similar (e.g. various instances of embezzlement by a bookkeeper), and the earlier instances may be used to establish the case. Otherwise, if the charges are neither identical nor similar (e.g. driving of company car under influence of alcohol as well as cheating on expense records) and no action has been taken on the earlier charge within the two-week period, these facts shall not be admitted when considering the merits of the case built on the more recent allegations.

The 'person entitled to give notice', i.e. the individual whose conclusive knowledge of the relevant facts shall be deemed decisive, is the superior in charge who is authorised by the company to give notice of termination of employment. It is debatable to what extent this person is responsible for 'imputed knowledge', i.e. for information not relayed to him but processed by third parties within the employer's organisation. According to more recent case law a third party's information shall suffice to constitute knowledge within the meaning of s. 626 BGB if, contrary to his duty, he does not report to his superior immediately, or timely reporting is delayed by internal administrative shortcomings.

Upon demand, the employer terminating the employment must submit to the employee, without delay and in writing, the cause for termination (s. 626(2) BGB).

German case law shows numerous examples of the kinds of actions or omissions which may justify termination of employment with immediate effect. The underlying principle is that the party giving notice should be able to prove that in the light of the serious cause any further continuation of the employment relationship, even during the ordinary notice period, is unacceptable.

Among the actions that may constitute grounds for immediate discharge for serious cause are the submitting of false certificates or diplomas, persistent and intentional refusal to work, or accepting kickbacks or bribes.

The Federal Labour Court has refused to permit an individual's contract to stipulate certain grounds which will be conclusively considered as 'serious cause'. Grounds for serious cause inserted in a contract may, however, indicate the kind of obligations the parties have deemed particularly significant and, thus, be useful when it comes to weighing the mutual interests of both parties.

¶905

(6) *Protection against unfair dismissal*

(a) *Protected employees.*   The basic rule is that giving notice without serious cause to an employee who has worked in the same firm or plant for more than six months is legally ineffective if it is socially unjustified (para. 1(1) KSchG).

Since the former minimum age limit of eighteen was abolished in 1976, the Code protects all employees including part-timers. It also applies to executives but not to corporate officers (board members, managing directors) or legal representatives of partnerships or other associations.

The law is only applicable to *Betriebe* with more than five regular employees (excluding apprentices). The term *Betrieb* (firm or plant or shop) in German law in general, and under the KSchG in particular, describes an independent organisational unit within one enterprise (*Unternehmen*), or belonging to several enterprises, which employs the business equipment and work force under the direction of the owner/manager for pursuing the business purpose defined by the controlling enterprise. Obviously, in larger organisations, where the employing shop does not meet the relevant number (six), the employee facing dismissal will attempt to come under the umbrella of the KSchG by arguing that the shop in fact lacks the organisational and managerial independence required to constitute a *Betrieb*, but must be regarded as a dependent part (*Teilbetrieb*) of a larger organisation which itself constitutes a *Betrieb* for the purpose of the KSchG.

Case law has afforded the protection provided by the Code to an employee who served with the German liaison-office of a foreign corporation which had only three regular employees on its domestic (German) payroll. The court took the view that the total number of the work force (world-wide, or at least in the foreign headquarters) was decisive as the liaison-office lacked the essential features of *Betrieb* and had to be regarded as a *Teilbetrieb* of the controlling enterprise.

As the *de minimis* exemption is meant to take the financial and administrative burden, being a consequence of this law, off the shoulders of small businesses, this decision would seems to be in line with what the legislature intended when introducing the Code Against Unfair Dismissal.

(b) *Social justification.*   The KSchG allows effective ordinary notice of termination only if the employer can establish 'social justification'. Social justification, within the meaning of the Code, is restricted to three lines of argument as spelled out in s. 1(2) KSchG:

> 'The termination of employment is socially unjustified if it is not caused by grounds related to (1) the person or (2) performance of the employee or (3) is not based on indispensable shop requirements which prevent the further employment of the individual . . .'.

The employer, bearing the burden of proof, has to establish the case and, if the dismissal is disputed by the employee, has to convince the Labour Court

¶905

that one of the above tests is met. Obviously, as the tests reflect a comprehensive concept of what the legislators had in mind rather than a concrete standard easy to handle in day-to-day business, attention should be paid to the vast body of case law when trying to arrive at a decision acceptable to both employer and employee. In essence, the tests require a review of all aspects in favour of the employee continuing employment and of the intent of the employer to effect the termination thereof. In general, the termination will be socially justified if, in the light of the existing grounds, the employer's decision can be considered as reasonable and adequate.

(i) *Personal grounds.* Personal grounds for dismissal include particular physical or mental defects, extensive absenteeism due to illness, or reduced working capacity because of old age.

If the dismissal is a result of repeated sickness of the employee, the employer, if the termination is challenged, must demonstrate that, in the light of the employee's medical record, repeated instances of further illness are to be expected in the future.

Termination on the grounds of illness is socially justified only if all factors to be considered on the part of the employer (such as extra costs for substitutes, availability of replacements at short notice, the willingness of the work force to work overtime when the individual concerned is on sick leave, etc.) allow the employer to come to a decision which is not to the detriment of the employee.

According to the statistics of the statutory health insurance scheme ('RVO'), sick leave exceeding not more than 6 to 7 per cent of annual working time is regarded as normal. As the laws request the employer to continue salary payments in the case of sick leave up to six weeks, it seems that the Federal Legislature itself considers up to 13 per cent time-off reasonable (base: 230 annual working days). Consequently, case law is only prepared to consider illness as a ground for termination if, on average during the last three years, the sick leave taken by the employee exceeds 14 per cent of his regular working time.

(ii) *Performance.* Among the reasons derived from the behaviour of the employee that may constitute social justification are embezzlement, working for a competitor, organising a wild cat strike, persistent and intentional refusal to work or to work properly, inexcusable absenteeism and faulty performance; it being understood, however, that a substantially lower level of lack of performance will be required than in extraordinary dismissal cases.

In numerous cases, the employer neglects to prove a history of attempts to secure the proper fulfilment by the employee of his contractual duties by warning him with regard to shortcomings prior to giving notice of termination. This duty to give advance warning, combined with the reminder that termination of employment will be considered unless the employee's attitude changes

¶905

drastically (*Abmahnung*), has been stressed by the Federal High Court for Labour Matters over the last few years and should now be considered as a prerequisite for establishing justifiable cause based on the non- or poor performance of the employee. The *Abmahnung* may be regarded as superfluous and may be omitted only where the behaviour of the employee is obviously unacceptable (e.g. cheque fraud) or where the intervention of the employer prior to notice of termination could not be reasonably expected (e.g. suspicion of the commital of a crime).

(iii) *Business reorganisation.* A dismissal will be socially justified if the grounds for it are due to changes in the employer's business organisation.

Business requirements which render termination unavoidable, such as a permanent lay-off due to the plant's closure, or reduction of the work force because of a shortage of orders, or corporate reorganisation in order to cut overheads and labour costs, are regarded as justifiable provided the employer's decision is based on valid commercial considerations. In this regard the Labour Court, if any, will accept as valid all motives and arguments (such as saving of costs, more convenient relocation of business activities) which exclude a merely arbitrary decision on the part of the employer.

In this context it should be stressed again, as discussed at ¶904, ('(4) *Assignment by operation of law*'), that the sale and transfer of a plant to another party is not considered as a social cause justifying a permanent lay-off, as the employee is transferred with the ongoing business to the assignee by operation of law in those cases where he is to continue employment (s. 613a BGB).

The crucial issue for determining social cause in the case of disputed dismissals due to plant reorganisation is the correct choice of the members of the work force to be made redundant. If a permanent lay-off concerns only a part of the work force, the termination of an employee or worker made redundant will be considered as socially unjustified if undue attention was paid to the personal situation of the employee (so-called 'social factors').

When applying the social 'factor-test' for selecting employees for redundancy, the employer has to consider all employees holding identical or comparable personal and technical qualifications and working in the same or similar jobs. In order to mitigate the detriments caused by a lay-off the employer must select those employees of a given category for redundancy for whom termination of employment lacks social hardship or is minimal. This selection process may require an individual to be picked who, for example, can immediately turn to a new job or can take advantage of early retirement. Social factors to be taken into consideration include age, term of employment, matrimonial status, alimony obligations (e.g. working spouse), personal assets, particularly high credit commitments (e.g. residence investment), remunerative side-lines,

¶905

workman's disability caused during the term of employment, labour market conditions and available job openings.

In practical terms this means that of, for example, two warehousemen the younger one with a shorter term of service will be made redundant and the older one who has been employed longer will stay on, in particular, as it seems to be the prevailing view among courts and legal scholars that other considerations such as performance and sick leave record may not determine the choice.

¶906   Labour Court review

(1) *Court action*

An ordinary notice of termination without social cause or, alternatively, extraordinary termination without serious cause will be null and void. The termination will become effective and binding, however, unless the employee objects by filing an action with the Labour Court (*Arbeitsgericht*) within three weeks of receiving notice of termination (ss. 4, 13(1) KSchG).

The first Labour Court hearing, which is restricted to an attempt to reconcile the matter, is set at very short notice and scheduled usually within two weeks of filing the action. If the reconciliation fails the matter goes to trial and, depending on the complications of the dispute and the evidence required, the judgment of the Labour Court at first instance may take between six and twelve months.

The unemployment rate prevailing over the last couple of years has alerted the labour force with the result that, in more than 70 per cent of cases, help is sought from the Labour Court to set a dismissal aside as unfair. The ever increasing work load of the lower Labour Court explains the tendency of legal proceedings, at least at first instance, to last even longer than mentioned above.

(2) *Labour Court decision*

At all times during the legal proceedings the Labour Court has to observe the statutory duty to reconcile the dispute (s. 57(2) *Arbeitsgerichtsgesetz*). If reconciliation should fail, the Labour Court shall:

(a) decide on the merits and render a judgment against one of the parties; or

(b) upon application of either party, decree the termination of the employment relationship and instruct the employer to make a severance payment.

(a) *Judgment on the merits.*   If the Labour Court takes the view that the termination is socially unjustified, the notice of termination shall be disregarded and the employment relationship shall continue unaffected beyond the termination date. The Code has anticipated that a judgment may be rendered or become final only long after the notice period has expired and the employee, in the meantime, may have signed up with a new employer. Section 12 KSchG affords the employee a right of first choice: He is at liberty to continue employment with the old employer and terminate his new employment by observing the applicable notice period; alternatively, he may wish to notify his old employer he does not want to take advantage of the judgment in his favour. In this case, the old employment relationship is finally terminated upon receipt of the employee's notification to discontinue. The employee has to make his choice within one week of the Labour Court judgment becoming final.

(b) *Court order for severance compensation.* If ordinary termination is socially unjustified, or if serious cause allowing extraordinary termination with immediate effect is absent, the parties can nevertheless achieve the dissolution of the employment relationship at the end of the applicable notice period if either of them submits an application to the Labour Court prior to the end of the final hearing (s. 9 KSchG).

Whether such application is heard depends on the applicant. The request of an employee is readily admissible. The employer's attitude as shown by the notice of termination and his defence of the Labour Court action usually allows the employee to argue that it should be considered unreasonable to keep him on the payroll against his will.

The test the employer's application for dissolution of employment by court order has to meet is somewhat more stringent as the court has to be convinced that there is no chance of mutually beneficial co-operation of the parties in the future. In this regard reference may be made to any instances of further lack of proper performance which occurred after the original notice was issued.

In any case, irrespective of the applicant, an application will only be granted where there is severance compensation in favour of the employee as the employer's notice of termination is regarded as null and void. If the motion is accepted, the employment relationship will be terminated at the end of the applicable notice period by court order, which also fixes the amount of the redundancy benefit in accordance with statutory guidelines.

According to s. 10 KSchG, the severance benefit may represent an amount of up to 12 months' salary and may be increased to 15 months' salary in the case of an employee aged 50 with a term of employment of 15 years and, further, to 18 months' salary in the case of an employee aged 55 with a term of service of 20 years.

Within this frame the exact figure of the severance compensation is determined on a case-by-case basis, taking into consideration the merits of the case

¶906

as well as the grounds submitted for the dissolution by court order. As a rule of thumb it seems safe to say that, on average, severance benefits equal between one half and one month's salary per year of employment.

(3) Severance agreement

Obviously, the legal terms in question, 'social justification' on the one hand and 'serious cause' on the other, have their equivalents in other legal systems, being drafted to cover the wide range of cases which make the outcome of Labour Court litigation, at least at times, unpredictable. Further, in view of the length of legal proceedings, and bearing in mind that lower Labour Court decisions may be appealed to the higher Labour Court (*Landesarbeitsgericht*) and, under certain circumstances, to the Federal High Court for Labour Matters (*Bundesarbeitsgericht*), the uncertainty resulting therefrom may prevent the parties from implementing their plans for the future.

In the light of these obstacles, it is not surprising that more than 90 per cent of all unfair dismissal cases are not contested, but are settled, either in court by court order or, more often, out of court by mutual agreement. If settlement is reached by out-of-court negotiations the parties may request to have it recorded before the Labour Court. A court-recorded settlement is enforceable like a final court judgment.

The inclination of parties to resolve labour disputes by mutually acceptable arrangements is favoured by the German Income Tax Act ('EStG'). According to s. 3, No. 9 EStG, severance payments of up to DM 24,000 are income tax exempt. This ceiling is increased to DM 30,000 for workers or employees aged 50 with a term of service of at least 15 years and to DM 36,000 for individuals aged 55 and a term of service of at least 20 years. For the balance of the severance benefits exceeding these limits a 50 per cent reduced tax rate may be available (ss. 34, 24 EStG).

(4) Employment pending court decision

Another incentive for resolving the dispute rapidly (i.e. to negotiate a severance agreement) is the constitutional right of the employee to furnish his services in kind, i.e. to insist on actual employment and to continue his job even after he has received ordinary notice of termination until the end of the notice period. If the employer does not comply with this basic right the employee may seek relief via an injunction.

The employer may be entitled to suspend the employee from rendering further service only for valid reasons, e.g. the alleged act (such as suspicion of embezzlement) has destroyed all confidence and trust in the employee or the

¶906

employer has to protect his future business (no further customer calls by a field service representative). However, although legally suspended, the employee shall remain entitled to receive his regular remuneration until the end of the notice period (s. 615 BGB).

Outside the scope of s. 102(5) BetrVG and s. 1(2) KSchG – non-existence of shop council or non-intervention of existing shop council (cf. ¶915 ((3)(e) *Dismissal of individual employees*)) – it has been widely disputed in case law and by legal scholars whether a right to post-notice employment exists. The situation has been clarified by the BAG in a decision of February 1985. In essence, the BAG denies the right of an employee to demand strict performance of his job assignment during the term following expiry of the notice period until the Labour Court decision is announced. If the lower Labour Court, however, grants the employee's motion and sets the termination aside as null and void, the employer is required to re-employ the worker for the time the judgment subsists. Thus, unless the judgment is overturned on appeal the employee is entitled to continued employment even before the case has been finally decided.

¶907   Mass dismissal

The labour market is controlled and monitored by Federal agencies at regional (Labour Office) and state level (State Labour Office) in order to minimise unemployment. For this reason the employer has to notify the Labour Office (*Arbeitsamt*) and the State Labour Office (*Landesarbeitsamt*) of so-called mass dismissals (*Massenentlassungen*).

(1) *Notification of Labour Office*
By definition (s. 17 KSchG), a mass dismissal exists any time an employer dismisses, within any given time of 30 calendar days:

(a) six or more employees (and/or workers) in a shop with more than 20 but less than 60 employees;

(b) 10 per cent or at least 25 employees in a shop with at least 60 and fewer than 500 employees; or

(c) at least 30 employees in a shop with at least 500 regular employees.

In order to meet this 30-calendar-days test neither the day when notice is given or received nor the length of the notice period is relevant; only the last day of the employment relationship. Thus, an employer with a work force coming within (a) above (more than 20 but less than 60 employees) and who pares down operations towards the end of a calendar year (31 December) would have to notify the *Arbeitsamt* having jurisdiction for his place of business if six or more employees receive notice of termination effective on 31 December. Obviously, compliance with the notification requirement may be avoided by phasing out operations in such a way that, for example, never more than five employees finish their job within a 30-calendar-days period but leave on the final day of the succeeding calendar months (31 December, 31 January etc.).

The notification required works as a time bar (*Sperrfrist*) as the termination of employment will not become effective within one month from the day the Labour Office was notified thereof. For the purpose of controlling the unemployment rate the State Labour Office has the discretion to extend the time bar to two months. Usually, this discretion is only exercised under exceptional circumstances, such as a substantial number of lay-offs in a geographical area or a business branch with a rate of unemployment already above average.

Provided the last day of employment falls within the time bar the employment relationship will be automatically extended by the unexpired balance thereof, i.e. in the above example notification would have to be received by the Labour Office on 30 November for the (basic one month) time bar to expire on 30 December in order to leave the last day of employment (31 December) unaffected thereby. Alternatively, if due to late notification of the Labour Office the time bar would only expire on 15 January, the employment would automatically be extended beyond 31 December to this date. Thus, prompt notification of the Labour Office, which is within the control of the employer, is essential in order to avoid an extension of notice periods by the mechanism of the law.

(2) *Notification of State Labour Office*

In addition to and apart from the notification of the Labour Office the employer has to report to the president of the State Labour Office in accordance with s. 8 of the Law Concerning Advancement of Employment (*Arbeitsförderungsgesetz*: AFG) where he anticipates that a cut-back of business operations within the next twelve months may cause a mass dismissal as defined above. If, due to intent or gross negligence, the employer has omitted to make such a report, he may be held liable for any costs and expenses the labour agencies may incur during a period of up to six months for job training or re-recruitment of dismissed employees which, in the case of proper notification, could have been avoided.

(3) *Participation of shop council*

For the participation of the shop council in case of mass dismissals and other business reorganisation measures see ¶915 ('Shop-floor representation') below.

¶907

¶908   Obligations upon termination

(1) *Personal records*

Upon termination of employment all wage and/or salary earners and apprentices are entitled to receive their personal records, which include, *inter alia*, the performance review (*Zeugnis*), the wage withholding tax card (*Lohnsteuerkarte*), the insurance card (*Versicherungskarte*) and the certificate of employment (*Arbeitsbescheinigung*), it being understood that all papers have to be properly completed and updated to document the employee's status (e.g. with regard to length of service, vacation taken, etc.) upon leaving.

According to s. 133 AFG the *Arbeitsbescheinigung* is to be submitted to the Labour Office with information concerning the length of service, the reason for termination and the total remuneration paid (including a redundancy payment, if any). These facts will determine whether and to what extent the employee is eligible for unemployment benefits.

As it is the normal practice of German employers when hiring employees to allow their decisions to be more or less influenced by earlier performance reviews, favourable reviews are of major concern for the majority of the work force. The *Zeugnis* to which the employee is entitled (ss. 630 BGB, 73 HGB, 113 GewO, 8 BBiG) must include a job description and an assessment of his or her performance. In this context 'performance' also requires the employee's attitude *vis-à-vis* his superiors and his degree of co-operation when dealing with colleagues, etc. to be assessed.

On the one hand the review must reflect a true and fair picture of the employee's record. On the other hand, case law requires the employer to be guided by a policy of goodwill, i.e. to avoid any comments or phrases which could have an unnecessarily detrimental effect on the future career of the employee. Obviously, it is a delicate matter for an employer to draft a paper meeting this 'double-standard', in particular as future employers may hold him liable for wrong statements or misrepresentation (s. 826 BGB). In this regard it has become standard practice to use artificial language when expressing the employer's view, e.g. the phrase ' . . . he used his best endeavours . . . ' would mean that the employee did not perform satisfactorily. Therefore, performance reviews may not be accepted at face value and careful reading between the lines is usually required to fully grasp their content.

(2) *Non-competition*

While it is generally understood that, during the term of an on-going employment relationship, the employee must not work simultaneously for a competitor of his employer, the situation is substantially different upon termination of the employment contract as the employee has to offer his services to another employer in an area where he can use his special skills, and this is most likely with the competitor of the former employer. Furthermore, if the employee should be precluded from working in his field of specialisation for more than a very brief period of time, he is likely to loose touch with its development, in particular in high technology jobs, and this will reduce his future employment chances. For these reasons, the validity of non-competition clauses for a period of time following the termination is recognised only if certain requirements are met.

First of all, the protection must be necessary for the employer and the area of its applicability must be defined to cover only the area where protection is most needed. This applies in particular to the geographical scope of the non-competition clause and the period of time for which it is to be effective; the maximum period of time for which a non-competition clause will be recognised is two years.

Secondly, the employer has to commit himself to pay to the employee during the term of the non-competition clause at least one half of his last remuneration, including all rewards in cash or in kind such as salary, vacation allowances, company car and other fringe benefits. Such a clause is void if it does not provide for any compensation at all and it is valid but unenforceable if the compensation does not equal 50 per cent of the last remuneration package. In the latter case, the employee may, however, elect to abide by the non-competition obligation and request payment of half of his last remuneration for the term of such obligation.

The employer, on the other hand, can waive his rights under the non-competition clause prior to the termination of the employment contract in writing, which means that the employee is immediately released from such obligation. The employer, however, will not be released from his obligation to pay the compensation until after one year has elapsed since the waiver.

The provisions of the Commercial Code dealing with post-employment non-competition commitments (ss. 74 to 75d HGB) are applicable to all employment contracts, except for legal representatives (officers/directors) of corporations or companies with limited liability. According to a decision of the Federal High Court for Civil Matters ('BGH') from 1984, corporate legal officers may not avail themselves automatically of the protection afforded under the Commercial Code and, thus, may be committed to post-employment competitive restrictions without compensation or beyond the statutory maximum term of two years. Non-competition clauses burdening corporate legal officers shall nevertheless be subject to court review and may be considered as null and void if, in the light of the missing or nominal consideration, the term and scope of the restriction with regard to territory, branch, line of products, etc. would be *contra bonos mores* (s. 138 BGB).

¶908

In practice, it is extremely difficult properly to police a non-competition arrangement and to evaluate its usefulness to the employer, particularly in view of the close economic integration among the Member States of the European Community. For example, take the case of a German sales subsidiary of a Dutch company that employs a salesman who is bound by a non-competition clause. After his termination he moves across the border to the Netherlands and starts to work for a competitor of the Dutch parent company. He may be able to collect one half of his former salary from the German sales subsidiary and his employment with a competitor of the Dutch parent company need not constitute a breach of his agreement not to compete, as the German sales subsidiary never effected sales into the Netherlands.

Finally, if the non-competition clause is agreed upon after 31 December 1981, there is a further disincentive for the employer: If the employee should not find a new job he can claim unemployment benefits and the employer has to refund such benefits to the state for the term of the obligation not to compete (s. 128a AFG).

GENERAL WORK RULES

¶909 Special protection

(1) *Women*

According to s. 611a BGB, the employer has to treat male and female employees equally, namely with regard to hiring and firing, working conditions and promotions. Advertisements for job openings must not differentiate between the sexes (s. 611b BGB). Practices arbitrarily favouring male workers and not justified by sex (e.g. fashion model) will be considered as discriminating and give rise to a claim for damages (e.g. loss of promotion).

Apart from the prohibition of discrimination, female employees are protected by a number of regulations as well as collective bargaining agreements. According to s. 16 *Arbeitszeitordnung* ('Regulation on Working Hours'), female employees may not be hired for hazardous work. On days before Sundays or legal holidays women may not work longer than eight hours (s. 17(2), sentence 2 AZO). Shift work during the night and later than 11 p.m. is illegal (s. 19(2) AZO).

Pregnant women are protected by the *Mutterschutzgesetz* ('Mother Protection Law'). They are entitled to a total of 14 weeks' leave of absence which, upon request of the mother, may be extended by an additional four-month period (ss. 3(2), 6, 8a MSchG). Employment of the expectant woman six weeks prior to the child's expected date of birth and eight weeks thereafter is prohibited, it being understood that the employer has to pay the balance between the regular net pay and the daily insurance benefit of DM 25 (ss. 13, 14 MSchG). After 14 weeks, i.e. during the extended four months maternity leave, no additional payments have to be made by the employer.

During pregnancy, employees cannot be required to perform tasks that might endanger their own health or that of the unborn child (s. 3(1), 4 MSchG).

Giving notice of termination of employment during the pregnancy until four months after giving birth, or eight months thereafter if the additional four months leave is taken, shall be null and void provided the employer is aware, or is notified within two weeks upon termination, of the pregnancy or the childbirth.

As this protection afforded to female workers depends on the state of knowledge of the employer, it is widely disputed whether inquiry as to any pregnancy when interviewing a job applicant is permissible. Although there exist valid reasons why such question should not be considered as discriminatory, the view taken by the Labour Courts is split. This makes it a matter of jurisdiction whether the inquiry and the probable consequences resulting therefrom – non-hiring, hiring but later rescission because of misrepresentation – should be upheld.

Release from the total prohibition of unilaterally dissolving the employment relationship with pregnant women or female workers on maternity leave, even if the dismissal would be based on serious cause, can only be sought by obtaining the prior approval of government agencies (*Gewerbeaufsichtsamt, Regierung*), the jurisdiction of which is determined by state law (s. 9(3) MSchG). Approval shall be granted only under exceptional circumstances, such as commital of a crime against the employer or total plant closure.

(2) *Minors*

Under the *Jugendarbeitsschutzgesetz* ('Law Concerning the Protection of Minors'), individuals under 18 years of age are regarded as minors. Minors below the age of 14 may not be employed with a few exceptions (e.g. minors of at least 13 years of age may distribute newspapers or do farm work for up to three hours on work days). Older minors may be employed subject to certain restrictions; in particular, they have to be allowed time off for visiting vocational training schools (s. 9 JArbSchG); the daily working time may not exceed eight hours and the weekly working time 40 hours (s. 8 JArbSchG), and not more than five days per week may be worked (s. 15 JArbSchG). Except for certain venues (e.g. restaurants) minors may not work on Saturdays, Sundays and statutory public holidays (ss. 16, 17, 18 JArbSchG) and they may not be

¶909

assigned to jobs considered particularly hazardous (e.g. poisonous chemicals) as specified by ss. 22 et seq. JArbSchG.

The vocational training of minors and others is dealt with under the *Berufs-bildungsgesetz* ('Law Concerning Vocational Training') which provides for minimum remuneration (s. 10 BBiG) and the obligation of the employer to continue the professional training (between two and three years depending on job qualification) until the apprentice has finally passed or failed to pass the exams (s. 14 BBiG). Before such time, the vocational training may not be terminated except during a short probation period which may be no longer than three months (s. 13 BBiG).

In plants with a shop council where more than five minors are regularly employed, a separate 'Minors' Representation Committee' (*Jugendver-tretung*) may be elected in accordance with s. 60 BetrVG. The *Jugendver-tretung* supervises, in particular, the compliance by the employer with all health, safety and other work regulations which are introduced for the protection of minors.

(3) Disabled persons

In order to promote the rehabilitation of disabled persons and their future employment, the *Schwerbehindertengesetz* ('Law Concerning the Disabled') provides for two measures:

(a) All employers with at least 16 members in the workforce must engage at least six per cent disabled persons (s. 4(1) SchwbG). Disabled persons, within the meaning of the law, are those who, due to physical or mental defects, have a minimum of 50 per cent reduced working capacity (s. 1 SchwbG). For each position in the handicapped quota which is not filled the employer has to pay monthly dues of DM 100 (s. 8(1) SchwbG). The penalty is paid into a public fund which is earmarked for the rehabilitation of the disabled (s. 8(3) SchwbG).

(b) Further, the dismissal of disabled persons requires the prior consent of the *Hauptfürsorgestelle* ('Principal Welfare Office'). In cases of serious cause not related to the disability this is a formality (s. 18 SchwbG). In all other cases, including ordinary termination, the Principal Welfare Office is called upon in order to carefully review and reconcile the interests of the disabled person with regard to continued employment and those of the employer with regard to rationalising operations.

¶910   Remuneration

As consideration for services rendered the employee is entitled to remuneration (s. 611 BGB) which is paid in arrears. In the absence of an express

¶910

stipulation the remuneration is deemed to be agreed upon if, under the circumstances given, the furnishing of services without consideration could not be expected (s. 612(1) BGB).

The parties are at liberty to agree on the rate of remuneration, provided collective bargaining or statutory minimum rates, if applicable, are not undercut. If the amount of the remuneration is neither agreed on, expressly or implicitly, nor stipulated by statutory regulation or collective bargaining agreements, the 'usual consideration' (usual for this kind of service in this type of branch and in this or a similar location) shall be deemed agreed upon (s. 612 (2) BGB).

The term, 'remuneration', comprises all benefits received by the employee, in cash or in kind, for his services including, but not limited to, commissions, premiums, vacation or Christmas allowances, bonuses and company cars, as well as corporate residences.

For the taxation of income from employment, including remuneration in kind, see Chapter 5 ('Taxation').

(1) *Payment period*

The remuneration must be paid when due, which is determined by statutes or agreements (ss. 271, 614 BGB). If the amount of remuneration is determined by the time worked (e.g. weekly, bi-weekly, monthly), payment has to be made at the end of each term (s. 614, sentence 2 BGB). For commercial employees the salary has to be paid monthly (s. 64 HGB). Bonuses and Christmas or vacation allowances, if any, are paid as contractually agreed.

(2) *Deductions*

The employer is under a statutory obligation to withhold income tax (wage tax) and social security dues from wages and salary (ss. 38, 41(c) EStG; ss. 394, 395, 1396, 1397 RVO; 118, 119 AVG; 114 RKG, 179 AFG) and to pay to the earners their net-wage (*Netto-Lohn*) or net-salary (*Netto-Gehalt*). Unless expressly stipulated otherwise the parties to an employment agreement agree on the gross remuneration (*Brutto-Vergütung*), i.e. the gross-wage (*Brutto-Lohn*) or gross-salary (*Brutto-Gehalt*), it being understood that it is subject to the above deductions.

Based on the revised income tax tariff and social security regulations effective from 1 January 1986, an employee (married, two children) with a monthly gross-salary of DM 4,400 would have to pay DM 554.80 wage withholding tax, DM 40.94 church tax and DM 770.90 for social security dues, which would leave him with a net salary of DM 3,003.63 to take home.

¶910

(3) *Commission*

Commission (*Provision*), as set forth in the Commercial Code ('HGB'), is the typical form of remuneration for (independent) commercial agents (cf. Chapter 3 : 'Commercial Intermediaries') for the soliciting of business and reflects a percentage of the consideration the principal gets for goods sold. According to s. 65 HGB, the provisions relating to the commission of commercial agents and dealing with the prerequisites for a commission claim (s. 87 HGB), its due date (s. 87a HGB) and the amount thereof (s. 87b HGB), as well as the furnishing of commission accounts (s. 87c HGB), are also applicable where commission as a variable income item is agreed upon for commercial employees, namely salary earners working as salesmen. They are not entitled, however, to the post-employment compensation granted to commercial agents (s. 89b HGB).

As this kind of compensation is not available for an employee it is debatable, in particular in the insurance business, whether a salesman's commission claim for automatic insurance renewals which becomes effective only after the term of employment has expired, may be excluded. According to the view taken by the BAG such exclusion is not invalid *per se* but it must be equitable, which fact is determined on a case-by-case basis. The exclusion of post-employment commission claims for insurance salesmen has been regarded as equitable where they were already compensated in advance during their term of employment by way of commission guarantees or lump-sum bonuses granted irrespective of their promotion efforts and marketing success.

(4) *Extra allowances*

If allowances such as Christmas bonuses or vacation pay are part of a collective bargaining agreement, or if they are individually stipulated by express or implied agreement, the workers or employees have a vested right. The allowance is regarded as part of the remuneration package and has to be paid *pro rata temporis* if the employment term is less than a full calendar year. However, even in the absence of such a provision, an employee who has received a bonus at least three times may consider it a vested right, unless the employer has the payments made expressly without prejudice.

A Christmas allowance paid voluntarily and considered a gratuity revocable at any time may be subject to certain conditions, namely continued employment, and may be recoverable if these conditions are not met. An employee receiving a Christmas bonus amounting to less than one month's salary but more than DM 200 may be requested to stay on until 31 March of the following year; if he receives more than one month's salary as bonus he may even be asked to continue until 30 June of the following year. If the employment

¶910

is left prematurely for reasons not caused by the employer, the Christmas bonus has to be paid back.

(5) Pension commitments

The employer has alternative methods of providing for retirement benefits for employees outside the state-run social security system:

(a) Types of pension commitments

(i) *Direct commitment by employer.* The employer may promise to pay certain retirement benefits to his employees. If he uses this method, he may set up pension reserves. In addition, he may (but needs not) purchase adequate life insurance to make sure that he is able to make such payments when they become due.

(ii) *Direct insurance scheme.* Alternatively, the employer does not promise to pay pensions but merely promises to buy life insurance on the life of the employee and to name the employee or his next of kin as the beneficiary under the life insurance policy. Upon retirement or death, the benefits may be paid either directly by the insurance company or via the employer. Employers normally favour the second alternative which permits them to demonstrate that they are in effect providing these benefits.

(iii) *Interposition of pension funds.* The employer may also set up a pension fund in the form of an independent legal entity which then extends the promise to pay pension to the workers and employees of the enterprise and its subsidiaries. This is attractive to the extent that payments by the enterprise to the pension fund constitute deductible expenses. Nevertheless, such pension funds are subject to German insurance regulations if they are set up in Germany and for this reason an independent pension fund is normally set up by major companies.

(iv) *Support and welfare funds.* Finally, and sometimes in addition to a pension fund, the employer may set up a support and welfare fund as a separate legal entity. The difference between a pension fund and a support and welfare fund is that the employees covered obtain a direct claim for the pension against the pension fund, whereas no such claim exists in the case of the support and welfare fund. The support and welfare fund has to set up a business plan, however, which outlines in detail when, under what circumstances and in what amounts payments will be made to the beneficiaries.

(b) Statutory regulations

All four methods outlined in (a) above are covered by a special statute enacted in 1974 (*Betriebsrentengesetz*), which introduced special provisions in three areas of the labour law in particular:

¶910

(i) *Vesting of rights in employee.*   In all four methods, the employee obtains a vested and enforceable right if his employment agreement terminates prior to death, disability or retirement, provided the employee is at least 36 years of age at that time and the pension promise has been extended to him for at least ten years prior to termination, or if he has been with the business for a least 12 years and the pension promise was extended to him at least three years prior to termination. In the case of a direct life insurance scheme, the employer has to commit himself not to revoke the insurance agreement after the above pre-requisites for vesting have been met and, in the case of a support or welfare fund, such employees are assured that they will remain beneficiaries of the fund even after termination of their employment contract. If they reach retirement, become disabled or die, they or their families are entitled to such part of the full pension benefit as corresponds to the ratio which the duration of their services in the company bears to the period of time between the beginning of their employment with the company and the end of their 65th year.

(ii) *Bankruptcy insurance.*   In order to protect the employee against the consequences of the insolvency or bankruptcy of the employer, a special bankruptcy insurance association has been organised (*Pensionssicherungs-verein*), which is subject to insurance regulations and which is financed by mandatory premiums paid by those employers who have granted direct pension promises, used the direct insurance alternative or who have set up a support and welfare fund; as the pension fund has to be managed in accordance with the rules for insurance companies, it does not have to be backed up by a special bankruptcy insurance.

(iii) *Subsequent adjustment of pension benefits.*   One of the most important and most controversial provisions of the *Betriebsrentengesetz* ('Law on Business Pension Schemes') requires the employer to review at three-yearly intervals whether and to what extent current payments under any of the four pension schemes should be adjusted. In this review, the interests of the retired employees and the economic situation of the employer have to be taken into account (s. 16 BetrAVG). Case law seems to be developing in a direction which requires the employer to increase the pension payments at three-yearly intervals by the same amount as the increase in the cost of living index in those same three years, unless the economic and financial situation of the employer prohibits such an adjustment. Because of the possible magnitude of future obligations which may result from such periodical adjustments this is an area of considerable dispute, and employers who have not already set up such a pension scheme are reluctant to institute a new one at the present time.

¶910

(6) *Attachments*

As the majority of the work force relies on its remuneration as its sole or, at least, principal source of income for securing a living, various statutory regulations have been introduced which are intended to shelter and protect the employee against third parties' claims or the bankruptcy of the employer.

Like the English Truck Acts, s. 115(1) GewO provides that workmen (including salary earners) shall not have unreasonable deductions made from their wages (as regards fines, damaged goods, materials or tools), nor have their wages paid otherwise than in current coin (i.e. cash, including bank transfer), nor be obliged to spend them in any particular place or manner.

Under the Civil Procedure Code ('ZPO'), a minimum amount of income derived from employment is exempted from seizure or attachment by creditors of the employee. A monthly net salary *above* DM 3,302 is fully seizable, whereas, of this base amount, a married employee with two children would be left with almost DM 2,780.

In the case of bankruptcy of the employer, wages and salaries which have been earned within six months before the date of the commencement of bankruptcy proceedings have priority over the payment of dividends to creditors, and will be paid in full out of the bankrupt estate (ss. 59, 60 Bankruptcy Act). Such amounts rank only below the costs and expenses of administration and preserving the estate subsequent to filing the petition. If the estate should be insufficient or exhausted by administrative expenses, up to three months' salary is guaranteed (*Konkursausfallgeld*) by a fund (s. 186(b) AFG) which is set up as a part of the workmens' compensation schemes (*Berufsgenossenschaften*).

¶911   Working hours

The prevailing practice of a 40-hour working week and an eight-hour working day (Monday to Friday) has over the years developed from the standards set by collective bargaining agreements nationwide or for particular branches. In 1984 the metal workers' union for the first time succeeded in having a 38-hour working week accepted in a collective bargaining agreement concluded with the automobile manufacturers' association. The metal workers, as well the other unions, have it made clear, however, that they are striving for a gradual reduction to a 35-hour week.

In the light of these developments, the statutory Regulation on Working Hours (*Arbeitszeitordnung*: AZO) has become outdated and superseded, with the exception of certain ceilings and minimum standards which are still in force. The AZO is not applicable for officers of corporations, legal representatives of associations, *Prokurists* or other executives responsible for a work force of at least 20 employees.

Section 3 AZO still allows a 48-hour working week, i.e. eight hours daily including Saturdays. Provided the weekly maximum (48 hours) is not exceeded, the daily working time may be allocated differently but must not exceed 10 hours (s. 4 AZO).

According to s. 5 AZO longer hours may be worked (up to 10 hours and in exceptional cases up to 12 hours daily) for certain preparatory or clean-up jobs in connection with the daily assignment or upon the demand of the employer for a maximum of 30 days per year (s. 6 AZO), or if provided by collective bargaining agreement (s. 7 AZO).

Shift work is permitted, and once during a three-week period a shift may last up to 16 hours in order constantly to continue operations, provided the employee is allowed 24 hours off twice during the same period (s. 10 AZO).

Still on the books to avoid excessive working hours, although heavily disputed by consumers, are regulations on the opening hours for retailers (*Ladenschlußgesetz*), according to which shops have to close at 6.30 p.m. Monday to Friday and at 2 p.m. on Saturdays (except for one Saturday per month) and may not open on Sundays.

During working hours half an hour break has to be allowed after six hours, and female workers are entitled to an extra half an hour after nine hours of work (ss. 12, 18 AZO).

Unless expressly exempted by law, working on Sundays or legal holidays is prohibited (s. 105a GewO). The exemptions are granted due to the nature of the business (e.g. petroleum refinery, hotels and restaurants, etc.) or if justified in emergency cases.

Any work performed beyond the regular work time is subject to overtime pay as provided for by law (s. 15 AZO, s. 612 BGB), or collective bargaining agreements or individual stipulation. Collective bargaining agreements usually provide for continuation of regular pay plus a premium to compensate for overtime. The premium may amount to 25 per cent of the regular pay as the base on a sliding scale which increases the premium with the number of overtime hours worked during a given period (week, month, etc.). If not individually agreed otherwise, these standards also determine the prevailing remuneration practice for overtime in employment relationships which do not come within the scope of collective bargaining agreements or which are outside s. 15 AZO, which, in this instance, is more or less obsolete anyhow.

¶912   Paid leave

(1) *Sick leave*

In cases of sickness preventing wage or salary earners from performing their services, they do not lose their claim for remuneration but commercial employees (s. 63 HGB), technical employees (s. 133c GewO), workers (s. 1

Lohnfortzahlungsgesetz), apprentices (s. 12 BBiG) and other employees (s. 616 BGB) are entitled to sick pay. Any claim for sick pay shall be excluded, however, if the incapacity to work is caused by a grossly negligent act or omission on the part of the employee, such as drunken driving or a car accident without the seat belt being fastened.

Sick pay, which equals the normal salary or wage, is received until recovery but not beyond six weeks, unless stipulated otherwise individually or by collective bargaining agreement. After six weeks the employee, if eligible, receives benefits from the state health insurance scheme.

(2) *Personal reasons*

Section 616(1), sentence 1 BGB, as interpreted by case law, does not exclude the employee's claim for remuneration if he is, without fault, prevented from attending work for a 'relatively short period' for reasons other than sickness. This provision, which is supplemented by the majority of collective bargaining agreements, secures paid leave on special occasions such as marriage, the birth of a child or the death of close relatives, jury duty, etc.

(3) *Vacation*

Under s. 3 of the Federal Law on Vacation (*Bundesurlaubsgesetz*), all employees are entitled to a minimum annual vacation of 18 working days, it being understood that all calendar days except Sundays and legal holidays are considered as work days. Again, this statute has been rendered more or less obsolete by collective bargaining agreements and general business practice. Since the end of 1985 the annual vacation has varied greatly from branch to branch but certainly exceeds the statutory minimum as Saturdays are no longer considered working days. On average, the work force is entitled to 22 to 25 working days (without Saturdays), with banks at the top of the list (28 days and more) and the restaurant business at the lower end of the scale (19 or 20 days).

The claim for full vacation exists for the first time after completing six months of service and will be prorated if the employment is terminated prior thereto (ss. 4, 5 BUrlG). Taking of vacation requires the prior consent of the employer who has to exercise his reasonable discretion (s. 7(1) BUrlG, s. 315 BGB) to reconcile conflicting interests (e.g. plant closure on the one hand and school holidays on the other). During his vacation the employee is entitled to vacation pay (*Urlaubsentgelt*) which equals his salary or wage, or, in the case of variable income, the average remuneration during the last 13 weeks before the commencement of vacation (s. 11(1), sentence 1 BUrlG).

For recreational purposes it is mandatory to actually take the vacation rather than accepting cash compensation, and, to the extent feasible, it must be taken

¶912

in one instalment (s. 6(2) BUrlG). Cash compensation is permissible only if, due to termination of employment, the vacation can no longer be taken.

At present only the states of Berlin, Bremen, Hamburg, Hesse and Lower Saxony have introduced statutory provisions giving employees the opportunity to take educational leave. At Federal level, members of a shop council and representatives of minors may avail themselves of paid leave for continued education for up to three weeks (up to four weeks if they are appointed for the first time) during their term of office (ss. 37(7), 65(1) BetrVG).

(4) *Legal holidays*

Legal holidays such as New Year's Day, Easter Monday, Labour Day (1 May), National Day (17 June), Ascension Day, Whit-Monday, All-Saints-Day (1 November), Christmas Days (December 25 and 26) and others are a matter of state law, with Bavaria leading with 14 statutory holidays.

¶913   Employee inventions

The 'Law Regarding Employees' Inventions' (*Arbeitnehmererfindungsgesetz*) provides the rights and obligations of employers and employees relating to inventions and technical improvements and suggestions which are made during the term of the employment relationship (s. 1 ArbnErfG). Section 4 ArbnErfG distinguishes between employment invention (*Diensterfindung*) and non-employment-related inventions (*freie Erfindung*). Employment inventions arise out of the job activities of the employee or are substantially derived from experience or the work of the firm; all others are non-employment-related inventions.

The employee must notify the employer of both types of inventions (ss. 5, 18 ArbnErfG) who has the discretion to claim an employment-related invention for his exclusive use. The law, and the supplementing regulations, provide a complicated formula to determine the amount of compensation due to an employee, which is dependent, *inter alia*, on the value of the invention, the duties and position of the employee and the division of the firm in which it was made (s. 9 ArbnErfG). If the invention is non-employment related, the employer has the first option to use the invention and, if the terms cannot be agreed on, the court will set a royalty figure (s. 19 ArbnErfG).

The provisions of the law regarding employee inventions cannot be changed by contract to the detriment of the employee.

COLLECTIVE LABOUR RELATIONS

¶914   Collective bargaining

(1) *Unions and employers' associations*

Article 9 of the German Constitution (*Grundgesetz*) guarantees the freedom of labour and management to form associations (*Koalitionen*) for the promotion of labour and economic conditions – namely, to conclude collective bargaining agreements (*Tarifverträge*) which are the regulatory instruments for remuneration, working conditions, work safety and similar matters.

Today there exist 17 unions in West Germany which are members of the German Federation of Unions (*Deutscher Gewerkschaftsbund*: DGB), each of which represents a particular branch of industrial activity such as coal mining (*IG Bergbau und Energie*), or printing (*IG Druck und Papier*) or heavy industry (*IG Metall*). These unions and the German Trade Union of Salaried Employees (*Deutsche Angestellten-Gewerkschaft*: DAG) are the major labour associations and representative of all industrial activities in the country.

As their counterpart there exist numerous employers' associations, one for each sector of industry or trade at local level, which form federations at state and Federal level such as the 'Federation of the Employers' Associations in Heavy Industry' (*Gesamtverband metallindustrieller Arbeitgeberverbände e. V.*).

All employers' federations belong to the 'Federal Organisation of Employers' Federations' (*Bundesvereinigung der deutschen Arbeitgeberverbände e. V.*: BDA).

At their various levels of representation labour and management exert considerable influence on West Germany's governmental, social and economic policies, it being understood that it is the primary task of trade unions and employers' associations to compromise on collective bargaining agreements.

(2) *Collective agreements*

According to s. 2 of the Law of Collective Bargaining Agreements (*Tarifvertragsgesetz*), collective agreements may be concluded between unions on one side and individual employers or employers' associations on the other side for a particular branch of industry (e.g. automobile manufacturers), or commerce (e.g. banking) at local, state or Federal level. Collective bargaining agreements must be put in writing (s. 1(2) TVG) and are usually negotiated annually or semi-annually with regard to salaries, wages and other items of remuneration (*Lohn-/Gehalts-Tarifvertrag*). More permanent provisions dealing with safety and health regulations, vacation, and working hours are dealt with in master agreements (*Manteltarifvertrag*) running for longer terms.

Section 1(1) TVG draws a distinction between the obligatory provisions of a collective agreement and so-called 'normative provisions' which may set guidelines or minimum standards for the conclusion, termination and contents of employment agreements, as well as for business organisation at shop floor level.

The nature of the provision determines its scope. Obligatory provisions, such as the prohibition of strikes or lock-outs (*Friedenspflicht*) during the term of a collective agreement, commit the unions and employers' association as signatories thereto but do not affect the individual members.

Normative provisions deal with individual aspects of employment such as remuneration, vacation, vacation pay, working hours or collective guidelines supplementing the Shop Constitution Law (*Betriebsverfassungsgesetz*) – namely, the scope of co-determination of the shop council with regard to personnel matters (s. 92 et seq. BetrVG), professional training (s. 96 et seq. BetrVG), and ordinary termination of employment (s. 102 BetrVG). Alternatively, they may deal with mutually administered pay compensation funds (*Lohnausgleichskassen*) as set up in the construction industry. Such normative provisions are binding for all members of the contracting union and employers' association until the end of the term of the collective bargaining agreement, irrespective of whether their membership with the association is terminated beforehand (s. 3(3) TVG). Provided 50 per cent of the work force of a branch falls under a collective bargaining agreement, either party thereto may request to have it made generally binding (s. 5 TVG) by a decree of the Federal Minister for Labour and Welfare (*Allgemeinverbindlicherklärung*). As a result, every employer or employee, whether or not a member of a signatory to the collective bargaining agreement, is bound thereby if he comes within the scope of the agreement. Finally, a collective bargaining agreement may become part of an individual employment contract by specific reference.

(3) *Strikes, lock-outs*

Provided a labour dispute cannot be settled by mutual agreement, and a *bona fide* attempt at reconciliation as normally required under collective bargaining agreements has failed, the work force can go on strike, which may be defended by management with a lock-out (*Abwehraussperrung*). 'Wild cat' strikes or strikes for matters other than those agreed on by collective bargaining (e.g. political concerns) are regarded as illegal and may allow immediate dismissal or a claim for damages.

During a legitimate strike employment is suspended and the participating employee loses his claim for remuneration. If the employer's operations are not directly involved but, for example, a car manufacturer has to close down because he is cut off from suppliers (e.g. tyre manufacturers) who are engaged

¶914

in a strike, the manufacturer's work force has no claim for compensation although they may be willing and prepared to render their services. In the leading case decided in 1980 the BAG agreed to the principle 'that the strike risk, i.e. the risk of losing compensation, has to be borne by labour, even if a particular part or branch of the work force is not itself on strike but its lay-off is caused by third party's labour dispute'.

This judicial law is supplemented by s. 116 AFG in connection with the Federal Labour Office's 'Guidelines on Neutrality in Case of Labour Disputes' (*Neutralitäts-Anordnung*), according to which no benefit may be granted (such as unemployment pay or reduced working time compensation (*Kurzarbeitsgeld*)) which may affect strikes or lock-outs.

Before this background the metal workers' union staged a strike in 1984 for the introduction of a 35-hour week in the automobile industry. The strategy followed by the union was determined by two considerations:

(a) the number of workers on strike must be kept to a minimum as the members were eligible for strike pay from the union; and

(b) suppliers in the automobile industry should be the prime strike target as automobile manufacturers rely heavily on suppliers, since only approximately 40 per cent of all spare parts and components of cars are originally produced by car manufacturers.

As a result of this strategy, the supplier's work force of 20,000 went on strike with the consequence that 400,000 employed by the car manufacturers had to be suspended.

The metal workers' union claimed unemployment benefits (DM 200 million) and, against the express instructions of the Federal Labour Office relying on its above Guidelines, prevailed in court on a technicality. The Social District Court in Frankfurt (Decree of 22 June 1984) took the view that under the Guidelines as drafted the metal workers' union was only excluded from unemployment benefits if the union was attempting to achieve for both branches of industry, suppliers and manufacturers, literally identical collective bargaining results. This test was not met as the union was striving, apart from the 35-hour week, for salary and wage increases at (minimally) different rates for suppliers and car manufacturers.

In substance, this decision points to Government-subsidised labour disputes and, thus, abolishes the balance of power between labour and management. At the beginning of 1986 the Federal legislator, being called upon by employers' associations and others concerned with the budget of the Federal Labour Office, enacted a revised s. 116 AFG for restating the principle of parity between labour and management, which, upon the initiative of the unions, is currently under review by the Federal Constitutional Court.

¶915　Shop-floor representation

(1)　*Organisation of shop council*

The shop council (*Betriebsrat*) can be formed in all plants which regularly employ at least five employees over 18 years of age, three of whom have to have been employed by the plant for at least six months (ss. 1, 7, 8 BetrVG). In plants with up to 20 employees, the functions of the shop council are performed by one employee. In larger plants, the number of shop council members increases gradually with the increasing number of employees (s. 9 BetrVG), i.e. to over 31 persons in case of more than 9,000 employees. In determining whether a shop council is required and how many members it should have, the legal representatives of the business (managing directors: *Geschäftsführer*; Officers: *Vorstandsmitglieder*) and executives (*Leitende Angestellte*) are not counted as employees (s. 5(3) BetrVG).

The members of the shop council, who hold office for a regular term of three years (s. 21 BetrVG), perform their function on an honorary basis, but they may perform their duties during normal working hours and this does not entitle the employer to reduce their salaries (s. 37 BetrVG). Moreover, in plants of 300 employees or more the gradually increasing number of members have to be completely released from their normal employment duties and continue to receive their normal salaries as if they had not been elected members of the shop council (s. 38 BetrVG). The employer also bears all the ancillary costs of the activities of the shop council; in particular, he has to provide meeting rooms, office supplies and personnel (s. 40 BetrVG).

(2)　*Duties of shop council*

The duties of the shop council as listed in s. 80 BetrVG, include, *inter alia*, ensuring that, for the protection of the employees, laws, collective bargaining agreements and other provisions are observed by the employer; recommending to management measures which would serve the plant and its employees; considering and passing on to management suggestions from employees and reporting back to them; promoting the inclusion of handicapped and other specially protected groups; and promoting the integration of foreign workers in the firm and understanding between them and the German employees.

In order to carry out these duties the shop council has different kinds of rights, ranging from co-determination concerning certain social matters (s. 87 BetrVG) to notification in case of dismissals (s. 102 BetrVG).

(3)　*Authority of shop council*

(a) *Social matters.*　The shop council may insist on co-determination in the fixing of working conditions generally, and this includes (s. 87 BetrVG) such social matters as the beginning and end of working time (but not the overall number of weekly working hours); a temporary reduction or increase of the usual working hours; time, place and manner of payment of wages; general rules regarding vacations and determination of vacation time for individual employees if they cannot agree with the employer; the form and administration of social welfare matters, in particular of pension or welfare and support funds at plant or company level; the conclusion and termination of rental agreements supplied by the company to individual employees; and the determination of basic rules concerning the nature and methods of employee remuneration.

(b) *General personnel matters.*   In accordance with ss. 92 to 95 BetrVG the shop council has to be informed in advance by the employer about his general personnel planning. In particular, the employer has to inform the shop council of his present and future needs for personnel and of his intended measures to meet these needs. If the employer fails to inform the shop council or does not make any plans concerning the future needs of the business, the shop council itself can put forward proposals for the introduction of such plans. Furthermore, the shop council can request that any vacancies be offered first to employees inside the plant. Hiring forms to be filled in by employees, as well as general directives concerning selection for employment, transfer and dismissal of employees, need the approval of the shop council in order to be effective.

(c) *Settlement of disputes.*   Employer and shop council have to consult with each other and try to find amicable solutions in the social and personnel matters discussed above. If agreement between the employer and shop council cannot be reached, the necessary agreement can then be imposed by a decision of a conciliation board (*Einigungsstelle*). This board, which is composed of an equal number of employer and shop council representatives with a neutral chairman, acts as an arbitrator (s. 76 BetrVG). The decision of the board must take into account the interests of both the plant and the employees concerned, but the board is vested with a wide discretion to find an equitable solution. Both employer and shop council can apply to the Labour Court for an additional review of whether the conciliation board exceeded in a particular instance the scope of the discretion given to it (s. 76(7) BetrVG).

The additional authority granted to the shop council in individual personnel matters concerns, in particular, the following two areas ((d) and (e) below).

(d) *Hiring, transfer and re-grouping of employees.*   In plants of more than 20 employees, the employer must seek the consent of the shop council for any new employment or for the transfer or re-grouping of employees (s. 99 BetrVG). He must submit all applications for employment and information about the applicant to the shop council. The shop council may deny its consent if the measure deviates from a general directive on personnel planning or if it could lead to an unjustified dismissal of other employees, causes unjustified detrimental treatment of the employees concerned or if the vacancy was not offered inside the plant before the employer looked for an outside applicant. If the shop council refuses to grant its consent, the employer may apply to the Labour Court and an affirmative decision of the court replaces the consent of the shop council.

In cases of urgency, the employer can take provisional measures before the shop council has had a chance to express its views on the contemplated action or after it has refused to grant its consent (s. 100 BetrVG). If the shop council is of the opinion that the action was not urgent and informs the employer accordingly, the employer may only maintain the new employment, transfer or re-grouping if he applies within three days to the Labour Court for its consent.

(e) *Dismissal of individual employees.* In all businesses which have a shop council, the employer may give notice to an employee only after he has notified the shop council of his intentions (s. 102 BetrVG). The shop council has one week upon notification to raise its objections. If the council does not react or not in time, it is deemed to have approved of the dismissal. The same rules apply to an immediate dismissal for cause. Here, however, the shop council must react within three days after the employer's notification. Because of this requirement it has virtually become impossible to effect extraordinary termination overnight, since the shop council will always be allowed a three-day period to consider the employer's notification.

As non-compliance with these notification requirements renders the termination null and void, their strict observation must be considered essential for the employer. Objections, if any, raised by the shop council shall not be conclusive, however, for the court when evaluating the circumstances for finding serious cause or establishing social justification.

In this context it should be noted that objections raised by the shop council because the termination of employment is, *inter alia*, contrary to personnel guidelines within the meaning of s. 95 BetrVG (dealing with hiring, firing, replacement, relocation), or because it does not take into consideration the fact that the employee could have been assigned to another job within the same shop or within another shop of the enterprise, may entitle the employee, provided he has instituted legal proceedings, to insist on continuing his employment and to perform his job during the notice period, and even thereafter, until the Labour Court judgment has become final (s. 102(5) BetrVG, s. 1(2) KSchG).

(f) *Business reorganisations.* In plants with more than 20 employees, corporate reorganisations require (ss. 111, 112 BetrVG):

    (i) the notification of the shop council; and

(ii) the amicable settlement of conflicting interests (*Interessenausgleich*) as well as, subject to certain conditions;

(iii) agreement on a severance compensation plan (*Sozialplan*).

(i) *Notification of shop council.* The shop council has to be *informed in advance* about changes of substance which may negatively affect the entire staff or substantial parts of the personnel, and the employer is under an obligation to consult with the shop council on such contemplated changes (s. 111 BetrVG). Such events include:

(aa) the cut-back or closing down of a plant or a significant part thereof;

(bb) the relocation of a plant or of a significant part thereof;

(cc) the consolidation of several plants into one;

(dd) substantial changes in the plant's organisation, or the corporate purpose of the plant or of the plant installations; and

(ee) the introduction of essentially new work methods and production processes.

Changes are considered 'significant' or 'substantial' if they cause mass dismissals within the meaning of the notification requirements dealt with in ¶907.

(ii) *Amicable settlement.* Further, employer and shop council have to find an *amicable solution* to harmonise the interests of the employer with the interests of the work force concerned (*Interessenausgleich*) so that any hardship for the work force resulting from the reorganisation may be avoided to an extent reasonably acceptable to management (s. 112 BetrVG).

Interessenausgleich is primarily concerned with the practical implementation of the operational measures intended by management, i.e. with the reconciliation of conflicting interests with regard to the why, when and how of the reduction. In practice, the amicable settlement may include an extension of notice periods for a part of the work force in order to become eligible for early retirement, or a reduction in the total number of firings, or an exemption therefrom for those most vulnerable to unemployment (old age, unskilled, etc.).

In essence, management's planning as a whole is subject to scrutiny by the shop council and the employer has to make a serious attempt to overcome its objections. Otherwise, if no amicable settlement can be reached, both parties may call upon the conciliation board (*Einigungsstelle*) to assist in the negotiations. The conciliation board has to make an effort to overcome the deadlock but does not have the power to force an *Interessenausgleich* upon the parties.

Pending the decision of the conciliation board, management is not entitled to implement any changes. Otherwise, according to a decision of the BAG published in early 1985, the employees are entitled to compensation (s. 113(3)

¶915

BetrVG) and, upon application of the shop council, the labour court may grant an order staying any action. The award to which the employee may be entitled must compensate for any loss of remuneration or for any other disadvantages during the 12-month period expiring after the unauthorised changes were implemented.

If the parties reach an amicable settlement, either with or without the help of the conciliation board, this has to be put in writing and forms a mutual guideline for the reorganisation. Alternatively, if the conciliation board returns its assignment with no compromise having been reached, management is at liberty to implement the cut-backs by unilateral action.

(iii) *Severance compensation plan.*   Apart from the *Interessenausgleich* the work force may be entitled to *severance benefits*, the details of which have to be negotiated with the shop council in order to agree on a severance compensation plan (*Sozialplan*). In essence, the employer has to set aside funds under the *Sozialplan* to compensate the employees for the economic disadvantages which the contemplated operational changes will cause to them. Until the beginning of 1985 the conciliation board had the authority to impose its decision on the parties in case no agreement on the severance benefits plan could be reached. Section 112a BetrVG, which was inserted by art. 2 *Beschäftigungsförderungsgesetz* 1985 (Law on the Advancement of Employment 1985), narrows the definition of a mass dismissal which mandatorily requires a severance compensation plan by increasing and scaling the percentages of dismissals caused by commercial reasons related to the company's size.

According to s. 112a(1) BetrVG, a severance compensation plan shall not be mandatory unless:

(aa)   in shops with regularly more than 20 but fewer than 60 employees 20 per cent, but at least six, are dismissed;

(bb)   in shops with regularly at least 60 and less than 250 employees 20 per cent or at least 37 employees are dismissed;

(cc)   in shops with regularly at least 250 but fewer than 500 employees 15 per cent or at least 60 employees are dismissed;

(dd)   in shops with regularly 500 employees 10 per cent or at least 60 are dismissed.

Furthermore, in the case of newly-established companies, shop-changes involving redundancies will not result in mandatory severance compensation plans during the first four years except where such new company had in fact been established as a result of a reorganisation of a previous company or a group of companies.

¶915

When reconciling the social interests of the employees concerned, as well as the economic concerns of the employer, the conciliation board, in the case of a mandatory severance compensation plan, has to observe the following principles which have been developed by case law and are now set forth in more detail in s. 112(5) BetrVG, as amended with effect from 1 May 1985:

- On a case-by-case basis, priority shall be given to specific payments compensating for or mitigating economic disadvantages due to reduction of income, loss of fringe benefits or future pension rights or because of moving expenses or increased commuting costs.

- The chances of layed-off employees on the labour market have to be evaluated. A generally high fluctuation rate, which is characteristic of, for example, the building industry, may suggest that less protection will be required; alternatively, highly qualified personnel (e.g. in the watch industry) may find it more difficult to find a new, adequate job. Employees refusing reasonable employment at the same firm, at another firm of the same or an affiliated company, or even at another location, shall be excluded from benefits.

- The benefits accorded by a severance compensation plan must be fixed at such amount that the continued existence of the company or the remaining jobs will not be jeopardised.

All these factors have to be taken into consideration when ultimately determining what share of the total amount of the *severance compensation plan* is allocable to each individual employee. It seems that the maximum severance pay which an employee can claim in an individual dismissal (i.e. one month's salary per year of service) should also be considered as the ceiling for benefits under a *Sozialplan*.

Nevertheless, these plans require substantial amounts as evidenced by the fact, that, for example, in an earlier plant closing in the textile industry in Southern Germany, the company offered a total of DM 4.5 million to its 630 employees which represented an average payment of approximately DM 7,200. The average severance compensation plan in the German industry in 1980 required payments of DM 6.7 million. The minimum amounted to about DM 4,200 and the maximum to DM 25,000 per employee, and the average of about DM 8,800 corresponded to about three months' salary.

In 1978 the BAG decided that all claims of employees under the severance compensation plan should have priority over any other claim in bankruptcy, although no such preference had been included in the relevant section of the *Konkursordnung* (Bankruptcy Act). The Federal Constitutional Court ('BVerfG') in 1983 held such judicial preference unconstitutional. In consequence, the Federal High Court for Labour Matters decided in 1984 that claims

¶915

under severance schemes are ordinary unsecured claims. The legislator reacted with the new Law on Severance Compensation Plan (*Sozialplangesetz*) and in essence provided for the priority of severance compensation plans to the extent they:

(aa) are established during bankruptcy, or no longer than three months prior to the opening of bankruptcy proceedings; and

(bb) neither in total exceed one-third of the total net assets of the bankrupt employer nor 2.5 months' salary and/or wage payments to all dismissed employees.

All other claims under compensation plans continue to be unprivileged. As a result of a political compromise the term of the above law has been limited to 31 December 1988. The legislator will have to enact the final law before such date or all severance schemes will again be unprivileged.

¶916   Board-level representation

Apart from labour participation at shop floor level, in West Germany the labour force has achieved an active role in formulating and implementing corporate policy by representation at board level. At the present time, there are three levels of consultation which can be described as follows:

(1) *Coal and Steel Co-Determination Code*

The *Gesetz über die Mitbestimmung der Arbeitnehmer in den Aufsichtsräten und Vorständen des Bergbaus und der eisen- und stahlerzeugenden Industrie* of 1951 provides for equal representation of shareholders and workers/employees on the supervisory board in the coal and steel industry. The majority of the employees' representatives are nominated by the unions; the union, in addition, can even object to the minority elected by the employees directly. The shareholders' and the employees' representatives together elect a neutral member as chairman to avoid a deadlock. In addition, the management board must have one member in charge of personnel affairs (director of labour) who cannot be appointed or removed without the approval of the majority of the employees' representatives.

(2) *Shop Constitution Code*

Since 1952, under the *Betriebsverfassungsgesetz*, corporations with more than 500 employees must have one-third of the members of the supervisory board elected by the employees. The board may consist of three or more members, any greater number, however, being always divisible by three. If, in the case of a three-member board, one member is elected by the employees, he must be an employee of the company itself; otherwise at least two labour representatives must be from within the company. They have the same rights as the shareholders' representatives on the supervisory board.

(3) Co-Determination Code

Under the *Mitbestimmungsgesetz* of 1976, the supervisory board of all German stock corporations and limited liability companies with more than 2,000 employees must consist of an equal number of shareholders and labour representatives. The statute does not apply to companies organised in other legal forms, such as partnerships, or to branches of foreign corporations. However, the law expressly includes limited partnerships where the general partner is a German corporation, as well as groups of affiliated companies where the parent is a German corporation.

The labour representatives of the supervisory board are directly elected by the employees, unless the employees resolve differently, in the case of companies with less than 8,000 employees, or indirectly via electors if the company has 8,000 or more employees. The elections are particularly complicated. They are either made jointly or in two groups, the workers (wage earners) and the employees (salary earners). The total size of the board depends on the number of employees. Two of the six or eight, or three of the ten, labour representatives must be elected from proposals made by the union (so-called union representatives). At least one of the white collar employees must be from the executive staff (*Leitende Angestellte*). The management board continues to be appointed by the supervisory board. One member, the director of labour, must be in charge of personnel and social matters. Unlike the Coal and Steel Co-Determination Code, the 1976 law does not expressly provide that the appointment or removal of the labour director cannot be made against labour or union objections. For all practical purposes, however, he requires the confidence of the labour representatives.

SOCIAL SECURITY

¶917   Coverage

The compulsory social security system in West Germany covers four principal areas: health insurance, old age benefits, workmen's compensation (s. 4 Social Security Law I; '*Sozialgesetzbuch I*: SGB I') and unemployment benefits (s. 100 AFG). Details of the coverage, contributions and benefits for health and occupational accidents insurance are provided for under the *Reichsversicherungsordnung* ('RVO') for workers and employees alike. Retirement benefits for workers are dealt with under the RVO as well, whereas employees come within the scope of the *Angestelltenversicherungsgesetz* ('AVG').

In principle, the social security system mandatorily includes all wage and salary earners working in West Germany (s. 3 Social Security Law IV; '*Sozialgesetzbuch IV*: SGB IV'), as well as temporary assignments by German employers abroad (s. 4 SGB IV). Temporary assignments to Germany by a foreign employer, however, do not come within the scope of the social security regulations (s. 5 SGB IV).

This principle of territorial restriction (*Territorialitätsprinzip*), which is of particular concern with regard to contributions to and benefits from the retirement scheme, has been supplemented by numerous bilateral treaties, namely with Italy, Belgium, Switzerland and the United States, in order to allow, in cases of labour assignments abroad, the accumulation of pension rights under the domestic and foreign social security system alike and to avoid double payments of social security dues.

Article 6 of the US-German Treaty on Social Security of 1 December 1979 provides, for example, that persons temporarily assigned to West Germany by their US employer shall not change their US social security status, i.e. they shall not come within the scope of the German social security system even if they are on the payroll of a German branch or subsidiary of the US corporation. Under Art. 7 of the same treaty terms of employment expiring under the German and US social security system may be counted for determining the qualification for retirement benefits under either system.

Commencement and termination of employment, as well as contractual (e.g. pay raise) or other changes (e.g. pregnancy) which may influence the social security coverage have to be notified to the local insurance office (AOK) through which all social security information is channelled (s. 317 RVO). The notification has to be made immediately upon commencement of employment, within six weeks after termination and annually on 31 March. A list of wage and salary earners employed on the preceeding 31 December must also be submitted.

¶918 Health insurance

Contributions to the health insurance scheme (in 1986 approximately 12 per cent of monthly pay) are shared 50:50 between employer and employees (s. 381 RVO) and are due only up to certain pay levels. For instance, as of 1 January 1986 a ceiling of DM 50,400 annually or DM 4,200 monthly applies to contributions toward health insurance, beyond which there is no compulsory health insurance. The employer has to withhold the employee's share for transfer with his contribution to the insurance office.

¶918

Benefits from health insurance include payment of medical expenses, hospitalisation and compensation for loss of pay (*Krankengeld*). As explained above, workers and employees are entitled to have their full remuneration paid by the employer during the first six weeks of sick leave. For the following period they receive 80 per cent of their regular pay from the insurance office but not more than their net income (s. 182 RVO). *Krankengeld* is paid until the employee becomes eligible for disability or retirement benefits, but not beyond a total of 78 weeks during a given three-year period (s. 183 RVO).

¶919   Unemployment benefits

Unemployment insurance contributions are paid by the employer and the employee at 2 per cent each for the period from 1 January 1986 (s. 174 AFG) up to a certain monthly pay ceiling (DM 5,600 for 1986). The payments have to be made by the employer to the insurance office (s. 176 AFG).

All unemployed persons are entitled to unemployment benefits provided they have been working for at least 360 calendar days during a three-year term preceeding unemployment (s. 104 AFG). The employment benefits amount to 63 per cent of net pay for unemployed persons without children and to 68 per cent of net pay for unemployed persons with at least one child (s. 111 AFG), and are paid for 156 days if the employee was employed for 360 calendar days within the three-year term, for 234 days if employed for 540 days and for 312 if employed for 720 days (*Arbeitslosengeld*). If the unemployed person is no longer eligible for *Arbeitslosengeld* he may apply for unemployment assistance (*Arbeitslosenhilfe*) which will be available at a rate of 56 per cent of his last net remuneration (in the case of at least one child, 58 per cent) (s. 136 AFG).

¶920   Old age benefits

Old age benefit contributions are shared by the employer and the employee at a rate of 19.2 per cent of the gross remuneration up to a ceiling of DM 67,200 annually or DM 5,600 monthly for 1986 (s. 1385 RVO, s. 12 AVG). The total amount of contribution is again transferred by the employer to the insurance office (s. 1396 RVO, s. 118 AVG). Workers or employees are eligible for retirement benefits at the age of 63 or, in the case of disability, at the age of 60, and they may take advantage of early retirement at the age of 60 (s. 1248 RVO, s. 25 AVG). The maximum amount of the retirement benefits equals 75 per cent of the gross remuneration after 50 years of reckonable service (s. 1254, 1255 RVO; s. 31, 32 AVG). The widow or survivor's benefits amount to 60 per cent of a disability pension (s. 1268 RVO, s. 45 AVG).

¶921 Workmen's compensation

Contributions to the workmen's compensation scheme, which is administered by associations set up for all branches of trade and industry (*Berufsgenossenschaften*), are solely made by the employers (s. 723 RVO). The amount of the contribution is fixed by the *Berufsgenossenschaften*, taking into consideration the risk of a work accident prevailing in the particular branch (e.g. banking compared to coal mining), the record of work accidents during the previous business year, and the total annual pay of all employees concerned (s. 725 RVO). The workers or employees become eligible for workmen's compensation in the case of a work accident which occurs during or in connection with their performance of services under their employment contract (s. 548 RVO). This definition would also cover an accident when the employee is commuting from the office to his residence. Provided the individual is totally unable to work he receives two thirds of his annual income as workmen's compensation or, otherwise, a percentage thereof which corresponds to his reduced working capability (s. 581 RVO).

10 German and EEC Competition Law

INTRODUCTION

¶1001   In general

Both German and European (i.e. EEC) antitrust laws are highly developed bodies of law. As they have parallel application businessmen, enterprises and legal advisers must be aware of both. There exists a wealth of literature on either, but for conceptual and other reasons few, if any, attempts have yet been made in treaties to combine them. In view of practical needs the following paragraphs attempt to bring them into closer contact, but a warning must immediately be added that, due to the conceptual differences described below, any antitrust problem must ultimately be resolved separately within its own legal framework without cross-reference. Consequently, any case with relevance under German antitrust law must also be examined under EEC competition rules, but the result may be identical, different or even contradicting (see ¶1002 below).

GERMAN AND EEC ANTITRUST LAW

¶1002   Sources of law

(1) *German cartel law (GWB)*

Prewar Germany has often been called a classical country of cartels. A first codification of cartel law consisted in the 1923 Cartel Regulation. Decartelisation and deconcentration had been a primary objective of the occupation period and resulted in US, British and French regulations prohibiting 'Excessive Concentration of German Economic Powers' and introduced US antitrust concepts.

Simultaneously the so-called *Freiburg School* developed the concept of a free market economy and, among others, in 1949 produced a draft antitrust law

¶1002

which preceded the first government bill of the *Gesetz gegen Wettbewerbsbe-schränkungen* ('GWB') of 1952. This bill was the subject of lengthy discussions and became law on 7 July 1957 only after significant compromises which included a number of exceptions from the cartel prohibition and a complete deletion of merger control. It has since been amended four times:

- in 1965, intensifying control over so-called market dominators and allowing specialisation cartels;

- in 1973, introducing merger controls, prohibition of price maintenance and expanding the definition of and further tightening control over dominant positions;

- in 1976, intensifying merger controls in the publishing industry;

- in 1980, resulting in more severe merger control and more detailed provisions for market domination.

The basic aim of the GWB is the protection of the freedom of competition. A restriction of competition is considered behaviour which reduces the options otherwise available to an enterprise on the same or opposite side of the market. The GWB regulates the following basic categories of enterpreneurial activity:

(a) horizontal restrictions (cartels) (s. 1), which are prohibited *per se* without any exemption provision, except those cartels expressly exempted by or on the basis of s. 2 et seq.;

(b) other (vertical) restrictions which would be legal, except as prohibited by or on the basis of s. 15 et seq.;

(c) abuses of market domination (ss. 22, 26);

(d) merger control (ss. 23–24a).

Of course, the above categories oversimplify a rather complicated law which effectively addresses all kinds of restriction and which also covers concerted actions, informal inducements (s. 25) and recommendations (ss. 38(2) and 38a).

In line with German legal tradition and constitutional law, the legislator, the authorities (primarily the Federal Cartel Office ('FCO': *Bundeskartellamt*) in Berlin) and the judiciary have used their efforts to develop a system of antitrust law with a high degree of sophistication and predictability.

The cartel law also applies to government-owned companies, but this applicability is excluded or modified with respect to certain areas (ss. 99–105):

(a) Federal post and railways;

(b) traffic and transportation;

(c) agriculture;

¶1002

(d) coal and steel;

(e) banking and insurance;

(f) copyright societies;

(g) public utilities.

(2) *EEC competition rules*

The Common Market's antitrust law, as applied by the Commission of the European Communities (the 'Commission') and interpreted by the European Court of Justice (the 'Court'), has developed in a way which could hardly have been predicted when the relatively short antitrust provisions of art. 85 and 86 found their way into the 1957 Treaty of Rome, and has a parallel only in comparing US antitrust law practice with the Sherman Act.

Antitrust law has turned out to be a much more effective tool for European unification than any other political movement or institution. In fact, the European Court, when interpreting art. 85 or 86, has often quoted the basic provisions of art. 2 and 3 of the Treaty, according to which:

'... the Community shall have as its task, by establishing a common market and progressively approximating the economic policies of Member States, to promote throughout the Community a harmonious development of economic activities, a continuous and balanced expansion, an increase in stability, an accelerated raising of standard of living and closer relations between the States belonging to it ... and for these purposes ... the activities of the Community shall include

(a) the elimination, as between Member States, of customs duties and quantitative restrictions on the import and export of goods, and of other measures having equivalent effect;

(b) the institution of a system ensuring that competition in the common market is not distorted; ...'.

It is, according to the European Court, in the light of the above provisions that art. 85(1) and 86 *prohibit*:

'All agreements between undertakings, associations of undertakings and concerted practices which may effect trade between Member States and which have as their object or effect the prevention, restriction or distortion of competition within the Common Market, ...'

(art. 85(1)); and

'any abuse by one or more undertakings of a dominant position within the Common Market or in a substantial part of it ... insofar as it may effect trade between Member States ...'

(art. 86).

European antitrust law may be categorised as follows:

(a) Agreements and other multipartite practices which violate art. 85(1) are automatically null and void unless covered by a group exemption or an individual exemption obtained pursuant to para. (3);

¶1002

(b) Unilateral action is prohibited if caught by art. 86, which is not self-executing but allows the Commission to impose sanctions. If such abuse of a dominant position is found to be present, no exemption can be granted.

Article 85 does not distinguish between horizontal and other agreements. There exists at present no general merger control and only acquisitions which could be considered an abuse of a dominant position are prohibited.

The above competition rules cover all sectors of economy except that:

(a) coal and steel are subject to the Treaty of Paris establishing the European Coal and Steel Community which includes similar competition rules and in addition provides for merger control (art. 65, 66);

(b) agricultural products, and traffic and transportation are subject only to very modified competition rules (art. 87(2)(c)).

Not directly part of Community competition law but closely related are art. 30 and 36 of the Treaty. Article 30 prohibits Member States imposing or applying 'quantitative restrictions on imports and all measures having equivalent effect'. However, art. 36 expressly allows prohibitions or restrictions on imports which are justified by reason of the protection of industrial and commercial property, provided they do not 'constitute a means of arbitrary discrimination or a disguised restriction on trade between member states'.

¶1003 Applicability of EEC rules

In practice, before analysing art. 85 and 86 in more detail, it is important to establish whether a restrictive covenant would in fact be caught by EEC law in spite of its primarily non-EEC aspects, (i.e. because it seems primarily to concern either a transaction with a non-EEC company or a 'purely' national transaction) or in spite of the apparently limited significance of the transaction.

(1) 'Ability to Affect Trade between Member States'

The above interstate trade clause of art. 85 and 86, which is also contained in a number of further provisions of the Treaty, is designed to draw a line between national and community law. Only actions which may affect trade between Member States will be caught by the antitrust law of the Community, whereas those the effect of which is limited to the territory of a Member State will be subject only to national law (EC 1979, 1869, *Hugin*; 1966 p. 321, *Grundig/Consten*).

Before the background of art. 2 and 3 of the Treaty the interstate trade clause is interpreted broadly. In spite of its critics the Commission, backed up by the Court, has in the past favoured jurisdiction over behaviour and transactions which, at first view, would appear to have merely national effects, the only further barrier being that such effect must be noticeable (see under *(b)* below).

The effect does not need to be negative nor does the effect have to be proven to be actual. It is sufficient that the interstate trade may develop differently as a result of the action in question.

(a) *National agreements.* A provision of an agreement between two Dutch associations of citrus fruit importers and wholesalers prohibiting wholesalers from directly importing third (i.e. non-EEC) country fruit outside the Rotterdam auction was held to be illegal (EC 1975 p. 563, '*Frubo*'). According to the court, the offending provision

> 'because it restricts the freedom... to import directly into the Netherlands,... is liable to interfere with the natural movement of trade and thus to effect trade between member countries'.

A cartel of four of the five Belgium wallpaper manufacturers providing for price fixing, retail prices, etc. because of aggregate rebates on total turnover may be liable to consolidate divisions between national markets and to hinder imports from other Member States. However, in such case of a national cartel, the Commission is required by the court to establish in detail the effect on trade between Member States (EC 1975, 1491, *Papiers Peints de Belgique*).

Only agreements between parties located in one Member State which do not, directly or indirectly, relate to imports or exports can be considered as purely domestic in scope (art. 4(2), reg. 17).

(b) *Third countries.* Agreements between companies within and outside the Common Market may violate art. 85 if they result in the isolation of the whole of the Common Market because the products concerned can not be obtained in other Member States by and from other retailers. Agreements between Common Market companies concerning exports to third countries will be critical if they affect reimportation (depending on customs, transportation and other cost items).

Agreements between non-Common Market companies restricting or regulating Common Market imports could fall under art. 85. In examining Japanese measures for the voluntary restraint of exports, the Commission decided that the main French and Japanese ball-bearing producers had concluded an agreement which infringed art. 85(1). As the restriction on competition, noticeably resulting in a price increase, 'covered the whole of the territory of France so that trade between France and the other Member States was likely to take place on conditions different from those which would have obtained in the absence of the agreement', the agreement was also liable to affect trade between Member States (OJ L 343 p. 19). The same position is taken by the Court when deciding that a selective distribution system which extends

¶1003

throughout the territory of a Member State may by its very nature have the effect of reinforcing the partitioning of the market on a national basis (EC 1981, 1963, *Salonia*).

(2) *Noticeable restriction*

The Court has stated that in order to violate art. 85 a restriction of competition must be noticeable, and even absolute territorial protection granted to an exclusive distributor for Belgium and Luxembourg by a German manufacturer with a market share of less than 1 per cent might not fulfil this requirement (EC 1969, p. 295, *Völk/Verwaecke*).

In its *de minimis* rule (Notices on Minor Agreements of 1970 and 1977) the Commission defines an agreement as being of minor importance and thus not violating art. 85 if:

(a) the products which are the subject of the agreement, including those considered to be similar by consumers, do not represent a market share of more than 5 per cent in all or a substantial part of the Common Market; and

(b) the aggregate annual turnover of the participating undertakings does not exceed 50 million Units of Account.

The 50 million mentioned in (b) above was 15 million for manufacturing and 20 million for distribution firms in 1970, but due to inflation should now be considerably higher. Of course, sales of affiliate companies must be included in such figure.

The unit of account (ECU) is a budget unit which is presently defined in terms of a basket of European currencies and which is quoted daily. On 29 April 1986 it was worth DM 2.15, £0.64, US $0.99.

The *de minimis* rule binds only the Commission, and not national courts when deciding whether an agreement may be void nor the European Court which so far has only decided cases involving 1 per cent or less market share. However, the Court has stated that a restriction (i.e. exclusivity) may not be 'noticeable', if it is necessary in order to allow a company to enter into a new market (EC 1966, p. 282, *Maschinenbau Ulm*), whereas the Commission in such case would be more likely to apply art. 85, para. (1), but consider an exemption under para. (3).

¶1004   Parallel application

(1) *Supremacy of Community law*

Community law has been created as a new body of public international law with priority over national laws of the Member States. Supremacy of Community law over national law means that the national court must not apply national law if it deviates from Community law.

Community law prevails, however, only insofar as it actually regulates the same facts and aspects as national law. Articles 85 and 86 address anti-competitive practices with respect to their effects on interstate trade. National law may regulate the same practices with respect to their domestic effects under different aspects. This being so, undertakings must comply with both laws and a cartel may consequently be subject to parallel proceedings (so-called *Zwei-schrankentheorie*, or two barriers doctrine) (EC 1969, p. 13, *Bayer Teer-farben* I).

According to the two barriers doctrine, national and Community law may have different objectives and may thus be applicable in parallel so that there may be cumulative consequences, the stricter law applying. However, parallel application of domestic law is permissible only to the extent that it would not impair the full effect of the measures adopted under Community law. Cases caught by both Community and national law can thus be categorised as follows:

(a) *'Same' conclusions.* No conflict will exist where both laws come to the same conclusions. In the case of parallel prohibition, however, a problem of double fines could arise. According to the Court, 'a general requirement of equity, . . . implies that any previous repressive decision should be taken into account when determining the sanction to be applied' (EC *supra*). In fact the later decision, be it from the FCO or from the Commission, must take the previous decision into consideration, i.e. deduct the amount of the previous fine from those to be imposed by itself. This would not be true, however, with respect to third country authorities, e.g. US antitrust authorities (EC 1972 p. 1291, *Böhringer*), as in such case the objects of the sanctions, because of their objective and geographic centre, are normally different (the Court allowed the enterprise, however, to prove identity, in which case the problem of double sanctions should presumably be dealt with as above).

(b) *Community law 'stricter'.* No conflict will exist where Community law is stricter than national law. In such situation Community law will prevail even where national law expressly provides for an exemption.

(c) *Community law 'neutral'.* No conflict appears to exist where Community law takes a neutral position as expressed by a negative clearance, a 'comfort letter' of the Commission or otherwise (EC rulings in the so-called perfume cases 1980, in particular EC 1980, 2327, *Guerlain*).

(d) *Community law 'positive'.* Conflict may arise where national law takes a negative and Community law a positive position, as expressed by an individual or a group exemption in accordance with art. 85, para. (3). This problem area is too complex to be conclusively answered by reference to the supremacy of

¶1004

Community law. Rather, it is necessary to analyse each decision carefully in order to establish whether a different national decision would be in conflict (in which case the Commission decision would take precedence) or can be reconciled. For instance, an individual exemption may be granted by the Commission because the restrictive covenant was necessary in order to improve production or rationalise distribution. In such case, the exemption would obviously be in conflict with the prohibition of the same agreement by the FCO. Conversely, a Community decision may exempt a distribution system which does not, or only marginally, effects intra-Community trade. A national prohibition would in such case not conflict with the exemption because in effect the decision of the Commission would come close to a restatement of neutrality ((c) above).

The German Federal Court has held that even where the BMW selective distribution systems had been exempted by the Commission, allowing BMW to terminate a dealer who also undertook to distribute the cars of a second manufacturer without prior approval, German cartel law may still apply if it considers such termination distriminatory (see ¶1014) (BGH WuW 1455). According to the FCO, a joint venture which may be exempted by the Commission would still be subject to national merger control provisions (1978 Activity Report p. 54).

(2) *Application of Community law by national authorities and courts*

The FCO has not, under German law, been given power to enforce Community competition rules, but does, of course, take EEC law into consideration and so advises companies in national antitrust procedures.

German courts will, of course, have to apply EEC competition law in the same way as national antitrust law. In doing so, they are not bound by any decision that the Commission may have taken informally, although they will have to take it into consideration when deciding whether or not an agreement is void because of art. 85, para. (1). Even an application for an exemption under para. (2) will normally only cause a court to consider the chances of an exemption being granted. An exemption granted, however, will automatically take the agreement out of art. 85, para. (1) and this will, of course, bind the national court.

If a court is in doubt about a question of Community law, it may decide on its own or submit the question to the European Court (art. 177). In the case of a court of last instance, i.e. the Federal Court, the question must be submitted to the European Court. The European Court does not decide the case itself, under this procedure, but rather answers abstract questions of law which the national court may have raised (but the Court may rephrase the question so raised).

¶1004

CARTEL AGREEMENTS

¶1005 German law

(1) *Cartel prohibition*

According to s. 1 GWB, cartel agreements shall be null and void. They are defined as 'agreements made for a common purpose by enterprises . . . insofar as they are able to influence production or market conditions . . . by restraining competition'. The practice of such an agreement is subject to fines (s. 38(1)). Equally prohibited are concerted actions with the same effect (s. 25(1), 38(1) No. 8).

The words 'for a common purpose' are meant to distinguish cartel agreements from so-called other (vertical or exchange) agreements, but reach beyond partnership-like agreements. All that is required is the pursuance of parallel interests, as a result of which even non-competition clauses in arm's length exchange agreements could be caught by s. 1. For instance, the Federal Court has decided that a non-competition clause binding a supplier of material *vis-à-vis* a manufacturer goes beyond mere exclusivity if the supplier is a potential competitor (BGH WuW 1458, *Fertigbeton* I). At the same time, the Federal Court has accepted non-competition clauses in exchange agreements if they could be considered as being merely ancillary to and not beyond the legitimate protection of what has been paid for, such as the acquisition of a company (BGH WuW 1600, *Frischbeton*).

In order to be prohibited, such cartel agreements must be 'able to influence market conditions', which has been interpreted by the Federal Court (*supra Fertigbeton*) as meaning 'noticeable'. Such effect would not be present where a cartel agreement with a non-competition clause would not cause reactions from competitors, or from suppliers or customers because there are a significant number of participants on both sides of the market and the parties only have a small market share. In order to be noticeable, theoretical effects are insufficient. Rather, it will be necessary to determine facts supporting the conclusion that the agreement is able to influence market conditions.

(2) *Statutory cartel exemptions*

German law provides neither for a rule of reason doctrine nor for an exemption procedure. Only the following listed types of cartels would be exempted under certain conditions, provided they are filed with and do not meet any objection by the Federal or competent State cartel authorities:

(a) *Condition cartels (s. 2).* These are cartels concerning the uniform application of general terms and conditions, except prices.

(b) *Discount cartels (s. 3).* These are cartels concerning rebates (discounts).

(c) *Standards and types cartels (s. 5(1)).* These types of cartels are of little practical significance because the highly developed standardisation in Germany is based on recommendations of specialised associations or institutes (DIN, RKW, VDO, VDE etc.) whose non-binding recommendations are legalised by s. 38(3) and supervised by the cartel authorities.

(d) *Rationalisation cartels (s. 5, para. (2) and (3)).* The cartel authorities may grant individual exemption for cartels which can be shown to increase substantially efficiency or productivity through rationalisation, provided the rationalisation effect is adequate in relation to the restriction of competition and, further, where joint purchasing or selling or price agreements are involved, that the positive purposes cannot be otherwise achieved. The number of cartels legalised this way is quite low.

(e) *Specialisation cartels (s. 5(a)).* Cartels which have as their purpose rationalisation through specialisation can be legalised, provided that, where prices or joint distribution are included, they can be shown to be indispensable and, further, that 'substantial competition' continues to be unaffected by such cartel. This provision has gained considerable practical significance. 'Substantial competition' cannot be defined generally. A rule of thumb may be that such cartel should not combine a market share of more than 25 per cent unless particularly strong competition exists outside the cartel or market entry barriers are particularly low. Normally the details are discussed in advance with the FCO.

(f) *Cartels of small and medium-sized companies (s. 5(b)).* Such cartels have gained considerable significance. They will be legal if they have as their purpose rationalisation by co-operation, such as joint supply and distribution, and will not combine more than 10–15 per cent of the market. In practice, even a large company may be included if this should prove to be the only way to bring about efficient co-operation of small companies. Instead of a binding co-operation agreement, small and medium-sized companies may agree on joint recommendations, provided they are expressly stated to be non-binding (s. 38(2) No. 1), which device is frequently used for purchasing associations of consumer goods.

In its Notice on Co-operation with Insignificant Anti-Competitive Effects of 8 July 1980, the FCO announced that it would tolerate restrictions on competition which:

(i) result in greater efficiency through co-ordination;

(ii) only comprise a small number of small or medium-sized companies; and

(iii) only comprise a total market share of 5 per cent or less.

¶1005

Even if such restrictions on competition would significantly affect the market condition of competitors or deteriorate the prices, terms, etc. of suppliers or customers, the FCO will only issue a seize and desist order, and not levy fines. The most important restrictions, i.e. relating to prices, quota or territories, or public tenders or biddings are expressly excluded, however.

(g) *Export cartels (s. 6).*   Cartels which only affect competition outside Germany need only to be filed. Cartels which also include domestic restrictions require the approval of the FCO, which will be granted if such restriction is necessary to protect or promote exports, and provided such restriction would not violate EEC law or any other free trade agreement to which Germany is a party, or the restraint of competition within Germany would be substantial and the interest in preserving such competition would prevail. The underlying reason for such export cartel privilege, which is similar to that of other Western countries, is that it is considered necessary to provide for some sort of counter-weighing powers in foreign markets with less developed antitrust laws. This way domestic manufacturers are allowed even to commit domestic exporters to jointly agreed prices and conditions or to provide for exclusive supply to a joint sales venture.

In a similar way the FCO could legalise import cartels in situations where the German importer when buying abroad could show himself to be confronted with no competition among the sellers (s. 7). However, this provision has virtually lost its significance.

¶1006   EEC cartel prohibition

(1) *Prohibition and exemption*
As discussed above, EEC law (if applicable in view of the interstate trade clause and the requirement of noticeability of anticompetitive effects (see ¶1003 above)) is at first view much more simple:

(a) art. 85, para. (1) does not distinguish between cartel and other (hori-zontal or vertical) restrictions;

(b) any restriction may be exempted by the Commission if the conditions of para. (3) are met.

Paragraph (3) allows the prohibition of para. (1) to be declared inapplicable in the case of any agreement, decision or concerted action or any category thereof:

'... which contributes to improving the production or distribution of goods or to promoting technical or economic progress while allowing consumers a fair share of the resulting benefit and which does not:

   (a) impose on the undertakings concerned restrictions which are not indispensable
to the attainment of this objective;

   (b) afford such undertakings the possibility of eliminating competition in respect
of a substantial part of the products in question.'

The Commission has adopted a number of categorical exemptions (Regulations on Group Exemptions) which are discussed separately in this chapter.
Individual exemption requires formal filing (using Form A/B as issued by the
Commission), setting forth in some detail why, in the applicant's opinion, the
agreement in question is considered not to violate para. (1) (application for
negative clearance) or how the conditions of para. (3) are met. In order to be
exempted, an agreement:

   (a) *must* –

      (i) improve production, distribution or technical economic progress,

      (ii) allow consumers a fair share of resulting benefits;

   (b) *must not* –

      (i) impose restrictions which are indispensable,

      (ii) in effect, eliminate competition on the market.

Subject to review by the Court, the Commission has in fact some discretion
in ruling on individual applications. In simple cases it may just send a 'comfort
letter' advising that it sees no reason to take further action. In other cases it may
press the parties to modify the agreement in order to qualify for an exemption.
A negative aspect of such procedure is that the decision will be published and
may be subject to conditions, and is always granted for a limited time only
(subject to renewal).

(2) *Group exemptions*

(a) *Specialisation agreements.* Specialisation agreements may fall under art.
85(1), but may at the same time provide for more efficiency and cheaper
products. Under reg. no. 417/85 (OJ 1985 L 53: valid until December 1997), the
Commission provides for the group exemption of agreements where the parties
accept reciprocal obligations not to manufacture certain products but to leave
it to the other party, or to manufacture or have them manufactured jointly,
including by a joint venture, provided that the agreement does not impose
restrictions of competition other than exclusivity, i.e.:

   (i) a prohibition on concluding with third parties specialisation agreements
relating to the same product;

   (ii) the obligation to procure the products only from the other party, except
where they are obtainable on more favourable terms which the other
party is not prepared to offer;

¶1006

   (iii) sole distribution, provided that intermediaries and users can also obtain the products from other sources and the parties do not render this difficult.

The agreement may also provide for the following product-related obligations:

   (iv) to supply and observe minimum quality;

   (v) to maintain a minimum stock of products and spare parts;

   (vi) to provide customer and guarantee services.

Further conditions include:

   (aa) the contractual products must not represent a market share of more than 20 per cent in the Common Market (or a substantial part thereof); and

   (bb) the aggregate annual turnover of the parties, including affiliates, must not exceed 500 million ECU (¶1003 above).

If the sales amount in (bb) above should be exceeded, exemption can be obtained through simplified filing, which means that the agreement would be exempted from the date of filing if the Commission does not object within six months, provided the notification expressly refers to art. 4 of reg. no. 417/85 and the information furnished with it is complete and correct. If the market share of (aa) above is exceeded, or if restrictions other than those listed under (i)–(vi) above are included, individual exemption is required. The regulation allows the Commission at any time to withdraw benefits of the block exemption, in particular if:

   (i) an agreement does not provide for significant rationalisation or consumers do not receive a fair share of benefits; or

   (ii) the contract products are not subject to effective competition from other products.

(b) *Research and development agreements.* Co-operation in research and development and in the exploitation of the results is generally considered to promote technical and economic progress by increasing the dissemination of technical knowledge and avoiding duplication of work. Under reg. no. 418/85 (OJ 1985 L 53: valid until 31 December 1997), the Commission provides for the group exemption of agreements for the purpose of joint research and development, including or excluding joint exploitation, 'joint' being defined as including joint ventures, joint subcontracting to a third party, or allocation and specialisation among the parties, on condition that:

   (i) the joint work is carried out within a defined programme;

   (ii) all parties have access to the results;

¶1006

   (iii) each party is free to exploit the results (except where joint exploitation is agreed);

   (iv) joint exploitation relates only to patented or otherwise qualified know-how (know-how which substantially contributes to progress) which is necessary for the manufacturer of the contract products or the application of the contract processes;

   (v) any joint venture or subcontractor is required to supply the products only to the parties;

   (vi) in the case of specialisation the relevant party must fulfil orders of all parties.

The exemption also applies to the following restrictions of competition ('white clauses'):

   (aa) prohibition of independent research and development in the contract and in closely related fields;

   (bb) prohibition on concluding research and development agreements with third parties in the same or closely related fields (exclusivity);

   (cc) exclusive supply;

   (dd) exclusive territory for manufacture by each party;

   (ee) restriction of manufacture to specified fields (except where parties are competitors);

   (ff) prohibition of active marketing in the other party's distribution territory for five years from the first marketing of the product (provided users and intermediaries can obtain the product from other suppliers without difficulties caused by the parties);

   (gg) exchange of information and non-exclusive improvement licences.

The agreement may also provide for the following obligations:

   (i) obligation to communicate necessary patented or secret technical knowledge;

   (ii) prohibition on the use of know-how received from another party for other purposes;

   (iii) obligation to obtain and maintain intellectual property rights;

   (iv) secrecy obligation also after expiry of the agreement;

   (v) obligation to inform of any patent infringements and to take or share in legal action against infringers;

   (vi) obligation to equalise unequal research and development or exploitation by royalties or services;

¶1006

(vii) sharing or third-party royalties;

(viii) minimum supply of products and minimum standards of quality.

The exemption will not apply in the case of ('black clauses'):

(i) restriction of research and development in unrelated fields or after completion of the programme;

(ii) prohibition on challenging intellectual property rights relevant to the programme after completion, or of the party's property rights protecting the results of the research and development after expiry of the agreement;

(iii) restriction on quantity of manufacture or sale or employment of contract process;

(iv) restriction on resale prices;

(v) restriction on customers;

(vi) sales restrictions or prohibition of active marketing in the other party's territory beyond the five-year period of (ff) above;

(vii) prohibition on selling to users or dealers within one party's territory for resale in other territories within the Common Market in the absence of joint manufacture, or an obligation to make it difficult for users or dealers to obtain products from other dealers, in particular by exercising intellectual property rights, or to take measures to prevent them from obtaining or putting on the market contract products.

A further condition is that where the parties are competing manufacturers of products capable of being improved or replaced by the contract products when entering into the agreement, their market share in the common market (or a substantial part thereof) must not exceed 20 per cent.

The exemption applies for the duration of the research and development programme and, in the case of joint exploitation, for five years from the time the products are first put on the market, and shall continue thereafter as long as the parties' combined market shares do not exceed 20 per cent.

Agreements which do not contain black or white clauses within the above meaning, but which otherwise provide for restrictions of competition, can be exempted through simplified filing, which means that the agreement would be exempted from the date of filing if the Commission does not object within six months, if the notification makes express reference to art. 7 of the regulation and the information furnished is complete and correct.

The Commission may at any time withdraw the benefits of the block exemption, in particular where:

¶1006

(i) the existence of the agreement substantially restricts third party research and development because of limited research capacity;

(ii) the existence of the agreement substantially restricts access of third
parties to the market because of the particular structure of supply;

(iii) without valid reason the parties do not exploit the results of the research
and development;

(iv) the contract products are not subject to effective competition.

¶1007   Typical problem areas

(1) *Lawful agreements*

(a) *Undertakings.*   Competition law is directed towards enterprises or undertakings, but the term 'undertakings' is broadly defined under both German and
EEC law. It would include private inventors and artists to the extent they are
exploiting their inventions and performances, but not private transactions
including employment or Government action, except where the Government
engages in commercial business. For commercial agents see under ¶1009 below.

Parent companies and subsidiaries would not normally be considered independent enterprises among which competition could be restricted. However,
both the FCO and the Commission have reserved a different view where the
relationship is such that both companies act independently on the market and
where the subsidiary is not in fact following the instructions of the parent.
Where the Commission finds that the parent company was involved in illegal
actions of the subsidiaries – even in the absence of positive evidence – it will fine
both companies jointly and severally (OJ 1980, L 377/16, *Johnson & Johnson*).

(b) *Ancillary restraints.*   While non-competition provisions in other sectors
of commercial law do not *per se* take precedence over the cartel prohibition,
any possible conflict must be reconciled on a case-by-case basis. At the same
time it is recognised that competition law is not violated by restrictions necessary
to secure the loyal performance of an agreement entered into for legitimate
purposes.

In the case of a partnership, commercial law would normally provide for, or
at least allow, the partners to agree on non-competition (see Chapter 4 ¶417).
The Federal Court, when analysing the conflict, has considered such a clause as
not violating the cartel prohibition if it restricts the general partner who is active
in the partnership and thus owes a particular degree of loyalty, but not in the
case of a partner whose only obligation is to make his capital contribution and
thus comes close to being a mere investor (BGH WuW 1517, *Gabelstapler*; cf.
WuW 2047, *Werbeagentur*, where the Federal Court accepted a non-competition clause of a limited partner who, however, held a majority participation).

A non-competition clause entered into in order to protect the buyer of a business from losing back to the seller what he has paid for would be legal, provided that it does not extend beyond, in scope and time, what could be considered reasonable and necessary. While this latter criterion depends on the individual case, the Commission indicates as a general guide, that:

'... where the transfer of a business also involves the transfer of good-will and know-how, a period of approximately five years will normally be acceptable, whereas a period of approximately two years will normally apply if the sale involves only the transfer of good-will'

(13th Report 1983, point 88). Any longer period will be reduced, and in *Nutricia/de Rooij* (which also involved a trademark licence which allowed the seller/licensor to use his trademark again after two years) the period was reduced to four years (OJ 1983, L 376 p. 22).

Under German law, the position of the Federal Court is similar, although there is still a risk that an agreement with an excessive non-competition clause may be immoral and entirely void (BGH WuW 1600, *Frischbeton*).

(2) *Market information*

(a) *Commission's view.*   Agreements on the exchange of information always raise suspicions that the purpose is to allow the parties to identify particular contracts and discounts. Where such discounts are made by one of only a few suppliers, competitors are likely to act in the same way next time. The consequence of such an information system would be to avoid any such discounts, whereas the purpose of competition law is to protect competitors even in making secret discounts.

In its Notice On Co-operation Agreements, the Commission held the joint production of 'neutral' statistics, market studies, etc. to be permitted ('neutral' meaning to exclude any disguised method of price fixing), but considered it contrary to art. 85(1) 'for a producer to communicate to his competitors the essential elements of his price policy, such as price lists, discounts and terms of trade he applies' (OJ 1974, L 160/1, IFTRA Rules on Glass Containers).

(b) *Federal Cartel Office.*   The FCO has issued the following principles (WuW 1977, p. 248):

(i) Industry-wide market statistics including information on prices do not violate antitrust law to the extent they only state maximum and minimum prices or average prices and do not allow conclusions on individual transactions;

(ii) Section 1 would be infringed if the system included an obligation to disclose details of quotations or transactions and resulted in the identification of suppliers, customers or latest data of individual transactions;

(iii) Also prohibited would be non-identifying systems which violated the prohibition of recommendations (s. 38(1), No. 11) or co-ordination (s. 25(1));

(iv) In individual cases the following aspects may require investigation—

- information on main prices between maximum and minimum prices,
- maximum and minimum prices together with related quantities,
- maximum and minimum prices related to geographic areas,
- excessive details on product groups,
- small number of available suppliers per product group,
- small number product quantities or transactions,
- maximum, minimum or average prices of only a few companies,
- only short information periods,
- maximum, minimum or average prices together with other transactions data;

(v) Illegal information systems may still be tolerated depending on the market conditions, e.g. in the case of small or medium-sized companies.

(3) *Joint ventures*

Joint ventures are generally described as companies with two or more parent companies and are of practical significance in many industries where two companies may want to combine capacities in order to obtain economies of scale or to enter into a market where entry might be difficult for each of them acting individually. The (usually two) parent companies collaborating in such joint venture are unlikely, if not expressly forbidden, to compete with the joint venture (and perhaps also with each other) on the market of the joint venture and/or neighbouring third markets (so-called group effect).

Whereas, under the Treaty of Paris (Coal & Steel), joint ventures have normally been reviewed under merger control aspects in EEC law (which does not recognize (yet) a merger control procedure), the Commission strictly applies the cartel prohibition and exemption provisions of art. 85. On the other hand the FCO applies either or both the cartel prohibition or merger control provisions, depending on each case.

(a) *Federal Cartel Office.* The FCO tries to distinguish between concentrative and co-operative joint ventures and follows the so-called 'double control' doctrine. In its annual report in 1978 (p. 23) the FCO established the following principle:

'In order to solve at least a part of the problem of double control, the FCO has established principles for those joint ventures which are of purely concentrative

¶1007

nature without co-operative elements. It follows an opinion increasingly voiced in legal literature, according to which it should be differentiated according to the actual structure of the legal relationship between the participating enterprises as well as purpose and nature of the joint venture. Joint ventures which primarily serve the purpose of joint investments for production of goods or services – either for the market or for the participating parent companies – shall be considered as at least overwhelmingly concentrative and subject only to merger control. If, however, the co-ordination of certain activities or the market behaviour of the parent companies is in front, then, according to such opinion, the underlying agreements shall exclusively be treated pursuant to s. 1.

The Federal Cartel Office considers a joint venture as purely concentrative if:

it is a fully functioning enterprise with all essential functions;

it performs market related activities and is not only active exclusively or primarily on behalf of the parent company on an upstream or downstream market; and

the parent company itself is not or is no longer active on the relevant market of the joint venture.

Under such conditions the FCO will not apply the cartel prohibition of s. 1; at least, not to the following provisions:

establishment of such purely concentrative joint venture;

prohibition on competing, to the extent it does not exceed the scope, territory or duration of the joint venture;

ancillary restrictions on competition which are necessary for the function of the joint venture.

In the case of joint ventures which differ from purely concentrative ones, merely because they serve the supply of the parent company on a preceding production level, the FCO will not apply the cartel prohibition to:

the establishment of the joint venture as such;

a non-competition clause and other incidental arrangements which restrict competition to the extent necessary for the functioning of the joint venture, e.g. the obligation of the shareholder to cover the relevant part of overheads in the case of insufficient use of the available capacity.'

The above principles have been confirmed by the Federal Court, which also confirmed that in order to determine whether a joint venture is or is not in fact established in order to co-ordinate and adjust the diverse interests of the shareholders, not only the wording of the articles but all underlying circumstances and facts shall be taken into account (WuW BGH 2169, *Mischwerke*).

(b) *Commission.* The Commission has applied the cartel prohibition to joint ventures with increased strictness while at the same time granting individual exemptions, in particular in the case of technically sophisticated products. It should be noted that such exemptions are always restricted with regard to duration, made subject to conditions (in particular, providing for efficient competition of the parent companies at the end of the joint venture) and subject to more or less continued supervision by the Commission.

¶1007

The Commission has recently circulated draft guidelines inviting the comments of national authorities, business and legal circles. These guidelines basically summarise previous decisions.

According to such guidelines, joint ventures are defined as undertakings jointly controlled by two or more independent firms, and joint control is said always to exist where neither parent can determine independently the joint venture's business activity.

Joint ventures do not fall within EEC competition rules if they either have effect only on the territory of one Member State, or the territories of third countries or have only negligible effect, which is indicated by a 5 per cent combined market share.

Further, art. 85(1) is not affected where the parent companies are neither actual nor potential competitors, i.e. where individual market entry cannot reasonably be expected considering factors such as financial, technical and management resources. Where competitors cease to be so as a result of the formation of the joint venture, it does not fall within art. 85, but may fall within art. 86 (concentrative joint venture). In applying art. 86, the Commission will consider whether an existing dominant position of one or several parent companies together is consolidated or strenghtened.

Under art. 85 the Commission distinguishes between horizontal, vertical and diagonal joint ventures:

(i) where parent companies and competitors and the joint venture will operate on the same market, a restriction of competition between the parents is likely, if not unavoidable;

(ii) where the parent companies are competitors and the joint venture will operate on an upstream or downstream market, competition between the parent companies will be less restricted the less the upstream product is of importance for the downstream product, but where it involves exclusive supply or purchasing market access of third companies may be affected;

(iii) where parents are competitors on a market that has nothing to do with the activities of the joint venture, competition will rarely be restricted.

The formation of a joint venture must be distinguished from restrictions on competition additionally agreed upon. The Commission strictly applies art. 85(1) to any restrictions going beyond what is necessary for the setting up and operation of the joint venture, such as restrictions on competition, supply or purchasing, prices, quantities or markets.

Under art. 85(3) (rather than (1)), the Commission states that if the partners' combined market share does not exceed 15 per cent, it can normally be assumed that the joint venture does not distort the competitive structure of the

¶1007

market, and this is also true if the joint venture includes distribution, although the closer the market share approximates such 15 per cent, the more detailed an analysis may be required. The Commission also states that joint ventures which lead to a reduction of structural over-capacity, and thus help undertakings in crisis sectors to return to viability, contribute as a rule to the attainment of the Community's general economic objectives.

VERTICAL RESTRICTIONS

¶1008   In general

Vertical restrictions are those between seller and buyer, lessor and lessee, manufacturer and distributor, contractor and subcontractor, licensor and licensee, etc. Under German law such vertical restrictions are not prohibited as generally and as strictly as horizontal restrictions among actual or potential competitors because the danger for competition is less imminent where a restriction is in essence part of the market strategy of only one undertaking.

Community law, on the other hand, does not expressly distinguish between horizontal and vertical restrictions, but tries to build some kind of rule of reason into the technique of adopting group exemptions in order to take into consideration that certain restrictions may have positive effects as defined by art. 85(3).

¶1009   Retail restrictions

(1) *General*

Neither Community nor German law prohibits unilateral refusals to deal, or customer selection or discrimination unless the undertaking is in a dominant position. In the absence of a dominant position any such action, in order to be prohibited, must be based on a bi- or multilateral concertation or agreement.

Section 15 GWB prohibits agreements concerning goods or services 'insofar as they restrict a party in its freedom to determine prices or terms in contracts for such goods or services with third parties', except those relating to foreign markets and except that publishing companies are permitted to practise price maintenance with respect to books and other publications (s. 16).

For s. 15 to apply, there must be two agreements among companies on different market levels: a first-tier agreement by which one party shall be restricted with respect to prices or terms which it shall agree (second-tier agreements) with its customers. Under Community law, art. 85(1) expressly prohibits 'direct or indirect fixing purchase or selling prices or of any other trading conditions'.

(2) *Commercial agents*

No such relationship exists in the case of commercial agencies, where the agent brings about agreements with customers in the name, on the account and at the risk of the principal (see Chapter 3, ¶303). The Federal Court has recognised this system for the distribution of gasoline (BGH WuW 877, *Shell-Tankstelle*; and for advertising media: BGH WuW 1103, *Context*).

Against this it is argued that s. 15 could thereby easily be evaded, and in fact the FCO has prohibited distribution systems for brown goods of Telefunken, whereby approx. 6,700 retailers had first been made commission agents and then commercial agents. Both decisions were upheld by the Berlin Court of Appeal. In its second decision (WuW OLG 3457), the Berlin Court held that in the case of a commercial agent who does in fact himself conclude the individual sales contracts on behalf of the principal (*Abschlußvertreter*), even the shift of the risk from such agent to the manufacturer would not be sufficient to take the agreement out of the scope of s. 15 where the balance of the relationship would correspond to that of a dealership. It found the following obligations untypical of commercial agency and thus s. 15 to apply:

- obligation of the principal to provide for price maintenance even if such obligation only results from mutual interest and the total of the system rather than express wording;
- lack of any non-competition clause;
- distribution of consumer goods to final customers;
- position and denomination of the agent as *Fachhaendler* (specialised dealer);
- warranty and repair services.

The Federal Court has recently reversed the above decision (its reasons still being unpublished at the time of publication of this book) and the Telefunken type distribution will thus be in line with German competition law.

In this context it should be noted that as early as 1962 the Commission published a notice on exclusive agents (OJ 1962, 2921), according to which art. 85(1) does not apply to agreements by which a commercial representative agrees in a specified territory to arrange for or conclude transactions for or on the account of another undertaking, provided that his functions are not in fact those of a dealer. The main criterion is expressly seen in the assumption of the risks of the transaction: only the normal credit risk may be shifted to the agent, whereas the obligation to provide for a significant stock of inventory at his risk, significant service at his cost or the right to determine prices and terms would make him a dealer.

Like German commercial law (see Chapter 3), that of most continental laws provides for detailed obligations and protection of the commercial agent.

(3) Most favourable prices and non-competition clauses

Section 15 GWB only relates to the freedom to determine prices or terms, but does not provide for restrictions on the conclusion of second-tier contracts as such. Unlike Community law, non-competition clauses or other clauses restricting the choice or allocating customers would not be prohibited by s. 15. The same is true with respect to field of use and tie-in and similar restrictions which do not even relate to a second-tier contract (in the case of 'market strength', however, see ¶1013).

On the other hand, s. 15 has been interpreted as not only prohibiting direct restrictions on terms and prices, but also indirect or economic restrictions. In particular, the Federal Court has held most-favourable treatment clauses to be invalid (WuW 1787, *Garant*). Presumably such most-favourable price clauses would still be valid as ancillary to a minimum quantity or similar requirement, but this is still undecided.

(4) Price recommendations

German cartel law makes it an offence for an undertaking to issue a recommendation which through uniform conduct would result in the circumvention of a prohibition (s. 38(1) No. 11). However, s. 38a allows price recommendations under conditions which are narrowly interpreted by the FCO:

(a) the price recommendation must only concern branded goods which are in price competition with similar goods of other manufacturers;

(b) the recommendation must be issued by the manufacturer or dealer or importer who legally attaches the trademark;

(c) the recommendation must expressly be stated as non-binding (the FCO insists on the use of the words *unverbindliche Preisempfehlung* or *unverbindlich empfohlener Preis*);

(d) no pressure or even influence must be exercised for the enforcement of the recommendation (anything beyond a mere recommendation will be interpreted as pressure);

(e) the recommendation must be issued with the expectation that it will correspond to the price likely to be charged (this will not be so where approximately 20 per cent of the retailers charge 10–15 per cent lower prices).

¶1009

¶1010 Distribution agreements

(1) *German law*

Restrictions on distribution, subcontracts and other vertical agreements as listed below need to be entered into in writing in order to be valid (see Chapter 1, ¶112). Such restrictions are not illegal *per se*, but may also be prohibited by the FCO under certain conditions. According to s. 18 these are restrictions included in 'agreements between undertakings concerning goods or services' which:

(a) restrict one party in the freedom to use the supplied goods, other goods or services;

(b) restrict a party in the purchase or supply of other goods or services from or to third parties;

(c) restrict a party in the sale of the supplied goods to third parties; or

(d) oblige a party to take normally unrelated goods or services.

Among such restrictions, exclusivity ((b) and (c)) is of particular practical significance. The cartel authorities may declare any such agreement null and void:

'. . . to the extent

(a) by such agreements a number of enterprises which is significant for competition on the market is similarly bound and unfairly restricted in its freedom of competition; or

(b) by such agreements market entry by other enterprises is unfairly restricted; or

(c) the extent of such restrictions significantly reduces competition on the market'.

Nevertheless, until such declaration is issued, the agreement will be valid and enforceable (in the case of market strength, however, see ¶1013).

(2) *EEC group exemption of exclusive distribution agreements*

EEC law recognises that certain restrictions may not violate competition law or may in general lead to an improvement in distribution, in particular in international trade. It may sometimes be the only way for a manufacturer to enter a market and compete with other manufacturers already present. Under reg. no. 1983/83 (valid until 31 December 1997) (OJ 1983 L 173) (replacing the previous reg. no. 1967/67), the Commission has exempted agreements between two parties whereby one (the supplier) agrees to supply contract products for resale within the whole, or a defined area, of the Common Market only to the other (the distributor). 'Resale' excludes any processing except packaging or only additions of insignificant value. 'Products' must not include services if the fees exceed the sales price for the product. Leasing would be considered as equivalent to an outright sale.

The supplier must not be subject to *restrictions*, except for the prohibition not to directly supply to users in the territory, and the distributor must not be subject to restrictions other than:

(a) a prohibition on manufacturing or distributing competitive products;

(b) a requirement to obtain contract products for resale only from the supplier;

(c) a prohibition on active marketing (seeking customers, establishing branches or maintaining distribution depots for the products) outside his territory.

No such restriction must exceed the term of the agreement, but the agreement may provide for non-restrictive *obligations* of the distributor such as:

(a) purchasing complete ranges of products or minimum quantities;

(b) selling the products under prescribed trademarks or packaging;

(c) providing for sales promotion, in particular advertising, maintaining a distribution network or stock of inventory, providing for after-sales and warranty services or/and employing qualified personnel.

In no case must the freedom to determine resale prices and terms or the choice of customers be restricted, but minimum quantities may normally be prescribed. Also, objective standards for dealers based on professional qualifications and quality (but not quantity of business premises) may be prescribed, provided that such criteria are uniformly applied without discrimination.

The exemption applies on *condition* that:

(a) exclusive distribution agreements between competing manufacturers (including affiliates) are not reciprocal; non-reciprocal agreements are permitted where either or both parties (including affiliates) have a total annual turnover of 100 million ECU (see ¶1003 above) or less;

(b) users can obtain the product in the territory from sources other than the distributor or have an alternative source of supply outside the territory (including the supplier if prepared to deliver on request);

(c) neither party makes it difficult for retailers or users to obtain the product from other dealers inside or, in their absence, outside the Common Market, in particular by exercising industrial property rights.

The regulation allows the Commission to withdraw the benefits of the group exemption, in particular where:

(a) contract products are not subject to effective competition from other products;

¶1010

   (b) access by other suppliers to the market is made significantly difficult;

   (c) it is difficult for retailers or users to obtain the products from dealers outside the territory for reasons other than those listed under (c) above; or

   (d) the distributor refuses to supply certain categories of purchasers with no alternative or supplies to them only at different prices or conditions of sale, or generally sells at excessive prices.

(3) *Group exemption of exclusive purchase*

The Commission has adopted a separate regulation (no. 1984/83 OJ 1983 L173/5) exempting categories of exclusive purchasing agreements. These are different from exclusive distribution agreements in that here the reseller is not protected against competition from other resellers, and in turn is free to distribute outside his sales area.

    The regulation only covers agreements where the reseller commits himself to purchase all the contract products he requires from the supplier, except that he may be permitted to buy from others at better terms or where the supplier cannot deliver. The supplier may only agree to a prohibition of direct competition (prohibition on distributing at the same distribution level within the reseller's main sales area). The reseller, in addition to the above exclusive supply commitment, may accept the restrictions and obligations referred to under (2) above, except for the prohibition on active marketing.

    In addition to the condition in (2) above (agreements among competitors), the exemption applies only on condition that:

   (a) the exclusive purchase commitment must not be agreed for different products, unless they are related to each other either by nature or according to commercial practice; and

   (b) the agreement is not entered into for an indefinite duration or for a period exceeding five years.

Special provisions apply for exclusive purchase of beer for resale in restaurants and for the exclusive purchase of gasoline for resale in service stations.

(4) *Selective distribution*

A manufacturer is basically free to determine his marketing and distribution policy. He may even decide arbitrarily where, when and for how long to appoint a distributor. Competition law would only apply where such policy becomes a matter of agreement, i.e. where the manufacturer commits himself *vis-à-vis* distributors to observe certain criteria (as discussed below) or if the manufacturer is in a market dominating or similar position (see 'Abuse of Market Domination or Market Strength' at ¶1012 et seq. below).

¶1010

(a) *EEC law*.   Selective distribution systems have been the subject of a large number of decisions, including the leading case ruled by the European Court (EC 1977, 1905 *Metro/Saba* I), which confirms a basic distinction between so-called open and closed systems or qualitative and quantitative restrictions (see also 5th Commission Report 1975, point 12).

To ensure that his goods are sold in a satisfactory manner, a manufacturer may choose his dealers by setting *objective qualitative requirements* as regards his own and his staff's qualifications and training and the nature of his premises, and require advertisement and after-sales services, but may not restrict the choice of the dealer to whom to sell.

Typically, an authorised dealer is *prohibited* to sell to other dealers *who do not meet the standards prescribed* by the manufacturer. Provided that such standards are reasonable in relation to the nature of the product and are uniformly applied without discrimination, such system would not be caught by art. 85(1). They must neither be designed nor practised in order to exclude certain types of dealers such as cash-and-carry outlets (EC OJ 1983 C 330 *AEG-Telefunken*). The Commission objected to distribution systems providing for the supply of plumbing fittings only to plumbers and not also to general retailers and department stores (OJ 1985 L 19, 20, *Grohe/Ideal Standard*).

A system requiring lengthy admission procedures and advance clearance of an appointed dealer before supplying another dealer may be found by the Commission to be too difficult to control discrimination; the Commission will in such cases require the manufacturer to allow distributors to appoint dealers or to accept automatic appointment procedures (see OJ 1984, L 118, *IBM Personal Computers*). The introduction of a code system by the manufacturer would be permitted, unless exceeding a legitimate purpose (e.g. in order to prevent and check exports).

Export and retail price restrictions are prohibited and unlikely to obtain *individual exemption*. Certain quantitative restrictions may be exempted due to the peculiarities of the product, e.g. automobiles or luxury products such as watches or perfumes. In addition, obligations such as the requirement to carry the full range of products, minimum sales or to further the distribution system, which would be harmless in a bi-lateral agreement, would be caught by art. 85(1) and require individual exemption in the case of a selective distribution system. This is certainly true for any non-competition clause. The dealer may be required to carry list prices, provided this does not result in any price cartel or price maintenance.

The Commission has become particularly vigilant in ensuring that, due to their cumulative effect, even national distribution systems will not reduce competition in an entire product market beyond a tolerable degree (14th Commission Report 1984, point 65).

¶1010

Taking into consideration peculiarities of the product, in particular safety aspects, the Commission has issued a special regulation on *group exemption for the distribution of motor vehicles* (reg. no. 123/85: OJ 1985 L 15/16), allowing systems combining exclusive and selective distribution. The supplier may agree only to supply one dealer in a given territory and only a specific number of undertakings within the distribution system. The dealer, on the other hand, may be prohibited from selling other manufacturer's vehicles, from seeking customers outside his territory and from supplying other dealers outside the distribution network. At the same time the regulation makes sure that the system will not be absolutely closed. The non-competition clause of the dealer does not extend to spare parts of equal quality (a point on which the Federal Court applying German law has been less strict considering difficulties in promptly detecting quality deficiencies: BGH WuW 1829, *Original VW Ersatz-teile* II). The dealer must be allowed to sell even to non-authorised intermediaries who can present a written purchase order from an end user (one of several clauses designed to assist direct importation of the cars within the Common Market).

The Commission may withdraw the benefits of the exemption where direct importation is made difficult, e.g. if authorised dealers refuse to perform guarantee services on cars which they have not sold or which have been imported from other member countries, or where particularly long delivery periods are applied, where agreements are used to set significantly different prices among Member States or where different national markets are the result of unreasonable differences in prices and terms.

(b) *German law.* In Germany, selective distribution traditionally is of particular significance. The range of products sold only in specialised stores (*Fachhandel*) extends well beyond technically sophisticated products and includes toys, china, cosmetics and sports equipment. In order for a manufacturer to protect such a system against outsiders ('free riders'), he must prove comprehensiveness (*Lückenlosigkeit*).

As explained in Chapter 11, ¶1109, a dealer can no longer be expected to honour the agreement and in particular not to supply outsiders when the system shows significant gaps or loopholes. The supplier is required therefore to take immediate legal steps against any infringements, not only of his authorised dealers but also of outsiders. Injunctions against outsiders are possible under German law only where the supplier is able to prove theoretical and practical comprehensiveness which allows the conclusion that the outsider must have obtained contract products through breach of contract or through other methods of unfair competition. In this context, the supplier must also prove that it is legally impossible to obtain the products by imports from other countries

¶1010

which, in turn, presupposes that at least within the Common Market all dealers are bound by similar agreements prohibiting supply to non-authorised dealers, that such agreements must not violate EEC competition rules and that they are equally enforced (as mentioned under (a) above, a code system identifying points of sale would normally be possible). Objections raised by the Commission against the distribution system in question do not automatically prejudice the national court, but require the supplier to convince it that such objections were unfounded under art. 85 (BGH WuW 2183, *Grundig*).

A separate, but important, problem exists in case of market strength, as defined by s. 26(2) (see ¶1013).

¶1011 Licence agreements

(1) *General*

Neither EEC nor national German antitrust law, in the absence of a dominant market position, restrict the owner's freedom to make use of his industrial property rights, and such rights include the state granted monopoly of a patentee to exploit a patented invention. In order to conflict with antitrust law, there must be some kind of multipartite action, in particular an agreement (and such agreement must normally go beyond a simple one-off sale or transfer of such right). The theory that art. 36 exempts industrial property rights entirely from the scope of art. 85 was rejected by the European Court in its first antitrust decision (1966, 322, *Grundig-Consten*). The Court has since repeated that industrial property rights must not be used to establish or reinforce export bans in private agreements.

With respect to agreements concerning the use of industrial property rights, the court in the *Maize Seed case* (EC 1982 p. 2015, *Nungesser*) objected to the position taken by the Commission that exclusivity provided for in a licence agreement would be caught by art. 85(1), and instead distinguished between an open exclusive licence prohibiting the licensor from exploiting the invention or from granting further licences within the licensed territory (not normally caught by art. 85) and an exclusive licence with absolute territorial protection which, in view of the significance of maize seeds for human and animal food, could not even be exempted under para. (3).

(2) *Group exemption of patent licences*

Under reg. no. 2349/84 (OJ 1984 L 219/15), the Commission accepted certain categories of exclusive licences which 'make patentees more willing to grant licences and licensees more inclined to undertake the investment required to manufacture, use and put on the market a new product or to use a new process'.

The regulation applies to licence agreements for patents, including patent applications (provided the application is made within one year after the date of the agreement) and utility models, with or without communication of know-how, sublicences and similar agreements, but excluding agreements relating to patent pools, joint ventures or reciprocal licences, except where the latter does not include any territorial restriction.

The list of exempted restrictions distinguishes between the licensor's reserved territory, the licensed territory and territories licensed to other licensees, provided the licensed product is protected in those territories (always within the Common Market) by parallel patents. Exempted are the following restrictions ('white clauses'):

(a) prohibition on the licensor within the licensed territory licensing others or exploiting the invention himself;

(b) prohibition on the licensee—
   — in the licensor's territory exploiting the licensed invention in any way,
   — in the territory of other licensees exploiting the invention (i.e. by manufacture or use; by an active sales policy; or, for the first five years after the product is first put on the market, even by any sale or delivery);

(c) obligation of the licensee to use only the licensor's trademark or packaging.

The above exemptions from restrictions on putting the licensed product on the market shall not apply in the case of mere distribution licences.

The regulation also contains a non-exhaustive list of further permitted obligations:

(i) obligation to procure goods services necessary for satisfactory exploitation;

(ii) minimum royalties and minimum quantities;

(iii) field of use restriction;

(iv) prohibition on exploiting patents after termination of the agreement;

(v) prohibition on licensee granting sub-licences;

(vi) secrecy obligation for know-how;

(vii) obligation to inform licensor of patent infringements, to take or assist in taking action against infringers;

(viii) minimum quality;

(ix) mutual non-exclusive licence on improvements;

(x) obligation of licensor to grant most-favourable treatment.

¶1011

Expressly prohibited are ('black clauses'):

- prohibition on challenging validity of patent (but the licensor may terminate the agreement in such event);

- automatic extension beyond expiry of patents initially licensed by inclusion of future patents, unless the agreement includes an annual notice provision (but the licensor may charge royalties for secret know-how used by the licensee after the life of the patents);

- non-competition clauses (but the licensee may be required to use his best endeavours to exploit the invention);

- royalties even on products which are not patented;

- restrictions on maximum quantities;

- restrictions on prices;

- restrictions on customers;

- instead of (ix) above, the obligation of the licensee to assign to the licensor improvement patents;

- inclusion of unwanted licences, products or services unless necessary for satisfactory exploitation;

- prohibition on delivery into other licensee's territory beyond the five-year period in (b) above;

- prohibition on selling to resellers within the territory for resale in other territories or a requirement making it otherwise difficult for users or resellers to obtain the product from other resellers within the Common Market.

The regulation also provides for a simplified (non-opposition) notification procedure with respect to agreements which include restrictions which are not part of the list of white or black clauses. Such agreements will be automatically exempted, unless the Commission opposes them within six months after notification, provided that such notification expressly referred to art. 4 of reg. no. 2349/84, and the information furnished was complete and correct.

The Commission may withdraw the benefits of the exemption if an agreement should turn out to have effects which are incompatible with the conditions of art. 85(3), in particular where:

(i) such effects arise from arbitration awards;

(ii) the licensed products are not exposed to effective competition;

(iii) if the licensor is not entitled to terminate the exclusivity at the latest after five years or at least annually thereafter, if the licensee fails to exploit the patent adequately;

¶1011

(iv) if the licensee fails to meet unsolicited orders from territories of other licensees, except as covered by (b) above, or either party refuses to sell for resale in other territories or makes it difficult for users or resellers to obtain the products from other resellers within the Common Market.

(3) *Other licences*

(a) *Copyright.* It is generally considered that the principles of patent licensing also apply to *other property rights* (see art. 4(2) 2. b reg. no. 17/62, which expressly includes utility patents and trademarks). In *Coditel II* (EC 1982, p. 3381), the European Court ruled that an agreement under which the owner of a copyright in a film granted the exclusive right to exhibit that film for a specific period in the territory of a Member State was not caught by art. 85. It must be ascertained further whether in the given circumstances the exclusive licence creates barriers which are artificial and unjustifiable in terms of the needs of the cinematographic industry, or the possibility of charging fees which exceed a fair return on investment or a disproportionate duration of exclusivity, or whether the geographic exclusivity otherwise restricts competition within the Common Market.

(b) *Know-how.* The Commission is not prepared to treat know-how in the same way as patents and patent licences, because in the latter case the monopoly is granted in consideration for the disclosure of the invention by the patentee. On the other hand, the technological significance of know-how is comparable to that of patents. Since the crucial element of know-how is its secrecy, clauses designed to protect secrecy and thereby the existence of such property rights are not considered as preventing competition.

(c) *Trademark.* The characteristic element of a trademark is its function in identifying the origin of a product. Trademark licences are closely related to distribution agreements and thus similar principles will apply (Commission OJ 1978 L 70 *Campari*).

(4) *German law*

Sections 20 and 21 GWB take out of the general rules of vertical restrictions those which are imposed on the licensee or assignee in agreements concerning the acquisition or licensing of patents, utility models, plant breeders' rights or unprotected inventions and know-how which can be considered patent-like business secrets (secret know-how), but not trademarks and copyrights. Restrictions placed on the licensor of the above-listed rights and any restrictions relating to rights other than those listed above are subject to the general rules of ss. 15 and 18 (see ¶1008 et seq. above).

¶1011

Sections 20 and 21 declare null and void restrictions on the licensee (assignee) 'which go beyond the scope of the protected right'. However, the law expressly states that:

> '. . . restrictions pertaining to the type, extent, quantity, territory or period of the exercise of such right shall not be deemed to go beyond its scope.'

It is unclear whether the above provision also applies to so-called mixed agreements, i.e. where the licence is only part of a broader agreement. It does not apply where the restrictions are not unilaterally imposed by the patentee, but where licensees have a collective right of approval, e.g. with respect to the granting of further licences, prices of the product, mutual restrictions concerning competitive products, etc. The same would be true with respect to patent pooling agreements, all of which would require to be reviewed under s. 1.

Where the licensor licenses another to copy technically sophisticated machinery without communicating technical secrets, the agreement would not be a licence agreement within the meaning of ss. 20 and 21, but would follow ss. 15 and 18, which would mean in practice that it would be valid unless including price and other second-tier restrictions as mentioned at ¶1008 et seq. above. On the other hand, where the licensor alleges patent rights which in fact no longer exist, the agreement will still have to be reviewed under ss. 20 and 21.

A typical clause going beyond the scope of the protected right would be a non-competition clause concerning unprotected products, including products which have become patent-free upon being put on the market by the patentee or licensee. As under EEC law, it would typically not be possible to provide for royalties based on sales of products of which only parts are patented. Also the obligation to pay royalties beyond the terms of the patent or the secrecy of the know-how would be void. A clause according to which royalties are due until the expiry of the last of several patents would be valid only if such last or substitute patent was of essential significance.

Section 20, para. (2) expressly permits:

(a) restrictions to the extent justified by the licensor's interest in technically satisfactory exploitation;

(b) obligations with respect to the price to be charged for the product;

(c) obligations to exchange experience or grant licences for improvements insofar as they meet with identical obligations of the licensor;

(d) prohibitions on challenging the patent;

(e) obligations concerning competition outside Germany to the extent not exceeding the duration of the patent or licence.

¶1011

Paragraph (3) provides for the authority of the FCO to authorize further restrictions provided they will neither restrict the licensee nor substantially impair competition in general. It is common practice for the FCO to discuss licence agreements informally, and, as long as the Commission has not instituted a procedure, the FCO will also informally advise on EEC law and accepting a clause according to (d) above only if it does not affect EEC law. Any such agreement needs to be entirely in writing (Chapter 1, ¶112), and the use of a clause which would be void for antitrust reasons would be subject to fines (s. 38(1) no. 1) and to injunction procedures by the FCO (s. 37a).

ABUSE OF MARKET DOMINATION OR MARKET STRENGTH

¶1012   Statutory provisions

Article 86 prohibits any abuse by 'undertakings of a dominant position within the Common Market or a substantial part of it'. It quotes as major examples:

(1) unfair prices or trading conditions;

(2) limiting production, market or technical development to the prejudice of consumers;

(3) applying dissimilar conditions to equivalent transactions with other trading parties, thereby placing them at a competitive disadvantage;

(4) making the conclusion of contracts subject to supplementary obligations with no connection according to their nature of commercial usage.

Prohibited practices would allow the Commission to interfere *ex officio* or upon application of the injured party who, in turn, may be entitled to damages to be tried under German law (s. 823(2) BGB).

German law does not only prohibit abuses of market dominators, but also of those of qualified market strength (see ¶1013 below).

According to s. 22(4), the cartel authorities may prohibit abusive practices and declare agreements to be of no effect insofar as enterprises abuse their dominant position. For example, if a market dominating supplier or purchaser:

'(a) impairs the competitive option of other enterprises in a manner relevant to competition on the market without justifying grounds;

(b) demands prices or other terms which are different from those to be expected with a high degree of likelihood from effective competition, taking into account practices of undertakings on comparable markets with effective competition;

(c) demands less favourable prices or other terms compared to those which it demands from similar buyers on comparable markets, unless the difference is justified.'

¶1012

¶1013 Definitions

(1) 'Market'

Under both Community and national law, in order to define the relevant market the products must be looked at with regard to their particular use and their interchangeability. All products which, according to their characteristics, their economic use and their price range, are so close to each other that a reasonable user would consider them as suitable for a specific need and which, when comparing them with each other, would normally be interchangeable, will form one market (*Bedarfsmarktkonzept* or *Konzept der funktionellen Austauschbarkeit*). One test may be whether or not a price increase for one product would be likely to result in customers switching to another product. Where a product is used for different purposes, the Federal Court will assume different markets only where the supplier is able to apply different strategies as well (price, rebate, etc.) (WuW BGH 1711, *Mannesmann/Brüninghaus*).

The market to be defined must be seen in close connection with the further question relating to any dominant position. Where the market has been defined particularly narrowly, competition from neighbouring markets (substitute competition) and low entry barriers (potential competition) may weaken the position of a company which would at first view appear to be dominant according to mere market share statistics. It is important, therefore, to establish how easily manufacturers of neighbouring products could switch their production and become serious competitors if this would appear profitable to them.

Hence, the market share as such may not be decisive, although particularly high shares (70–80 per cent) would under normal circumstances indicate a market dominating position, whereas lower shares (40–45 per cent) would, under Community law, call for further investigation as to the position of the next strongest competitors, size of the company, range of products, financial resources, sources of supplies, and vertical integration, etc.

(2) 'Domination'

Section 22 of the Cartel Law defines an enterprise to be market dominating insofar as it:

(a) is without substantial competition in the relevant market;

(b) has a paramount market position in relation to its competitors, taking into account in addition to its market share its financial strength, access to supply or sales markets, affiliation with other enterprises and market entry barriers;

(c) is one of a group of companies which would jointly fall under (a) or (b) if no substantial competition existed between them in general or on specific markets.

Whereas (c) above refers to members of an oligopoly, (b) is designed to catch conglomerates (as not only market shares but also financial strength, resources, integration and market entry barriers have to be taken into account).

(3) 'Presumptions' for market domination

German law (in s. 22(3)) presumes the presence of market domination in the case of:

(a) a single company which commands one third or more of a market, except where its annual sales are less than DM 250 million;

(b) not more than three enterprises which together command one half or more of the market, but excluding companies with annual sales of less than DM 100 million;

(c) no more than five enterprises which command two thirds or more of the market, but excluding companies with annual sales of less than DM 100 million.

Where one oligopolist does not reach the above sales figure it is debatable whether this would make the entire presumption ineffective or only exempt that particular company.

It should be noted that 'presumption' in the above context does not discharge the FCO of its general obligation to investigate all relevant facts, including those in favour of the alleged market dominator. The presumption will, however, operate effectively where neither the FCO nor the company, having used their best efforts, were able to rebut the presumption (*prima facie* market domination).

(4) 'Market strength'

In addition to the above general market domination, the Cartel Law has (in s. 26(2) sentence 2) introduced so-called 'relative market domination' operating only in respect to customers or suppliers who are without acceptable and reasonable alternatives to such relevant market domination.

According to s. 26(2), market dominating enterprises:

'... must not unfairly hinder, directly or indirectly, another enterprise in business activities which are usually open to similar enterprises nor, in the absence of justification for differentiation, treat such enterprise differently from similar enterprises. Sentence 1 shall also apply to enterprises ... insofar as suppliers or purchasers of certain types of goods or services depend on them to such extent that adequate business alternatives do not exist.'

¶1013

These latter provisions have become the most significant in the practice of German competition law.

In its fundamental decision, the Federal Court held an important sports store to be dependent on Rossignol skis, in spite of their German market share of only 8 per cent, because the store would not, due to the superior reputation of this brand, be considered as a serious competitor without them (BGH WuW 1391; see also, with respect to the sports shoes 'Adidas', WuW 1885, and for a liquor store with respect to the brand 'Asbach-Uralt', WuW 1429).

¶1014 Forms of abuse

Abuse is any use of the market dominating position contrary to the objective of the Treaty:

(a) in order to achieve market results which could not be obtained under competative circumstances (exploitation);

(b) by impairing remaining competition (action against competitors);

(c) by action against the market structure.

(1) 'Monopolising'

According to the so-called 'Continental Can' doctrine of the Court (EC 1973, 245), art. 86 is not only aimed at practices which may cause damage to consumers directly, but also at those which are detrimental to them through their impact on an effective competition structure, such as is mentioned in art. 3(f) of the Treaty.

Abuse therefore occurs if an undertaking in a dominant position strengthens such position in such a way that the degree of dominance substantially fetters competition, i.e. that only undertakings remain in the market whose behaviour depends on the dominant undertaking. It is thus abusive for a market dominator to acquire the last major competitor. In practice, however, the Commission has not found a case in which to apply its powers in this way to control mergers, and a proposed merger control regulation has not yet been adopted by the European Council.

In 1980, the Commission opened proceedings against IBM for alleged abuses of a market dominating position by failing to supply other manufacturers with interface information required for competitive products to be used with IBM's system/370, by practising memory and software bundling for its system/370 CPUs and by discriminating between its software users, i.e. refusing to supply certain installation and other services to users of non-IBM CPUs. In August 1984, the Commission accepted a unilateral undertaking from IBM, pursuant to which it had undertaken to:

(a) offer its system/370 CPUs in the EEC either without main memory or with only such capacity as strictly required;

(b) disclose, in a timely manner, sufficient interface information to enable competing companies in the EEC to attach both hardware and software products of their design to system/370;

(c) disclose adequate and timely information to competitors to enable them to interconnect their systems or networks with system/370.

Timely disclosure for interfaces to hardware products must be made within four months of the date of announcement of the product concerned, and for software interfaces as soon as it is reasonably stable, but no later than general availability. The duration of the undertaking is for an indefinite period, but IBM has reserved the right to terminate it giving one year's notice, at the earliest as of 1 January 1990. The Commission hopes that competition can thus be expected to be strengthened and made more effective, and users may be free to choose from a wider selection of products.

(2) *Pricing*

The Commission had fined General Motors because it had abused its dominant position by charging an excessive price for inspecting new Opel vehicles which had not been marketed through its own distribution network in Belgium but which had been brought in as parallel imports from other countries. 'Excessive' had been defined in relation to the 'economic value' of a service (OJ 75 L 29). To carry this premise further, it would be necessary to determine the costs exactly, which may be difficult in the case of multi-product manufacturer, and to determine whether such costs are justified and what should be a fair profit margin.

In *United Brands* (OJ 76 L 95), the Commission found prices for Chiquita bananas in Benelux, Denmark and Germany excessive because they exceeded prices in Ireland (they were 30–40 per cent higher than prices for unbranded bananas, of which only half the difference could be justified by quality and advertising costs) and were higher than for other brands. On appeal, the court had considered it to be decisive whether the company could be found to have used its position 'in such a way as to reap trading benefits which it would not have reaped if there had been normal and sufficiently effective competition'.

Under German law this is called *Vergleichsmarktkonzept*, obliging the authorities to establish a hypothetical price which could conceivably come about under competitive circumstances (*als-ob Wettbewerbspreis*). It is certainly questionable whether it is easier to determine reasonable or just costs, profits and prices or a fictitious price resulting from competition. However, only the last alternative appears to be in line with the theory of competition law.

¶1014

The Federal Court has confirmed that the excess of the actual price over the fictitious competition price must be significant in order to qualify as abusive (WuW 1445, *Valium* I). In the case of highway gas stations the FCO considers a price abusive which exceeds the per litre price charged by the surrounding non-highway stations by more than DM 0.02.

(3) *Rebate and bonus systems*

Rebates beyond normal quantity rebates are likely to have the object of forcing customers to place additional orders with the market dominator, thereby expanding the latter's market share. Loyalty rebates are thus prohibited, even if appearing as mere quantity rebates (EC 1979, 1869 *Hoffmann-LaRoche*).

Rebate systems based on sales objectives in a given reference period would be prohibited if the terms and criteria were such as to result in undue pressure, also in comparison to similar systems of competitors. The length of the reference period and any discrimination in the system would be of particular significance (EC 1983, 3461, *Michelin*).

The FCO has fined a manufacturer who granted additional discounts on his main products for sales in secondary, less competitive products (WuW BKartA 1805, *International Harvester*). It also prohibited annual sales rebates, but the court of appeal expressly allowed sales rebates for short reference periods of some weeks or months (WuW OLG 2401, *Effem*).

In addition, rebates with drastic quantity progression may have the effect of concentrating additional orders with market dominators to the disadvantage of competitors.

(4) *Refusal to deal*

Market dominators must be particularly careful not to go beyond objective criteria for the selection of distributors and must not practice exclusivity (Commission's statement of objections, 8th Competition Report 1978, point 114).

Prior to the *Grohe* decision of the Commission referred at ¶1010 above (but after application for exemption), the FCO prohibited distribution systems where wholesalers who were held to be dependent on manufacturers of sanitary installation fittings (market strength – see ¶1013) were prohibited to supply to anyone other than installation plumbers thereby excluding, in particular, department stores and other general retailers (WuW 2010, *Grohe*). The FCO found a logical gap in the distribution agreement, according to which the manufacturer required pre-sales consultation and services and installation of the products by experts, but at the same time expressly allowed uncontrolled retail business by plumbers in their retail stores. Where a manufacturer considers expert services an essential part of his distribution policy, he must carry this logic through to the end or otherwise be found guilty of discrimination. As a secondary argument, however, the FCO questioned the authority of the manufacturer to decide who should be allowed to install his products. In its opinion, the reasonableness of qualification criteria should depend primarily on the quality of the product and the expectation of the users. (The FCO expressly stated that notification of the agreement to the Commission and the initiation of proceedings would not exclude a negative decision under the Cartel Law; there might be a duty to suspend the proceedings if the Commission had already indicated its likely decision, but in this case this was not so.)

GERMAN MERGER CONTROL

¶1015   General

Section 23(2) GWB defines mergers and acquisitions (*Zusammenschluß*) broadly. The definition covers in particular the acquisition of:

(1) all or a significant part of the assets of another enterprise;

(2) the shares of another enterprise if such shares alone or together with other shares already owned by the acquiring enterprise –

   (a) equal 25 per cent of the voting capital of the other enterprise, or

   (b) equal 50 per cent of the voting capital of the other enterprise, or

   (c) give the acquiring enterprise a majority participation within the meaning of s. 16(1) of the Stock Corporation Law.

The definition also includes certain enterprise agreements (creation of a combine, profit and loss transfers and similar arrangements), as well as the acquisition of shares to the extent that, through agreement, bylaws or resolutions, the acquiring enterprise is granted the position of a shareholder in a stock corporation with a blocking majority (i.e. more than 25 per cent voting rights). In the case of partnerships, the FCO considers almost any minority interest (together with some partnership rights) as comparable to a blocking minority. The definition concludes with a 'catch-all' clause to sweep in the creation of 'every other combination of enterprises through which one or more enterprises can directly or indirectly exercise a dominating influence on another enterprise'. Such dominating influence may be found to be vested in each of several shareholders where identity of interests is reasonably assumed, e.g. due to a prohibition on transfers of shares to third parties, obligations to make active contributions, and the shareholders being from within the same industry (WuW BGH 1810, *Transportbeton Sauerland*). The possibility of divided voting would be a counter-argument only if such different voting actually occurred.

A joint venture would not only be a merger between the parent companies and the joint venture but, according to specific wording of s. 23(2), also among the parent companies as regards the market of the joint venture. Also, a merger of parent companies (in particular if occuring outside Germany) is deemed to be a merger among their (domestic) subsidiaries (e.g. see ¶1019 below).

¶1016   Pre-merger filing ('Anmeldung')

Any merger plan may be filed with the FCO for advance clearance. It must be filed according to s. 24a (1) if during the last fiscal year:

(1) one of the participating enterprises had sales of DM 2 billion or more; or

(2) at least two participating enterprises had sales of DM 1 billion or more.

It should be noted that the seller of the assets or of all the shares of a company is not considered to 'participate' within the meaning of this provision. However, sales of affiliated companies need to be included in the computation. Special rules apply with respect to 'sales' of distribution companies, banks, insurance companies and publishing houses.

The FCO excludes from such pre-merger filing only the acquisition of an independent business with annual sales of DM 4 million or less.

The notification sets in motion certain relatively short (one to four months) deadlines for action by the FCO, during which time it must either approve or disapprove the plan. The deadline only starts once such reporting can be considered as complete (see ¶1017 below). The deadlines may be extended with the consent of the parties concerned. Prior consummation of the merger is subject to fines (s. 38(1)3) and any agreement to the contrary would be null and void. It is thus recommended that such an agreement should be entered into only under a condition precedent. Failure to provide for pre-merger filing would further set in motion the one-year period for prohibition after post-merger filing (¶1017 below).

¶1017   Post-merger filing ('Anzeige')

Any merger or acquisition must be filed without delay after its conclusion (s. 23(1)) if:

(1) the participating companies, taken together during the last fiscal year, had sales of DM 500 million or more or 10,000 or more employees;

(2) after the merger a market share of 20 per cent is reached or increased; or

(3) one participating company already has a share of 20 per cent or more of another market.

The seller does not need to be taken into account when calculating the above figures, except where continuing to be affiliated by holding 25 per cent or more of the shares, but all affiliate companies of the buyer and the purchased company must be included (affiliation normally requiring majority participation). With respect to the market definition see ¶1013 above.

All parties, directly or indirectly, concerned (and this includes the seller and the purchased company) are obliged to report the merger, but this obligation can be, and normally is, satisfied by one of them. Reporting must be correct and complete and must include:

(1) the firm name, location and kind of business;

(2) the form of the merger, including, in the case of a share deal, the amount of shares acquired and total participation;

(3) the market share, sales and number of employees, to the extent the above ceilings are reached, of all participating companies and their affiliates (but the FCO also accepts consolidated figures).

Prohibition of a merger or acquisition is possible only within one year upon its filing with the FCO.

The notice of the reporting is published in the Federal Gazette. Failure to report or incorrect reporting is subject to fines.

¶1018   Prohibition of mergers

(1) *Principle*

According to s. 24(1), the FCO must prohibit a merger or acquisition:

> '. . . if it is anticipated that it will create or strengthen a market dominating position, unless the participating enterprises demonstrate that the merger will also result in improvements to competition and that such improvements will outweigh the disadvantages of market domination.'

This means that in cases of market domination the FCO has not been given discretionary powers.

In the case of joint ventures the cartel prohibition of s. 1 is also applicable if the joint venture qualifies as co-operative (see ¶1007-(3) *Joint ventures* above).

No prohibition will be possible in certain *de minimis* cases (s. 24(8)), i.e. if:

(a) the participating companies together had sales of less than DM 500 million; or

(b) a company which is not an affiliated company and which had sales of less than DM 50 million is acquired, except where it had sales of DM 4 million or more and the acquiring enterprise had sales of DM 1 billion or more; or

(c) the market concerned exists for five years or more and, during the last calendar year, comprised sales of less than DM 10 million.

Much stricter rules apply to the press market (newspapers and periodicals).

The term 'market domination' has been outlined at ¶1013 above and the statutory presumptions there mentioned are of particular significance in the context of merger control. The FCO may issue specific questions to competitors, suppliers or customers in order to establish the market structure and the likely effects of the merger. General statements are difficult to make. Even the absence of price competition does not necessarily prove market domination where quality, terms and service competition can be shown to be effective. Where the company in question has a significantly higher market share than its next competitor, market domination is likely to be assumed.

In the case of an oligopoly the presumptions in ¶1013(3) above will make it easier for the FCO to prove absence of effective competition both within and outside the group.

(2) Special presumptions

For the purpose of merger control, s. 23(a) provides for additional presumptions that a merger or acquisition will result in the creation or strengthening of a superior market position, if:

(a) the participating enterprises together have annual sales of DM 12 billion or more and at least two of them have sales of DM 1 billion or more. The presumption will not apply with respect to joint ventures, except where the joint venture is active on a small market which comprises sales of DM 750 million or less (this presumption is designed to catch so-called 'elephants' marriages');

(b) an enterprise with annual sales of DM 2 billion or more acquires a company which either –

    (i) is active on a market on which small or medium-sized companies have a market share of two-thirds or more and the participating companies together have a market share of 5 per cent or more ('giants' penetrating small company markets), or

    (ii) is dominating on one or more markets which comprise annual sales of DM 150 million or more (combination of size and market domination);

(c) oligopolists with annual sales of each DM 150 million or more are presumed to be market dominating if the participating companies taken together achieve a market share of 15 per cent or more, provided that –

    (i) the oligopoly consists of three or less enterprises which have the highest market shares and together achieve one half, or

> (ii) the oligopoly consists of five or less enterprises with the highest market shares which together achieve two-thirds,
>
> except where the companies prove either that the competitive conditions are likely to result in significant competition among them even after the merger or acquisition or that the oligopolists taken together are not in a superior position *vis-à-vis* the other competitors.

The above presumptions are interpreted so as to shift the burden of proof from the FCO to the companies, but in view of the obligation of the FCO to investigate *ex officio* in both directions the presumptions will only operate if, in spite of best efforts, neither the presence nor the absence of market domination can be established. Competitive behaviour in the past may allow conclusions for the future to be drawn. In either event it is still left to the companies under s. 24(1) to establish that the merger will also cause competition to improve and that such improvements will outweigh the disadvantages of market domination. This is not meant to restate the failing company defence because the market share of such failing company is normally expected to spread even to all other competitors.

(3) *Result of prohibition*

If a merger or acquisition is prohibited by the FCO, then the Federal Minister of Economics may still allow it to proceed if the restriction on competition is outweighed by general economic advantages of the merger or acquisition or if the merger or acquisition is justified by an overwhelming public interest. In order to avoid a total prohibition, the parties may enter into certain commitments with the FCO, e.g. to divest a subsidiary in a market domination position.

Negative decisions of the FCO (and the Minister) are subject to judicial review, but such appeal does not normally have suspensive effect.

A merger which has been prohibited must not be carried out and transactions to the contrary are null and void. However, the prohibition order does not itself dissolve the merger, it rather forms the basis for a dissolution order where the FCO may specify how a prohibited merger shall be dissolved or how anticompetitive effects shall otherwise be eliminated, but the parties shall first be given an opportunity to dissolve voluntarily or restructure the merger. For example, where the FCO has prohibited the acquisition of 50 per cent of the voting capital, no dissolution or divesture may subsequently be ordered by the FCO if the parties in the meantime have reduced the acquisition to only 24.9 per cent (no 'merger' according to ¶1015 above) (BGH WuW 2031, *Springer/Elbe-W.* II). Where, during an appeal against a prohibition order, the parties restructure the merger so that the initial transaction is not only modified but essentially

¶1018

changed, the proceedings must start all over again, provided the FCO has prohibited the 'new' merger as well (BGH DB 86, 850, *Morris/Rothmans*).

A prohibition order which has become final allows the FCO to order partial or total divesture, e.g. by ordering the parties to sell a business through a broker, and in the meantime to withdraw directors and to abstain from exercising voting rights. The FCO may also order the parties to cancel agreements or declare certain provisions as null and void. No such order must go beyond what is to be considered reasonable and adequate (s. 24(b)3). Enforcement will be secured by imposing enforcement fines.

¶1019   'Foreign mergers'

The application of German merger control to foreign mergers is particularly disputed as regards pre-merger filing and prohibition. Section 98(2) establishes the so-called 'effects doctrine', according to which the Cartel Law applies to all restrictions of competition with domestic effects, regardless of where caused. According to the Federal Court, such effects must be noticeable and must be established in connection with each provision of the Cartel Law separately (WuW 1613, *Organische Pigmente*).

(1) *Domestic effects*

In its memorandum of 1975 (Activity Report p. 45), the FCO established the following criteria:

  (a) In the case of mergers, except joint ventures, realised abroad

   (i) domestic effects will be present if both participating enterprises have been active in Germany directly or through subsidiaries, branches or importers already prior to the merger;

   (ii) domestic effects may exist where only one enterprise had been active in Germany but, e.g., if after the merger deliveries of the foreign enterprise into Germany are likely because of the relationship to the domestic participant, or if the know-how of the domestic participant is increased, or if the latter will receive additional industrial property rights.

  (b) In the case of foreign ventures, domestic effects will primarily depend on its actual and geographic activities (likely deliveries into Germany or additional production capacities available to a participant with domestic activities).

¶1019

(2) *Post-merger filing*

The Federal Court (WuW 1631, *Organische Pigmente*) has held that the post-merger filing provision must be seen separately from any prohibition possibility, and has as its object providing the FCO and the public with information. It is thus applicable also to a foreign merger which meets the required criteria, as long as such merger has any noticeable effect in Germany, and the Court has found this to be so in a case where the merger caused the acquiring company's market share to increase by 0.23 per cent, to gain additional know-how and to eliminate the acquired company as a competitor.

(3) *Pre-merger filing*

The FCO takes the same position with respect to pre-merger filing, although pre-merger filing has a very different meaning in that it makes it illegal and subject to fines to proceed with mergers of a certain size in the absence of FCO clearance. The FCO has been heavily criticised, and it may indeed violate principles of international comity to control foreign mergers for mere sales amounts which may be significant if taking place within Germany, but not if almost entirely outside Germany. In order to avoid undue complications, the FCO has been instructed by the Federal Ministry of Economics in obvious cases to inform foreign filing parties immediately (WuW 1980 p. 591). The situation has not arisen where fines have been levied for late filing in such cases, although the FCO reserves the right to do so in 'provocative cases'.

(4) *Prohibition*

In *Morris/Rothmans*, the FCO had prohibited the acquisition of 50 per cent of the voting capital of Rothmans Tobacco (Holdings) Ltd. by Philip Morris Inc. because both had German subsidiaries which rank among the five largest manufacturers of cigarettes on the German market (WuW 1943). The Berlin Court of Appeal partially quashed the decision and only upheld the prohibition of the (fictitious) merger among the German subsidiaries because s. 98(2) and international comity only allowed the prohibition of domestic effects of foreign mergers (WuW OLG 3051). It is debatable whether:

(a) a foreign merger can be split this way and how such partial prohibition can be implemented in practice; and

(b) whether a foreign merger which cannot be split into a domestic and a foreign part can be prohibited.

During an appeal to the Federal Court, the parties restructured the acquisition to result in an acquisition of 30.8 per cent of the nominal shares with only 24.9 per cent of the voting rights of Rothmans International by Philip Morris.

¶1019

The FCO, in analysing the agreements and underlying circumstances, found that Philip Morris had in fact obtained a stronger position than reflected by 24.9 per cent of the voting rights and again prohibited the merger entirely (WuW 2204). The Federal Court decided that the initial prohibition procedure did not cover the restructure (see ¶1018). The new prohibition, initially ordered by the FCO as a precaution, is again pending appeal and the international aspects of the case are thus still unsettled.

GERMAN AND EEC ANTITRUST PROCEDURE

¶1020   Powers of the FCO

The FCO (and the antitrust authorities of the German States) have clearly defined powers which differ depending on whether part of an administrative or of a criminal procedure. The objectives of an administrative procedure are injunction (prohibition), exemption, declaration of invalidity or objection against certain anticompetitive practices, as provided for by the individual provisions of the Cartel Law. Criminal procedures are directed toward the fixing of administrative fines. The FCO must at an early stage determine whether a given case may result in an administrative or a criminal procedure. It may, however, in good faith change from an initially administrative procedure to a criminal procedure, and would in such case not be prohibited from using information so obtained.

(1) *Powers in administrative procedures*

(a) *Initial suspicion.*   The basic powers of the FCO are laid down in s. 46 and do not allow for a general investigation ('fishing expedition'). The FCO will rather have to establish a so-called 'initial suspicion' (*Anfangsverdacht*), and such suspicion must reasonably cover all legal aspects of a case before any official action can be taken. The case must be such that where all facts which the FCO has reason to suspect can be proved, the FCO would be entitled to issue a specific prohibition, etc. order.

(b) *Addressee.*   Only undertakings (enterprises), associations of enterprises and natural persons legally representing such enterprises (the owner of a sole proprietorship or the directors of a legal entity) are subject to official powers. Such addressees would include third parties (customers, suppliers, competitors, etc.) and their legal representatives, but no other natural persons (such as procurists or other employees). Such other persons could only be ordered to act as witnesses (see (g) below).

(c) *Request for information.*   The powers of the FCO to obtain information are those of most practical significance. Pursuant to s. 46 (1), the FCO may:

'. . . to the extent as is necessary to carry out its duties under this Law

   (1) request from undertakings and associations of undertakings information about their economic relationship;'.

The FCO may request information from an undertaking only about its own relations (or those of subsidiaries to the extent available), but not of third companies.

An official information request must be formally resolved by the FCO, specify the information and give written reasons. Such formal request is subject to appeal to the courts. The appeal has no suspensive effect, but a fine for withholding information officially ordered will not be enforced before the appeal has been decided.

In practice, the FCO usually relies on informal requests and only where not, or not correctly or completely, answered will issue a formal request.

(d) *Inspection.*   Section 46 (1) No. 2 further allows the FCO to inspect and examine business documents on the premises of undertakings and associations of undertakings during normal business hours. The owner or directors of the undertaking must submit the documents so ordered and permit inspection. The officials need not wait until the arrival of the company lawyer, but the owner/ directors are not required to make any statements with respect to the subject matter of the investigation.

Any search of the premises will require a court order. Any refusal to submit requested documents would cause suspicion of removal of the documents, in which case the official of the FCO has the immediate right to search without court order. Documents so obtained may be seized.

(e) *Self-incrimination and legal privilege.*   Section 46, para. (5) allows a person to refuse to answer questions which would expose him or a relative to the danger of criminal prosecution, including prosecution for fines. As fines in antitrust cases are usually levied for violation of supervisory duties, and as no one can be expected to incriminate his company (although this is disputed), the defence against self-incrimination is reasonably protected. The person concerned must raise such defence in general and only if the FCO fixes fines for unjustified withholding of information, then on court appeal he must substantiate why the information could result in prosecution.

The FCO recognises a legal privilege only to the extent documents have been prepared for or by a lawyer in the context of criminal procedures (see (2) below), i.e. where procedures for administrative fines have been commenced, and even in such case the FCO will check whether the document in question is actually privileged (statement of the President of the FCO, WuW 83 p. 283).

¶1020

(f) *Confidentiality.* The FCO must observe business secrets. Practical difficulties may arise in a later procedure where adversary third parties would be included and would have a right to inspect the files.

Section 46(9) allows the authorities to use information so obtained for tax purposes, provided 'public interest mandatorily demands' prosecution for tax defraud or where the person concerned had deliberately given incorrect information.

(g) *Witnesses and experts.* The FCO may, as part of its administrative procedure, hear witnesses or experts, and such witnesses have the right to refuse testimony, but only insofar as they could do so in civil court procedures (s. 54). Instead of personal appearances, the FCO may be satisfied with written affidavits.

(2) *Procedure for fines*

FCO procedures for fines follow the Law for Procedure for Administrative Fines (OWiG) and the Criminal Procedure Code (StPO). Under such laws the FCO has the position of the district attorney (public prosecutor). Unlike the administrative procedure, the FCO here has the power to order the court hearing of witnesses, in which case incorrect testimony would be subject to criminal prosecution. As mentioned under 1(e) above, legal privilege and the defence against self-incrimination are protected under this procedure.

Procedures for fines are, under German law, not technically directed against a company as such but only against natural persons. Only where a director of a company is found liable for having violated competition rules could a fine be fixed against the company itself as a secondary participant (*Nebenbeteiligter*) in addition to the fine for the director (ss. 30, 130 OWiG). In practice, however, such a fine against the company is a main objective of the procedure and it is therefore crucial for the FCO to establish at least a violation of supervisory duties. In addition to fines, the company is also punished by having its name published, although this practice is under attack for lacking a legal basis. With respect to the amounts of fines, see ¶1022.

¶1021 Powers of the Commission

(1) *General*

The powers of the Commission for the purpose of applying the competition rules of art. 85 and 86 are contained in reg. no. 17 and include the power to:

(a) require undertakings to terminate infringements;

(b) take interim measures to bring to an immediate halt damaging behaviour;

(c) exempt notified agreements from the prohibition of art. 85(1);

(d) impose administrative fines.

In addition, the Commission may take informal or formal procedural measures and in particular request information or inspect books and records of undertakings.

Proceedings may start *ex officio* or following a complaint. Only relatively few cases (about a dozen per year) terminate in a final decision; the vast majority of cases are settled informally or by administrative letters.

(2) *Exemption procedure*

In order to obtain exemption, an agreement must be formally notified using the prescribed Form A/B in thirteen copies (one for the Commission and one for each Member State) attaching a written power of attorney of the legal representative.

Detailed information is required to be given and the entire agreement should normally be attached as well. Any incorrect or incomplete information is subject to fines. The procedure may take years, and sometimes never ends (the Commission may not give the case particular priority, there may be additional questions to be answered or changes to the agreement required, which may lead to difficult discussions between the undertaking and the Commission and, finally, formal decisions internally involve the antitrust authorities of the Member States and all members of the Commission).

Where the Commission believes art. 85(1) not to have been violated and no exemption required, it may grant negative clearance, and Form A/B automatically includes an application to do so. Negative clearance is not a decision and thus not binding on national courts or the European Court.

The advantage of notification is that the parties do not risk fines from the date of notification unless the Commission, in a provisional decision, expresses a warning to the contrary and the parties fail to observe such warning. Furthermore, the notification will be evaluated by the national courts and where an exemption is granted, this even binds the courts.

(3) *Complaints*

Whosoever has a legitimate interest in the determination of any behaviour by an undertaking that is objectionable under competition rules is entitled to complain to the Commission (art. 3(1), reg. 17). A special form (Form C) is available, but a simple letter including names and addresses, a description of the substance of the complaint and the legitimate interest (usually damages being suffered) and the written power of attorney of the legal representative will suffice. The Commission must attend to the complaint and either take action or inform the complainant of the reasons for not pursuing the matter. In such latter case, the complainant must be allowed sufficient time to submit further comments before the Commission definitely rejects the complaint. Such final decision will be subject to appeal to the Court. The complainant will be fully informed on all defences raised by the undertaking concerned. The Commission will also consider anonymous complaints, but is not obliged to do so.

(4) *Obtaining information*

(a) *Request for information.*   Pursuant to art. 11, reg. 17, the Commission 'may obtain all necessary information' from governments and competent authorities of Member States (i.e. the FCO) and from undertakings and associations of undertakings. Undertakings include third parties who may be in a position to clarify matters, but no natural persons. The procedure is in two stages:

   (i) written (including telex) requests: if the undertaking replies, it must do so correctly and completely in order to avoid fines and within the prescribed (or extended) deadline;

   (ii) if the undertaking does not reply, or only partly replies, the Commission may take a formal decision, and failure to comply fully will be subject to daily default fines (some undertakings prefer to be obstructive under the initial request, relying on the internal difficulties for the Commission in producing a formal decision, but risk annoying the *rapporteur* who will have considerable influence on the final decision).

(b) *Inspection.*   Article 14, reg. 17 gives the Commission the power to send inspectors to enter the premises of undertakings and:

   (i) to examine books and other business records;

   (ii) to take copies or extracts; and

   (iii) to ask for oral explanations on the spot.

There is a similar two-stage procedure as under (a) above, but where inspectors arrive unexpectedly, they are likely to have a formal decision with them (the Court having held that there is no need first to investigate on the basis of a simple mandate – EC 1980, 2033, *National Panasonic*). If necessary, admission of the inspectors could be enforced under national German law through police action.

Upon assurance that the documents will not be removed, the inspectors may be requested to wait for the arrival of a lawyer, unless such waiting time would go beyond the necessary minimum or the company has an in-house legal department.

¶1021

The undertaking owes the Commission co-operation, i.e. inspectors must be advised of the location of the records concerned and of the meaning of certain documents, but 'oral explanations on the spot' do not need to include the subject matter in general.

'Records' do not include those which are either irrelevant, private or privileged (see under (c) below), but records not available at the premises need to be procured. The Commission has no right to seize records, but in order to avoid lengthy copying by hand, the undertaking may prefer to allow the use of its copying machine.

(c) *Self-incrimination and legal privilege.* Unlike national German law, the Commission does not recognise the defence against self-incrimination but, following a decision of the Court, legal privilege is protected (EC 1982 p. 1575, *AMS*). Such protection against self-incrimination is denied because investigations and decisions are not directed against private persons but against undertakings, who are said not to enjoy any such constitutional right.

The legal privilege is extended to any correspondence between the undertaking and a lawyer which has a bearing on the subject matter of the procedure. The lawyer must be independent and admitted within the EEC, thus excluding salaried house counsel and third country lawyers. The privilege must be raised, and in case of dispute the relevant records are to be sealed until the court has given its decision.

(5) *Cease and desist order/fines*

When the court reaches a preliminary conclusion that competition rules are violated, it will send the parties a statement of objections and annex a list of documents which constitute the Commission's file. This file, except documents of a confidential nature (business secrets of another undertaking and internal notes of the Commission), may be examined by the parties before preparing a response to be given within a relatively short deadline (usually one to two months). Thereafter the parties may request an oral hearing to be conducted by the Hearing Officer (recently introduced to ensure that the rights of the defence are respected, which introduction was in partial response to criticism that the Commission more or less decides its own case without there being a prior appeal on facts to the European Court).

Where the infringement has been terminated, the Commission's decision may consist of a simple declaration stating the infringement. The decision may also be positive, e.g. requiring an undertaking in a dominant position to supply another.

The Commission may also take so-called interim measures to stop objectionable behaviour immediately. Such measures must be of a temporary nature aimed at safeguarding the status quo, and not determine the final outcome of the case.

If the Commission finds an undertaking liable for negligent or deliberate infringement, it will impose a fine. With respect to the amount, see ¶1022.

(6) Informal settlements

As mentioned above, most cases are concluded by way of informal settlement, notably where the undertakings involved voluntarily desist any objectionable practice. Informal settlements may take place by way of administrative letters informing the parties that the Commission sees no reason to take action and that the file will be closed. Such letters are not legally binding decisions, but will serve as guidelines. Recently, the Commission instituted the practice of publishing a notice of its intention to issue an administrative letter, allowing third parties to react before it takes further steps, thus enhancing the value of such administrative letters.

(7) Publicity/confidentiality

Decisions granting negative clearance, exemption, or ordering the termination of an infringement, as well as interim measures and provisional decisions, must be published in the Official Journal.

Procedural decisions, such as those formally requesting information, need not be published, but the Commission nevertheless will do so if it considers the case to be of general interest. Decisions and informal settlements may also be reported by the Commission in its monthly bulletin, as well as in its annual Report on Competition Policy.

The Commission must protect business secrets (art. 20, reg. 17). In order to enable a company to defend itself or to justify a complaint, the Commission may present excerpts of those parts of its files which include confidential information (EC 1979, 461, *Hoffman-La Roche*).

¶1022 Amount of fines

(1) Commission

The Commission has the power to impose fines of up to ECU 1 million or 10 per cent of the worldwide annual sales in the preceding fiscal year for infringements of competition rules (art. 15(2), reg. 17). The amount will depend, among other things, on the seriousness of the behaviour, how long it went on, the size of the companies, whether the infringement was deliberate or negligent, and whether it was of a kind already frequently attacked by the Commission in the past. Of course, any such amount would be subject to appeal.

In the case of *AEG-Telefunken* (OJ 1982 L 117), the Commission imposed a fine of ECU 1 million because it found that in 1973 the company had filed a distribution system stating that any dealer who satisfied the condition would be admitted, whereas in fact admission was refused or rendered difficult to dealers who practised an aggressive pricing policy. The company had also exercised substantial influence on the setting of retail prices. In setting the amount of the fine, the Commission took account of the fact that the company was a major manufacturer of electronic leisure equipment, and that the infringement had a substantial effect on the market. As mitigating circumstances the Commission took account of the fact that this was the first case of a decision on the application of a selective distribution system, which in itself was not objectional, and the level of discrimination and influence on prices initiated by the dealers.

In *Hasselblad* (OJ 1982 L 161), the Swedish camera manufacturer was fined ECU 65,000 and its UK distributor ECU 165,000 when found to have taken steps to support the partitioning-off of national markets. The infringement was considered particularly serious. Much smaller fines were imposed on the Belgian, French and Irish sole distributors who took an active part in the market partitioning, but under pressure from the manufacturer.

The highest fines so far imposed amounted to ECU 6.9 million against the four most important peroxide manufacturers who had been found to have practised the so-called 'home market rule' following national frontiers, if not on the basis of agreements, then of concerted action. The Commission also found bilateral agreements relating to special national and export markets. The Commission considered the infringements particularly serious in view of their lengthy duration and their effect of virtually eliminating competition in a market with a volume of several hundred million ECU (OJ 1985 L 35 p. 1, *Peroxyd*).

Michelin's fine for the practice of a prohibited rebate system in the Netherlands (¶1014) was reduced by the court from ECU 680,000 to ECU 300,000.

(2) Federal Cartel Office

Major infringements of the Cartel Law are subject to fines of up to DM 1 million or three times the proceeds resulting from such infringements (whichever amount is the higher) (s. 38(4) GWB). The proceeds may be estimated. Other infringements will be fined up to DM 50,000. In case of not deliberate but negligent infringements, only one half of the above maximum amounts shall apply.

The fine will be imposed on each person who participated in an infringement, and where the sole proprietor, managing partner or director of an incorporated

¶1022

undertaking was liable (at least in neglecting supervisory duties), the undertaking itself will also be fined as a secondary participant. The fine to the undertaking is normally significantly higher than that of the relevant natural person and such amount is not tax deductible. In order to discharge supervisory duties, it will not normally be sufficient generally to advise the employees of competition rules, but, depending on the nature and size of the business, the FCO may require the introduction and monitoring of policies preventing antitrust infringements. However, the Federal Court considers it as excessive to require sales personnel of construction companies to prepare memoranda for files on each contact with a competitor in connection with bidding procedure (as yet unpublished).

In general, the mitigating and aggravating factors follow those described under (1) above. Fines for natural persons will also depend on their annual income.

Where competitors had agreed on joint price increases, the FCO fixed fines of between DM 5,000 to 70,000 at a time when the statutory maximum was still DM 100,000 because the companies had a strong market position, significant sales amounts had been effected and the price increases also caused other prices to rise (WuW 119 *Farbenhersteller*). In this case the European Court subsequently held that the FCO and the Commission must take each other's decision on fines into account (see ¶1004).

The Federal Court confirmed a DM 20,000 fine on the sales manager of a TV manufacturer who refused to supply a department store, because it was considered discriminatory to insist on significantly higher requirements for the supply of a department store than for other retailers (WuW 2145, *Nordmende*). The managing director was acquitted because, not being sufficiently versed in the German market conditions and language, he had done what could be expected from him by appointing an experienced representative and instructing him to take legal advice in the given case (the representative, however, should not have followed such legal advice in view of apparent risks and contradiction with the position taken by the FCO 'consisting of no less expert lawyers').

The managing director and sales manager of the newly-established sales subsidiary of a Japanese Hi-Fi manufacturer, as well as the company itself, were fined because the sales manager had issued a circular letter to local dealers asking them to see to it that all products exhibited the new prices and advising the dealers that their pricing would be checked. The prices as such were expressly stated to be non-binding recommendations, but the wording of the letter was contradictory. The fines amounted to DM 20,000 for the company because it was still in its initial phase and not yet making profits, DM 4,000 for the sales manager (monthly salary of DM 4,000), and DM 6,000 for the managing director (annual salary DM 90,000). The court stated the fines to be

particularly low also because the effect of the infringement was limited to the
Frankfurt area (WuW OLG 2477, *Fisher HiFi*).

¶1023   Private enforcement

In the absence of particular incentives like triple damages under US law, private
enforcement of competition rules is not of primary significance. Litigation
involving antitrust law basically follows general rules of civil procedure (see
Chapter 13, ¶1304 et seq.), except that the venue in antitrust matters is
exclusively vested in special commercial chambers of certain regional courts
and courts of appeal which are bound to advise the FCO of any such case and
give it an opportunity to submit briefs and to participate at any hearing (s. 90).
Typical antitrust matters would include actions for damages resulting from
infringements of competition rules, provided the relevant provision of the
Cartel Law is one which is also meant to protect individuals (s. 35). The same
applies where the plaintiff, for example, seeks supply, arguing that refusal to
deal violates s. 26(2).

EEC competition rules are undisputedly meant also to protect individuals
who would consequently be entitled to sue for damages under German law
(WuW BGH 1646, *BMW-Importe*). Payments made under an agreement which
is void under art. 85 (2) can be claimed back applying principles of unjust
enrichment (WuW OLG 3248, *Zement-import*). In such cases normal jurisdiction rules would apply rather than the above exclusive venue for antitrust
matters under the Cartel Law.

Whereas German law does not provide for the right of a claimant to sue the
FCO for failure to take action on his behalf, the European Court grants a
claimant the right to sue the Commission in a similar case (EC 83, 3045, *Demo-
Studio Schmidt*).

11 Unfair Competition Law; Restrictions on Commercial Advertising

PROTECTION OF FREE COMPETITION

¶1101   Introduction

In addition to the antitrust rules outlined in Chapter 10, the unfair competition law is designed to be a second method of protection of free competition. Its fundamental concept is (as it will be in most other civilised countries) that everybody who participates in trade or business as a commercial seller or buyer of goods or services has to comply with the rules of fair play.

This principle was given general statutory expression in the Act against Unfair Competition which was enacted as early as 7 June 1909, and which has been amended several times since then (*Gesetz gegen den unlauteren Wettbewerb*: UWG), but also in several other laws aiming at specific competitive practices, e.g. the Act Concerning Price Discounts, limiting the discretion of the seller to grant discounts on his list prices (*Rabattgesetz*); the Regulation on Complementary Extras, prohibiting the combination of the sale of goods or services with a free gift (*Zugabeverordnung*); the Regulation on Seasonal Sales, regulating the time and duration of seasonal sales (*Verordnung über Sommer- und Winterschlußverkäufe*); the Decree concerning Special Promotional Sales, strictly limiting 'for-sale' events (*Anordnung betreffend Sonderveranstaltungen*); and the Regulation concerning the Quotation of Prices, committing the seller of merchandise or services to quote and advertise only final prices, including VAT and all other duties to be paid (*Preisangabenverordnung*).

For the pharmaceutical and drug business, which is considered a particularly sensitive commercial area, the Drug Advertising Act (*Heilmittelwerbegesetz*: HWG) sets forth special standards of advertising.

Labelling requirements under the Food Law (*Lebensmittel- und Bedarfsgegenständegesetz*: LMBG) the Wine Law (*Weingesetz*) and the Cosmetics Law

(*Kosmetikverordnung: KosmetikVO*) are of particular significance in this context, as a violation of these laws often encompasses an act of unfair competition. Another relevant area is the Act concerning the Closing Time of Stores (*Ladenschlußgesetz*).

The following paragraphs briefly demonstrate that competition in Germany is subject to a large number of restrictions and prohibitions, presumably more than in most other countries, and certainly more than in the common law countries. It is a legitimate question whether all of them in fact *protect* the freedom of competition and fit into the modern economical system. Some of them may rather give the impression that they *limit* the freedom of competition, merely maintaining historical privileges or the conservative ethical standards of certain groups.

LIMITS TO THE FREEDOM OF COMPETITION

¶1102   General rights

The equal rights of everyone to participate in trade and business, to make business decisions and to compete in any market at his or her own discretion is considered to be a constitutional right granted by art. 2, para. 1 of the Constitution of the Federal Republic of Germany (*Grundgesetz*: GG) guaranteeing the free development of personality, and by art. 12 GG guaranteeing the freedom to enter into the business, occupation or profession of one's choice. Such rights and freedom are, however, automatically limited by the concurrent rights and freedom of others with the same scope.

Consequently, the freedom of competition must not impair:

(1) the right of a potential customer to make a purchase decision at his free discretion without being misled by the promotional activities of the seller or by being put under psychological pressure; and

(2) the right of a competitor to compete under equal terms and conditions.

Thus, 'freedom of competition' may not be interpreted as 'unrestricted competition' but rather as the commitment of each competitor to concentrate his or her competitive efforts exclusively on the quality and price of his or her own products or services. See *Nordemann*, 4th Ed. 1984, p. 38, ann. 20 *et seq.*

GENERAL ASPECTS AND SYSTEM OF GERMAN UNFAIR COMPETITION LAW

¶1103   Competitive actions

While a number of specific unfair practices are addressed in the long list of individual provisions of the UWG and special regulations (some of which are mentioned in ¶1101), the most important provision of German unfair competition law is the general clause in s. 1 UWG which reads as follows (in translation):

> 'A person who in the course of trade or business acts with competitive purposes *contra bonos mores* is subject to an action to cease and desist from such act as well as to damage compensation claims.'

This provision sets forth the general standards for all promotional and advertising practices in Germany. Due to its broad language the courts have had to interpret it and draw from its general principle more specific rules. This is why unfair competition law is one of the few areas of the German civil law system which has, to a great extent, been developed by case law.

Section 1 UWG expresses the basic requirement which must be present for any action or claim under unfair competition rules, i.e. the 'competitive purpose' of an act which implies a 'competitive relationship' to other parties.

A competitive relationship is not only found among competitors in the common sense; it was, in the past, held by German courts to exist, for example, between a broadcasting station and the press (see *OLG München*, 1958 NJW 1298, 1302), between a manufacturer and a retailer (since the customers of the retailer are, indirectly, potential customers of the manufacturer (see *Baumbach/ Hefermehl, Wettbewerbsrecht*, 14th Ed. 1983, Einl. UWG, ann. 220)), and even between such different businesses as the retailers of coffee and of flowers; expressed in a case in which a coffee dealer promoted his products with the slogan '. . . instead of flowers' (see *BGH*, 1972 GRUR, 553).

With respect to the competitive relationship and regional distances, the motion of a real estate broker in Munich, Bavaria, against an illegal advertisement of a broker in Northrhine-Westfalia some 400 miles away was recently granted. The court ruled that a competitive relationship may only be denied if a conflict of the business interests of both competitors cannot be anticipated under any circumstances. It may, however, not be stated with any certainty that the broker in Munich may not in the future address customers in Northrhine-Westfalia (see *OLG München*, 1984 GRUR, 373). It becomes obvious from the foregoing, that courts in Germany interpret the 'competitive relationship' quite extensively.

The *purpose of a competitive action* may be either the promotion of one's own business interest or that of another party. In this respect it must be noted that even scientific reports or editorial articles may be incriminated under unfair competition rules. This is the case if evidence exists that the author himself is economically interested in the promotion of the product in question, e.g. if a physician who is employed with a pharmacological enterprise publishes an article in favour of a new medical drug of his employer and at the same time discriminates, in the guise of scientific research, against the product of a competitor (see *Baumbach/Hefermehl, supra*, Einl. UWG, ann. 229).

¶1104   Unlawfulness of competitive actions

A competitive practice is illegal under German law, whether or not it is committed intentionally or negligently or with the awareness of the violation of law, if it:

(1) either violates one of the individual competition rules of the UWG or the annex regulations addressing certain specific practices or the protection of certain market areas;

(2) constitutes an act *contra bonos mores* under s. 1 UWG.

The German Federal Supreme Court ('*BGH*') has ruled that the latter requires conduct that violates the 'sense of decency' of the reasonable average businessman or most reasonable people. See *BGH*, 1981 GRUR, 665, 666.

¶1105   Applicability

German unfair competition law is applicable to all competitive acts occuring on the German market, whether they were committed by a German or a foreign businessman. Based on international treaties and conventions, in particular the Paris Convention for the Protection of Industrial Property Rights, the citizens of most foreign civilised countries are entitled to pursue the protection of their industrial property rights (name, firm, trademarks, etc.) in Germany under the applicable provisions, including those of unfair competition law, even if they do not maintain a branch or subsidiary in West Germany but have competitive interest in this country. See *Godin, Wettbewerbsrecht*, 2nd ed. 1974, s. 28 ann. 4, 5.

¶1106   System

Considering the vague statutory formula on the one hand and the variety of individual competition rules on the other, it is difficult to establish the general characteristics of German unfair competition law to help a foreign business man to understand what is allowed and what is not in promoting his products on the German market. Several attempts have been made to develop a system of typical unlawful practices. See *Baumbach/Hefermehl, supra*, Einl. UWG, ann. 152 *et seq*; *Nordemann, supra*, p. 34, ann. 25 *et seq*; *Emmerich, Das Recht des unlauteren Wettbewerbs*, 1982, p. 56 *et seq.*, para. 5 no. 7. Objections were raised against all of them, since it is impossible to clearly attribute each case to a certain group (see *Nordemann, supra; Emmerich, supra*, p. 57).

For the general survey which this outline aims to provide, it seems appropriate to structure the various forms of unfair practices according to the different parties who may be affected, i.e. customers, one or several competitor(s), or the general public.

IMPORTANT ISSUES OF UNFAIR COMPETITION

¶1107   Unfair influence on customers

(1) *Misleading advertising*

Obviously, advertising statements must, in any event, be true and correct. However, even true and correct statements may be illegal if they are misleading (see s. 3 UWG). The deception of customers was also held to be *contra bonos mores* under sec. 1 UWG. The German courts are strict in this regard, ruling that an advertisement is misleading where more than merely an insignificant number of the addressed customers are likely to misunderstand its content (see *BGH*, 1983 GRUR, 293, 294). Case law indicates that the courts determine the possible misunderstanding with a hasty, superficial or naive reader or listener of the advertisement in mind. On the other hand, typical promotional exaggerations are not considered illegal, since the average customer recognises them as merely sales-puff.

The determination of whether a certain practice is misleading is made either by the court itself, if a product designed for day-to-day use is concerned and the judges are themselves customers addressed by the advertisement, or, if the judges do not have enough factual experience of their own, by public opinion polls.

In order to be judged as illegal under unfair competition law, misleading statements must play a part in the customer's decision to purchase. This may be the case if they refer to: (a) the size, significance and trustworthiness of the enterprise addressing itself to the market; (b) the quality of the products or services offered; or (c) their prices.

(a) It is considered to be a misrepresentation of the advertising enterprise if a name or certain terms in connection with the name are used which the average customer would believe to be attributes that the enterprise in fact does not have. For example, the term *Akademie* (academy) is not permitted for an institution which is not a governmentally approved school (see *OLG Bremen*, 1972 NJW, 164, 165); *Deutsch* (German) is misleading, if the size, the facilities, the number of employees and the turnover of a company indicate that it does not in fact cover the whole (West) German market (see *BGH*, 1982 GRUR, 239, 240). Similarly, *Europa* (Europe), *europäisch* (European) or *international* may only be used if the enterprise has in fact commercial interests in several European countries or is engaged in international trade or business (see *BGH* 1978 GRUR, 251, 252; *OLG Stuttgart*, 1970 GRUR, 36, 37). Terms like 'the best', 'the largest', etc. must be true in the sense that an evident lead on all competitors must be able to be proven (see *BGH*, 1968 GRUR, 440 *et seq.*). The term 'centre' similarly indicates an outstanding market position (see *BGH* 1977 GRUR, 503, 504; *OLG Köln*, 1979 WRP, 575).

(b) The quality of a product is, in view of the customer, to a large extent dependent upon its origin. 'Made in Germany' is considered by some customers to be an indication of quality. Therefore, it may only be added if in fact the essential steps of the manufacturing process were made in Germany (see *Baumbach/Hefermehl*, *supra*, para. 3 ann. 210, 213). 'Scotch Whisky' not only requires the advertised whisky to have been in fact distilled in Scotland, but also the minimum storage period of three years required under British law must have been observed, since it is the storage period which primarily led to the fine reputation of Scotch Whisky (see *BGH*, 1969 GRUR, 280, 282). *Münchner Bier* (Munich beer) obviously must be from Munich, but it must also be brewed in compliance with the pureness requirements applicable in Bavaria (*Reinheitsgebot*) (see *Baumbach/Hefermehl*, *supra*, para. 3 ann. 239).

On the other hand, geographical terms may, from the viewpoint of the consumer, change to a mere quality standard. 'Mocca' no longer indicates coffee from Arabia or Abyssinia but strong coffee in general (see *OLG Düsseldorf*, 1961 GRUR, 365). Moreover, delocalising additions may remove the misleading effect of a certain term. Case law has accepted the name 'Pilsener' or 'Pils' for beer not brewed in Pilsen, if this name is used in connection with a term clarifying that the beer is actually not from Pilsen, such as *Königs-Pilsener*, *Club-Pilsener*, *Bitburger Pils*, etc. (see *Baumbach/Hefermehl*, *supra*, para. 3 ann. 238, with critical remarks).

National, bilateral and multilateral regulations and treaties, including EEC-regulations, are focused on preventing misleading indications of the origin of certain products. This is especially true for food products like cheese (see German-Swiss Treaty of 7 March 1967, 1967 GRUR Int., 347 Exh. B II), wine, champagne and liquors (see the German Wine Act: *Weingesetz* of 27 August 1982, BGBl. 1982 I, 196; art. 18c, 43 of

EEC Order No. 355/79 of 5 February 1979; German-French Treaty of 8 March 1960, 1960 GRUR Ausl., 431 Exh. B I, BGBl. 1961 II, 23).

As already mentioned, misleading product information may also be caused by scientific opinions or newspaper articles not published by independent experts or journalists, or issued for remuneration or by an employee of the manufacturer. It is illegal under German law to use such an opinion or article for advertising purposes, unless it is pointed out that it is not the opinion of an independent third party (see *Emmerich*, *supra*, p. 124, para. 10 no. 2). Moreover, a true scientific report must not be used in advertising if it presents scientific opinions which may be seriously contested as proven facts. If a scientific opinion is included in a third party's advertisement, the advertiser is responsible for any incorrect or misleading impression which the public may receive from the 'advertised' scientific statements (see *BGH*, 1971 GRUR, 153/155; 1958 GRUR, 485, 486).

(c) There is a wide variety of misrepresentations of prices.

It is illegal to advertise a 'discount price', if the price is in fact not a special low price.

If certain products are advertised at low prices, such products must in fact be available in the stores of the advertiser for a reasonable period of time (see *BGH*, 1984 GRUR, 593 *Adidas-Sportartikel*). It is not permitted to attract customers with low price articles, which are not in fact, or not in a reasonable number, available. A special low price offer must be marked as such, in order to avoid the assumption that the entire collection of the promoter is particularly low-priced (see *Baumbach/ Hefermehl*, *supra*, para. 3 ann. 273a *et seq.*).

A comparison of the actual prices with former (higher) prices implies that the higher price was in fact applied to the product for a reasonable period of time (see *BGH*, 1975 GRUR, 78, 79).

Similarly, comparison of the store's own prices with the (higher) retail prices recommended by the manufacturer is only permissible if those recommended prices are not arbitrarily determined but the result of actual market conditions (*Baumbach/Hefermehl*, *supra*, para. 3 ann. 290).

The Regulation concerning the Quotation of Prices (*PreisangabenVO*) requires all offers to ultimate customers indicating prices to quote the final price, including all taxes and other duties. A violation of this duty is regarded as unfair competition because the advertiser gains a competitive advantage by means of a breach of the law.

(d) Finally, it must be pointed out that the advertiser is, generally, not obliged to disclose any negative features of his products. However, if certain characteristics of the product are essential in the mind of the consumer and likely to influence the purchase decision, the public may expect any such (negative) characteristics, such as the year of production, the existence of a more current design, etc. to be disclosed, and the seller must include a statement to such effect. This applies to most fashion articles, to cars, and to skis and skiboots if the model has been discontinued and replaced by a new model (see *BGH*, 1982, GRUR 374 – *Ski-Auslaufmodelle*).

(2) *Psychological pressure*

It is the aim of any competitive action to influence the purchase decision of the customer. As long as such influence is limited to the endeavours of the advertiser to convince a potential purchaser of the quality and price of his products, it has no relevancy under unfair competition law. As soon as, however, the advertising practices of a seller put the customer under psychological pressure which impairs his freedom to make purchase decisions of his own choice, the competitive behaviour of the seller no longer complies with the rules of fair competition.

(a) Such pressure exerted by an agressive approach to the customer may make it difficult for the customer to refuse a particular offer in which he otherwise might not have been interested.

A typical situation of this kind is created if people in the street are individually addressed by the representative of a business in order to persuade them to enter a store, or if victims of a car accident are approached immediately after its occurrence in order to offer professional assistance (car repairs, legal advice, etc.). The fear of appearing impolite in the first instance, and the emotional tension after a car accident in the second are likely to be the true reasons for the acceptance of an offer, rather than a reasonable evaluation of the advantages and disadvantages of the product or service offered (see *BGH*, 1960 GRUR, 431, 432, 1980 GRUR, 790 *et seq.* – *Werbung am Unfallort* III; *Nordemann, supra*, ann. 177 *et seq.*, p. 94).

Similarly, a customer may find it difficult to refuse a sales offer if the sales representative simultaneously hands him a prize which the customer has won in a competition (*BGH*, 1973 GRUR, 81 – *Gewinnübermittlung*).

Promotional approaches to relatives of recently deceased persons do not only evidence bad taste but also constitute a violation of *bonos mores* and illegal exploitation of emotional distress (*OLG Düsseldorf*, 1982 WRP, 274 *et seq.*).

¶1107

Another example of exerting unlawful pressure on a customer is the delivery of unordered merchandise. Obviously, the customer addressed is not obliged to pay for such merchandise. Nevertheless, he may feel obliged to do so. Even an explicit note attached to the respective product, clarifying the fact that no duty to pay, store or return the delivered merchandise exists, does not eliminate the psychological pressure, unless goods of virtually no value are concerned (see *BGH*, 1959 GRUR, 277 *et seq. – Künstlerpost-karten*).

(b) Appealing purposefully to the emotions of the customer also constitutes an unlawful promotional practice, unless those emotions are directly related to the offered product or service. Of course, it is permissible for an institution supporting starving children in Africa to appeal to the pity and readiness of the people to help. Nevertheless, it constitutes unfair competition if former prisoners are employed for the promotion of magazines who emphasize their poor financial and social conditions in order to convince a customer to subscribe (see *Nordemann*, *supra*, ann. 191, p. 99; *OLG Hamburg*, 1981 WRP, 469 *et seq.*).

Free-gift advertising impairs the ability of the customer to make an unbiased purchase decision, if the value of the gifts and/or the manner of their distribution would make the customer feel guilty, if he did not express his gratitude. Usually, this is the case if one has to enter a store in order to collect the gift or a prize or if a businessman offers free, individual transportation to the sale facilities (see *BGH*, 1972, GRUR, 603, 605 – *Kunden-Einzelbeförderung*; *OLG Stuttgart*, 1970, GRUR, 192, 193).

To make a gift contingent upon a certain purchase is prohibited by the *Zugabenverordnung* of 9 March 1932 (Regulation Concerning Complementary Extras), as amended. Correspondingly, the *Rabattgesetz* of 25 November 1933 (Act concerning Price Discounts), as amended, strictly limits the right to offer discounts on generally announced and listed sales prices. The only material exception is a discount of up to 3 per cent for instant cash payment.

An interesting issue in this context was raised by coffee-shop chains in West Germany. They started to sell low-priced goods entirely unrelated to their coffee products (books, household articles, even bicycles and furniture). In order to acquire those products, the customer had to also buy as a 'package' a certain quantity of coffee. The Federal Supreme Court considered this practice an undue influence on the customer (see *BGH*, BGHZ vol. 65, p. 68, 74 – *Vorspannangebot*). Since then, the coffee-shop chains have continued the sale of low-priced, unrelated

¶1107

products but no longer insist on a combined purchase. This was held to be permissible, although there might still be psychological pressure on the buyer of low-priced goods if he was to leave the coffee-shop without buying coffee (*BGH*, 1979 GRUR 56 *et seq. – Tierbuch*).

(c) Section 12, 13 and 22 UWG explicitly prohibit the offering of bribes to employees of potential customers as well as the acceptance of bribes for the purpose of giving preference to the offeror over his competitors. Such behaviour is even prosecuted as a criminal offence (s. 12, 22 UWG).

(d) It is also an unfair practice under s. 1 UWG to arouse fear or panic in order to convince the customer to accept an offer, e.g. by suggesting an extreme price increase in the near future if this is in fact unpredictable.

(e) Unfair pressure may not only be exerted by the seller but also by a powerful customer, like a big foodstore-chain requesting so-called 'entrance fees' or other benefits from a supplier before the products of the latter are displayed on the shelves in the stores. Such abuse of economical power may put psychological pressure on the supplier either to accept the unfair conditions or to lose an important customer (see *Loewenheim*, 1976 GRUR, 242).

¶1108   Unfair restraint of competitors

The restraint, or even the elimination, of one or several competitors by means other than better performance or lower prices constitutes a violation of *bonos mores* under s. 1 UWG. On the other hand the restraint or elimination of a competitor as a result of the better quality or lower price of the products or services offered is, in general, not objectionable under unfair competition rules.

(1) *Destructive competition (Vernichtungswettbewerb)*

Even a restraint of competitors due to better performance may constitute an unfair practice if it:

(a) is aimed at obstructing or eliminating competitors; or

(b) causes substantial risks for the continued existence of free competition in the respective market area.

(a) *Undercutting of prices.*   The attempt to offer products or services at a lower price than a competitor is simply a normal feature of a functioning competition. Even the sale of merchandise under prime cost may, under normal circumstances, not be regarded as an unfair practice. It is not up to the courts to determine whether a price is economically reasonable or not.

Only if the price cutting is directed at the systematic elimination of individual competitors (outsiders) or the entire competition in a certain market segment, does it violate *bonos mores* under s. 1 UWG (see *OLG Düsseldorf*, 1982 WRP, 582). Needless to say it is often difficult to provide enough evidence to prove such unfair intentions of a low price offerer.

(b) *Enticement of customers and employees.*   Soliciting new customers, as well as recruiting capable employees, is normal practice for a businessman in a free market. If he approaches the customers or employees of a competitor, however, this inevitably implies detrimental effects for the latter. Nevertheless, such behaviour is an essential element of free competition and, thus, in principle, legitimate. It becomes illegal only if improper methods are applied or if it serves unjust purposes. A businessman who induces potential customers or employees to breach a valid contract with a competitor acts unfairly. If he only takes advantage of a committed breach of contract, he may nevertheless violate *bonos mores* under s. 1 UWG, provided he does so with the intention of damaging the competitor. Even inducing a potential employee or customer to properly terminate his agreement with a competitor may constitute unfair competition if such influence is purposefully directed against a specific enterprise and systematically exercised to an extent which actually jeopardises the existence of such competitor (see *BGH*, 1976 GRUR, 306, 307).

(c) *Unfair hindrance of operation and marketing.*   The call for a boycott of a competitor is expressly prohibited by s. 26, para. 1 GWB. Also, a third party (e.g. a trade association) promoting the competitive position of a specific enterprise acts unfairly if it explicitly or implicitly calls for a boycott of a competitor of such enterprise.

Often, a call for a boycott has no competitive targets, but is only supposed to influence public opinion with respect to political, social or economical issues. In these cases, it is covered by the constitutional freedom of speech (art. 5 GG) if all facts are stated correctly and no pressure is exerted on the addressees (see *Federal Constitutional Supreme Court* BVerfGEm, Vol. 25, 256, 269-*Blinkführ*).

Competition may also be eliminated by swamping a market with free products of a certain kind. Such a practice, which actually may clog the market for competitors, is unfair. Free samples of a new product in smaller quantities may be distributed in order to simply open up the market and develop competition (see *BGH*, 1969, GRUR, 295, 297-*Goldener Oktober*).

An obviously illegal restraint on the marketing efforts of a competitor is the obstruction of his advertisements by tearing down or pasting over advertising posters. It is debatable whether the removal of trademarks, manufacturers'

¶1108

names or other marks of origin from a product by a retailer may be treated similarly. In the case of obstruction of goodwill of the manufacturer, this should be actionable only if such practice is followed to an extent relevant in view of the total sales of the manufacturer and not only in individual cases.

In particular, on the market for cosmetics and drugs the removal of control numbers recently became a serious issue. In order to fight against grey market ('*Graumarkt*') activities, and to control their distribution channels, manufacturers affix certain code numbers to their products. The removal of such code numbers by grey marketeers or their suppliers was not considered to constitute an unfair restraint of the manufacturer's marketing efforts, however. Only if the number is required in order to provide proper repair and warranty services, and its removal causes the loss of warranty rights to the customer, does the retailer mislead the consumers if he does not inform them about this negative feature of his product (see *BGH*, 1978 GRUR, 364, 366 *Golfrasenmäher*).

(2) *Comparing advertising*

The purpose of any advertisement is to emphasise the advantages of the product or service concerned. Obviously, the customer is likely to be particularly impressed if the manufacturer is able to underline those advantages by comparing its own efficiency with that of a competitor. In contrast to the liberal practice in the United States, the German courts are rather restrictive in allowing advertisements comparing products, even if the statements about the competitor or its products are true and correct. As a statement of principle, nobody is allowed to promote his products by means of disparaging those of the competitor.

(a) *Disparagement of competitors.* Section 14 UWG explicitly forbids detrimental statements about the business, the owner or the products of a competitive enterprise which cannot be shown to be true. Knowingly making false statements about a competitor is even considered a criminal offence under s. 15 UWG. Moreover, misleading information concerning a competitor may be pursued under ss. 1 and 3 UWG.

(b) *True comparing advertising.* As a general rule, advertising comparing products is only permissible if there are sufficient reasonable grounds for a comparison, in particular if it serves the need for objective information to the customer. See *Nordemann, supra*, ann. 337, p. 149.

A reference to the person of the competitor is virtually never required in order to inform the customer about the merits of the products or services. Thus, a reference (oblique or otherwise) to previous unfair practices or convictions of the competitor is illegal under s. 1 UWG, even if it is true. Exceptionally, a legitimate interest in a reference to personal affairs may exist, if it serves as a

¶1108

reasonable defence against an illegal act by the competitor, e.g. a call to boycott the advertiser.

Advertisements comparing products by their very nature make implied or actual reference to one or more individual competitors. Simple comparisons of different systems of products are generally allowed, unless it is obvious to the customer to which competitor the compared system is attributed.

A reference correctly comparing the products of a competitor with those of the advertiser was held to be legitimate by German courts if it was necessary to show the technical progress of the advertiser's own new product ('progress comparison') , if it was used to defend an illegal offence by a competitor, e.g. an untrue comparison of systems ('defence comparison'), if it was made upon the explicit request of the customer, or if it improves market transparency.

Moreover, a (correct) comparison of the advertiser's own price with the (higher) price which is recommended by the manufacturer is also permissible.

Since it was the idea of promoting more factual and informative advertising that led the courts to adopt a more liberal approach towards comparing advertisements in recent years, case law is still very strict in prohibiting comparisons which rely on suggestive catchwords or unnecessary disparagement of competitors.

(3) *Unfair exploitation of work results and marketing efforts of competitors*

The work results and creative achievements of a businessman may be protected under applicable patent, trademark, business name and copyright laws (described in detail in the subsequent Chapter dealing with industrial property rights). Where no such protection exists, everybody, in principle, is free to reproduce, copy or even plagiarise the products of a competitor. Under unfair competition rules, such behaviour becomes relevant only if its potential effect on the competitor, as well as the underlying intentions of the 'sponger', render it an unfair competitive practice.

(a) *Unfair exploitation of products of competitors.* The simple appropriation of a competitor's achievement without any manufacturing efforts and costs of one's own, e.g. by means of duplicating papers on a photocopier, implies the intention to obstruct the marketing efforts of the competitor and, thus, is, as a rule, prohibited by s. 1 UWG.

The reproduction of work results constitutes an unfair practice under s. 1 UWG if the reproduced item has certain characteristics which are known to the public and, therefore, stand for its specific high quality, the origin of such object or its low price, and if the reproducer does not make all reasonable efforts to avoid the possibility of confusion between the original and the copied products. Unfair competition law does not, however, protect day-to-day and common

¶1108

products which are marketed by several manufacturers of basically the same quality so that the origin of the respective merchandise is without importance to the public (see *BGH*, BGHZ vol. 50, 125, 130 – *Pulverbehälter*).

(b) *Unfair imitation of advertisements of competitors.*   Similar criteria are applied to the question of whether the imitation of advertisements of a competitor is relevant under unfair competition law or not. This is the case if a commercial advertisement includes certain characteristics which are recognised by the public and associated with a specific product or manufacturer. This might include a specific slogan (usually not subject to copyright) or a characteristic design expressing a certain advertising idea. The imitator acts unfairly if he causes the possibility of confusion without a reasonable motive.

Even without the possibility of confusion the imitation of an advertising measure may violate *bonos mores* under s. 1 UWG, if it involves the 'delusion' of a famous advertising idea (see *Baumbach/Hefermehl*, *supra*, para. 1, ann. 456, 463).

(c) *Exploitation of reputation of a competitor.*   Often the public associates with a certain product a specific standard of quality which a competitor may wish to exploit.

The exploitation of the special reputation of a competitor can take place in the form of an open reference. In such a case, a businessman advertises his product with terms like 'substitute for . . .' or 'same quality as . . .', and refers to the product of the competitor. Here, the advertiser takes advantage of the goodwill of a competitor which, possibly, was built up after considerable effort. At the same time he obstructs the marketing of the competitor, since the consumer may believe that he does not need the products of the competitor anymore, since those of the advertiser are of the same quality. Such practice is considered unfair under s. 1 UWG.

Another method of exploitation of a competitor's reputation is the hidden approximation of competitive products. It constitutes an unfair practice if a businessman markets products which the public may confuse with other (original) products with which it associates a certain standard of quality, unless all reasonable efforts to reduce the possibility of confusion are made by the newcomer.

(d) *Exploitation of business secrets.*   The exploitation of the achievements of a competitor which was made possible by commercial espionage or the misuse of trust is considered, and may be prosecuted as, a criminal offence under ss. 17 to 20a UWG.

¶1109   Breach of law

As mentioned before, the commercial activities of a businessman are subject to a multitude of legal regulations and restrictions. Some of them are clearly related to certain competitive practices. Others do not directly concern questions of unfair competition, but constitute the expression of certain ethical values, so that their breach violates substantial interests of the public and, thus, may be considered *contra bonos mores*. Again, others merely contain certain organisational principles. Their breach does not constitute unfair competition by itself but only if it is aimed at gaining an unlawful advantage over competitors. In this context the breach of contractual commitments also may be relevant.

(1) *Special unfair competition regulations*

Certain specific competitive practices are addressed in the UWG, as well as in related legislative acts. The most important provisions are the following:

(a) *Act Concerning Price Discounts (Rabattgesetz).* Discounts and rebates on listed prices can be used to solicit customers. The Act Concerning Price Discounts of 25 November 1933, as amended, strictly limits the discretion of a retailer to offer such discounts and rebates to the final consumer with respect to products for day-to-day use.

The Act does not prevent a businessman from modifying (in particular reducing) his prices, as long as such reduction is generally applied to all customers. It limits, however, the right to offer special rebates to certain customers based on personal relations. The idea behind it is to guarantee a reliable comparison of prices and thereby of the efficiency of competitors. The price tag which must be attached to displayed goods would be meaningless if the price shown could be reduced at the whim of the seller by a discount. In essence, the consumer of day-to-day goods cannot bargain with the seller, he can only shop around to find a better general offer from another seller if he thinks the price of one offer to be too high. Furthermore, a discount (in the view of the legislature) would give the buyer the misleading impression that a discount constitutes a personal favour or privilege while in fact every customer asking for the same is granted it.

The *Rabattgesetz* only applies if products for day-to-day use are sold to a final customer. The term 'day-to-day use' is construed rather broadly and includes, *inter alia*, TV sets, cars, motorcycles, electric equipment, holiday trips, etc. However, the sale of luxury goods, land, works of art and antiques is not subject to the Act. 'Final consumer' may also cover a businessman who uses a product for his own business purposes and does not resell the same.

Under the *Rabattgesetz* only expressly listed discounts are permissible, i.e.:

(i) a discount of up to 3 per cent for instant cash payment (ss. 2 to 5 of the Law);

(ii) a discount for the sale of larger quantities of products to the extent that such discount is customary (ss. 7 and 8 of the *Rabattgesetz*);

(iii) special discounts to persons utilising the merchandise or service for their business activities to the extent that such discount is customary (s. 9 No. 1), or to bulk purchasers (s. 9 No. 2) or to employees of the enterprise with respect to products or services obtained for their own household (s. 9 No. 3 of the *Rabattgesetz).*

Any other discount or rebate is illegal and subject to a fine of up to DM 10,000 (s. 11), and can give rise to claims of competitors to cease and desist from such practices (s. 12 of the *Rabattgesetz).*

(b) *Regulation Concerning Complementary Extras (Zugabeverordnung).* Complementary extras imply an undue influence on the purchase decision of the consumer which is made under the impression that a special advantage is to be gained, although the cost for the extra is commonly included in the price calculation for the main merchandise. The Regulation Concerning Complementary Extras (*Zugabeverordnung*) of 9 March 1932, as amended, prohibits the offering or announcement of complementary extras if they are made dependent upon the purchase of the main merchandise. The *Zugabeverordnung* is also applicable (according to s. 1(1)) if only an insubstantial consideration is requested for the extra (i.e. a 'fictitious' amount which is requested in order to suggest that a consideration attaches to a service, etc. which is in fact complementary) or if its complementary character is disguised under a combined total price for the joint-sale of the product or service and the extra.

The prohibition on combining the sale of a product with a free gift does not, under s. 1(2) of the *Zugabenverordnung*, apply to promotional items of immaterial value, small items of virtually no value (up to about DM 1: see *OLG Hamburg*, 1984 WRP, 33) or customary appurtenances or customary supplementary services. 'Customary' in this sense means not only what corresponds to the established customs of a certain branch, but includes further developments of business practices, e.g. the packaging of the goods which may also be usable for other purposes (see *BGH*, 1975 GRUR, 199 – *Senf-Henkelglas*: drinking glass from a container for mustard)).

Under s. 2 of the *Zugabeverordnung*, competitors may ask the court for a cease and desist order against a violator of the provisions of the Act. Under s. 3 of the Act, such breach may also be subject to fines of up to DM 10,000.

(c) *Special 'sales'.* Businessmen familiar with common law practices may be surprised to learn that German unfair competition law strictly limits all 'for-sale' events. The idea behind this is to curtail wildcat canvassing methods as well as excessive dumping competition.

Special 'sales', within the meaning of the law, do not fall within the regular course of business. Rather, they interrupt the regular course of business and are advertised in a way such that the consumer expects an extraordinary event. Thus, special promotional offers concerning individual products or product types taking place without a time limit within the regular course of business are not affected by the restrictions outlined below (see s. 1(2) of the Decree Concerning Special Promotional Sales (*Anordnung betreffend Sonderveranstaltungen*) of 4 July 1935). Obviously, distinguishing special 'sales' from special promotional offers may be sometimes difficult, as in the case where a promotional offer includes almost complete product lines. The most important criterion is the prohibition of a time limit. Case law is very strict in this regard and does not even accept limitations like 'summer offer' or 'holiday offer' (see *BGH*, 1973 GRUR, 653).

The following restrictive conditions exist for special 'sales' in Germany:

- *Winding-up sales* are permissible under s. 7 UWG only if either the total business or a branch of the business closes down, or a certain kind of merchandise is completely sold off. The reason for the event must be indicated in any advertisements. It must be notified to the Chamber for Industry and Commerce or the municipal trade office, respectively, and must not exceed the period of two months.

- *Clearance sales* under s. 7(a) UWG, must have as their purpose the clearance of a certain stock of merchandise due to renovation or other building alterations, the reduction of business or a similar event. Case law is restrictive in this regard and prohibits clearance sales if the merchandise may reasonably be stored temporarily outside the business premises. A clearance sale may not exceed the period of one month, unless it is extended for one additional month by the Chamber of Industry and Commerce.

- *Seasonal sales* (summer sales and winter sales) may only take place for the period of 12 working days beginning on the last Monday in January and the last Monday in July of each calendar year (s. 9 UWG in connection with the Regulation on Seasonal Sales of 13 July 1950). Case law has often had to deal with promotional offers and price reductions occurring shortly before or after the seasonal sales. If they give the impression of being extended seasonal sales, they may constitute an unlawful 'for-sale' event (see BGH, 1976 GRUR, 702 – *Sparpreis*).

Apart from the aforementioned special sales, the *Anordung betreffend Sonderveranstaltungen* only permits anniversary sales after the expiration of 25, 50, 75, etc. years of the existence of the enterprise (s. 3), and special rummage sales during the last three days of seasonal sales.

Violations of the aforementioned regulations may be subject to fines under s. 10 UWG (up to DM 10,000). The restrictions only apply to retailers who are

¶1109

selling products, not to wholesale dealers or to service enterprises like banks and transportation companies (which may, however, be subject to special regulations).

(2) Other statutory regulations

The breach of laws other than those directly related to unfair practices may only be relevant under unfair competition rules if the breach is caused by a competitive action and has an effect on the competition. On the other hand, not every breach of law with a competitive impact automatically contravenes *bonos mores* under s. 1 UWG.

(a) *Fundamental ethical principles.*   The violation of laws which are the expression of a generally accepted fundamental ethical value, and which aim at the protection of an important public interest, constitutes an unfair practice. In this context, particularly the statutes related to public health, such as the Drug Law (*Arzneimittelgesetz*: AMG) of 24 August 1976, the Drug Advertising Act (*Heilmittelwerbegesetz*: HWG) of 18 October 1978, the Act Concerning Pharmacies (*Apothekengesetz*) of 15 October 1980, as well as those provisions of the Food Law (*Lebensmittel- und Bedarfsgegenständegesetz*: LMBG) of 15 August 1974 which concern the protection of human health, should be noted.

(b) *Organising and administrative regulations.*   The majority of statutory provisions do not contain or express substantial ethical standards or fundamental public interests, but merely serve the expedient administration or organisation of the commercial field. This group of laws includes notification duties with respect to the setting up of a trade or business, the duty to quote final prices under the Regulation Concerning the Quotation of Prices (*Preisangabenverordnung*) of 14 March 1985, and the Act Concerning the Closing Time of Stores (*Ladenschlußgesetz*) of 28 November 1956.

The non-observance of these administrative requirements may only constitute an act *contra bonos mores* if a competitor wilfully and systematically disregards them in order to gain an unfair advantage over others. This implies that the same restrictions must be applicable to the relevant competitors and be actually observed by these competitors. The breach must cause a competitive advantage in the sense of lower prices or improved efficiency. If a businessman keeps his store open under violation of the time restrictions of the *Ladenschlußgesetz* and, thus, offers to customers the possibility of making purchases at a time when other stores are closed, he offers special efficiency. 'Wilfully and systematically' in this context means that not only an occasional breach of these laws is committed and that the acting person is aware of all the circumstances of the unlawful behaviour. Case law has concluded from the fact that a violating party did not immediately submit to a cease and desist request of a competitor

¶1109

that the breach of law was committed wilfully and systematically (see *OLG Nürnberg*, 1983 GRUR, 666).

(3) *Breach of contracts*

The breach of contractual commitments has become the subject of unfair competition disputes, in particular with respect to controlled distribution and marketing systems. Case law has ruled that the breach of a controlled distribution system where the commitment is to sell only to final customers (as well as the solicitation or exploitation of such breach by an outsider) may constitute an unfair practice and therefore entitle the parties observing the controlled systems to stop any further selling by outsiders, provided the system is in fact comprehensive. This means that all relevant competitors must be equally bound by the conditions of the distribution contracts. Otherwise a violation is no longer unfair.

Case law requires theoretical, as well as practical, comprehensiveness. Theoretical comprehensiveness exists if the distribution system and the underlying contracts equally bind all partners and legally prevent any distribution of the products concerned outside the system, even by the way of 'grey' imports from foreign countries. Practical comprehensiveness requires the manufacturer to supervise the system and immediately prosecute any subsequent breaches. As soon as an outsider can prove that the controlled products are available on the free market notwithstanding the distribution restrictions, the courts deny the relevancy of the breach under unfair competition law (see *BGH*, 1964 GRUR, 629 – *Grauer Markt*; 1968 GRUR, 272 – *Trockenrasierer* III).

LEGAL PROTECTION AGAINST UNFAIR PRACTICES

¶1110   In general

In Germany, the prosecution of unfair practices and, thus, the protection of fair competition is, primarily, a matter of private law. The competitors control each other. Therefore, s. 13, para. 1 UWG concedes the right to take action against unfair practices primarily to competitors on the same market. In order to effectively protect fair competition in the event that the competitors are not able or willing to pursue their rights, s. 13, para. 1 and 1(a) UWG authorises associations whose purpose is the promotion of trade interests or the protection of consumer interests, to proceed against a businessman who does not observe the restrictions set out in the UWG and auxiliary legislation. Unfortunately, this right is often abused by dubious associations whose only true goal is to earn legal fees and not to support the interests of the consumers. Courts are becoming more and more reluctant to accept lawsuits from such associations (see LG *München* I, 1981 WRP, 424 – *Concurrencia aeterna*). However, legislative measures would be necessary, and have indeed been mooted for a long time, in order to effectively restrain the activities of these so-called 'warning clubs' (*Abmahnvereine*).

The individual consumer does not have a right to claim under unfair competition law. He is considered sufficiently protected by contract or tort law to which he might resort in connection with, for example, a misleading advertising statement.

The defendant in any unfair competition action is the violating party. If the violation was committed by an employee or an agent, the owner of the enterprise may also be held liable (s. 13, para. 3; s. 14, para. 3 UWG: s. 2, para. 1 *Zugabeverordnung*: s. 12, para. 2 *Rabattgesetz*).

Criminal or quasi-criminal sanctions provided in the unfair competition laws (e.g. in s. 4 UWG for a knowingly false advertising statement, in s. 12 UWG for the offering or acceptance of bribes, in s. 15 for the disparagement of competitors, in ss. 17, 18 and 20 UWG for commercial espionage or in s. 11 *Rabattgesetz* and s. 3 *Zugabeverordnung* for the non-observance of the provisions of those laws) are merely of a supplementary nature and do not have any substantial practical significance. It should be noted that the general clause in s. 1 UWG (which is by far the most important basis for unfair competition claims) does not provide for any criminal or quasi-criminal sanction.

¶1111 Important claims under unfair competition laws

(1) Cease and desist claim

The most important legal remedy in order to secure the observance of the rules and obligations imposed on competitors is the cease and desist claim. The claim is raised to prevent repetition of an unfair practice in the future and, thus, implies that a certain illegal action in fact is likely to reoccur. Such danger is assumed if the same action was committed once by a competitor. This assumption cannot be eliminated by the violating party merely stating that it will abstain from such behaviour in the future. It is necessary for such competitor to agree that an adequate contractual fine may be levied against him in the event that he breaches his undertaking. Depending upon the severity and economical significance of the unfair practice, such contractual fine may amount to between DM 500 and DM 10,000 for each future violation.

As long as the violating party has not given an explicit undertaking to cease and desist (combined with the submission to an adequate contractual fine for further violations), a competitor may take legal action against such party. This is true even if the unfair act was committed without negligence or wilful misconduct. A cease and desist claim only requires a violation of the competition rules to exist.

(2) *Remedy claim*

The commitment of an unfair act does not only give rise to a cease and desist claim (to prevent its repetition), it also obliges the violating party to remedy the detriment or damage caused to the competitor. If a businessman distributes advertising materials which contain incorrect or misleading statements, he is under an obligation to delete, or even destroy, the relevant statements in the entire remaining stock of such materials.

The most important remedy is the right to claim an order revoking or rectifying untrue detrimental statements about a competitor or his business. Moreover, under s. 23, para. 2 and 3 UWG, the courts may grant the competitor concerned the right to publish the court decision if there is a justifiable interest in such publication.

(3) *Damage claim*

Unfair practices may also result in the injured competitor claiming damages. Such claims require negligence or wilful misconduct in the sense that the acting party must have known or been in a position to know that its action was illegal. Under case law, negligence only requires the violating party to have been aware of all the circumstances which rendered its behaviour unfair (see *BGH*, 1969 GRUR, 418, 422 – *Standesbeamte*). Not even misunderstanding the legal restrictions can discharge the violating party from liability (see *BGH*, 1975 GRUR, 667 – *Reichswehrprozess*).

The damage claim includes all expenses of the damaged competitor actually incurred in connection with the unfair practice, such as legal fees and additional advertising costs which were necessary in order to eliminate any confusion among the consumers due to a misleading advertising statement, and even lost profits. A claim for loss of profit is often quite difficult to establish because the problems involved in calculating and proving the amount of such loss caused by the competitor are usually great.

Only in the case of the violation of industrial property rights is the calculation of damages simplified, insofar as case law accepts the assertion of:

(a) a fictitious licence fee, which would have been payable under a licence agreement executed under comparable circumstances; or

(b) the profits of the violating party attributable to the infringed industrial property right.

¶1111

(4) *Disclosure and account claim*

Often, there is no way for the damaged competitor to obtain the information necessary to prepare his remedy or damage claim other than from the violating party. This is why case law acknowledges a 'discovery and accounts' claim to the extent necessary to determine and calculate the respective claims.

In the case of the violation of industrial property rights, the discovery includes not only the volumes and prices of the infringing sales but also names and addresses of customers and the dates of delivery in order to make the information verifiable. For the protection of the violating party the court may require a chartered public accountant to be appointed who shall not disclose the names of the competitor's customers.

(5) *Statute of limitation*

All claims under unfair competition law are barred by the statute of limitation after a period of six months from the time the plaintiff became aware of the unfair practice or the occurrence of damage, and the identity of the violating party, and where such knowledge is lacking, after a period of three years respectively. It must be noted that, according to the BGH, a temporary injunction (see below) does not interrupt the running of the statute of limitation (see *BGH*, 1979 GRUR, 121 – *Verjährungsunterbrechung*). Therefore, a regular lawsuit must be commenced within the six-month period, notwithstanding pending injunctive proceedings, unless the violating party effectively undertakes to accept the temporary injunction as final.

¶1112   Procedural aspects

Generally, unfair competition claims are pursued, as any other private law claims, by suing the violating party in court. In practice, however, a special unfair competition procedure has been established with the result that 90 per cent of the disputes falling within the scope of the unfair competition laws are finally settled in injunctive proceedings (see *Nirk, Gewerblicher Rechtsschutz*, 1981, Teil V., para. 11, I. 5).

(1) *Warning letter*

There is no legal obligation to send a warning letter to the violating party prior to the initiation of court proceedings. However, it is customary and advisable to give the potential defendant the chance to remedy the unfair action out of court by submitting a cease and desist statement combined with an agreement to pay a contractual penalty as mentioned in ¶1111 above. In the absence of such a statement and agreement, the plaintiff is likely to have to pay all legal fees, including court fees and those of the defendant, if the latter immediately acknowledges the claim in court and, thus, can argue that he did not give cause for a court action (s. 93 of the German Code of Civil Procedure: ZPO).

(2) *Temporary injunction*

If the violating party does not sign an appropriate cease and desist statement within a reasonable period set by the applicant, the applicant may apply for a temporary injunction under s. 945 ZPO. Such injunction will be granted by the court under the following conditions:

(a) There must be sufficient cause for an injunction, which is the case if the matter is urgent. Urgency is statutorily assumed in unfair competition disputes (s. 25 UWG), which assumption may, however, be disproved by the applicant's own behaviour which may show that he himself does not consider the matter urgent. Case law is not uniform in this regard. The court of appeal in Munich denies urgency if the applicant did not apply for an injunction within a period of (only) one month after he became aware of all relevant circumstances (1983 WRP, 943, 644), while other courts of appeal consider an application after a period of two months still to be within the time limits (1980 WRP, 491; 1981 WRP, 224, 225), and some courts of appeal will even accept an application within a period of six months (1976 WRP, 483, 485). This leads to the unpleasant conclusion that the chances of an effective defence of unfair practices can substantially depend upon regional aspects, and often some 'forum shopping' by the applicant may be called for.

(b) Furthermore, the applicant must establish the underlying claim for the injunction. Since injunctive proceedings are designed to provide a temporary settlement, damage claims and related discovery and account claims, which would lead to final satisfaction of the applicant or plaintiff, cannot be raised in injunctive proceedings which are primarily reserved for cease and desist claims. The correct formulation of such a claim is often complicated, since it must be related to the actual unfair act in question, but, on the other hand, should be wide enough to prevent the opponent from continuing his unfair practices in a slightly modified form.

(c) If the applicant establishes the cause for the injunction (urgency), as well as the injunction claim, to the satisfaction of the court, the injunction may be granted even without an oral hearing. In practice such an injunction may often be obtained on the same day on which the application was filed. It can be enforced immediately. The defendant, however,

¶1112

may subsequently apply for an oral hearing, after which the initial court order may or may not be reversed by a formal judgment.

If, at the discretion of the court (which will take into consideration the legitimate interest of both parties and, in particular, the urgency of the matter), an oral hearing prior to the granting of the injunction is called for, the court will schedule such hearing for a date within the next few days or weeks. Immediately after such hearing a judgment is given which either grants or denies the injunction.

Both parties may appeal against the judgment. It is the great danger of any injunction (and must therefore be considered carefully by both the plaintiff and applicant) that, when an injunction is later lifted, the plaintiff will have to compensate the defendant for all damages suffered by the injunction and its implementation, independent of any fault or negligence of the plaintiff or applicant (s. 945 ZPO).

(3) Termination letter

After a temporary injunction is granted, the plaintiff usually will request a statement from the defendant in which the defendant acknowledges the injunction as final and binding. This statement is called a termination letter and, if issued by the defendant, will make a regular lawsuit dispensable.

(4) Lawsuit

If the defendant refuses to acknowledge the finalty of the injunction, the plaintiff must file a regular lawsuit in order to bring the matter to an end and to interrupt the statute of limitation. As mentioned above, damage claims (as well as the related discovery and account claims and the remedy claims) may only be asserted by way of a regular lawsuit. If damages can only finally be determined in the future, the plaintiff can also ask for a declaratory judgment which will hold that the defendant must compensate him for all future and further damages resulting from the unfair act.

(5) Venue

The principal venue for unfair competition claims is the domicile or seat of the defendant (s. 24, para. 1 UWG). Much more important in practice, however, is the alternative venue of the place where the unfair act was committed (s. 24, para. 2 UWG). This latter venue includes the place where the unfair act was actually initiated, as well as all the places where the violation was realised. Therefore, in the case of an illegal advertisement in a newspaper, the unfair act is committed in the entire area of distribution of such newspaper, which means that the plaintiff has the choice between all the venues falling within such area ('flying venue').

¶1112

12 Industrial Property Rights

PATENTS

¶1201 Introduction

Patent applications in Germany are governed by the Patent Act of 16 December 1980. This latest revision of the Act, which first came into effect in 1891, takes full account of the 1973 European Patent Convention. Since 1903 the Federal Republic has been a member of the 1883 Paris Union Convention, and it currently applies the Stockholm Version of this Convention which became effective in Germany in 1970. This Convention rules on the industrial property rights of foreign nationals of other member states to the Convention if they apply for industrial property rights protection in Germany.

The Patent Co-operation Treaty, which came into force for the Federal Republic in 1978, the Strasbourg Convention on the International Classification of Patents, the Budapest Treaty of 1977 (dealing with patents for micro-organisms), and many other major international treaties in the field of industrial property rights have been signed and ratified by Germany. The Luxembourg Convention on the Patent for the Common Market of 1975, signed by the EC Member States, will eventually lead to a common patent for all EC countries, but before a law to that effect is enacted for the EC states, some more political stumbling blocks have to be cleared out of the way.

¶1202 Domestic patents

(1) *Grant of patent*

A patent in Germany is granted for an invention, provided it is:

- made in a technical field;
- new;
- susceptible of industrial use;
- based on an inventive activity;
- technically advanced;

- sufficiently clearly and completely described; and
- useful.

Of these criteria the newness, technical advancement and inventive activity (which latter requirement means the high level of inventiveness) are the real yardstick for the Patent Office to either grant a patent or reject an application.

(2) *Exclusion of patentability*

The above named requirements for the grant of a patent also delineate the limits beyond which no patent can be granted (s. 1(2) Patent Act).

(a) A discovery is not an invention where something already existing, but not generally known, is found. The discovery can become an invention if it is used for a certain technical purpose. The discovery, for instance, of a new metal in the earth's crust cannot be patented, but the use of the metal for a certain product can lead to a patent.

(b) Scientific theories and mathematical methods are also not inventions but a special type of discovery. Again, neither the theory nor the method can be patented, but they form the basis for a patentable invention if practical use of the scientific findings can be made.

(c) Aesthetic designs which are meant to animate the sense of colour or forms can be protected by a design patent (*Geschmacksmuster*), but a technical patent is not available. If, on the other hand, the technical means are used to create a particular aesthetic effect, that use could be a patentable invention.

(d) Plans, rules, procedures for intellectual activities, games or business activities are barred from being patented as they are 'instructions to the human intellect' but not technically orientated.

(e) Programs for data processing equipment are excluded from patent protection (s. 1(2) No. 3 Patent Act).

A very small area where exceptions to the above rule might be possible is open to patents, insofar as software can be patentable if it requires a new and inventive construction of data processing equipment or shows new methods to use such equipment in a novel, uncommon and not obvious manner. For example, a fairly complicated self-modulating algorism in a vehicle anti-skid braking system was held to meet these criteria. The key to German patent protection for software seems to be a very high degree of incorporation in a 'device'.

(f) Reproduction of information (tables, forms, writing patterns) cannot be patented. They are a sub-group of (d) above.

¶1202

(g) Forms and methods of medical treatment are not patentable because they are not susceptible of 'industrial' use. This rather formalistic view is in support of the real, ethical reason that such treatment should be free for everybody. Products for medical treatment, such as pharmaceutica, medical instruments or medical equipment, can be patented.

(3) *The main patent criteria*

(a) An invention is no longer new, and thus not patentable, if it has been described anywhere in the world at any time in any manner accessible to the public (publication, lecture, discussion, radio or television, any patent applications which have not yet been published, etc.).

(b) Technical advancement must be achieved by the invention. The state of the art is the foundation for any enhancement.

(c) The requirement of the 'level of invention' ensures that a patent is only granted for achievements considerably above the state of the art. A creative act of the inventor has to lead him beyond the point which an average man skilled in the art with normal working methods is likely to reach. This is the point where many patent applications fail. The difficulty for the Patent Office in its evaluation process lies in the fact that the state of the art has to be determined without knowledge of the invention, while in fact the invention has been disclosed to the Office by the patent application.

(4) *The filing of the patent application*

(a) The filing of the patent application with the German Patent Office in Munich requires an application for the patent, the description of the invention (usually with drawings), and one or more patent claims. A special form supplied by the Patent Office is commonly used, the filing usually being done by a patent attorney. The Patent Office has published a Memorandum on the filing formalities.

The description of the invention must disclose the technical achievement in such a manner that the average man skilled in the art can understand it. The patent claims must show what, in the opinion of the applicant, will be protected by the patent. Here lies the real difficulty of a patent application. If the claims are drafted too narrowly, the later scope of protection is only narrow, while if they are too broad, the application may fail the test of newness or may not reach the required level of inventiveness.

¶1202

(b) After the patent is filed, the Patent Office initially checks the application for its formalities and, if a mistake, incompleteness or ambiguity is found, will request the applicant to remedy the situation.

Following the preliminary examination, but not before 18 months after the date of application (or an earlier priority date, if a patent was first filed in the foreign jurisdiction of a Paris Union Convention member state), the Patent Office publishes the application. The applicant may request a search to be made by the Patent Office, which he can do either together with his initial application or within a maximum period of seven years after the application date. During the search, the Patent Office, in constant communication with the applicant, will examine the application for the newness and level of the invention by considering all publications which are known to the public prior to the application date. If the application survives the examination, the patent will be granted. The Patent Office gives notice of such grant in the official Patent Journal and it publishes the patent.

(c) Within three months after the publication of the patent any third party can challenge the validity of the patent by filing an objection with the Patent Office. Contested proceedings between the applicant and the objecting party take place before the Patent Office which will either confirm, limit or revoke the patent.

(d) The patent fees payable to the German Patent Office accrue in stages:

- DM 100 become due when the applicant files his application with the Patent Office;
- DM 200 become due when the request to the Patent Office is made to search for publications which may be of importance for the question of the patentability of the invention; and
- DM 400 become due when the request for the examination of the application is made.

Finally, DM 150 must be paid when the patent is granted.

For each patent and application an annual fee for each year starting with the third year after the filing of the application must be paid. The fee for the third and fourth year is DM 100 for each of those years, but it increases each following year and the fee for the twentieth year amounts to DM 3,300.

(5) Effects of the patent

The patent awards to its owner a monopoly to exclusively exploit the invention. The owner is the only person who can manufacture, offer or sell the patented

¶1202

product or use the patented process. This monopoly includes the right to prevent unauthorised exploitation of the patented goods or process by a third party. How far this negative right of defending the monopolised technical area against intruders will reach depends on the scope of protection of the patent, which in turn is determined by the patent claims expressed in the patent grant.

(6) *Licensing or transfer*

Instead of exploiting the patent himself by manufacturing the patented product or employing the process, the owner may make commercial use of the patent by having others exploit the invention.

(a) The patent holder can grant an exclusive licence to a third party which will allow the latter full use of the invention and prevent others, including the patent holder, from doing the same.

(b) The patent holder may restrict the grant to a simple licence which will permit the licensee one or more alternatives of patent use but not exclusivity. Such simple licence may be restricted to a certain territory, to a limited period of time, to a specific product incorporating the patented invention, or to restricted activities such as distribution but not manufacture.

(c) The owner of the patent can sell and transfer the patent. No special form of contract or registration in the Patent Register is required, although usually employed.

(7) *Infringement litigation*

If someone uses the patent rights without the authorisation of the owner, he infringes an industrial property right and can be enjoined to desist by the courts.

(a) The most effective and rapid help from the courts is given by way of a preliminary injunction for which the patent holder may apply. The preliminary proceedings allow the applicant an easier way of proving his facts to the court because affidavits are allowed. Difficult technical issues, however, do not lend themselves to 'first reaction' proceedings. There is also the danger that, in the main proceedings which may follow the injunctive relief, the injunction will be lifted, in which case the applicant has to compensate the other side for all damages created by the injunction. If the defendant was forced to halt production as a result of the (unjustified) injunction, the damages may be substantial.

(b) The patent owner can seek to enjoin an infringer by way of normal lawsuit where experts can clarify technical issues and where the danger

¶1202

of having to pay damages is under control. In such a suit the patent owner or exclusive licensee may also recover damages for any infringing acts committed during the past. The lawsuit is commenced in the civil courts and the proceedings are much the same as described in Chapter 13.

(8) *Termination of patent*

The patent is limited in time. Patents applied for after 1 January 1978 run for 20 years from the day following the date of their application; earlier applications limit the life of the patent to 18 years.

A patent can terminate prior to its expiration date either if the annual patent fees are not paid or if the patent holder waives the right to the patent by written notice to the Patent Office.

Once the patent has been granted and not successfully challenged within the three months' objection period, it can only be defeated by a plea of nullity to the Federal Patent Court made by a third party. These proceedings are conducted by way of a normal lawsuit directed against the patent holder, and the reasons for the plea of nullity can be the same as those which could have been advanced in an objection to the Patent Office. If the Court declares the patent to be null and void, it will be retroactively cancelled.

¶1203   European patent law

The European Patent Convention (EPC) signed in 1973, and in force since 1976, achieves a higher degree of unification and centralisation than the Patent Co-operation Treaty (PCT), but is restricted to countries in Europe. The Federal Republic is a signatory to both the EPC and the PCT. It was the main achievement of the PCT to allow the inventor to file one international application for the protection of his invention in more than one country and to lead to a uniform international search, but the PCT leaves the final examination of the patentability and the granting of the patent to the countries which the inventor has selected for patent protection. The EPC goes further than the PCT and provides for the full procedure from the filing of the patent application to the grant of the patent conducted centrally by and before the European Patent Office in Munich. When the procedure is completed and a patent granted, it is subject to the various national laws of the countries for which patent protection is sought. The patent is divided into a 'bundle of national patents' and the further life of these patents is territorily restricted and governed by the various national bodies of patent law.

The advantage of the centralised procedure under the EPC is that the patent granted by the European Patent Office has the same wording in all member countries for which the applicant requests protection. The cost of the procedure before the European Patent Office is about four times as much as for a German national procedure. A European patent which, for example, was submitted for registration in three member countries will cost about DM 5,000 in total. Therefore, the EPC is cost-effective only if the applicant intends to register his patent in at least four member states.

While the EPC leads to a 'bundle of national patents', the Convention on the Patent for the Common Market of 1975 will eventually allow for the grant of a European patent valid in all the member countries of the EC. The European patent will be one uniform patent for the European Community which will avoid competitive distortion within the territory of the EC otherwise created by the different national patents of the EC countries with their various degrees of protection.

The European Community patent will only be granted for the entire EC territory, may only be transferred in total and will come to an end in its entirety. It will be completely independent from any national patent laws of the Member States and it will co-exist with the national patents. To achieve this supra-national patent, the Convention will contain the substantive patent law to create and govern the life of the patent. It will enact all the provisions dealing with the object of a patent, its extent of protection, the rights it will afford and the effect of the protection, its maintenance and termination, and the restriction and nullity of the patent.

The Convention has not become law yet.

UTILITY PATENTS

¶1204   Overview

Although the grant of a utility patent has to meet the same conditions as a patent and excludes the same unpatentable areas, a utility patent can only be received in a segment of the technical field where patents can be granted. Only articles of daily use, work utensils and parts thereof can be the object of a utility patent. The invention must be perceptible in tangible form. Under this requirement, the invention of a procedure (work or manufacturing procedure) cannot be protected by a utility patent but only by a regular patent. The article of daily use or utensil must be one unit which is a single, connected and moveable object. A multitude of objects cannot be the subject of a utility patent.

The invention must be new, technically advanced and inventive. The principles of patent law apply to a large extent. The requirements as to the level of the invention are lower than those of the patent, which is understandable in view of the six years' maximum protection period of a utility patent.

The filing of the utility patent is more or less the same as for the regular patent, but the Patent Office examines only the formal requirements and leaves it to the competitors to challenge the utility patent if and when the holder thereof attempts to use his 'monopoly' against the competition.

The fees payable to the Patent Office for the application amount to DM 50 , and the extension fee after three years for a one-time possible extension for a further three years of protection is DM 350.

The effect of the utility patent once it is granted, its commercial exploitation and its defence in court are the same as for a regular patent (¶1202 (8) above).

TRADEMARKS

¶1205   Trademark Act

The Trademark Act of 1968 recognises that the name which a manufacturer or distributor has given to his product, and which he promotes to advertise this product, is in itself of considerable value to the business. By protecting such names and granting a monopoly on their use promotional activities are encouraged. The name of the goods will allow the buyer to link the goods to a certain manufacturer or distributor (whom he does not necessarily have to know by name), will give him reason to expect goods of the same name to be of equal quality and will lead him to buy the same 'name' again if he was satisfied with such goods in the past.

The Trademark Act considers the trademark to be an instrument suited to distinguish the goods of one business from those of another. It must distinguish the goods according to their origin and not their type or nature.

Service marks, which have existed in Germany since 1979, have the same function for services as trademarks have for goods.

¶1206   Registration of trademarks

Only the owner of a business which engages in the manufacture, treatment or distribution of goods can register a trademark so that such goods may compete under the trademark with other goods.

Trademarks which are to be registered in the Trademark Register must be described in a two-dimensional manner (word, picture, logogram, pattern) and must appear on the goods or their container. The trademark cannot be the goods itself, e.g. a special form of a soap bar, but it can be impressed into, or stuck on or appended to the goods, and it can be the form of the container (*Coca-Cola* bottle which can be registered as a drawing) or a coloured stripe in textiles.

As it is the function of a trademark to distinguish goods according to their origin of manufacture or distribution, a trademark must have distinctive characteristics. This would not be the case if the trademark simply copied the goods for which it is being registered. Some of the absolute impediments against the registration of a trademark are based on this lack of distinctiveness.

¶1207 Absolute impediments against registration

In the interests of the general public, limits against a totally unrestricted choice of trademarks have been set. Section 4 of the Trademark Act lists a number of absolute impediments which the Trademark Registration Office, a department of the German Patent Office in Munich, must observe *ex officio* and which, if present, will lead to a rejection of the application for registration. This rule is intended to keep certain words, data, pictures and signs out of the Register and not grant a monopoly on their use to a single trademark holder because the business community needs the words or signs in its everyday dealings, the Government and its administrative bodies have reserved them to themselves or they run contrary to the public interest.

(1) Marks common to a particular trade (general marks: *Freizeichen*) cannot be registered (s. 4(1) Trademark Act). An example would be the *caduceus* used in pharmaceuticals. Although general marks might have sufficient distinctiveness to be registered, they are used by a multitude of unconnected businesses for the same kind of goods and can therefore no longer point to the particular origin of such goods. The Patent Office, with the help of the trade associations and Chambers of Industry and Commerce, determines when a mark has become common for a specific product and it then publishes the general mark in the Trademark Gazette. A general mark can lose its described characteristics again by lack of use in the trade, and it can then become available for registration as a trademark.

(2) Lack of distinctiveness of the requested trademark is the most common reason for the rejection of an application by the Patent Office (s. 4(2) No. 1 Trademark Act). Simple geometric forms like a circle or triangle, ornaments and plain stripes can usually not be said to distinguish one business from another.

Marks composed exclusively of numerical figures or individual letters which cannot be read as a word must remain free for the business community and fail the test of distinctiveness.

Descriptive marks which also cannot be registered include all marks containing information exclusively on the nature, time or place of manufacture of the goods, on their quality, designation or their price, or on the quantity or weight of the product. This is a wide field for rejection by the Patent Office as the Office applies the term 'descriptiveness' very extensively.

(3) Marks containing (even as a part) the coat of arms, national flags or emblems of a state, or armoreal bearings of a domestic town or municipality must not be used to promote business in order to avoid a devaluation of their heraldic character.

(4) Marks offensive to the public can no more be registered than misleading marks. A mark is misleading if it is likely to create a misunderstanding about the goods by that part of the public which will be in contact with those particular goods.

(5) Trademarks which are equal or similar to famous marks known by the public to be used for similar goods cannot be registered. The registration alone of a mark in the Trademark Register does not make it a well-known mark. Therefore, the Patent Office will register identical marks of different applicants, provided the older mark is not well-known, and will leave it to the prior trademark holder to object to the newcomer's mark.

¶1208   Relative impediments against registration

Once the application has passed the barrier of the absolute registration impediments, the Patent Office will publish the application in the Trademark Gazette. This will designate the beginning of the three months' objection period during which any third party who believes himself to have better (because older) rights than the applicant can object to the registration of the trademark. The date of application to the Patent Office, not the date of the eventual registration of the trademark, is crucial for determining the priority date. The Patent Office does not itself investigate any prior claims of others in the trademark register, but leaves it to the owners of such rights to assert their priority.

If an objection is raised, the Office compares the older (objecting) trademark with that of the applicant. The marks need not be equal, but a similarity confusing to the public will suffice for the rejection of the application, provided the objecting trademark and that of the applicant are to be used for goods of the same or similar kind.

The scope of the protection granted by a trademark can be used to attack not only an identical mark of a newcomer, but also similar marks which could lead the public to confuse one with the other and which will make the public believe that the goods of the newcomer identified by his mark are manufactured or distributed by the prior holder. An indirect risk of confusion, which will suffice to defeat the application of the newcomer, exists if the two trademarks have one distinct, similar feature that will cause the public to think that, although the two marks identify different goods, they come from the same source. The Patent Office has gone even further and has rejected applications for a trademark containing similarities to the objecting mark of a kind which allowed the public to see the difference between the business and the origins of the goods, but which created the appearance of the two independent businesses having commercial or organisational ties.

The danger of confusion of two marks can be based on visual, tonal or conceptual components. If one of the three gives rise to confusion, it will lead to the rejection of the application. As a standard for its determination of whether two marks are likely to be confusing, the Patent Office applies the view of a member of the public who will probably only glance at the trademarks. This fictitious person will rarely have both the old and the new trademarks before him at any one time for purposes of comparison, but, when confronted with the new mark, he may be vaguely reminded of the old one and confuse the two. Therefore, it is easy to see why even a very distant resemblance can be declared 'confusingly similar'.

The danger of confusion is increased or decreased if the goods for which the two marks are or will be registered are identical, similar or only related. The greater the dissimilarity of the goods the less likely the public will be to confuse two similar marks. A shirt maker with the trademark 'Arrow' is not going to be considered to be the source of origin for bicycles sold under 'Double-Arrow', while the maker of overcoats using the latter trademark would, if challenged by 'Arrow', not be successful in pleading that both trademarks are sufficiently distinct and will not confuse the public.

The objecting mark, in order to be successful against the application, must be registered for identical or similar goods. The trademark must prevent any confusion about the origin of the goods. Similarity of goods, therefore, exists in the eyes of the law if both goods, each identified by their mark and offered in competition, would lead the public to believe that both products would come from the same source because of their identification through the trademarks. Again, the conception or misconception of the public to whom the goods will be offered determines the test of similarity/dissimilarity. Thus, goods offered to a small group of experts, who tend to look at a product more carefully and who will recognize small differences, can be 'closer' to other products and still will be regarded as dissimilar, while a greater distance between goods offered to the general public must be maintained.

¶1208

¶1209   Defence of applicant

If the trademark application is challenged by a prior holder, the applicant may have a sweeping defence. Only if the prior holder has used his own trademark in his business within the last five years will he be allowed to rely on it in his attack. If he has not used his trademark during that period, he can be challenged by any third party (and, therefore, also by the applicant) for non-use which will lead to the deregistration of his mark by the Patent Office. A prior trademark which is less than five years old cannot be defeated by the defence of non-use.

¶1210   Formalities of registration

The filing of an application for registration of a trademark to the Patent Office must be made in duplicate and must state, in addition to the data of the applicant, the particular business or industry of the applicant. The list of goods for which the trademark protection is sought must be included, and the manufacture or distribution of these goods must be covered by the business or industry of the applicant indicated in the application.

The requested trademark must be incorporated in the application form. If the trademark contains a picture or emblem, if its script deviates from the usual antiqua type face, or if colours form part of the registration, twelve or twenty copies, respectively, of the trademark in its desired form or colour must be furnished.

There will be a basic fee of DM 300 for each trademark application, which is payable to the Patent Office. A further fee, which depends on the number of classes of goods for which the application is made, must be paid to the Patent Office. If the trademark is for only one or two classes of goods, an additional DM 60 must be paid; if it is filed for three or four classes, an additional DM 90 (DM 150 altogether) must be paid. If more than four classes are requested, DM 120 must be paid for each class starting with the fifth in addition to the DM 150 for classes 1 to 4. A typographical block will be charged extra if the trademark is registered in colour or cannot be copied in the Trademark Gazette and the Trademark Register by means of a simple photocopying process.

Once the applicant has filed his application to the Patent Office, the Office checks the application for its formalities and for the existence of absolute impediments. Any objections raised by the Patent Office are first discussed with the applicant. If they are not dropped or eliminated, the official in charge will reject the application. Since in trademark matters the official in charge is usually from the middle-tier hierarchy, an 'appeal' against his decision constitutes a second examination of the same issues by a legally trained official of the higher echelon. His decision, if negative, can be challenged by an appeal to the Federal Patent Court.

If no absolute impediment exists the trademark application is registered in the Federal Gazette and the three months' period for an objection by a prior holder is thereby opened.

An alternative to the above procedure is 'accelerated registration'. It is the aim of accelerated registration to avoid priority drawbacks to the applicant in the case of an international registration of a trademark. An international registration requires as a basis national registration in one of the member countries of the Madrid Convention of 1891 (Stockholm Version in force in Germany since 1970) and an extension thereof to other member countries via the World Organisation for Intellectual Property (OMPI/WIPO) in Geneva, Switzerland. As the normal period from the filing of the application to the registration of the trademark can easily run for two or more years if heavy opposition by one or more prior holders has to be overcome, international registration (which must be filed within one year after the application of the 'basic' national registration) would not be able to meet this deadline. Therefore, accelerated registration allows for the national registration of the trademark instead of the publication of the application, and any prior holder can challenge the registration within the three months following. Meanwhile, the application for international registration can be based on the accelerated registration. The international registration will collapse if, through the objection of a prior holder against the national registration, the latter is defeated.

¶1211 Term of the trademark

Unlike other industrial property rights, a trademark can be renewed over and over again for ten-year periods. A fee for each extension must be paid, which is slightly higher than the initial registration fees. If the extension fees are not paid in time, the Patent Office will send a reminder and set a deadline for payment. If the deadline is not met, the trademark will be deregistered.

The holder of the trademark can cancel his registration at any time by written notice to the Patent Office.

Any third party, whether he holds a trademark of his own or not, can at any time challenge the trademark by filing an application for deregistration with the Patent Office (s. 10 Trademark Act). His reasons for such application can be the existence of an absolute impediment or the lack of general registration requirements. The Patent Office will notify the registered holder about the application for deregistration. If the trademark holder does not object within one month, the trademark will be extinguished without further discussion. Upon his objection, the matter will be examined and discussed with the participants by the Patent Office which will then either reject or pursue the application for deregistration. An appeal to the Federal Patent Court is available against this decision.

Only the holder of a registered trademark can file a complaint in the civil courts for the deregistration of another registered trademark. Four reasons will permit the success of such a lawsuit: better (prior) trademark of the plaintiff; a lack of business of the defendant which the trademark could serve; the deceptiveness of the defendant's trademark; and the defendant's lack of use of his trademark during the last five years of his registration. This lawsuit is conducted in the same way as any other civil litigation and the same appeals are available.

¶1212   Licensing and transfer

A trademark can be licensed in the same manner as any other industrial property right. It can, however, only be transferred together with the business or part of the business to which the trademark applies (s. 8(1) Trademark Act). If no loss of priority is to be feared, the statutory prohibition can be legally overcome by the 'acquiring' party registering the same trademark in its own name, after which the 'transferring' party will deregister its existing trademark.

¶1213   Trademark litigation

Because of the Patent Office's extensive interpretation of 'similarity' of trademarks and of goods, trademark disputes are quite common. Many of them are settled by a so-called 'delimitation agreement' where the challenged party undertakes to use its trademark only in a restricted manner (only for certain goods, only in connection with specific additions, etc.). Such delimitation agreements are also used to make a prior holder withdraw his objection against the registration of the applicant's trademark.

¶1214   Service marks

Service marks are available for services rendered as a main business purpose. A service mark cannot be registered for the auxiliary activities of selling or packing goods by the manufacturer, as these will be covered by the trademark.

In general, the service mark is treated in a similar way to the trademark.

¶1215   European trademark law

At present, rules governing the registration and protection of trademarks are a purely national affair and a trademark registered in one country is usually not recognized in another. The international registration of trademarks by way of the Madrid Convention (and with the help of the World Organisation for Intellectual Property (see ¶1210 above)) is no more than an easy way to process a number of national registrations in various countries, but each country applies its own national trademark laws to a mark deposited in its territory. Due to the territorial restrictions on a trademark, identical marks may be used in different countries by different manufacturers for similar or entirely different products. This can cause confusion to the consumers and, even more importantly, national trademarks may be used as barriers to the free movement of goods and services. This latter reason in particular has caused the EC Commission to present two drafts on trademarks to the Council, to which the European Parliament requested some amendments in 1984 but gave its general support.

(1) The first draft is a regulation which provides for the creation of a uniform EC trademark and an EC Trademark Office, which will allow the applicant to file one trademark application for all EC Member States and which will create one supra-national trademark for the entire territory of the EC.

The draft includes many detailed provisions on the definition of the EC trademark, on the procedure to apply for such trademark, on grounds for refusal of an application by the EC Trademark Office, the opposition procedure and all the other aspects of trademark law.

(2) The second draft of the EC Commission is a directive which aims to harmonise the national laws of the EC Member States. It provides for common criteria for the granting of a trademark and the refusal of an application which must be incorporated into the national laws. The scope of protection of the various national trademarks, their use and the disputes over such trademarks will become more or less the same in all EC jurisdictions so that territorial restrictions created by trademarks within the EC will disappear.

The creation of the EC trademark will not dwarf national registrations. It is expected that only a fairly small proportion of trademarks will be registered under EC law, partly because the majority of all trademark users have only localised commercial interests and partly because many existing trademarks could not be used throughout the EC territory because of language differences which will make many trademarks which are registerable in one country confusing, objectionable or unattractive in another country's language.

DESIGN PATENT

¶1216   Coverage

The design patent is a non-technical property right (*Geschmacksmuster*). The Design Patent Law of 1876 protects accomplishment in the aesthetic field. In this it is related to the copyright laws. However, it does not protect the artistic creation as such, but the industrial exploitation of a design. The object of the protection is the aesthetic form which can be commercially used and which aims to address the human sense for colour and forms. This form must have been incorporated in a two- or three-dimensional pattern or model which can serve as an example for the repetition of the commercially exploitable product.

The creator of an aesthetic form of a pattern or model, or, in a business where the creator works as an employee, the employer, can apply for a design patent. German residents apply to the Local Court (*Amtsgericht*) which maintains the Commercial Register, foreign applicants must apply to the German Patent Office. The model or pattern is to be deposited with the application. The cost for such application and deposit is minimal.

Neither the court nor the Patent Office examines the application for its compliance with the law. The application fixes the 'priority' date of the design patent. The question of whether the design patent complies with substantive law and exists will be determined when this industrial property right is asserted against a third party who will then challenge its existence in court. The court has to decide whether or not the model or pattern:

- can be commercially used;
- has an aesthetic content which is not only dictated by the intended use of the object;
- is new, i.e. was at the time of its application and deposit neither known among experts nor reasonably could have been known when taking into account the existing design variety. The greatest enemy of the requirement of newness is often the applicant himself because a model or pattern is no longer new if the applicant has shown it to the public (exhibition, sale in small quantities, etc.) prior to the application date;
- is original.

The pattern or model must be sufficiently different from generally existing designs. The degree of originality required here differs from that necessary for art covered by copyright. While the copyright law protects the creation of the individual intellect of the artist, the Design Patent Law is content with a form which, though it must be original, meets the common taste. The reward for an original form of an industrial (mass) product is the monopoly of the design patent.

¶1216

The owner of a design patent which meets the above conditions has the exclusive right to manufacture his goods as a copy of the pattern or model. He can prevent other businessmen, but not a non-commercial user, from copying his design for business exploitation. He may not only object against identical imitations, but he can also prevent imitations of parts of the design in a changed form as long as the characteristic effect on the human sense of colour and form is the same in the infringing model. However, a three-dimensional model (e.g. lamp-shade) deposited for a design patent cannot prevent the two-dimensional pattern of the same form (e.g. the form of a lamp-shade as a design on wallpaper).

The exploitation of a design patent by licensing or transferring the industrial property right is the same as in the case of the regular patent or utility patent.

COPYRIGHT

¶1217   Overview

Although the copyright is not an industrial, but rather an intellectual, property right, it is used to protect commercial interests.

The subject of a copyright can be works of literature, science or art. The protected works constitute, in particular, linguistic works, such as publications and speeches, works of music, pantomime and dance, works of fine art (including those of architecture and applied art), film, and presentations of a scientific or technical nature, such as drawings, plans, tables and sketches.

Computer programs have expressly been added by a 1985 revision of the Copyright Act (s. 2).

The Act lists various protected works by way of example, but not exclusively. Any new type of work that may be developed in the future will be protected if it can meet the standards of the Act.

The sole condition for a copyright is the existence of an individual intellectual creation. This means any such works which represent something new and original. The work must be the result of intellectual creativeness. The scientific or technical idea or discovery will not be protected, but only the individual form which the writer or artist gives to the description of such idea or discovery. Copyright does not require the incorporation of the work into solid material; a speech, a performance on stage or a composition played on a musical instrument can all be protected by copyright if they show a personal intellectual creation. Copyright protection does not require any form of registration with the authorities or a deposit of the work, but exists automatically with the creative act.

The copyright holder of a work is its creator. If more than one individual created the work, and their individual contributions cannot be used separately, they are co-creators. Where several creators join their work for mutual exploitation (text and pictures in a book), each can request from the other creator consent for the publication and exploitation of the joined work, but can also make use of and exploit his individual work.

Many authors prefer to publish under pseudonyms or anonyms. Such publications are protected, and to this end, the only register in connection with copyright, the copyright roll at the German Patent Office, is maintained.

Unlike the United States and some other countries, the basic principle that the copyright is generated only in the individual who creates the work also prevails in the case of the employed creator. The employee becomes the holder of the copyright by his creative act, but he is under an obligation to transfer the rights of exploitation to his employer.

The copyright protects the creator in his intellectual and personal relationship to his own work and in its commercial exploitation.

(1) The creator's personal rights allow him to decide whether and how his work is to be made public, they recognise his authorship in the work and his right to prevent distortion or other impairments of his work.

(2) The Copyright Act does not list all forms of commercial exploitation of the work by the author, but gives a number of examples. New, future means of exploitation are always reserved to the creator. He has the right to copy, to distribute and to exhibit his work; he alone may recite, perform, display or transmit his work by radio or television. Copying in that sense is a very broadly defined term. A piece of music is copied when a sound carrier is made (pressing of the disk, recording of the tape), and it is copied again when the sound carrier is played. Feeding a computer with copyright-protected works is an act of copying, the outprint or display of the work by the computer is another.

The rights of exploitation can either be exercised by the author himself or, more commonly, licensed to others. The licensing, as the commercial side of the copyright, is not very different from a patent or other licence. An exclusive copyright licence will allow the licensee the full and sole commercial exploitation of the work in a particular fashion and will give him the right to exclude the author himself from such exploitation. Commonly different forms of exploitation of a work (book, film, television) are given on an exclusive basis to different licensees for their exploitation. The copyright itself cannot be transferred by the author except by way of inheritance.

¶1217

The copyright protection is limited in time to seventy years after the death of the creator. The copyright and its protection is defended by the copyright holder or his exclusive licensee in the same way as if he held a patent or other kind of industrial property right.

¶1217

13 Litigation and Arbitration

COURT SYSTEM

¶1301 Branches of courts

The German Constitution (art. 95 *Grundgesetz*), established five branches of courts:

(1) ordinary courts (*ordentliche Gerichte*);

(2) administrative courts (*Verwaltungsgerichte*);

(3) tax courts (*Finanzgerichte*);

(4) labour courts (*Arbeitsgerichte*); and

(5) courts for social matters (*Sozialgerichte*).

These courts are independent from each other and equal in rank. In addition, the Federal Constitutional Court (*Bundesverfassungsgericht*) exercises jurisdiction (art. 93 *Grundgesetz*). The question of which case is dealt by which branch is answered by statutory provisions, which refer to the legal issue in dispute. They always allocate the suit exclusively to one special branch. There is no concurrent jurisdiction between them. Tax litigation, for example, has to be brought before the tax courts, labour litigation before the labour courts, etc.

Ordinary courts comprise sections for criminal and for civil matters. The distinction of jurisdiction between ordinary courts for civil matters and administrative courts is made by taking into consideration the rules of law relevant in deciding the merits of the dispute. If these rules of law are related to public law, the matter in dispute has to be brought to the administrative courts or, in special cases, to the constitutional court. Otherwise, the suit falls within the ordinary courts' jurisdiction.

¶1302 Civil jurisdiction

Jurisdiction in civil matters is exercised generally by ordinary courts. They consist of local courts (*Amtsgerichte*), regional courts (*Landgerichte*), the courts of appeals (*Oberlandesgerichte*) and the Federal Court (or Federal Court of Justice) (*Bundesgerichtshof*).

The local courts deal with financial actions up to DM 5,000 and, regardless of the amount in dispute, landlord-tenant matters, divorces, family relations, bankruptcy, the enforcement of judgments, and certain non-litigious proceedings (e.g. the commercial and land registers). A single judge presides over civil matters in the local court. All other civil actions must be brought before the regional court, acting as the court of first instance. Appeals from the local courts are also heard by the regional courts. Decisions are made by chambers of three professional judges. Special chambers are established to deal with commercial matters (*Kammer für Handelssachen*). They consist of one professionally educated judge and two lay judges experienced in business.

The court of appeals hear appeals from regional courts, as well as from local courts in matters of family, parent and child law.

All the courts mentioned above are state courts, although they apply Federal law, virtually all civil law being Federal.

The Federal Court, located in *Karlsruhe*, is exclusively competent to hear appeals on law only from decisions of the courts of appeal.

¶1303   Special jurisdictions

Actions dealing with public law are generally decided by administrative courts (*Verwaltungsgerichte*). Special arrangements exist for constitutional, social and tax law. The administrative court of first instance sits with panels of three professional judges and two lay judges. Appeals against a first instance decision are brought before the superior administrative court (*Oberverwaltungsgericht* or *Verwaltungsgerichtshof*), appeals on law only are heard by the Federal Administrative Court (*Bundesverwaltungsgericht*).

Unlike civil jurisdiction, the source of law in dispute (i.e. whether state or Federal) decides the jurisdiction of the court.

Social security matters are heard by the social courts which are organised in three levels, the social court, the regional court and the Federal Social Court in Kassel.

The fiscal court system consists of only two stages. The court of first instance is the tax court; appeals are brought before the Federal Tax Court (*Bundesfinanzhof*) in Munich.

LITIGATION IN CIVIL COURTS

¶1304 Court procedure leading to a judgment

(1) *Jurisdiction*

German law distinguishes between local and international jurisdiction.

(a) *Local jurisdiction.* Local jurisdiction (venue) is regulated by the Civil Procedure Code (s. 12 et seq. *Zivilprozessordnung* of 30 January 1877, as amended: 'ZPO'), according to which general jurisdiction, where all actions against a person can be tried, is determined by the residence of the defendant. The legal person's equivalent is their registered domicile (seat) (s. 17(1) ZPO). The venue for *special* jurisdiction is the place of performance of a contractual obligation and the place of the commission (action or effect) of a tort. The plaintiff has the right to choose between general and special jurisdictions, if no exclusive jurisdiction is applicable. Actions on property rights covering, for example, chattels or real estate can be brought exclusively before the court within the district where the property is located (s. 24 ZPO).

As German civil procedure does not contain special provisions for international jurisdiction, German courts also apply the rules of local jurisdiction in determining international jurisdiction. Questions of international jurisdiction are always relevant if the suit has a foreign reference, e.g. a foreign company, domiciled abroad, intends to sue a local company. International jurisdiction determines whether a German court is competent to hear the case.

(b) *International jurisdiction.* Under German law international jurisdiction follows local jurisdiction. However, the location of any property is of particular relevance for foreigners in determining the venue for an action (s. 23 ZPO). Under German courts practice, any financial claim against the owner of the property may be litigated in the place where the property is situated, regardless of the property's value, if the defendant has no residence within Germany. This practice, regarded as excessive, is comparable to 'long arm' statutes in the United States or (in the United Kingdom) to jurisdictional grounds being based on the presence of property belonging to the defendant. Unlike in the United States or the United Kingdom, there is no doctrine of *forum non convenience* in Germany which enables the court to reject an inconvenient suit based on such grounds as a lack of jurisdiction.

(c) *EEC Convention.* International jurisdiction in civil and commercial matters between the initial EEC members (Italy, France, the Netherlands, Belgium, Luxembourg and Germany) is governed by the Brussels Convention on Jurisdiction and the Enforcement of Judgments in Civil and Commercial

Matters of 27 September 1968. A revised version of this Convention will soon come into force covering the United Kingdom, Ireland, Denmark and Greece.

The Convention contains jurisdictional rules which all courts in the contracting states are obliged to obey. Under art. 3, s. 2 of the Convention, the location of property as a jurisdictional ground is expressly barred from application in cases where the defendant is domiciled in another Member State. On the other hand, the Convention is dangerous for defendants domiciled in other contracting states, as German judgments are easily enforceable in their home country because the court which decides on the enforcement of the judgment is not permitted to consider whether the judgment-granting court actually had jurisdiction.

(2) *Access to court*

(a) *Security deposit.* A party to a civil lawsuit can be a natural person or a legal entity. Legal persons under foreign laws are generally accepted, if their domestic law so provides. There is no restriction on foreigners suing Germans in German courts but, at the defendant's request, foreign plaintiffs must deposit a security for court costs and attorney's fees except where German plaintiffs would not be required to furnish security in the alien's home state. This exception applies basically to the United States of America, the United Kingdom and Canada, provided the plaintiff has his residence or domicile within the jurisdiction of the court. If his residence is outside Germany, or elsewhere, such security deposit may be required. Another exception applies to summary proceedings such as injunctions, attachments and procedures involving bills of exchange or claims on documentary evidence only.

(b) *Representation by lawyer.* In civil litigation any party has to be represented by an attorney admitted to the bar of that particular court, except in the local courts. Generally, only attorneys are permitted to represent litigants before a court. As attorneys are admitted only to the regional court of their domicile, they are competent to represent a client only before the courts of that district. However, there is no territorial restriction on advising and counselling out of court.

(3) *Ordinary course of a civil lawsuit*

(a) *Briefs to court.* A civil lawsuit in Germany is initiated by serving a statement of claim to the defendant (s. 253(1) ZPO). The service will be effected by the court after the plaintiff's advancement of the initial court fees. Generally, the court will fix the date of the hearing at once and summon the parties together with the service of the statement of claim to the defendant.

¶1304

Both parties are obliged to specify and substantiate their claims and defences and to offer evidence as part of conclusive written briefs. Any subsequent introduction of additional facts or evidence may be precluded. The law requires the judge to try to ascertain at the earliest possible hearing which evidence has to be admitted. Unlike English judges, the German judge is acquainted with all written statements.

(b) *Evidence.* The oral trial will always refer to the written statements. It is at the parties' discretion to determine the facts and evidence to be presented to the court. Everything that remains uncontested is considered as proven and only contested facts are subject to evidence. Whether a witness will in fact be heard or other evidence taken is to be decided by the judge, depending upon what he considers to be relevant and within one or other of the parties' burden of proof.

For the purposes of preparation, the court may (for example) issue orders regarding the production of a document, but this does not constitute pre-trial discovery procedure and such orders are not enforceable.

Generally each party is burdened with the proof of contested facts on which their allegations are based. These principles apply to any kind of evidence, including documentary evidence. Even if the document concerned is in the other party's custody, the other party is only required to produce the document if such obligation results from general statutory or contractual law or it itself referred to such document as part of its claim or defence. If the court is convinced that the party intentionally does not meet such obligation, or even concealed the document, it will consider the consequences of such failure in its evaluation of the evidence. Any type of discovery procedure would be against basic principles of German procedural law.

German procedural rules provide for five different kinds of evidence: witness, expert, documentary evidence, inspection by the court and the parties' testimony. As there is no fixed rule of evidence, except for documentary evidence, it is at the court's discretion whether it considers a fact proven because of lack of reasonable doubt.

(c) *Termination of lawsuit.* A lawsuit may be terminated in several different ways. The plaintiff may withdraw his suit but, as from the first oral hearing, only with the consent of the defendant. Such withdrawal terminates the suit. On the motion of the defendant, the court will render an enforceable decision that the defendant may recover all costs (¶1306) from the plaintiff (s. 269 ZPO).

If the claim is resolved because the debtor performs while the suit is pending, both parties may make identical motions regarding its obsolescence. The court will render a cost order, taking into consideration the hypothetical chances of the claim's success without the disposing incident (para. 91a ZPO).

¶1304

Lawsuits are frequently terminated by settlement in court. Such settlement will be recorded in the minutes of the court and thus become an executory title on which a writ of execution may be issued. The wording of the settlement is at the parties' discretion; the judge will only advise them.

Usually a lawsuit is terminated by judgment. Judgment may be rendered on questions of procedure only, e.g. in cases of lack of jurisdiction, or as a decision on the merits. No decision will be made upon anything which was not subject to the parties' motions (s. 308(1) ZPO). An exception is made regarding costs and stay of execution.

Judgments may be challenged by an appeal on facts and law (*Berufung*) by any party burdened by the judgment by more than DM 700. Non-financial suits can always be appealed. An appeal on matters of law only to the Federal Court is restricted to cases specifically admitted by the courts of appeal or to actions concerning disputes with a value exceeding DM 40,000.

¶1305   Special procedures

(1) *Payment order*

Claims for the collection of money may be pursued in quick, summary proceedings. The least expensive way to obtain an enforceable award is to file a motion for a summary payment order (*Mahnbescheid*) with the local court of the plaintiff's domicile. If he has no domicile within the Federal Republic, generally the local court in Berlin-Schöneberg is competent to deal with the motion (s. 689(2) ZPO). If the defendant is not domiciled within Germany, a payment order can only be obtained from a court of jurisdiction according to the general rules (BGH NJW 1981 p. 264), provided that the motion can be served on the defendant within Germany or within member countries of the Brussels Convention (see ¶1304 above) (currently the Netherlands, Italy, Belgium, Luxembourg, France, and, shortly, the United Kingdom, Ireland, Denmark and Greece).

The subject of such payment order can only be a specific amount of money. The plaintiff needs only to state that the money is due and payable and does not depend on any further performance on his side. The court will issue the payment order without examination of its merits and serve it upon the defendant. If the defendant files an objection within two weeks of service, the suit will automatically proceed like an ordinary lawsuit. Otherwise, the court will grant an executory award (*Vollstreckungsbescheid*). If the defendant does not object within the two weeks following service such award becomes *res judicata* (i.e. a matter which has been adjudicated upon).

(2) *Documentary proceedings*

Another way of collecting money due without delay consists in documentary proceedings (*Urkundsprozeß*), if conclusive documentary evidence is available. These proceedings also apply to claims upon cheques or bills of exchange (promissory notes). If the defendant objects to the claim, the court will render only a preliminary judgment which reserves the defendant's rights to an ordinary suit. Such preliminary judgment, however, is enforceable without the deposition of security (s. 708 No. 5 ZPO).

(3) *Injunctions*

Provisional and protective measures are available as seizure attachments (*Arrest*) or interlocutory injunctions (*einstweilige Verfügungen*). Like the Mareva injunction in the United Kingdom, the *Arrest* is normally granted *ex parte*, if there is reason to believe that during the ordinary court procedure the defendant might deal with his assets with the intention of avoiding the expected judgment. This is always assumed if the expected judgment would have to be executed outside Germany (s. 917(2) ZPO). (It is debatable whether 'outside Germany' in this sense would include the EEC.) In order to obtain such an injunction, etc. the underlying claim does not need to be fully proven, but substantiation will be required and will be sufficient.

Arrest is restricted to securing money claims. Other claims are secured by interlocutory injunctions (*einstweilige Verfügungen*). The terms of the injunction are at the court's discretion, provided that an injunction must never finally dispose of, but only secure, a claim. Again, the plaintiff has to show *prima facie* that the alleged claim exists, and that without the granting of the injunction his rights are in danger of being irrecoverably lost.

Interlocutory injunctions taking the form of seize and desist orders are normally applied to cases involving industrial property rights and unfair competition law. Only in exceptional cases are monetary claims enforceable by interlocutory injunction, e.g. urgent support claims. German civil procedure provides no equivalent of interim payment orders.

¶1306 Costs

(1) *Court and counsel fees*

The costs of litigation and fees for legal advice are regulated by statute, i.e. court costs by the Court Cost Act (*Gerichtskostengesetz*) and attorneys' fees by the Attorneys' Fees Act (*Bundesrechtsanwaltsgebührenordnung*). Under both statutes the costs of civil actions depend on the value of the subject matter.

Increasing the value of the disputed subject matter results in a disproportionately decreasing ratio between costs and value. While in small cases costs can even be higher than the value of the case, costs are comparatively low if high value assets are in dispute.

In addition to the value of the subject matter, costs depend on the *kind* of action performed by the court or the attorney, e.g. initiation of a suit, taking of evidence or termination of a suit by compromise. Nevertheless, the *extent* of the work connected with such action has no bearing on the amount of costs.

Attorneys are permitted to agree on fees calculated on a different basis, such as time, although the latter has not been common practice in the past. Furthermore, it would be unethical for an attorney to agree to undercut the statutory fees. Finally, fee arrangements related to the success of the suit (contingency fees) would be illegal.

(2) *Allocation of costs*

According to s. 91(1) ZPO the distribution of costs in civil litigation is governed by the principle that the loser bears all costs, provided that such costs would include only attorneys' fees provided by the Attorneys' Fees Act. Any agreed fees exceeding the statutory fees can not be claimed to be reimbursable by the other side.

If a party has partly lost a case the costs are shared between the parties according to the value-ratio of losing and winning. This forces every party to sue only for such amount as can realistically be expected to be adjudicated. Inflated law suits are thus less frequent in Germany than in the US.

In any event, the plaintiff always has to advance court fees and expenses, and risks being left to pay all court costs without reimbursement if the losing defendant should be without assets.

Any court decision terminating an action contains a ruling on the apportionment of the costs (s. 308(2) ZPO). On application the court will separately fix the exact amount of costs to be reimbursed by enforceable order (s. 103 ZPO).

RECOGNITION AND ENFORCEMENT OF FOREIGN JUDGMENTS

¶1307   Recognition

Foreign judgments are recognised automatically without special procedure if they comply with the statutory requirements of s. 328 ZPO, i.e. that:

(1) the foreign court had jurisdiction following German jurisdiction principles;

(2) the defendant was served with the writ, etc. within the country of origin of the judgment or by judicial assistance of the German authorities;

(3) in the same situation a German court decision would be enforced within such foreign country (reciprocity); and

(4) recognition would not be against public policy (for example, a foreign judgment providing for exorbitant amounts of damages in tort would not be recognised).

¶1308 Enforcement

Execution of foreign judgments in Germany requires a court procedure leading to an executory decision issued by a German court. Such a decision will be rendered if the foreign court decision is final and conclusive under the laws of the country of its origin and if it is recognised in Germany under the conditions listed in ¶1307 above.

Many countries have entered into recognition and enforcement conventions with the Federal Republic. These treaties mainly contain provisions simplifying the recognition and enforcement of foreign judgments in civil matters. The most important is the Brussels Convention (see ¶1304(1)(c) above).

MUTUAL JUDICIAL ASSISTANCE

¶1309 Service of documents

The service of foreign documents within the Federal Republic of Germany is governed by the provisions of the Convention on the Service Abroad of Judicial and Extrajudicial Documents in Civil or Commercial Matters of 15 November 1965, as far as the documents concerned are issued by the authorities of member states, which include France, the United States of America and the United Kingdom.

Under the rules of that Convention the central judicial authority of each state of the Federal Republic within which service is sought will serve the document, provided the conditions set forth in the Convention are met. Direct service or service by attorney, for example, are regarded as violations of German sovereignty, even if they comply with the procedural rules of the country of the document's origin.

¶1310   Support of foreign civil court procedures

Requests by foreign courts to obtain evidence are executed under the provisions of the Convention on Taking Evidence Abroad in Civil or Commercial Matters of 18 March 1970 (member states include the United States, the United Kingdom and France).

Letters of request are to be addressed to the central authority of the state of the Federal Republic concerned. This authority will transmit the request to the court having jurisdiction, if the request complies with the provisions of the Convention. In executing the request the court will generally apply German law, but, as far as compatible with German law, it will follow any special method or procedure specified in the request. However, letters of request concerning the pre-trial discovery of documents are expressly excluded from mutual judicial assistance within the Federal Republic.

ARBITRATION

¶1311   General

Basic rules of arbitration are set out in the Civil Procedural Code (s. 1025 et seq. ZPO). Arbitration in Germany is quite common in commercial (especially in international) transactions. The advantages and disadvantages of arbitration are varied. Whereas state court hearings are open to the public, arbitration procedures are held in private. Arbitrators are chosen freely by the parties, depending on the provisions of the arbitration agreement, and may be legal specialists in the disputed matter. There may also be a time-saving factor in favour of arbitration; while the Civil Procedural Code provides for two or three instances (levels of court), the arbitral award is generally final and not subject to appeal. On the other hand, arbitration has the reputation of forcing a type of compromise upon the parties, whereas court procedure is not likely to result in a decision under strict rules of law.

In the international field it may be easier to agree on arbitration under one of the established arbitration organisations than on jurisdiction of any of the state courts at the place of domicile of one of the contracting parties. Because the majority of industrialised countries signed multilateral treaties on arbitration, including the United Nations Convention (1958), arbitral awards are normally easier to recognise and be enforced than foreign judgments of state courts, which may not meet the reciprocity or other tests referred to under ¶1307 above (as in the case of some US states).

¶1312 Arbitration agreement

Under German law there is no distinction between an arbitration agreement concerning a dispute which has already arisen or a dispute which has still to arise, provided that, in the latter case, the arbitration agreement refers to a specific legal relationship. It is at the parties' discretion to determine the law governing the arbitration agreement.

German law requires the arbitration agreement to be in writing and to be set forth in a separate document or clearly separated from the main contract which is also signed (BGHZ 38 p. 165). This requirement is not applicable to full merchants (see under Chapter I, ¶114 above). Like any other contractual obligation under the rules applying to merchants, a binding arbitration agreement may under German law result even from not objecting to the other party's commercial letter of confirmation which contains a customary arbitration clause (BGH RIW/AWD 1970 p. 417).

The validity of an arbitration agreement is, furthermore, dependent on whether the subject matter is suitable for arbitration, and, hence, a private settlement is excluded, e.g. for disputes about the validity of a marriage, about future statutory support and alimony claims between relatives or about proceedings for the annulment of stockholders meetings' resolutions. Arbitration concerning rooms rented for residential purposes is restricted to single claims but not to the validity of the contractual relationship as a whole (s. 1025a ZPO). Arbitration clauses concerning disputes under agreements qualifying as cartel agreements under German antitrust law would be valid only if providing for the free option to choose between arbitration and ordinary court procedure (s. 91 GWB).

A valid arbitration agreement creates a bar to ordinary court procedures, but such bar must be explicitly raised (s. 1027a ZPO). This bar to ordinary court procedure does not apply to interim protective measures like attachments or interlocutory injunctions.

Generally an arbitration agreement binds only the parties who entered into it. Third parties are bound only if they are successors to one of the parties to the arbitration agreement.

¶1313 Procedure

The parties enjoy great freedom in agreeing on the procedural rules to which the arbitrators shall be subject. Normally the appointment of the arbitrators is either provided for in the arbitration agreement itself, or by reference to the rules of an institutional court of arbitration, which would then also determine the procedure to be observed. If no provisions are contained each party can initiate the arbitration procedure by the appointment of one arbitrator (s. 1028

ZPO). The code does not provide for a third arbitrator, and if the parties do not provide for one, the arbitration risks failing if there should be internal disagreement between the two arbitrators.

The other party is obliged to appoint another arbitrator within one week of receiving the request to do so. After the expiration of that period the missing arbitrator will be appointed by the ordinary court (s. 1029(2) ZPO). Once a party has given notice regarding the appointment of an arbitrator it cannot remove him without the consent of the other party (s. 1030 ZPO).

Although the parties are quite free to prescribe the procedure to be observed by the arbitrators, some basic statutory rules are mandatory. For example, before the final award is made the arbitral court has to hear the parties either orally or (at least) in writing (s. 1034(1) ZPO). The parties may always be represented by attorneys (s. 1034(1) ZPO). Any open procedural issues are left to the arbitral court's discretion (s. 1034(2) ZPO).

As the appearance of witnesses and experts in front of the arbitration court is voluntary, and the administration of oaths is reserved to ordinary courts, either party may apply for any assistance which the arbitrators may deem necessary (s. 1036 ZPO).

¶1314   Settlement and award

Like ordinary court procedure, arbitration procedure can be terminated by arbitral award or by settlement. In fact, arbitral procedures are much more likely to result in a settlement than ordinary court disputes. However, only settlements with the participation of the arbitration tribunal are enforceable. In order to be enforceable the settlement needs not only to be signed by the arbitrators and both parties, but must also include a clause according to which both parties submit to its execution (s. 1044 ZPO).

The arbitrators decide by a majority of votes (s. 1038 ZPO). In order to be enforceable the award requires the signature of all arbitrators, service upon the parties and the deposition of the award and proof of service with the competent court. The award itself must include the names of the parties, the wording of the decision and, if not prescribed otherwise in the agreement, the reasons for the decision.

An arbitral award may be challenged by ordinary court procedure only for certain specified reasons (s. 1041 ZPO): if the arbitration was not based on a valid arbitration agreement, or the arbitration procedure was in violation of mandatory procedural principles, such as lack of due process, or if the award is contrary to public policy (public policy is reserved to fundamental principles which would, however, include provisions of antitrust law).

¶1315 Enforcement

(1) *German award*

Enforcement of an arbitral award requires a declaration of enforceability by an ordinary court. On the application of a party such a decision will basically be rendered if none of the above reasons for setting it aside (see ¶1314) are present and the formal requirements are met. The court will decide by resolution (*Beschluß*) or by judgment (*Urteil*), depending on whether the defendant has been heard in writing or orally. If the application for declaration of enforceability is rejected, the award is set aside by the same decision (s. 1042(2) ZPO). The decision is subject to normal appeal.

(2) *Foreign award*

Execution of foreign awards is governed by similar rules to (1) above. However, unlike in common law countries, the distinction between foreign and domestic awards is not dependent on the place of arbitration but on the procedural law applied by the arbitrators. If they decide to apply foreign procedural rules the award is deemed to be foreign. Awards rendered by institutional arbitration bodies applying their own procedural rules are basically deemed to be foreign if the institution is domiciled abroad.

A foreign award is declared enforceable if it is final, binding and valid, including the expiration of any period for appeal, all as to be determined under the applicable foreign law.

An application for a declaration of enforcement for such an award can only be rejected if:

- the award violates public policy;
- the party was not properly represented;
- principles of due process were infringed (s. 1044(2), ZPO).

Unlike domestic awards foreign awards will not technically be set aside by a German court; rather, they have to be declared as not recognised in Germany (s. 1044(3) ZPO).

A recent change in German case law produced another alternative to give effect to foreign arbitral awards (BGH NJW 1984 p. 2765). If a foreign award is already confirmed by a decision of an ordinary court of law of the country of origin, the claimant may choose between an application for recognition and enforcement of that court decision or the award itself. The procedure concerning recognition and enforcement of the ordinary court decision follows the usual rules of recognition and enforcement of foreign judgments.

(3) *International Conventions*

For awards made under the laws of states including the United States of America, Japan and the EEC Member States, the United Nations Convention (1958) on the Recognition and Enforcement of Foreign Arbitral Awards is of particular relevance. The rules of the Convention prevail against national rules regarding the enforcement and recognition of foreign awards, but to apply the Convention is optional, and if the party seeking enforcement believes that recognition and enforcement can be more easily obtained by other rules he may pursue his claim under such procedure.

The Convention contains special definitions of foreign awards as it is only applicable to these awards. The national courts are obliged to recognise and enforce a foreign award governed by the UN Convention, regardless of its foreign origin, provided certain listed requirements are met.

Enforcement based on an arbitration agreement between German and American nationals also may be sought under the 1954 Treaty of Friendship, Commerce and Navigation between Germany and the United States. As this Convention contains fewer conditions than the United Nations Convention it might be advantageous for a claimant to pursue his action under those rules.

The procedure concerning the recognition and enforcement of the ordinary court decision follows the usual rules of recognition and enforcement of foreign judgments.

14 Personal Business

INTRODUCTION

¶1401   Foreign nationals

A foreign national who wants to take up residence and employment in Germany should be aware of the rules and regulations that apply to foreigners. Knowing about the required permits and registration is a must, and information about apartment leases and cars may prove valuable.

RESIDENCE PERMIT

¶1402   General principle

The general principle set forth in s. 2(1) of the Aliens Act of 28 April 1965 (*Ausländergesetz*) provides that all foreigners who wish to enter Germany for any reason must have a residence permit. The most significant statutory exceptions to the rule are:

   (1) tourists, who may enter Germany for the purposes of travel for up to three months; and

   (2) employees of a foreign employer, who may work for that employer without formal requirements for up to a maximum of two months.

It is a prerequisite, however, that the person concerned must be a citizen of a country which has entered into a non-visa treaty with Germany (e.g. USA, Japan). Nationals of EC Member States are practically exempt. They are entitled to the permit and, thus, for them the application is only a formality (see ¶1403).

¶1403   Prerequisites for the permit

The requirements for the granting of a residence permit depend on whether the foreigner is a citizen of a Common Market Member State or not.

(1) *Non-Common Market citizens*

The Aliens Act expressly allows wide discretion to the authorities in granting or denying the residence permit as such permit 'may only be conferred if the residence of a foreigner will not jeopardise the interests of the Federal Republic of Germany'. The vagueness of such a condition explains the difficulties in listing definite and precise circumstances under which the residence permit will be granted or denied. In fact, it is the purpose of the law to give the authorities the opportunity to take into consideration the specific political and/or economic situation when the application for a residence permit is decided. An application will always be rejected if the foreigner was convicted for a criminal offence (which, if committed in Germany, would also be subject to criminal prosecution), if he has a contagious disease or if he has violated the Aliens Act, e.g. if he is found to have entered in Germany without a visa (if required) or stays in Germany without the necessary residence permit.

An often quoted doctrine of German alien law is that 'Germany is not a country of immigration'. Therefore, under the doctrine the residence of a foreigner in Germany is generally not considered to be in the interests of the Federal Republic. Although this basic rule of interpretation was neglected, or at least applied very liberally, until the mid 1970s, it has now found its way back into practice. Consequently, it may be stated as a general rule that residence permits will not be granted unless exceptional circumstances exist permitting preferential treatment. The following exceptions should be noted as being particularly significant.

(a) *Treaties of Friendship, Commerce and Navigation.* Depending on the details of the applicable treaty between Germany and the country of which the applicant is a citizen, that citizen can count on the favourable treatment of his residence application, or will be treated in the same way as a citizen of a most-favoured-nation or may even enjoy complete freedom of residence as long as he has no intention to immigrate.

Most-favoured-nation clauses exist, for example, in the Treaties of Friendship, Commerce and Navigation with Ceylon, Iran, Japan, Spain and Thailand. Nationals of these countries will be treated as 'most-favoured foreigners'. Comparison cannot be made with citizens of EC member countries, because of the supra-national character of the EEC Treaty, but the benefits granted to such 'most-favoured foreigners' may be compared with those accorded under the most favourable bilateral treaty. As such, the Treaty of Residence with Greece (which is still valid parallel to the EC Treaty, as in the case of all other Treaty members) is normally applied by the German authorities and courts as providing the most benevolent treatment for the applicant.

Treatment equal to that experienced by German nationals, combined with a most-favoured-nation clause, is contained solely in the Treaty of Friendship,

¶1403

Commerce and Navigation with the USA. However, even this treaty does not give the foreigner an enforceable right to a residence permit. The authorities still have a certain discretionary power, although it has to be exercised in the applicant's favour.

Furthermore, the so-called 'privileged foreigner' must prove that he is able to support himself either by his independent means or due to a business, a profession or an employment which he is permitted to exercise in Germany.

(b) *European nationality.* Residence permits for Europeans (for example Swiss or Swedish nationals), but not Eastern Europeans, are granted more readily than for other foreigners. The more or less identical cultural background, which permits easy integration into the German way of life, plus:

(i) the comparatively small number of applications; and

(ii) the experience that most of them will return to their home states after some years;

allow the authorities to consider their residence applications as generally not likely to jeopardise the interests of the Federal Republic.

(c) *Investors.* The residence of a foreign investor who is willing to establish an employment-intensive or a high-tech business is normally considered as not contrary to German concerns but in the German interest.

(d) *Educational purposes.* Finally, residence permits for educational purposes are conferred in general, provided the applicant is able to prove:

(i) his admission to a school, university or other educational institution; and

(ii) his sufficiently independent means for the time he intends to stay in Germany.

Nevertheless, even if all the requirements are met, a residence permit may be denied if the applicant intends not only to live but also to work in Germany (see ¶1406, 'Work Permit'). If he wants to work as an employee, his residence permit will depend on the receipt of a work permit. Where the applicant is independent, the business or profession he intends to exercise will influence the granting of his residence permit, as the application will be examined with regard to labour market aspects. No problems should occur if the applicant is an investor or if he sets up a business as described in (c) above. Further, the residence permit will be granted to the independent individual if the bilateral treaty concerned also displays a most-favoured-nation or equal national clause with respect to the establishment of a business or the exercise of a profession. This is the case for Iran, Japan, Thailand and the USA.

(2) *Nationals of Common Market countries*

Based on the EC Treaty and on various EC Regulations and Directives, nationals of member countries enjoy residence rights in the Federal Republic if

¶1403

they are entitled to free movement according to the EC Treaty. This freedom is accorded to workers (wage earners and salaried employees), to self-employed persons who have made their domicile in the Federal Republic (or intend to do so), and to persons who market or buy services without taking up residence in Germany. Accordingly, the Residence Act /EEC (*Aufenthaltsgesetz/EWG*) provides for a full right of residence for this group of individuals (ss. 1(1) and 2–6 Residence Act/ EEC). In fact, the residence permit for nationals of Common Market countries has a solely declaratory effect, though its application is mandatory. Non-compliance is subject to fines.

(3) *Treaty of Association with Turkey*

Based on the Treaty of Association between the EC and Turkey, freedom of movement as to EC nationals is to be accorded to Turkish citizens by the EC member countries as from 30 November 1986. Whether equal status will indeed be granted will depend on the political arrangements to be reached between Turkey and Germany. Furthermore, it will be decisive to what extent the EC members and Turkey come to an understanding at the Council of Association.

In the meantime, the regulations of the common Aliens Act apply as stated in (1) above. Provisions facilitating the granting of work permits exist, however (see ¶1406 below).

¶1404 Procedures

Generally, the law provides for the application for a residence permit at the German consulate or embassy in the foreigner's home country. With the exception of nationals of the Common Market countries and citizens of the United States, the foreigner must apply before he enters the country.

Consequently, unless the foreigner is able to prove that he did not intend to stay for longer than three months in Germany, and only as a tourist at the time of his entry, he will be deemed to have concealed this intent from the authorities and will be considered as having violated German law by entering the country under false pretences when he was actually intending to stay for much longer or even to take up employment. This presumption can (but does not have to) be used as an argument in denying a residence permit after his arrival. Cases of late application have been known where the foreigner had to return to his home country in order to file his application again with the local German consulate and, in other instances, residence permits have been issued without any difficulty in spite of clear evidence that the applicant intended to stay longer than three months in Germany or even to work.

Nationals of Common Market countries may apply for the residence permit after having entered the Federal Republic (s. 5(3) Executive Order/Aliens

Act). Citizens of the United States enjoy the same favourable treatment under the existing Treaty of Friendship, Commerce and Navigation (s. 5(2) Executive Order/Aliens Act).

A period of three to four months from the application should be expected before the residence permit is granted by the German consulate or embassy in charge.

¶1405   Term of permit

The initial residence permit is generally granted for one year. Continued extensions are possible and are normally granted for up to four to four and a half years in total, although the foreigner is not entitled to an extension. A foreign national who has lawfully lived in Germany for at least five years, and who has adapted to the economic and social life of the country, can receive a permit which gives him the unlimited privilege to stay in Germany. This privilege can be revoked only under very narrow circumstances, e.g. if he loses or changes his nationality, has no valid passport, leaves the country not only temporarily or if he is deported.

The holder of a residence permit or privilege may be deported and sent back to his home country if, among other reasons, he is convicted of a felony, violates tax or customs rules or the statutes regulating the exercise of a profession or other occupation, or if he cannot provide a living for himself and his family.

WORK PERMIT

¶1406   General principle

In principle, all non-German nationals who want to work in the Federal Republic need (according to s. 19 *Arbeitsförderungsgesetz*: Law for the Enforcement of Employment) a work permit in addition to the residence permit. An important exception should be noted in that members of boards of directors (*Vorstandsmitglieder*) of German stock corporations, managing directors (*Geschäftsführer*) of German limited liability companies and managerial staff members with broad powers to represent their employer-company (*Prokurist*) do not need a work permit, even though they are legally employees of the corporation. Yet, this is only true for the *Geschäftsführer* and the *Prokurist* if their internal position (in relation to the shareholders) can be characterised as independent. However, it is normally considered as sufficient by the Aliens and Labour Authorities in charge if this is confirmed by the employing company. Such 'independent' managerial staff, however, are then often deemed to be independent business entrepreneurs and therefore need a trade permit, which usually encounters the same difficulties as a work permit.

¶1407 Conditions of issue

While nationals of Common Market Member States are entitled to work permits, other foreign nationals, as a general rule, do not have a statutory right to receive such a permit. The labour authorities will consider an application on the basis of the general situation existing on the labour market, thereby taking into account the individual situation. They would particularly examine the place of employment and any labour shortage or over-supply in the particular field in which the applicant intends to work, as well as the economy as a whole. Also taken into account is the kind of work to be performed and whether it can be performed by domestic employees or EC nationals in a similar manner. As an exception, it should be noted that, according to Resolution 1/80 of the Council of Association, Turks are entitled to an extension of the work permit with their present employer after one year of employment, if the position is still available.

In practice, the wide discretion left to the authorities has led – at least in recent years – to the rejection of applications for work permits in most cases. Though the granting of permits is facilitated if a bilateral treaty shows corresponding stipulations (as they do in the Treaties with the USA and Austria), German and EC nationals still enjoy priority. Based on Resolution 1/80 of the Council of Association, since 1980 certain preferences are also granted to Turkish nationals. Only if no German, EC or Turkish national candidate has been offered as an alternative by the Labour Office (*Arbeitsamt*) within one month of the request will the national of the treaty member state be granted a work permit.

¶1408 Procedure and categories of work permits

The application must be filed with the local *Arbeitsamt* (Labour Office) in the district where the foreigner resides or will reside. The issuing of the work permit is dependent on the existence of a residence permit. The two application procedures are interwoven. If an individual applies for a residence permit with the intention of working in Germany, the Alien Office, before granting the residence permit, will contact the Labour Office to ascertain whether it is likely to issue a work permit. Only after this Office has given an affirmative answer will a residence permit be issued. Once the residence permit is obtained, the work permit will follow.

The work permit will be either issued for a special type of employment, or for a special type of employment in a certain area or for a special type of employment with respect to a given employer.

¶1409 Period of validity

The work permit can be issued for a maximum period of two years, but it generally will not be granted for the maximum period when the first application is made. Work permits are usually extended upon application, but again the applicant has no enforceable right to it. If the residence permit has expired, is not extended or if the foreigner is expelled, the work permit will also be terminated.

LOCAL REGISTRATION

¶1410 Requirement

All foreign nationals must register with the local authorities (*Einwohnermeldeamt*), just as German citizens must do. Registration has to take place within one week of permanent living quarters having been found. When the resident moves, he must notify the authorities of his departure. If he moves within Germany, he must re-register at the *Einwohnermeldeamt* at his destination. This second registration is subject to proof that the first *Einwohnermeldeamt* was notified of the departure. A change of address within the same area must also be registered.

LEASE OF HOME OR APARTMENT

¶1411 In general

Lease agreements are generally concluded in written form but are also valid if only verbally made. Because of the shortage of housing, at least in the main cities in Germany, the lessor is usually in a strong position to insist on the terms of the contract. Bargaining and negotiating substantial alterations to the usual standard form leases is therefore not often open to the lessee.

¶1412   Terms of lease

(1) *Duration*

Lease contracts may be concluded for a fixed term or with unlimited duration. Both are common. If the lessee contracts for a fixed period, he will be responsible for the rent due for the unexpired term, even if he moves out or tries to terminate the lease earlier. Therefore, the foreign lessee should at least try to negotiate the right to sublet and/or assign the lease in case he is repatriated before the contracted term of the lease expires.

(2) *'Schönheitsreparaturen'*

The lessee should look out for a very common clause in lease contracts which provides that *Schönheitsreparaturen* (Decorative Repairs or the painting of walls, window and door frames) must be carried out by the lessee at the end of the lease period. This is standard practice in German lease contracts. In particular, if the lessee is likely to stay for only a few months in his apartment and then leave Germany, this obligation can be very costly. Depending on where the lessee is going to live in Germany this condition is sometimes open to negotiation.

(3) *Repairs and replacements*

Since the lessee is responsible for damages to the apartment or house which occur during the term of his lease, it is recommended that he should insist on a survey being made with the lessor and on a written statement regarding the condition of the leased premises before he signs the lease, and again before he vacates and returns the premises. The statement should list all defects in the apartment (cracks in the walls, defective windows, faulty plumbing, damaged furniture etc.), should be signed by lessor and lessee in duplicate and one copy should be kept by the lessee. This list will act as a safeguard against possible later claims of the lessor for repairs or replacements not caused by the lessee.

(4) *Deposit*

A deposit (*Kaution*) (normally a bank guarantee or cash amount equivalent to three-months' rent) left as security with the lessor until the lease has ended, is so common in Germany that very few lessors will waive its payment or be bargained out of this demand.

¶1413   Rent increases

The fixed indexation of housing rents in accordance with the increases, for example, of the official consumer price index, with rare exceptions, is not possible under German law. However, the landlord is allowed to increase the rent by up to 30 per cent within a period of three years, even if not expressly determined in the lease contract. Nevertheless, the lessee very often is able to fix the rent for a certain period in the agreement.

¶1414   Termination

Statutory law provides for a three-month period for the notice of termination to become effective at the end of a calendar month. If the lease contract is unlimited, this period of notice may not be shortened for the lessor. In the case of leases for a fixed period of time (which often provide for the extension of the contract), provided neither party terminates the lease, the notice period is usually the same as the statutory period. If such lease does not provide for the possibility of an extension, no notice has to be given to terminate the contract, but it terminates automatically. If the lease of living quarters is not limited in time, the lessor may only terminate the contract if he needs the premises for his personal (including his family's) occupation or if the continuation of the lease affects the marketability of the premises.

DRIVERS LICENCE AND CAR REGISTRATION

¶1415   Drivers licence

The law permits a foreign national to use a foreign or an international drivers licence as a valid licence within Germany for a period of one year. This period commences on the date of the driver's arrival in Germany. The date of his residence permit or the registration of a car in Germany has no relevance to the beginning of the one-year period.

It should be noted that after the year has elapsed, every driver who has not received a German drivers licence will be considered as driving without a licence. Unlicensed driving is not only a criminal offence, punishable with a maximum of one year's imprisonment, but it also invalidates the driver's liability insurance and other car insurance contracts. Thus, every foreign driver who suspects that he will remain in Germany for more than one year should apply in time for a German drivers licence.

The holder of a foreign or international drivers licence can receive the German licence quite easily. He will first have to obtain a translation and classification of his foreign licence. This is done by the *Allgemeiner Deutscher Automobil Club* (ADAC), which has offices in major cities all over Germany. With the exception of EC nationals, the applicant must furnish some kind of proof that he has driving experience in Germany. The confirmation of his company or any third person will be sufficient. Further, an eye test made by a licensed optician is required, but, again, not for EC nationals.

The confirmation, the translations of the licence, a passport, a passport photo, the eye test certificate, the certificate from the *Einwohnermeldeamt* (see ¶1410 'Local Registration' above) and the required fee must be handed to the *Amt für Öffentliche Ordnung, Führerscheinstelle*. This office will process the papers and, after a period of time (generally at least one month), issue the German licence.

¶1416 Car registration

Often, a foreign employee who intends to stay in Germany for a longer period of time wants to buy a car for his business or private use. A number of customs and registration requirements arise which are outlined below to facilitate the buyer's decision.

In principle, all car purchases made in Germany are subject to the 14 per cent turnover tax, based on the sales price. If the car is (later) exported, turnover tax is still payable but may be refunded under a statutory exemption. In order to qualify for the exemption the owner must take the car across the German border within 30 days after delivery. A compulsory liability insurance must be obtained before customs plates are issued for the car. An exception applies, however, to foreign nationals who buy a car in Germany and have no residence there at the time of purchase. They may drive their car with customs plates for one year within Germany (as well as other countries), after which time they must either finally export the car or register it with normal German licence plates. Nevertheless, this means that car insurance for the one-year period is necessary, which is currently provided by only one insurance company in Germany and at a much higher price than for a normally registered car.

If the car is exported within the 30 day or one-year period no turnover tax will have to be borne. Although the tax is initially billed by, and must be paid to, the car dealer (or factory in the case of a direct factory purchase), it is refunded by the seller upon proof of export.

Proof of export is obtained at the German border from the German customs officer, who certifies that the car has been exported. An export certificate (*Ausfuhrbescheinigung*) will be issued which can then be mailed to the dealer for the refund of the tax. This 'export' does not prevent the car owner from returning with his car to Germany if the period for the validity of the customs plates has not expired.

It must be noted, however, that a car which has been exported to obtain the tax refund can neither be sold nor driven in Germany after the customs plates have expired unless the car is reimported to Germany. Such reimport is subject to import duty. Furthermore, the car buyer has to refund the turnover tax and he has to pay the German car taxes for the time in which he drove the car with customs plates in Germany.

This fact and the reimport customs duty make it advisable to drive the car under customs plates and to export it for the sake of the turnover tax refund only if the car owner is certain that the car will finally be exported before the one-year period of the customs plates' validity expires. If the owner can foresee that he may need the car in Germany for a longer period, he should make a very careful calculation, including insurance premiums, possible customs duty, and the devaluation of the car within the year's period, to determine whether he would not be better off registering the car with German licence plates immediately after its purchase.

Premiums for the compulsory liability insurance of a car driven with customs plates are about 100 per cent higher than the insurance rates for nationally registered cars. Premiums for a car with normal German plates to be paid by a foreigner are about 200 per cent more expensive if the foreigner has no German drivers licence or if he possesses one but for a shorter time than three years. A foreign national with an accident-free driving record in his home country would be well advised to inquire with his German car insurer whether a more favourable liability insurance rate can be obtained. Some auto insurers will take this into consideration. A statement from the insurer in the home country attesting to the accident-free record over a stated period of time would be required. The type of previous insurance must also be stated. This rate reduction applies to residents only, however, and not to tourist insurance.

¶1416

Index

References are to paragraph numbers

AMM

DAT

DAT

LOC